THE PICKERING MASTERS

THE WORKS OF DANIEL DEFOE

General Editors:
W. R. Owens and P. N. Furbank

POLITICAL AND ECONOMIC WRITINGS
OF DANIEL DEFOE

POLITICAL AND ECONOMIC WRITINGS OF DANIEL DEFOE

General Editors: W. R. Owens and P. N. Furbank

Volume 8: SOCIAL REFORM

Edited by
W. R. Owens

Routledge
Taylor & Francis Group

LONDON AND NEW YORK

First published 2000 by Pickering & Chatto (Publishers) Limited

Published 2016 by Routledge
2 Park Square, Milton Park, Abingdon, Oxon OX14 4RN
711 Third Avenue, New York, NY 10017, USA

Routledge is an imprint of the Taylor & Francis Group, an informa business

© Taylor & Francis 2000

BRITISH LIBRARY CATALOGUING IN PUBLICATION DATA
Defoe, Daniel, 1660 or 1–1731
Political and economic writings of Daniel Defoe. – (The Pickering Masters)
1. Political science – Great Britain – Early works to 1800 2. Economics – Great
Britain – Early works to 1800 3. Great Britain – Politics and Government –
1714–1760 4. Great Britain – Politics and Government – 1660–1714 5. Great
Britain – Economic conditions – 17th century 6. Great Britain – Economic
conditions – 18th century I. Title II. Owens, W. R. III. Furbank, P. N. (Philip
Nicholas) 320.9′41′09032

LIBRARY OF CONGRESS CATALOGING-IN-PUBLICATION DATA
A catalogue record for this title is available from the Library of Congress.

ISBN-13: 978-1-85196-465-9 (set)

Typset by Florence Production Ltd,
Stoodleigh, Devon

CONTENTS

ACKNOWLEDGEMENTS

I wish to thank the Faculty of Arts Research Committee and the University Research Committee at the Open University for the provision of generous financial support towards my work on this edition. I am grateful also to the staff of the Open University Library for their help.

INTRODUCTION

An Essay upon Projects was the first full-length book published by Defoe, and it was also the first of many works he was to write on questions of social reform. It appeared in January 1697, representing, so he tells us in the Preface, the fruit of nearly five years' work. In the *Essay* he puts forward impressively detailed and far-reaching proposals for country branch banks; building, repairing and maintaining highways; insurance schemes and friendly societies; a Pension Office; humane treatment of the mentally handicapped; a reform of the laws on bankruptcy; the establishment of a military academy and an academy for women; and an improved system for recruiting seamen for the navy. Some of these proposals were in fact taken up, and Defoe was actively involved in the promotion of a Bill to Prevent Frauds Frequently Committed by Bankrupts which became law in 1706, and in submitting proposals to a House of Lords committee looking into the problem of naval recruitment.[1]

Other areas where Defoe was to make notable and often highly original contributions included regulation of the press, relief of the poor, and the law on imprisonment for debt. In his old age, in the *persona* of the elderly and curmudgeonly 'Andrew Moreton', he put forward a further series of reforming schemes: for regulating the employment of servants and other groups of workers; retirement homes for the aged; a university for London; a hospital for foundlings; an academy for music; state-run institutions for the care of the insane; and better protection against street robbery. Many of his Victorian admirers regarded these writings on social reform as being among Defoe's most significant achievements. William Minto thought that the *Essay upon Projects* 'might alone be adduced in proof of Defoe's title to genius', and went on to claim that Defoe's 'powerful advocacy was enlisted in favour of almost

---

[1] See *The Letters of Daniel Defoe*, ed. George Harris Healey (Oxford, 1955), pp. 73–7.

every practicable scheme of social improvement that came to the front in his time'.[2] For Walter Wilson, likewise, Defoe was pre-eminently 'a rational reformer ... his schemes were not only practicable, but, in the highest degree, benevolent and useful'.[3] William Lee, who before becoming a biographer of Defoe in the mid-1860s had behind him a career as a pioneering Surveyor of Highways in Sheffield and then as a Superintending Inspector on Edwin Chadwick's General Board of Health, praised the 'foresight and sagacity' of Defoe's proposals for social reform, many of which, Lee said, with a touch of pride, 'are no longer projects, but ... existing Institutions, indispensable to the well-being of the country'.[4]

An Essay upon Projects

Although in many ways a highly individual book, and certainly one very characteristic of the mind and outlook of its author, *An Essay upon Projects* is also very much a book of the 1690s. This was a period which saw an intense interest in economic and social questions, with many writers putting forward ideas on how the prosperity and well-being of the country might be increased. Some of these writers suggested, for example, practical schemes to improve internal communication by water and road; others advocated changes in the laws governing trade and commerce; still others focused on finance, proposing various methods of establishing banks and improving credit facilities.[5] It was indeed, as Defoe says in his Introduction, a 'Projecting Age'. As he also recognises, the long war with France which England had entered in 1689 enormously stimulated new developments in English commerce and industry. This was the great period of flotation of joint-stock companies, set up to manufacture not only a range of armaments needed for the war, but commodities such as paper, fabrics and glass. Others were set up to engage in activities such as mining for coal, copper, lead, salt, alum and tin, or to supply water,

[2] William Minto, *Daniel Defoe* (London, 1879), pp. 18, 167.

[3] Walter Wilson, *Memoirs of the Life and Times of Daniel De Foe*, 3 vols (London, 1830), vol. III, p. 592.

[4] William Lee, *Daniel Defoe: His Life, and Recently Discovered Writings*, 3 vols (London, 1869), vol. I, p. 434. For Lee's earlier career, see P. N. Furbank and W. R. Owens, 'William Lee of Sheffield: Sanitary Reformer and Defoe Bibliographer', *The Book Collector*, 37 (1988), pp. 185–206.

[5] See P. G. M. Dickson, *The Financial Revolution in England* (London and New York, 1967), pp. 4–7.

particularly in London. By 1695 something like 150 such companies had been established in England.[6]

However, the cost of the war also strained the economy to its limits, and led to unprecedently high levels of taxation. Public expenditure rose nearly threefold, and between 1689 and 1702 was running at between £5,000,000 and £6,000,000 a year.[7] Various expedients were adopted to help finance the war effort. The most important source of revenue was the Land Tax which was introduced in 1692. Although, as Defoe points out, there were various problems with assessment procedures and collection of the Land Tax, which allowed many wealthy landowners to evade paying the full amount, there was in fact, by seventeenth-century standards, a remarkable degree of compliance with the tax. According to David Ogg, it raised about £19,000,000 during William's reign, far outstripping the £13,000,000 raised each from Customs and Excise.[8] As well as direct taxation levied through the Land Tax, there was a great expansion of indirect taxation. Taxes were imposed or increased on many basic items of consumption, such as salt, leather, spices, tea, coffee, beer, cider, brandy, tobacco pipes and waterborne coal. There were also experiments with poll taxes and taxes on births, deaths, and marriages, though these raised little and were short-lived. One of the most striking features of the *Essay upon Projects* is Defoe's insistence on the need for a progressive system of taxation, '*in which every man may be tax'd in the due proportion to his Estate*'. He calls for the setting up of a national body of tax assessors, with powers to enquire into the personal wealth of every citizen and ensure that each paid an appropriate amount of tax.[9]

In addition to levying new taxes and trying to increase revenue from excise duties, William's ministers also experimented with new ways of raising money by the creation of lotteries and annuities which were attractive to both large and small investors. In March 1694, for example, Parliament passed an Act authorising the 'Million Lottery'. This was essentially a government loan, to which was added a lottery element. There were 100,000 numbered tickets costing £10, of which 2500 paid out prizes. The establishment a month later of the Bank of England was designed to raise an even larger sum of money, with subscribers being invited to lend a total of £1,200,000. Such was the interest that

---

[6] See William Robert Scott, *The Constitution and Finance of English, Scottish and Irish Joint-Stock Companies to 1720*, 3 vols (Cambridge, 1910–12), vol. I, p. 334.

[7] Dickson, *Financial Revolution*, p. 46.

[8] David Ogg, *England in the Reigns of James II and William III* (Oxford, 1955), p. 405.

[9] See *An Essay upon Projects*, below, p. 31.

the subscription was filled within ten days of opening, and the new bank received its charter on 27 July 1694.

Defoe himself was directly involved in some of these new financial enterprises, and was acquainted with prominent 'projectors' of the time. One of his early associates was Thomas Neale, Groom Porter to the King, Master of the Mint and an enthusiastic sponsor of private lotteries and other schemes for raising money. In 1695 Defoe was listed among the thirteen 'Managers trustees' of 'The Profitable Adventure for the Fortunate for 50000*l*. at 20*s*. per Ticket', a lottery organised by Neale.[10] Another acquaintance was Dalby Thomas, to whom the *Essay* is dedicated. As Defoe remarks, Thomas was an energetic projector, who had put forward various schemes, including a proposal for a 'General Fishery', and for setting up land banks.[11] He was one of the managers of the Million Lottery, and in 1695 was appointed one of three commissioners of the newly imposed Glass Duty, a tax on glasswares, stone and earthen bottles (6 & 7 William and Mary, c. 18). He recruited Defoe to serve as 'Accomptant to the Commissioners', a post worth £100 and later £150 a year, and which Defoe held until the Glass Duty was abolished in 1699.[12] In the Preface to the *Essay* Defoe acknowledges his indebtedness to Thomas for some of the ideas included in his chapter on banks.

The title Defoe chose for his book is worth examination. The term 'project' was in bad odour at this time, as Defoe recognises in speaking of '*the Despicable Title of a* Projector' (p. 29), because of the recent proliferation of over-speculative or downright fraudulent schemes. There was, therefore, a hint of deliberate paradox in his title here – in which it would resemble many of his titles.[13] In fact, in his 'Introduction' and his opening chapters on 'The History of Projects' and 'Of Projectors' he is at pains to make semantic distinctions. He is explicit that by 'projects' he does not mean the same as 'improvements'. In his view, the history of humankind was, in an important sense, the history of 'improvements': for instance, in ancient times, the discovery or invention of wine, writing, the sail, agriculture and metalworking, and more recently of the compass, gunpowder and printing. He was to write of this at length in a *General History of Discoveries and Improvements* (1725–6). 'Improvements', though

---

[10] See F. Bastian, *Defoe's Early Life* (London, 1981), pp. 188–9.

[11] See *A Proposal for a General Fishery* [London, 1694?]; *Propositions for General Land-Banks* [London, 1695].

[12] See John M. Parkinson, 'Daniel Defoe: Accomptant to the Commissioners of the Glass Duty', *Notes & Queries*, 243 (1998), pp. 455–6.

[13] Consider such titles as *Conjugal Lewdness, The Protestant Monastery, Reasons against the Succession*.

often credited to some legendary, perhaps semi-divine, inventor, were essentially anonymous and part of the general patrimony of mankind. A 'project', on the other hand, was most typically promoted, at least in part, for private profit (as well as being clearly associated with an individual promoter). According to the verbal usage that Defoe has in mind, even in the case of an honest project its author could be allowed 'to aim primarily at his own Advantage', though this would not prevent him from aiming at 'Publick Benefit' (p. 36), and he writes later of beneficial schemes to supply water as 'Perfect Projects, adventur'd on the risque of Success' (p. 41). As for dishonest projects, Defoe's account gives a vivid picture of what, some twenty years later, would be the staple of the South Sea Bubble:

> —new Inventions, Engines, and I know not what, which being advanc'd in Notion, and talk'd up to great things to be perform'd when such and such Sums of Money shall be advanc'd, and such and such Engines are made, have rais'd the Fancies of Credulous People to such height, that meerly on the shadow of Expectation, they have form'd Companies, chose Committees, appointed Officers, Shares, and Books, rais'd great Stocks, and cri'd up an empty Notion to that degree, that People have been betray'd to part with their Money for Shares in a *New-Nothing*. (p. 37)

What, however, we come to notice when actually reading Defoe's *Essay* is that few of his so-called 'projects' are actually for private profit (any more than the schemes of his 'Andrew Moreton' later on).[14] The fact is expressive. The truth is that Defoe was deeply ambivalent in his feelings about projects. This, indeed, is not very surprising for, as he ruefully mentions in passing in the *Essay* (p. 37), he himself had been inveigled into an ill-planned commercial diving venture and lost a considerable sum of money over it.[15] Yet in 1687 an even riskier diving enterprise conducted by Sir William Phipps had, against all probability, turned out a triumphant success. ''Twas a mere Project', writes Defoe, in a wonderfully spirited sentence,

> a Lottery of a Hundred thousand to One odds; a hazard, which if it had fail'd, every body wou'd have been asham'd to have own'd themselves concern'd in; a Voyage that wou'd have been as much ridicul'd as *Don Quixot's Adventure upon the Windmill*: Bless us! that Folks should go Three

---

[14] He says of his grandiose scheme for the repair of highways that it is certainly a project for which it would be easy to find 'Undertakers' (p. 57), though he is not offering to be one of these himself.

[15] See Paula R. Backscheider, *Daniel Defoe: His Life* (Baltimore and London, 1989), pp. 56–7.

thousand Miles to Angle in the open Sea for Pieces of Eight! why, they wou'd have made Ballads of it, and the Merchants wou'd have said of every unlikely Adventure, 'Twas like *Phips* his Wreck-Voyage; but it had Success, and who reflects upon the Project? (p. 38)

On its weak side, 'projecting', as Defoe could see, led directly into stock-jobbing and monopoly. Yet it remained true that, in an altogether favourable sense, 'Every new Voyage the Merchant contrives, is a Project' (p. 36). Projecting, and the paradoxes associated with it would intrigue Defoe throughout his career.

His opening chapter in the *Essay*, 'Of Banks', deals with a highly topical subject, because the Bank of England had only been established, under Whig auspices, in 1694, and a Tory rival, known as the National Land Bank of England, had been set up in 1696. Defoe approves of the establishment of the Bank of England, but he wants its activities to be greatly expanded. He recommends that its stock be increased to at least £5,000,000 (which indeed happened a few years later), that it operate more as a central clearing-house, with separate offices dealing with matters such as foreign and inland exchange, and that it be linked to a network of banks in all the major county towns throughout England.[16]

The following chapter, 'Of the Highways', takes a similarly large view of the subject. It is one of Defoe's most elaborately worked-out proposals, and rather than try to discuss all his schemes, it may be worth examining this one in a certain amount of detail. The state of English roads was widely recognised to be deplorable. A statute of 1555 had thrown responsibility for the maintenance of existing roads on the parishes through which they passed. Every inhabitant was required to perform six days' labour on the roads, under the direction of one or more surveyors who were elected for a year at a time. Various laws were passed to give surveyors more authority and to regulate such matters as the width of roads, the weight of carts and even the width of wheels, but the system was never very effective. Meanwhile traffic on the roads was increasing and compounding the problem. It was not until the introduction of the turnpike system, under which users paid a toll, that improvements would begin to be made, but there were very few turnpike roads before the eighteenth century.[17]

---

[16] See J. Keith Horsfield, *British Monetary Experiments 1650–1710* (London, 1960), p. 140. For further discussion of Defoe's ideas about banking, and financial matters more generally, see John McVeagh, Introduction, *Political and Economic Writings*, vol. 6.

[17] For details, see W. T. Jackman, *The Development of Transport in Modern England* (1916; third edition, London, 1966), pp. 58–65.

Defoe's proposal for dealing with this great problem is a radical one: nothing less than a national road building and maintenance programme. The scheme would require legislation, with Parliament passing laws to authorise 'undertakers', working with representatives of each county, who would arrange for the compulsory purchase and enclosure of land, and would press 'Wagons, Carts, and Horses, Oxen and Men' into service for the task of construction. Local labour would need to be supplemented, and Defoe recommends that sentences of corporal punishment might be commuted into so many days work on the highways, and criminals be sent to work for a year on the highways as an alternative to transportation. Negro slaves could also be purchased from the Guinea Company. He goes into considerable detail about his plans for the new highways. All main roads within a ten-mile radius of London are to be forty feet wide, thereafter narrowing to thirty feet, and with ditches on either side eight feet broad and six feet deep. Stone, chalk or gravel should be used for paving. Land compulsorily purchased beside the highways could be exploited for agriculture, and the rent would provide a source of funding for the future maintenance of the roads. Maintenance should be carried out by workmen who would live in specially built cottages, two miles apart, and these cottages would serve the further purpose of helping or protecting travellers. The cost of the programme Defoe thinks might easily be raised through taxation, perhaps employing banks to assist in the raising of loans.

The vision is breathtaking in its boldness, and most inventive in its detail, and we can certainly agree with Defoe when he exclaims: 'What a Kingdom wou'd *England* be if this were perform'd in all the Counties of it!' Equally, however, it is not very surprising to learn that his ideas were never taken up. As William Minto observed, Defoe's plans were 'on a scale worthy of Baron Haussman',[18] or, as one might equally say, they foreshadow the building of the Victorian railway system. There was never the remotest chance that any British government in the eighteenth century would set aside property rights and impose taxation to the extent envisaged in the *Essay*.

If proposals to extend the banking system and to improve the roads were designed to facilitate economic development, Defoe's next group of proposals are designed to improve the lives of the poor and vulnerable in society. He was particularly interested in the potential of insurance schemes. As he acknowledges, insurance against fire and shipping loss

---

[18] Minto, *Daniel Defoe*, p. 18.

was already available, and indeed he himself had been involved in the provision of marine insurance.[19] Similarly, friendly societies were beginning to be established, and Defoe regards these developments as an extension of the biblical injunction to help fellow creatures in distress: 'it must be commendable to bind our selves by Agreement to Obey that Command' (p. 73). In Defoe's eyes, insurance was 'a Project that we are led to by the Divine Rule', and it held out the prospect that mankind might be 'secur'd from all the Miseries, Indigences, and Distresses that happen in the World' (ibid.). He proceeds to outline detailed insurance schemes for groups such as seamen and widows, though oddly enough, and without giving any reasons, he rules out the possibility of life insurance (p. 71). Perhaps his grandest proposal is for the provision of sickness benefit and old-age pensions: in effect a national insurance scheme to which everyone would be obliged to contribute, and from which all would benefit according to their need. It is a noble and humane vision, and Defoe is confident that it can be made to work:

> I desire any Man to consider the present State of this Kingdom, and tell me, if all the People of *England*, Old and Young, Rich and Poor, were to Pay into one common Bank, 4 *s. per Ann.* a Head, and that 4 *s.* duly and honestly manag'd, Whether the overplus paid by those who Die off, and by those who never came to Want, wou'd not in all probability Maintain all that shou'd be Poor, and for ever Banish Beggery and Poverty out of the Kingdom. (p. 89)

A final group of proposals concern the spread of education. The best known of these is Defoe's proposal for the establishment of an academy for women, which shows his thinking at its most progressive. But what may perhaps slightly surprise the reader is to find him claiming earlier in the chapter 'Of Academies' that 'War is the best Academy in the World' (p. 115), and drawing up detailed plans for a military academy (as the next best thing to a literary academy, such as the one for which England envies France). The clue to this does in fact lie in France, and we see here the beginnings of a piece of social criticism which would underlie much of Defoe's writing. It was an essential truth for him that France, however one might dislike its arbitrary system of government, stood at a higher cultural level than England. Equally, it was a basic social difference between the two countries that the French nobility saw military service as the natural path to honour and influence, whereas it

---

[19] See Scott, *Constitution and Finance of . . . Joint-Stock Companies*, vol. III, pp. 372–4 for details of early insurance schemes.

was a convention among the English nobility and squirearchy that the army was a career only for younger sons; and that, for similar reasons, only younger sons had any need to acquire education and culture. The eldest son and heir to an estate felt himself to be above such things (Defoe is satirical, and very funny, about the incapacity of eldest sons for anything but 'dog-language' and the arts of the stable).[20] His observation that King William's chief generals and engineers were all foreign (p. 116) is closely related to this. It is nicely illustrated in an exchange in the *Review* for 30 October 1708 between 'Mr. Review' and 'Madman', in which Madman remarks that we should not blame English engineers for any deficiencies during the siege of Lille. And why is that, asks Mr Review? Because, says Madman, there was not a single one there. The illiteracy of eldest sons in England is a theme which Defoe is still hammering at in his unpublished *Compleat English Gentleman* at the very end of his life.

Regulation of the Press

On 3 May 1695, the Licensing Act of 1662 lapsed and was not renewed.[21] Under the terms of this Act the press had been restricted in three important ways: the number of master printers was limited to twenty; all published works had to be entered in the Registers of the Stationers' Company; and it was illegal to publish any material which had not been licensed by the Lord Chancellor, the Archbishop of Canterbury, or one of the Secretaries of State. The expiry of the Act did not mean that henceforth the press was free – existing laws against treason, seditious libel, blasphemy and obscenity continued to be used to control what was printed[22] – but it did mean that the Stationers' Company lost its monopoly over the book trade, and during the next few years printers and booksellers joined with some politicians to demand a restoration of press regulation.

In December 1703, when party conflict was running high over the attempt to outlaw the practice of Occasional Conformity, the issue of press freedom once again flared up. The Whig journalist John Tutchin

---

[20] Defoe, *Review*, 20 November 1708 in *Defoe's Review*, facsimile ed. Arthur W. Secord, 22 vols (New York, 1938).

[21] 13 & 14 Charles II, c. 33.

[22] See John Feather, 'The English Book Trade and the Law 1695–1799', *Publishing History*, 12 (1982), pp. 51–75.

gave offence to High-flying Tories by his hostile comments in the *Observator* on the new Occasional Conformity bill which had recently passed the Commons but had been thrown out by the Lords. Tutchin was immediately arrested, and at the same time a Licensing bill was introduced in the Commons. It was given a first reading on 13 January 1704 and a second reading on 18 January, but was subsequently lost in committee and never became law. Defoe, who had recently been imprisoned for writing *The Shortest Way with the Dissenters* and was now in the employ of Robert Harley, responded to the debate with a pamphlet, *An Essay on the Regulation of the Press*, which appeared on 7 January 1704. A few weeks later he also produced for private circulation among his Dissenting friends a brief satirical address *To the Honourable, the C—s of England . . . Relating to the Bill for Restraining the Press*.

An Essay on the Regulation of the Press puts forward a moderate set of arguments. Defoe grants that there must be some restrictions on the press, in order to prevent the circulation of books 'tending to Atheism, Heresie, and Irreligion', and agrees that authors who break the laws of libel or blasphemy should be punished.[23] However he is against bringing back a system of licensing before publication, for the simple reason that this would make the press 'a slave to a Party': which-ever party was in power would be able to name the licenser and thus prevent the publication of anything that was not to their liking. To put into the hands of 'one or a few Men . . . an absolute Negative on the Press' would, Defoe said, be 'the first step to restore Arbitrary Power in this Nation' (pp. 146–8). In a situation where more than one political party exists, 'every Side ought to have an equal Advantage in the use of the Press' (p. 152).

The only acceptable way to restrain the press, Defoe argues, is first of all to pass a law specifying which matters of church and state are not to be criticised, and then to punish offending authors *after* publication. To facilitate the discovery of offenders he also proposes a law which would require the name of the author, or the printer, or the bookseller, to be placed on the title page. Anyone selling an anonymous work would be deemed to be the author, and held responsible for it.

Although Defoe argues his case extremely effectively, his general line of thought is not altogether original. Milton in his *Areopagitica* and Locke in a 'Memorandum' written in 1693 had argued against pre-publication censorship, and had called for laws to outlaw anonymous publication.[24]

---

[23] *An Essay on the Regulation of the Press*, below, p. 145.
[24] See Mark Rose, *Authors and Owners: The Invention of Copyright* (Cambridge, Mass. and London, 1993), pp. 28–30, 32–3.

What was original about Defoe's contribution was the emphasis he placed upon the rights of authors. A law requiring publication of the author's name, he said, would not only serve to restrain those who would abuse the freedom of the press, it would establish authorial copyright in the work and end the pernicious trade in piracies:

> every Author being oblig'd to set his Name to the Book he writes, has, by this Law, an undoubted exclusive Right to the Property of it. The Clause in the Law is a Patent to the Author, and settles the Propriety [i.e. property] of the Work wholly in himself, or in such to whom he shall assign it. (p. 158)

According to Mark Rose, this call for a law to protect authorial property rights 'may be the earliest such advocacy in English'.[25] As Rose notes, Defoe went on campaigning in his *Review* on behalf of the rights of authors. In late 1709 and early 1710, when what was to become the famous Copyright Act of 1710 was being discussed, he published a stream of articles urging Parliament to pass a law 'to secure to the Authors of Books their Right of Property'.[26] In the event, as John Feather has pointed out, the main beneficiaries of the first Copyright Act were not authors, but the booksellers who owned the copyrights.[27]

Defoe's contribution to the debate over licensing in 1704 was not confined to his soberly argued *Essay on the Regulation of the Press*. At much the same time he also composed and had printed for private distribution a satirical broadsheet addressed *To the Honourable, the House of C—s of England*. In this an imaginary High-Church author urges the House of Commons to bring in laws to restrain the press, so as to silence the 'Clamours' of 'Whigs and Moderate Church-men' about such 'Trifles' as 'Law, Liberty, Property and Conscience'. Although written in the manner of *The Shortest Way with the Dissenters*, there is no attempt here to fool the reader. As J. A. Downie, who first discovered the broadsheet, points out, 'here the writer's true stance is never in doubt: [Defoe] was clearly ridiculing the character he had created, who felt it to be "absolutely necessary" for the preservation of the church that the press was silenced'.[28]

---

[25] Ibid., p. 35.

[26] *Review*, 26 November 1709.

[27] John Feather, 'The Book Trade in Politics: The Making of the Copyright Act of 1710', *Publishing History*, 8 (1980), pp. 19–44 (p. 20).

[28] J. A. Downie, 'An Unknown Defoe Broadsheet on the Regulation of the Press?', *The Library*, 33 (1978), pp. 51–8.

Poor Relief

On 2 November 1704, the Tory MP Sir Humphrey Mackworth introduced in the House of Commons a Bill for the Better Relief, Employment, and Settlement of the Poor. This would have extended the existing workhouse system by authorizing the Overseers of the Poor in every parish to set up a public workhouse and provide the resources, both financial and material, to set the destitute poor to work at spinning, weaving, and manufacturing woollen goods. The goods they produced would be sold in the market, thus helping to finance the workhouses and relieve the poor rates.

The bill was at first well received, and passed through all its stages in the Commons. About two weeks later, however, Defoe published *Giving Alms no Charity*, a devastating counterblast to Mackworth's scheme, declaring it to be quite fatal, calculated to ruin the English wool trade and liable, rather than to relieve the poor, to add to their number. The effect was to kill the bill stone dead; it was thrown out when it reached the House of Lords. When there was an attempt to revive Mackworth's scheme in 1707, Defoe came back to the attack with even more vehemence. He wrote in the *Review* for 22 February 1707:

> I would think my self happy to be led out to immediate Execution, rather than to have the Curses of a whole Nations Poor follow me to a Grave more remote, or have it wrote on my Grave-stone, that here lyes *D. F.* that projected the Destruction of the *English* Manufactures, and ruin'd the Poor of this Kingdom.

According to Defoe's view of the matter, there was no shortage of work for beggars and vagrants to do. On the contrary, '*There is in* England *more Labour than Hands to perform it, and consequently a want of People, not of Employment*'.[29] The remedy for unemployment was not to create work for the workless, but rather to compel them to look for work themselves, by enforcing the laws against beggars. '"Tis the Men that *won't work*, not the Men that *can get no work*, which makes the numbers of our Poor; all the Work-Houses in *England*, all the Overseers setting up Stocks and Manufactures won't reach this Case' (p. 190). To set up a manufacture in every parish, as Mackworth was proposing, was a sure way to wreck the delicate mechanism of English trade. It would increase supply without creating any new trade or new market, and would simply deprive some other poor man of similar work somewhere else: for every skein of worsted

---

[29] *Giving Alms no Charity*, below, p. 174.

spun in a workhouse there must be 'a Skein the less Spun by some poor Family or Person that spun it before' (p. 180). Moreover, there were 'Arcanas' or secrets explaining why particular manufactures have flourished in particular regions, and this regional specialism carried with it all the huge benefits of circulation of trade. Set up the same trades everywhere, Defoe says, and you will ruin all the innkeepers and carters and other intermediaries who serve this circulation and gain their living by it.

In the volume on the history of the Poor Law in their great work, *English Local Government*, Sidney and Beatrice Webb are shocked at what they see as Defoe's harshness towards the unemployed in *Giving Alms no Charity*, and it is not hard to see why. Nevertheless, as they themselves admit, Defoe's arguments about the use of workhouses to deal with unemployment were well founded, and attempts to set up such workhouses on a profit-making basis were a complete flop.[30] In the *Review* for 1 March 1707 Defoe criticises the English for their mistaken ideas about charity: 'People have such a Notion in *England* of being pitiful and charitable, that they encourage Vagrants, and by a mistaken Zeal, do more Harm than Good'. It is not the case, however, that he was against all charity. In *Giving Alms no Charity* it is clear that where poor families have been deprived of the labour of the father through illness or death, they should be relieved (p. 177).

There is no doubt that in attacking what he believed to be a deeply mistaken idea, however charitable the motives, Defoe was being perfectly sincere. As Peter Earle has argued, Defoe believed in a high-wage, high-employment economy, and central to this was the concept of circulation: 'The more hands a commodity passed through on its way from raw material to final consumer, the more employment each article gave rise to and the more wages or profits could be earned on the way'.[31] There was thus no inconsistency in Defoe's praise for workhouses where the goods that were being produced were goods which would otherwise be imported, or which entailed the teaching of new skills, because these contributed to the great chain of distribution rather than diminishing it. In the *Review* for 6 and 8 March 1707, for example, he suggests that if new markets for English cloth could be opened up, manufacture could be increased, or alternatively the English could set up an entirely new manufacture, such as calicoes. Where Defoe might more justly be faulted,

[30] Sidney and Beatrice Webb, *English Local Government*, vol. 7: *English Poor Law History, Part I. The Old Poor Law* (London, 1927), pp. 114–16, 233–7.
[31] Peter Earle, *The World of Defoe* (London, 1976), p. 109.

paradoxically, is in his opposition to labour-saving innovations, whether in equipment or in methods of distribution and sale. As he puts it in *Giving Alms no Charity*, 'All Methods to bring our Trade to be manag'd by fewer hands than it was before, are in themselves pernicious to *England* in general, as it lessens the Employment of the Poor, unhinges their Hands from the Labour, and tends to bring our Hands to be superior to our Employ, which as yet it is not' (p. 183).

Bankruptcy and Imprisonment for Debt

An area of social policy that preoccupied Defoe throughout his writing career was reform of the laws on bankruptcy and the treatment of insolvent debtors. This is perhaps not surprising, in view of his own experience of going bankrupt as a trader, and of finding himself on several occasions in a debtors' prison. In *An Essay upon Projects* he proposed a radical overhaul of the existing laws on bankruptcy, and in 1705–6 he took an active part in the promotion of a Bill to Prevent Frauds Frequently Committed by Bankrupts.[32] He devoted many numbers of his *Review* to detailed discussions of the bill, and published a closely argued pamphlet, *Remarks on the Bill to Prevent Frauds Committed by Bankrupts* (1706), supporting the legislation, though with reservations. Near the end of his life he returned again to the subject of insolvent debtors, in *Some Objections Humbly Offered to the Consideration of the Hon. House of Commons, Relating to the Present Intended Relief of Prisoners* (1729).

England was somewhat of an exception among European nations in regard to the laws of debt. Ever since the thirteenth century creditors in England had had the right to have debtors put in prison and kept there until they paid their debts. As a result, it came to be a practice among debtors to take refuge in a sanctuary, or flee the country, and it was only during Defoe's lifetime that steps were finally taken to suppress the most notorious of these sanctuaries, such as the Mint and Whitefriars. But what was even more distinctive about English law was that, in England, a creditor, by obtaining a warrant from a sheriff, could have a debtor arrested in the street. The victim would then, normally, be taken off by bailiffs to a 'sponging house' (a place of detention, privately run, but to all intents and purposes a prison). Here, the more fortunate debtor might get himself bailed out, or have his debt paid for him, by his friends

---

[32] Enacted as 4 & 5 Anne, c. 4.

(though meanwhile paying an extortionate price for his accommodation); whilst for the less fortunate it could be the prelude to trial, and perhaps to long-term incarceration in a debtors' prison.[33]

In his *Essay upon Projects* Defoe concerns himself specifically with the form of debt which leads to bankruptcy. (An Act of 1570 first made a clear distinction between bankrupts and other insolvent debtors, laying it down that only traders and merchants, who earned their living by 'buying and selling', could be declared bankrupt. The reason for this distinction, according to Blackstone, was that non-traders *choose* to get into debt, while traders are *obliged* to contract debts as a necessary part of their business.)[34] The laws of bankruptcy as they existed when Defoe was writing the *Essay*, so he argues there, benefited neither debtors nor creditors. Once a 'statute' of bankruptcy had been taken out against a debtor, it was impossible for him to try to get back on his feet again, because anything he subsequently earned could be taken by his creditors. Equally, the ease with which dishonest debtors could evade their creditors, and the ways in which what remained of a debtor's estate could be wasted in the process of taking out a commission for bankruptcy, often meant that creditors recovered very little of the money owing to them.

Defoe's proposal in the *Essay* is for the establishment of an independent 'Commission of Enquiry' with a membership including at least twelve merchants, which would sit at the Guildhall and would have statutory powers to examine the affairs of bankrupts. Upon surrender of all estate and effects to the commission, five per cent of the value of the estate would be returned to the debtor, and he would be given a complete discharge from all his creditors. The remainder of the estate would be divided proportionately among the creditors.

In 1697, soon after the publication of Defoe's *Essay*, Parliament passed an Act for the More Effectual Relief of Creditors in Cases of Escapes, and for Preventing Abuses in Prisons and Pretended Privileged Places, and a related Act, for the Better Preventing Escapes out of the

---

[33] For a general account of the law, see Jay Cohen, 'The History of Imprisonment for Debt and its Relation to the Development of Discharge in Bankruptcy', *Journal of Legal History*, 3 (1982), pp. 153–71. See also Joanna Innes, 'The King's Bench Prison in the later Eighteenth Century', in *An Ungovernable People: The English and their Law in the Seventeenth and Eighteenth Centuries*, eds John Brewer and John Styles (London, 1980), pp. 250–98; Paul H. Haagen, 'Eighteenth-century English Society and the Debt Law', in *Social Control and the State*, eds Stanley Cohen and Andrew Scull (Oxford, 1983), pp. 222–47.

[34] Blackstone, *Commentaries on the Laws of England*, 4 vols (1765–9), vol. II, pp. 473–4, cited in Cohen, 'History of Imprisonment for Debt', pp. 160–1.

Queen's Bench and Fleet Prisons (1 Anne, sess. 2, c. 6) was passed in 1702. It was aimed at preventing the practice, which had grown very rife, of prisoners for debt bribing their way out of the Queen's Bench and Fleet prisons, and prescribed that fresh warrants could be obtained against any prisoner who had escaped in this way and that he could forthwith be committed to a common gaol in any part of the country. Defoe refers to this as the 'Escape Act' and also as 'the Law lately made for the Perpetual Imprisonment of Debtors without Bail', and, though he admits that it may have been felt to be necessary at the time, he argues that it has made the situation of honest debtors even worse. It is 'Barbarous and Inhumane, in Practice Unjust, and Unequal in its Nature' and quickly became 'as great a Grievance as the Crime'.[35]

Defoe thus had a great deal to say when, early in 1706, a new bankruptcy bill was going through Parliament, entitled A Bill to Prevent Frauds Frequently Committed by Bankrupts; indeed he claimed to have had some influence on the wording of the bill. The crucial feature of the bill was that for the first time it gave encouragement to honest bankrupts to come forward and make a settlement with their creditors. In return for making a full and honest declaration of their financial affairs, they would be discharged from their former debts, and would be allowed to keep five percent of the net estate, up to a maximum of £200, if the dividend paid to creditors was more than eight shillings in the pound. In a word, the Act would give an honest bankrupt his freedom to resume trading.

In his *Remarks on the Bill to Prevent Frauds Committed by Bankrupts*, published just a few weeks after the Act became law, Defoe explained that it had become an urgent necessity because of the ruin caused to merchants and tradesmen by the war and by the great storm of November 1703, which had led to the prisons being filled with unfortunate debtors. However the event which had finally impelled Parliament to take action was the notorious case of Thomas Pitkin, a linen draper from Cheapside, who had gone bankrupt owing enormous sums of money, and who had fled to Holland taking with him, it was said, 'Effects and Money to the value of near One Hundred Thousand Pounds'.[36] As Defoe pointed out, under the terms of the new bill bankrupts like Pitkin who attempted to defraud their creditors by flying to a refuge or leaving the country, could be sent to the gallows as felons. The new bill, he said, would benefit

---

[35] *Review*, 12 February 1706.
[36] See *An Account of the Apprehending and Taking of Mr. Thomas Pitkin* (n. p., 1705).

everyone. He predicted that there would be fewer bankrupts because more debtors would make voluntary settlements; less money which should go to creditors would be wasted on costly commissions of bankruptcy, law suits, and bribes paid to court officials and prison warders. Indeed the only losers, Defoe remarks with irony, would be the 'poor industrious Families, who are now maintain'd by the laudable Employment of *Bayliffs*, Bayliffs *Followers*, *Sergeants* ... *Appraisers*, *Brokers*, *Spunging Houses*, private *Prisons*, and the like'.[37]

In his commentary on the new bill in the *Review*, Defoe became for a time despondent that it was going in a wrong direction. He thought it essential that it should compel *all* creditors to come into a 'composition' with the debtor, for otherwise the latter could never be sure that he would not later suffer prosecution by some further claimant; however it did not appear that this, though perhaps implied, was going to be spelled out in the bill. Further, the bill seemed to be going to allow the Commissioners, who were appointed without external scrutiny by the creditors themselves, to refuse to grant the debtor a Certificate of clearance without giving their reasons.

In the event, however, when the bill was finally passed, Defoe warmed to it, declaring that it was 'one of the best Bills, that ever was produc'd in Parliament, since the *Habeas Corpus* Act', though it would, he thought, remain a weakness in it that creditors were not forced to give good reasons why the debtor should not be granted his Certificate.[38]

Defoe's writings on bankruptcy show him at his best as a social critic. He was able to picture where bad law might, in practice, hurt; and he was very good on the psychology of bankruptcy. He writes, with insight: 'At the Beginning of a Disaster, when a Trades-man falls, he is generally tender, willing to be fair, open, and forward to make a free Offer; Retreats and Time, put Men upon Shiftings and Subterfuges' (p. 205). One remembers, too, his famous description in the *Review* for 19 February 1706, of 'the Infinite Mazes of a Bankrupt, before he comes to the *Crisis*':

> what Shifts, what Turnings, and Windings in Trade, to support his Dying Credit; what Buying of one, to raise Money to Pay another; What Discounting of Bills, Pledgings and Pawnings; what Selling to Loss for present Supply; What Strange and Unaccountable Methods, to buoy up sinking Credit!

[37] *Remarks on the Bill to Prevent Frauds Committed by Bankrupts*, below, p. 214.
[38] *Review*, 23 March 1706. Defoe was to have trouble himself over the fact that, when in 1706 he had made a composition with his creditors, he failed to obtain a Certificate. See Backscheider, *Daniel Defoe*, pp. 201–2.

As he very frankly admits here, he is speaking from painful experience: 'I freely rank my self with those, that are ready to own, that they have in the Extremities and Embarrassments in Trade, done those things, which their own Principles Condemn'd, which they are not Asham'd to Blush for, which they look back on with Regret, and strive to make Reparation for, with their utmost Diligence'. His advice to potential bankrupts is clear:

> BREAK, GENTLEMEN, for God sake, for your own sake, for your Creditors sake, for your Wife and Childrens sake, and for the Publick Good; BREAK, while you have something to Pay, something to show the Honest Man with, something to Bribe your Creditors, to be Civil to you with, something to Tempt them to Refrain a Statute of Bankrupt, to the Ruine both of your Family and their Debts.

With the last of the pamphlets reprinted in this volume, *Some Objections Humbly Offered*, our scope widens and we are made to consider Defoe's attitude towards not merely bankruptcy but debt, and imprisonment for debt, in general. Throughout his writings on the subject of bankruptcy and the treatment of debtors Defoe passionately and eloquently condemned the abuse of the law by which creditors could 'Confine Men to Perpetual Imprisonment for Debt'. In the *Review* for 21 February 1706, for example, he described it as a disgrace to the English nation:

> To talk of Humanity and Mercy, and Confine Men to Perpetual Imprisonment for Debt, and that Men who cannot pay too, as well as they that can, Men Ruin'd by known Disaster, as well as men of Fraud; to put Men to Torture and Famine, and neither let them Work to Pay, nor to Live; to smother Men in Noysome Dungeons, and Crowd them with Murtherers and Thieves; to Condemn them to the Temporal Hell of a Gaol, and barr them up from all the helps of Art, Industry, and Time to Restore their Families, and pay: For Shame, let us no more Reproach the *Dutch*, Amboyna *is a Fool to this*...

Thus, in the light of this humanitarian stance, it perhaps comes as something of a shock to a modern reader to discover that Defoe was by no means in favour of abolishing the whole system of surprise arrest and imprisonment for debt. On the contrary, he believed it essential to the support of credit and to the prosperity of a trading nation. In such a great commercial nation as England, he wrote in the *Review* of 6 May 1707, 'it is absolutely necessary to make the Recovery of small Debts as well as great, as easie as possible, and to give the Creditor all possible Security, both on the Person as well as the Effects of his Debtor'. In his view, indeed, the great superiority of England over Scotland as a commercial nation was closely related to the difference between English and Scottish law in regard to arrest and imprisonment for debt (the Scottish system being more slow and cumbrous and not allowing for the surprise arrest of a debtor or surprise seizure of his goods, and requiring the creditor to pay for the upkeep of an imprisoned debtor).[39] The Scottish system, Defoe thought, 'is a Cheque to Trade, and helps to keep the People down, as it hinders petty Credit, and prevents People launching freely out in Trade'.[40]

It seems clear that there is no contradiction in Defoe's position, nor does it imply any inhumanity on his part. It did not mean, for example, that he was opposed to the recurrent Acts of Grace passed to discharge small insolvent debtors – on the contrary, he was strongly in favour of these. Such Acts he considered to be beneficial, in that they released thousands of 'Honest, Distress'd, Industrious Trading-Men ... whose Restraint before, tho' ruinous to them, was no real advantage to their Creditors, and a very great Injury to the Publick Stock of the Nation'. Furthermore,

> tho' *it is True*, and it is reasonable it should be so, *that* a Debtor ought to be Imprisoned, in order to oblige him to pay his Debts; yet, when that Payment becomes really impossible, the end of Imprisonment is answered; for Imprisonment for Debt, is not *as a Punishment* to the Debtor, but as the properest Method to make him Honest, when then, he is, *bona fide*, uncapable, he ought not to be detain'd.[41]

The whole issue of imprisonment for debt, though of perennial concern in the early years of the century, became a particularly burning one at the beginning of 1729. In anticipation of another Act of Grace, there was a flood of petitions to the House of Commons from the oppressed debtors in gaols up and down the country.[42] More dramatically, in February 1729 James Oglethorpe drew the attention of the House to the truly scandalous condition of the Fleet prison, under its barbarous Warden, Thomas Bambridge. As a result, a committee of inquiry into the state of English prisons was set up under Oglethorpe. The committee's investigations revealed that prison officials were thoroughly corrupt and

---

[39] See William Chambers, *The Book of Scotland* (Edinburgh, 1830), pp. 150–73.
[40] *Review*, 6 May 1707.
[41] *Review*, 29 January 1713.
[42] See works listed in the section on imprisonment for debt in *A Bibliography of Eighteenth-Century Legal Literature*, eds J. N. Adams and G. Averley (Newcastle upon Tyne, 1982).

that debtors were kept in appalling conditions. Oglethorpe reported the findings of the committee on 14 May 1729 and on the same day two Acts, one for the 'Relief of Insolvent Debtors' (2 Geo. II, c. 20) and one for the 'Relief of Debtors, with respect to the Imprisonment of their Persons' (2 Geo. II, c. 22), received the royal assent.[43]

In response to this public and parliamentary debate, Defoe published a pamphlet entitled *Some Objections Humbly Offered to the Consideration of the Hon. House of Commons, Relating to the Present Intended Relief of Prisoners.* In this, although he strongly supports the action being taken against Bambridge and is in favour of the proposed relief for debtors who have nothing to pay, he argues that safeguards should be built into the proposed Act of Grace to ensure that it is not taken advantage of by fraudulent debtors, who 'boldly run into Mens Books, with a Dependance upon such *Acts of Grace*, and with an evident Design to cheat and defraud their Creditors, and this *several* Times over'.[44] But the heart of the pamphlet is a clear statement of the reasons why creditors needed to be able to arrest debtors and have them locked up. According to Defoe's view of the matter, the giving of credit depends upon the threat of imprisonment for debtors: 'If you destroy this Power of *Coercion*, you destroy the *Credit in Trade*; for if the Man cannot be *credited*, he cannot *buy*; and if the Tradesman cannot *arrest* him, he will not sell' (p. 297).

The 'Andrew Moreton' Pamphlets

Three pamphlets included here – *Every-Body's Business is No-Body's Business* (1725), *The Protestant Monastery* (1727), and *Augusta Triumphans* (1728) – formed part of a series published by Defoe under the pseudonym 'Andrew Moreton, Esq.', which also included *Parochial Tyranny* and *Second Thoughts are Best.*[45] The invented *persona* of 'Andrew Moreton' – a public-spirited but irritable old bachelor with a pawky sense of humour, unpractised in the use of the pen, and who lives in a modest way with

[43] The reports of the Oglethorpe committee are given in Cobbett's *Parliamentary History*, 36 vols (1806–20), vol. VIII, pp. 708–31, 744–54; see also the *Historical Register* for 1729, pp. 127–8, 157–78, and the *Commons Journals* for 20 March and 14 May 1729.

[44] *Some Objections Humbly Offered*, below, p. 293.

[45] *Parochial Tyranny*, which appeared in December 1727, was an attack on the self-perpetuating select vestries, calling for their abolition and replacement by more democratically elected bodies. *Second Thoughts are Best*, published in October 1728, included an expansion of the scheme for prevention of street robberies put forward in *Augusta Triumphans*, as well as discussing other social problems such as the opening hours of drinking establishments, prostitution, and the extortionate price-fixing of certain tradesmen.

his sister in Highgate – is very well sustained in the three pamphlets. It was a nicely conceived device of Defoe's for comment on a whole range of contemporary social issues, and 'Squire Moreton' evidently caught on with the public. *Every-Body's Business* was particularly popular, running through five editions within a year.

The largest part of *Every-Body's Business* is devoted to a plea for legislation to deal with the insolence and vanity of women servants, who at present, so Moreton grumbles, shift about from employer to employer as they please, in an effort to raise their wages, and who aim to become a finer '*London*-Madam' than their mistresses. If they are at all handsome, they may seduce some apprentice or the young master of the house; and since they have no idea of saving, they will very probably end up as thieves or prostitutes. The answer, Moreton argues, is legislation to fix their wages, make them wear a uniform, and require them to enter into written contracts, before a Justice of the Peace, which would prevent them leaving their jobs before a fixed term had expired.

'Andrew Moreton' was, of course, far from being alone in his strictures on maidservants. Evidence seems to confirm his belief that their wages were rising, and the fact that there was a growing demand for servants meant that they were in a stronger bargaining position.[46] Judging by the volume of complaints about their behaviour it seems that many were indeed quite insubordinate. There were numerous allegations about servants pilfering, adding sums to bills, neglecting guests who failed to tip generously enough, and quitting their posts. Many proposals for tighter controls on servants were being put forward, such as Christopher Tancred's *Scheme for an Act of Parliament for the Better Regulating Servants, and Ascertaining their Wages*, published just a year before *Every-Body's Business*. Other commentators also claimed, like Moreton, that maid servants were prone to ideas above their station. Eliza Haywood warned them against 'imitating your Betters in point of Dress': 'The greatest Pleasure you take is in being called *Madam* by such as do not know you; and you fear nothing so much as being taken for what you are'.[47]

One of Moreton's fantasies is that, as soon as a country girl arrives in London to enter domestic service, she is seized upon by 'a Committee of Servant Wenches', who advise her on how to screw her wages up to

---

[46] According to figures given in J. Jean Hecht, *The Domestic Servant Class in Eighteenth-Century England* (London, 1956), a lady's maid would have been paid £6 a year in 1705, and £10 in 1720. Cf. Peter Earle, *The Making of the English Middle Class* (London, 1989), pp. 219–20, 376n.

[47] [Eliza Haywood,] *A Present for a Servant-Maid* (London, 1743), p. 22.

the maximum.[48] This, no doubt, was what prompted a facetious anonymous retort to *Every-Body's Business*, entitled *Everybody's Business is Nobody's Business. Answered Paragraph by Paragraph. By a Committee of Women-Servants and Footmen* (1725). Indeed Defoe's first 'Moreton' pamphlet made quite a stir, and provoked several other replies, such as *The Maid-Servants Modest Defence* (1725), and *Every Man Mind his Own Business* (1725). These were anonymous, but in 1729 the footman-poet Robert Dodsley published a poem, *Servitude*, to which he prefixed an Introduction on the servant question and added a Postscript 'Occasion'd by a late Trifling Pamphlet, entitl'd, *Every Body's Business is No Body's*'. Dodsley is scathing about Moreton's 'trifling and ridiculous' remarks on the ill consequences of maidservants wearing printed linens and cottons, and particularly, apropos of Moreton's complaint about the extravagance of maids over the washing of their own clothes, his 'pitifully taking Notice of its enhancing the Article of Sope'. Nothing in the world, he writes, 'could have more betray'd his mean and sordid Temper, than this low ungentlemanlike Remark'. He ends with a 'sincere Wish' to his fellow-servants 'that those of my Brethren, who do actually resemble the Picture which Squire *Moreton* has drawn of them, may never meet with a better Master than he to encourage them' – a neat tit for tat.[49]

Another of Moreton's pet hates, it is revealed in *Every-Body's Business*, is that 'Race of Caterpillars' known as shoe-blacks. With their excuse for roving the city streets or calling for work at gentlemen's houses, they have abundant opportunity for theft, and with their profane language and retinue of trulls they are, he holds, the enemies of public decency. They must, he suggests, be placed under government-appointed 'taskmasters' and either put to a wholesome trade, such as wool-combing, or made to work down the mines or help to clear the sandbanks in the Thames. But how will we then get our shoes cleaned? Moreton's solution here, as elsewhere, is thoroughly 'interventionist'. 'Ancient persons' and poor widows should be authorised, under a strict system of licensing, to act as shoe-cleaners in a particular 'walk or stand', thus removing a burden from the parish.

In *The Protestant Monastery* Moreton's subject is the congenial one of treatment of the elderly, and how they are now despised by the young. He describes with feeling the miserable fate of one of his old friends, a merchant, who had settled his money on his daughter and her husband

---

[48] *Every-Body's Business*, below, p. 221.
[49] [Robert Dodsley,] *Servitude* (London, [1729]), pp. 29, 32.

and hoped to spend his last years happily in their house, but found himself abused and neglected by them, and even tyrannised over and insulted by the servants. (Moreton's account of a visit to this appalling household, and the despairing letter from his friend a week later, are in Defoe's best novelistic vein.) Moreton's proposal is for a 'Protestant monastery', or joint-stock association of elderly people of either sex and of any religious denomination, to set up their own 'College', furnished with servants, chaplains, doctors and an infirmary. Very much in the manner of Defoe's early *Essays upon Projects*, 'Moreton' goes into some detail as to how the scheme could be financed, though begging his readers' forgiveness for his 'immethodical Manner of calculating'.[50]

This 'monastery' strikes one as an altogether feasible scheme, and a remarkably untraditional one. The force of the story of Moreton's unfortunate old friend is clear: the old must keep complete control of their lives. They must eschew any of the usual dependence on the clergy, or City bigwigs, or professional philanthropists, or condescending Lady Bountifuls. Their refuge is to be neither a charitable nor a religious institution, but a purely secular and pragmatic self-help organisation. This, indeed, is the character of many of Defoe's reformist schemes.

Augusta Triumphans is in some ways Moreton's most characteristic and ambitious piece. The first part of the pamphlet could almost be described as an *Essay upon Projects* in miniature, for it is framed as a series of proposals for social reforms of various kinds. These include the establishment of a university in London, in separate colleges across the city and paid for by fees; an academy of music which would nurture English talent; the abolition of private madhouses; the suppression of prostitution and gambling; a reorganisation and expansion of the Watch to help prevent street crime; and an improved system of street lighting.

The proposal for a University of London is a particularly interesting and far-sighted one. Moreton thinks that standards have declined at Oxford and Cambridge, with students going there 'not to study, but to drink; not for Furniture for the Head, but a Feather for the Cap'.[51] He sees no reason why 'such a Metropolis as *London*' should not sustain a university made up of several colleges located conveniently in various parts of the city. It would have the advantage that students could live at home under the supervision of their parents instead of having to be sent away. Moreton does not in fact mention that Dissenters were excluded

---

[50] *The Protestant Monastery*, below, p. 253.
[51] *Augusta Triumphans*, below, p. 259.

from Oxford and Cambridge. It was, of course, the need to provide un-denominational higher education for Dissenters that led to the foundation of University College in 1828, and eventually to the establishment of the University of London in 1836.

By contrast, Moreton's next proposal, for a Hospital for Foundlings, had already been anticipated, as he himself notes. As long ago as 1713, Addison had called for provision to be made for the care of foundlings, noting that such provision already existed in Paris, Madrid, Lisbon and Rome.[52] Ever since the early 1720s, the philanthropist Thomas Coram had been campaigning on behalf of abandoned infants, and eventually, in 1741, with the approval of George II and the support of such notable figures as Hogarth and Handel, the first children would be admitted to the Foundling Hospital. To those who argued that caring for foundlings would encourage vice, Moreton responds with passion: 'the Fault . . . is in the Parents, not the Child; and we ought to shew our Charity towards it as a Fellow-Creature and Christian, without any regard to its Legitimacy or otherwise' (p. 264).

Later in the pamphlet he speaks out eloquently against the practice of sending wives to madhouses. Private madhouses had been in existence since the seventeenth century, but their numbers were increasing, and they attracted much criticism. As early as 1706 in the *Review*, Defoe had related the case of a young woman wrongly detained in a madhouse run by Dr Edward Tyson, the physician at Bethlem Hospital, and had advocated the official regulation of such madhouses.[53] In *Augusta Triumphans*, Moreton calls for the suppression of all private madhouses and their replacement with licensed houses which would be subject to regular inspection. In a florid apostrophe to Queen Caroline, he calls on her to lead the campaign to 'rescue your injur'd Sex from this Tyranny', and ensure that it would no longer 'be in the Power of every brutal Husband to Cage and Confine his Wife at pleasure' (p. 275). Defoe was here far ahead of his time. It was not until 1774 that the first Act for regulating madhouses was passed, requiring the production of a medical certificate confirming insanity before a non-pauper could be admitted.

The final part of *Augusta Triumphans* is devoted to a scheme for preventing street robberies. This would involve a reorganisation and expansion of the watch. Current watchmen are simply too old and feeble to be of any use, and should be replaced by young, able-bodied, well-

[52] *Guardian*, no. 105, 11 July 1713.
[53] *Review*, 8 June 1706.

armed men, at least three times as many as at present in order to provide a man for every forty houses. They should carry a bugle to sound in case of an alarm. Street lighting should be improved, and rewards should be paid out promptly for the conviction of offenders.

This scheme of Moreton's attracted a certain amount of comment. The author of *Villany Exploded*, an account of the activities of a gang of street robbers recently caught and sent to Newgate, warmly supported Moreton's proposals. He noted, however, that 'The Notion of Mr. *Moreton's* Horn, is laugh'd at by some malicious or foolish People; but a grave Alderman, was pleased to say, on this Occasion, *That the very Thought deserved a Horn to be placed in the Escutcheon of Esq; Moreton'.*[54] Then, on 21 September 1728, a letter signed 'Andrew Moreton' appeared in *Applebee's Journal*, complaining of how the Press, recently, has been puffing a certain 'Projector', who lays claim to a 'Discovery to prevent street robberies', which he promises to offer to Parliament. Moreton strongly suspects, he says, that this is his own scheme, as outlined in *Augusta Triumphans*, and he challenges the 'Projector' to publish his plan, to prove that he is not an imposter. If his proposals really are different from Moreton's, he will be happy for their author to be rewarded for them. As for himself, he says, he asks for no reward, merely for recognition and gratitude. Nevertheless, when Parliament assembles, he intends to give a copy of his own scheme to 'divers honourable worthy members of both Houses'. This letter is then reprinted, a week or two later, in a further 'Andrew Moreton' pamphlet about street robberies, entitled *Second Thoughts are Best*. On 12 October 1728 *Read's Journal*, and one or two other papers, report that 'On Sunday last Andrew Moreton Esq. presented to their Majesties at Windsor, his Scheme for preventing Street-Robberies'.

Now, since there was no such person as Andrew Moreton, and *a fortiori* he could not possibly have presented himself at Windsor, one begins to have a strong feeling that the whole thing – the letter signed 'Andrew Moreton', the rival 'Projector' and the supposed visit to Windsor – may have been a fabrication and a publicity stunt, designed to boost the sales of *Second Thoughts are Best*.[55] The whole episode, however, helps us in understanding how the *persona* of 'Andrew Moreton' is being exploited by Defoe.

---

[54] *Villany Exploded* (London, 1728), pp. 52–54.
[55] The bibliographical story is even more complicated, in that a 'Proposal for Preventing Street-robberies', in places close in its wording both to the relevant portion of *Augusta Triumphans* and to *Second Thoughts are Best*, was printed in *Read's Journal* for 5 October 1728, and there is also a broadsheet in the British Library, entitled *Proposals to Suppress Robberies all over England*, which also echoes the two 'Andrew Moreton' works quite closely.

It is important not to take 'Andrew Moreton' as a mere synonym for Defoe himself, as some of his biographers have done. In his preface to *The Protestant Monastery*, for instance, Moreton explains how he could not persuade any of the journals to publish his scheme for an old-people's home without being paid, and so, in his old age, he has had to 'turn Author' and bring out his own pamphlet. Defoe's Victorian biographer William Lee quaintly took all this quite literally as referring to a recent boycott of Defoe by the journalistic fraternity – occasioned by their discovery, very belatedly, that he had been working for the Government. Poor Defoe, according to Lee, now finds it impossible to place his articles – a sad situation for a man with so much still to offer.[56]

The importance of recognising that the old grumbler 'Andrew Moreton' is a fictional creation of Defoe's can be illustrated by reference to an apparent contradiction between what he says about gin drinking in *Augusta Triumphans*, and what Defoe had written two years earlier, in *A Brief Case of the Distillers* (1726). In the earlier pamphlet Defoe had offered a defence of the distilling trade as a valuable part of the national economy, and had argued there that 'Geneva', i.e. Dutch-style gin, was not necessarily unwholesome: what is ruinous to health is *adulterated* gin, and the vice of drinking too much of it. In *Augusta Triumphans*, by contrast, Moreton launches into a furious diatribe against gin ('There is not in Nature so unhealthy a Liquour as *Geneva*'). This has been taken by some critics as a naked self-contradiction on Defoe's part,[57] but it is perhaps, rather, a contradiction between two quite different kinds of speaker, one of them at least (i.e. Andrew Moreton) being a fictional creation and not simply to be identified with Defoe. He rants about the evils of gin in his own special unbridled and Moretonesque way.

Conclusion

The projects and schemes advocated by Defoe during his long career are a mixed bag, but it is safe to say that no one else in the England of his day competes with him in his range and ambition as a social reformer. It is not surprising that it was in the age of Bentham (or, as the history books style it, 'The Age of Reform') that Defoe's reputation finally took off.

[56] Lee, *Daniel Defoe*, vol. I, pp. 418–19.
[57] Earle, *The World of Defoe*, p. 152.

AN

ESSAY

UPON

Projects.

LONDON:
Printed by *R. R.* for *Tho. Cockerill,*
at the *Three Legs* in the *Poultrey.*
M DC XC VII.

Preface to Dalby Thomas,[1] Esq;
One of the Commissioners for Managing His Majesty's
Duties on Glass, &c.

SIR,

THIS Preface comes Directed to you, not as Commissioner, &c. under whom I have the Honour to serve his Majesty; nor as a Friend; though I have great Obligations of that sort also; but as the most proper Judge of the Subjects Treated of, and more Capable than the greatest part of Mankind to Distinguish and Understand them.

Books are useful only to such whose Genius are suitable to the Subject of them: And to Dedicate a Book of Projects to a Person who had never concern'd himself to Think that way, would be like Musick to one that has no Ear.

And yet Your having a Capacity to Judge of these things, no way brings You under the Despicable Title of a Projector,[2] *any more than knowing the Practices and Subtleties of Wicked Men, makes a Man guilty of their Crimes.*

The several Chapters of this Book, are the results of particular Thoughts, occasion'd by Conversing with the Publick Affairs during the present War with France. *The Losses and Casualties which attend all Trading Nations in the World, when involved in so Cruel a War as this, have reach'd us all, and I am none of the least Sufferers;[3] if this has put me, as well as others, on Inventions and Projects, so much the Subject of this Book, 'tis no more than a proof of the Reason I give for the general Projecting Humour of the Nation.*

One unhappiness I lie under in the following Book, viz. That having kept the greatest Part of it by me for near Five Years, several of the Thoughts seem to be hit by other Hands, and some by the Publick; which turns the tables upon me, as if I had Borrow'd from them.

As particularly that of the Seamen, which you know well I had contriv'd long before the Act for Registring Seamen[4] was Propos'd. And that of Educating Women, which I think my self bound to Declare, was form'd long before the Book call'd Advice to the Ladies,[5] *was made Publick; and yet I do not Write this to Magnify my own Invention, but to acquit my self from Grafting on other People's Thoughts. If I have Trespass'd upon any Person in the World, 'tis upon Your self, from whom I had some of the Notions about County Banks,[6] and Factories for Goods, in the Chapter of Banks; and yet I do not think that my Proposal for the Women, or the Seamen, clashes at all, either with that Book, or the Publick method of Registring Seamen.*

I have been told since this was done, That my Proposal for a Commission of Enquiries into Bankrupt Estates, *is Borrow'd from the* Dutch; *if there is any thing like it among the* Dutch, *'tis more than ever I knew, or know yet; but if so, I hope 'tis no Objection against our having the same here, especially if it be true, that 'twou'd be so publickly Beneficial as is express'd.*

What is said of Friendly Societies, *I think no Man will Dispute with me, since one has met with so much Success already in the Practice of it, I mean,* The Friendly Society for Widows,[7] *of which you have been pleas'd to be a Governor.*

Friendly Societies are very extensive, and as I have hinted, might be carri'd on to many Particulars. I have omitted one which was mention'd in Discourse with your self; where a Hundred Tradesmen, all of several Trades, Agree together to Buy whatever they want of one another, and no where else, Prices *and* Payments *to be settled among themselves; whereby every Man is sure to have Ninety nine Customers, and can never want a Trade: And I cou'd have fill'd up the Book with Instances of like nature, but I never design'd to tire the Reader with Particulars.*

The Proposal of the Pension-Office *you will soon see offer'd to the Publick, as an Attempt for the Relief of the Poor; which if it meets with Encouragement, will every way answer all the great Things I have said of it.*

I had Wrote a great many Sheets about the Coin, about bringing in Plate to the Mint, and about our Standard; but so many great Heads[8] being upon it, with some of whom my Opinion does not agree, I wou'd not adventure to appear in Print upon that Subject.

Ways and Means[9] also I have laid by on the same score. Only adhering to this one Point, That be it by Taxing the Wares they Sell, be it by Taxing them in Stock, be it by Composition,[10] which, by the way, I believe is the best; be it by what way soever the Parliament please, the Retailers are the Men who seem to call upon us to be Tax'd; if not by their own extraordinary good Circumstances, though that might bear it, yet by the contrary in all other Degrees of the Kingdom.

Besides, the Retailers are the only men who cou'd pay it with least damage, because it is in their power to levy it again upon their Customers in the Prices of their Goods, and is no more than paying a higher Rent for their Shops.

The Retailers of Manufactures, especially so far as relates to the Inland Trade, have never been tax'd yet, and their Wealth or Number is not easily calculated: Trade and Land has been handled roughly enough; and these are the men who now lye as a Reserve to carry on the Burthen of the War.

These are the Men, who, were the Land-Tax[11] *collected as it shou'd be, ought to pay the King more than that whole Bill ever produc'd; and yet these are the men who I think I may venture to say, do not pay a Twentieth part in that Bill.*

Shou'd the King appoint a Survey over the Assessors, and Indict all those who were found faulty; allowing a Reward to any Discoverer of an Assessment made lower than the literal Sense of the Act implies, What a Register of Frauds and Connivances wou'd be found out!

In a General Tax, if any shou'd be excus'd, it shou'd be the Poor, who are not able to pay, or at least are pinch'd in the necessary parts of Life by paying: And yet here a poor Labourer who works for Twelve-Pence or Eighteen-Pence a Day, does not drink a Pot of Beer, but pays the King a Tenth part for Excise; and really pays more to the King's Taxes in a year, than a Countrey Shopkeeper, who is Alderman of the Town, worth perhaps Two or Three Thousand Pounds, brews his own Beer, pays no Excise, and in the Land-Tax is rated it may be 100 l. *and pays* 1 l. 4 s. per Annum: *But ought, if the Act were put in due execution, to pay* 36 l. per Ann. *to the King.*

If I were to be ask'd how I wou'd remedy this? I wou'd answer, It shou'd be by some Method in which every man may be tax'd in the due proportion to his Estate, and the Act put in execution, according to the true Intent and Meaning of it; in order to which a Commission of Assessment *shou'd be granted to Twelve Men, such as His Majesty shou'd be well satisfied of, who shou'd go through the whole Kingdom, Three in a Body, and shou'd make a new Assessment of Personal Estates,* not to meddle with Land.

To these Assessors shou'd all the Old Rates, Parish-Books, Poor-Rates, and Highway-Rates also be delivered; and upon due Enquiry to be made into the Manner of Living, and reputed Wealth of the People, the Stock or Personal Estate of every man shou'd be assess'd, without Connivance; and he who is reputed to be worth a Thousand Pound, shou'd be tax'd at a Thousand Pound; and so on: And he who was an over-grown Rich Tradesman of Twenty or Thirty thousand Pounds Estate, shou'd be tax'd so, and Plain English *and Plain Dealing be practis'd indifferently throughout the Kingdom; Tradesmen and Landed men shou'd have Neighbours Fare, as we call it; and a Rich Man shou'd not be pass'd by when a Poor Man pays.*

We read of the Inhabitants of Constantinople,[12] *that they suffer'd their City to be lost, for want of contributing in time for its Defence; and pleaded Poverty to their Generous Emperor, when he went from House to House to persuade them; and yet when the* Turks *took it, the Prodigious Immense Wealth they found in it, made 'em wonder at the sordid Temper of the Citizens.*

England *(with due Exceptions to the Parliament, and the Freedom where-with they have given to the Publick Charge) is much like* Constantinople; *we are involv'd in a Dangerous, a Chargeable, but withal a most Just and Necessary War,*[13] *and the Richest and Money'd Men in the Kingdom plead Poverty; and the* French, *or King* James, *or the* Devil *may come for them, if they can but conceal their Estates from the Publick Notice, and get the Assessors to tax them at an Under-Rate.*

These are the men this Commission wou'd discover; and here they shou'd find men tax'd at 500 l. *Stock, who are worth* 20000 l. *Here they shou'd find a certain Rich Man near* Hackney, *rated to day in the Tax-Book at* 1000 l. *Stock, and to morrow offering* 27000 l. *for an Estate.*

Here they shou'd find Sir J— C—[14] *perhaps tax'd to the King at* 5000 l. *stock, perhaps not so much, whose Cash no man can guess at: And multitudes of Instances I cou'd give by name, without wrong to the Gentlemen.*

And not to run on in Particulars, I affirm, That in the Land-Tax Ten certain Gentlemen in London *put together, did not pay for half so much Personal Estate, call'd* Stock, *as the poorest of them is reputed really to possess.*

I do not enquire at whose door this Fraud must lye, 'tis none of my business.

I wish they wou'd search into it, whose Power can punish it. But this with Submission I presume to say;

The King is thereby defrauded and horribly abus'd; the true Intent and Meaning of Acts of Parliament evaded; the Nation involv'd in Debt by fatal Deficiencies and Interests; Fellow-Subjects abus'd, and new Inventions for Taxes occasion'd.

The last Chapter in this Book is a Proposal about entring all the Seamen in England *into the King's Pay; a Subject which deserves to be enlarg'd into a Book it self; and I have a little Volume of Calculations and Particulars by me on that Head, but I thought them too long to publish. In short, I am persuaded, was that Method propos'd to those Gentlemen to whom such things belong, the greatest Sum of Money might be rais'd by it, with the least Injury to those who pay it, that ever was or will be during the War.*

Projectors, they say, are generally to be taken with allowance of one half at least; they always have their mouths full of Millions, and talk big of their own Proposals; and therefore I have not expos'd the vast Sums my Calculations amount to, but I venture to say I could procure a Farm[15] *on such a Proposal as this at Three Millions* per Ann. *and give very good Security for Payment; such an Opinion I have of the Value of such a Method; and when that is done, the Nation wou'd get Three more by paying it; which is very strange, but might easily be made out.*

In the Chapter of Academies, I have ventur'd to reprove the Vicious Custom of Swearing: I shall make no Apology for the Fact; for no man ought to be asham'd of exposing what all men ought to be asham'd of practising: But methinks I stand corrected by my own Laws a little, in forcing the Reader to repeat some of the worst of our Vulgar Imprecations, in reading my Thoughts against it: To which, however, I have this to reply;

First, *I did not find it easy to express what I mean, without putting down the very Words, at least not so as to be very Intelligible.*

Secondly, *Why should Words repeated only to expose the Vice, taint the Reader, more than a Sermon preach'd against Lewdness should the Assembly; for of necessity it leads the Hearer to the Thoughts of the Fact; but the Morality of every Action lies in the End; and if the Reader by ill use renders himself guilty of the Fact in Reading, which I design'd to expose by Writing, the Fault is his, not mine.*

I have endeavour'd every where in this Book to be as Concise as possible, except where Calculations oblig'd me to be particular; and having avoided Impertinence in the Book, *I wou'd avoid it too in the* Preface; *and therefore shall break off with subscribing my self,*

SIR,

Your most Obliged,
Humble Servant,
D. F.

Introduction.

Necessity, which is allow'd to be the Mother of Invention, has so violently agitated the Wits of men at this time, that it seems not at all improper, by way of distinction, to call it, *The Projecting Age*. For tho' in times of War and Publick Confusions, the like Humour of Invention has seem'd to stir; yet, without being partial to the present, it is, I think, no Injury to say, the past Ages have never come up to the degree of Projecting and Inventing, as it refers to Matters of Negoce,[16] and Methods of Civil Polity, which we see this Age arriv'd to.

Nor is it a hard matter to assign probable Causes of the Perfection in this Modern Art. I am not of their melancholy Opinion, who ascribe it to the general Poverty of the Nation; since I believe 'tis easy to prove, the Nation it self, taking it as one General Stock, is not at all diminish'd or impoverish'd by this Long, this Chargeable War;[17] but on the contrary, was never Richer, since it was inhabited.

Nor am I absolutely of the Opinion, that we are so happy as to be Wiser in this Age, than our Fore-fathers; tho' at the same time I must own, some parts of Knowledge in Science as well as Art, has received Improvements in this Age, altogether conceal'd from the former.

The Art of War, which I take to be the highest Perfection of Human Knowledge, is a sufficient Proof of what I say, especially in conducting Armies, and in offensive Engines; *witness* the new ways of Mines, Fougades,[18] Entrenchments, Attacks, Lodgments,[19] and a long *Et Cetera* of New Inventions which want Names, practised in Sieges and Encampments; *witness* the new sorts of Bombs and unheard-of Mortars, of Seven to Ten Ton Weight, with which our Fleets standing two or three Miles off at Sea, can imitate God Almighty himself, and rain *Fire and Brimstone* out of Heaven, as it were, upon Towns built on the firm Land; *witness also* our new-invented *Child of Hell*, the Machine, which carries Thunder, Lightning, and Earthquakes in its Bowels, and tears up the most impregnable Fortifications.

But if I would search for a Cause, from whence it comes to pass that this Age swarms with such a multitude of Projectors more than usual; who besides the Innumerable Conceptions which dye in the bringing forth, and (like Abortions of the Brain) only come into the Air, and dissolve, do really every day produce new Contrivances, Engines, and Projects to get Money, never before thought of; if, I say, I would examine whence this comes to pass, it must be thus:

The Losses and Depredations which this War brought with it at first, were exceeding many, suffer'd chiefly by the Ill Conduct of Merchants themselves, who did not apprehend the Danger to be really what it was: For before our Admiralty could possibly settle Convoys, Cruisers, and Stations for Men of War all over the World, the *French* cover'd the Sea with their Privateers, and took an incredible number of our Ships. I have heard the Loss computed by those who pretended they were able to guess, at above Fifteen Millions of Pounds *sterling*, in Ships and Goods, in the first two or three Years of the War: A Sum, which if put into *French*, would make such a rumbling Sound of great Numbers, as would fright a weak Accomptant out of his belief, being no less than One hundred and Ninety Millions of *Livres*. The weight of this Loss fell chiefly on the Trading Part of the Nation; and amongst them, on the Merchants; and amongst them again upon the most refin'd Capacities, as the Insurers, *&c.* And an incredible number of the best Merchants in the Kingdom sunk under the Load; as may appear a little by a Bill which once pass'd the House of Commons, for the Relief of Merchant-Insurers,[20] who had suffered by the War with *France*. If a great many fell, much greater were the number of those who felt a sensible Ebb of their Fortunes, and with difficulty bore up under the Loss of great part of their Estates. These, prompted by Necessity, rack their Wits for New Contrivances, New Inventions, New Trades, Stocks, Projects, and any thing to retrieve the desperate Credit of their Fortunes. That this is probable to be the Cause, will appear further thus; *France*, tho' I do not believe all the great Outcries we make of their Misery and Distress, if one half of which be true, they are certainly the best Subjects in the world; yet without question has felt its share of the Losses and Damages of the War; But the Poverty there falling chiefly on the Poorer sort of People, they have not been so fruitful in Inventions and Practices of this nature, their Genius being quite of another strain. As for the Gentry and more capable sort, the first thing a *French* man flies to in his distress, is the Army; and he seldom comes back from thence to Get an Estate by painful Industry, but either has his Brains knock'd out, or makes his Fortune there.

If Industry be in any Business rewarded with success, 'tis in the Merchandizing Part of the World, who indeed may more truly be said to live by their Wits than any people whatsoever. All Foreign Negoce, tho' to some 'tis a plain road by the help of Custom, yet it is in its beginning all Project, Contrivance, and Invention. Every new Voyage the Merchant contrives, is a Project; and Ships are sent from Port to Port, as Markets and Merchandizes differ, by the help of strange and Universal Intelligence; wherein some are so exquisite, so swift, and so exact, that a Merchant sitting at home in his Counting-house, at once converses with all Parts of the known World. This, and Travel, makes a True-bred Merchant the most Intelligent Man in the World, and consequently the most capable, when urg'd by Necessity, to Contrive New Ways to live. And from hence, I humbly conceive, may very properly be deriv'd the *Projects*, so much the Subject of the present Discourse. And to this sort of men 'tis easy to trace the Original of Banks, Stocks, Stock-jobbing, Assurances, Friendly Societies, Lotteries, and the like.

To this may be added, the long annual Enquiry in the House of Commons for Ways and Means, which has been a particular movement to set all the Heads of the Nation at work; and I appeal, with submission, to the Gentlemen of that Honourable House, if the greatest part of all the Ways and Means, out of the common road of Land-Taxes, Polls, and the like, have not been handed to them from the Merchant, and in a great measure Paid by 'em too.

However I offer this but as an Essay at the Original of this prevailing Humour of the People; and as 'tis probable, so, 'tis also possible to be otherwise; which I submit to future demonstration.

Of the several ways this Faculty of Projecting have exerted it self, and of the various Methods, as the Genius of the Authors has inclin'd, I have been a diligent Observer, and in most an unconcern'd Spectator; and, perhaps, have some advantage from thence more easily to discover the *faux Pas* of the Actors. If I have given an Essay towards any thing New, or made Discovery to advantage of any Contrivance now on foot, all Men are at the liberty to make use of the Improvement; if any Fraud is discover'd, as now practis'd, 'tis without any particular Reflection upon Parties or Persons.

Projects of the nature I Treat about, are doubtless in general of publick Advantage, as they tend to Improvement of Trade, and Employment of the Poor, and the Circulation and Increase of the publick Stock of the Kingdom; but this is suppos'd of such as are built on the honest Basis of Ingenuity and Improvement; in which, tho' I'le[21] allow the Author to aim primarily at his own Advantage, yet with the circumstances of Publick Benefit added.

Wherefore 'tis necessary to distinguish among the Projects of the present times, between the Honest and the Dishonest.

There are, and that too many, fair pretences of fine Discoveries, new Inventions, Engines, and I know not what, which being advanc'd in Notion, and talk'd up to great things to be perform'd when such and such Sums of Money shall be advanc'd, and such and such Engines are made, have rais'd the Fancies of Credulous People to such height, that meerly on the shadow of Expectation, they have form'd Companies, chose Committees, appointed Officers, Shares, and Books, rais'd great Stocks, and cri'd up an empty Notion to that degree, that People have been betray'd to part with their Money for Shares in a *New-Nothing*; and when the Inventors have carri'd on the Jest till they have Sold all their own Interest, they leave the Cloud to vanish of it self, and the poor Purchasers to Quarrel with one another, and go to Law about Settlements, Transferrings, and some Bone or other thrown among 'em by the Subtlety of the Author, to lay the blame of the Miscarriage upon themselves. Thus the Shares at first begin to fall by degrees, and happy is he that Sells in time; till like Brass Money it will go at last for nothing at all. So have I seen Shares in Joint-Stocks, Patents, Engines, and Undertakings, blown up by the air of great Words, and the Name of some Man of Credit concerned, to 100 *l.* for a 500*th.* Part, or Share, some more, and at last dwindle away, till it has been Stock-Jobb'd down to 10, 12, 9, 8 *l.* a Share, and at last no Buyer; that is, in short, the fine new word for Nothing-worth, and many Families ruin'd by the Purchase. If I should name *Linnen-Manufactures, Saltpeter-Works, Copper-Mines, Diving-Engines, Dipping,*[22] and the like, for instances of this, I shou'd, I believe, do no wrong to Truth, or to some Persons too visibly guilty.

I might go on upon this Subject to expose the Frauds and Tricks of *Stock-Jobbers, Engineers, Patentees, Committees,* with those *Exchange-Mountebanks* we very properly call *Brokers*; but I have not Gaul enough for such a work; but as a general rule of caution to those who wou'd not be Trick'd out of their Estates by such Pretenders to New Inventions, let them observe, That all such People who may be suspected of Design, have assuredly this in their Proposal, Your Money to the Author must go before the Experiment: And here I could give a very diverting History of a Patent-Monger,[23] whose Cully[24] was no body but my self; but I refer it to another occasion.

But this is no reason why Invention upon honest foundations, and to fair purposes, shou'd not be encourag'd; no, nor why the Author of any such fair Contrivances should not reap the harvest of his own Ingenuity; our Acts of Parliament for granting Patents[25] to first Inventors for Fourteen years, is a sufficient acknowledgement of the due regard which ought to be had to such as find out any thing which may be of publick Advantage; new Discoveries in Trade, in Arts and Mysteries,[26] of Manufacturing Goods, or Improvement of Land, are without question of as great benefit, as any Discoveries made in the Works of Nature by all the *Academies* and *Royal Societies* in the world.

There is, 'tis true, a great difference between *New Inventions* and *Projects*, between Improvement of Manufactures or Lands, which tend to the immediate Benefit of the Publick, and Imploying of the Poor; and Projects fram'd by subtle Heads, with a sort of a *Deceptio Visus*,[27] and *Legerdemain*, to bring People to run needless and unusual hazards: I grant it, and give a due preference to the first, and yet Success has so sancti-fi'd some of those other sorts of Projects, that 'twou'd be a kind of Blasphemy against Fortune to disallow 'em; witness Sir *William Phips*'s Voyage[28] to the Wreck; 'twas a mere Project, a Lottery of a Hundred thousand to One odds; a hazard, which if it had fail'd, every body wou'd have been asham'd to have own'd themselves concern'd in; a Voyage that wou'd have been as much ridicul'd as *Don Quixot's Adventure upon the Windmill*: Bless us! that Folks should go Three thousand Miles to Angle in the open Sea for Pieces of Eight! why, they wou'd have made Ballads of it, and the Merchants wou'd have said of every unlikely Adventure, 'Twas like *Phips* his Wreck-Voyage; but it had Success, and who reflects upon the Project?

> *Nothing's so partial as the Laws of Fate,*
> *Erecting Blockheads to suppress the Great.*
> *Sir* Francis Drake *the* Spanish *Plate-Fleet Won,*
> *He had been a Pyrate if he had got none.*
> *Sir* Walter Rawleigh *strove, but miss'd the Plate,*
> *And therefore Di'd a Traytor to the State.*
>
> *Endeavour bears a Value more or less,*
> *Just as 'tis recommended by Success:*
> *The lucky Coxcomb ev'ry Man will prize,*
> *And Prosp'rous Actions always pass for Wise.*[29]

However, this sort of Projects comes under no Reflection as to their Honesty, save that there is a kind of Honesty a Man owes to himself and to his Family, that prohibits him throwing away his Estate in imprac-ticable, improbable Adventures; but still some hit even of the most unlikely, of which this was one, of Sir *William Phips*, who brought home a Cargo of Silver of near 200,000 *l. sterling*, in Pieces of Eight, fish'd up out of the open Sea remote from any shore, from an old *Spanish* Ship which had been sunk above Forty Years.

THE HISTORY OF PROJECTS.

WHEN I speak of Writing a *History of Projects*, I do not mean either of the Introduction of, or Continuing necessary Inventions, or the Improvement of Arts and Sciences before known; but a short Account of Projects, and Projecting, as the Word is allow'd in the general Acceptation at this present time, and I need not go far back for the Original of the Practice.

Invention of Arts with Engines and Handycraft Instruments for their Improvement, requires a Chronology as far back as the Eldest Son of *Adam*, and has to this day afforded some new Discovery in every Age.

The Building of the Ark by *Noah*, so far as you will allow it a human Work, was the first Project I read of; and no question seem'd so ridiculous to the Graver Heads of that Wise, tho' Wicked Age, that poor *Noah* was sufficiently banter'd for it; and had he not been set on work by a very peculiar Direction from Heaven, the Good old Man would certainly have been laugh'd out of it, as a most senseless ridiculous Project.

The Building of *Babel*[30] was a Right Project; for indeed the true definition of a Project, according to Modern Acceptation, is, as is said before, a vast Undertaking too big to be manag'd, and therefore likely enough to come to nothing; and yet as great as they are, 'tis certainly true of 'em all, even as the Projectors propose; that according to the old tale, If so many Eggs are hatch'd, there will be so many Chickens, and those Chickens may lay so many Eggs more, and those Eggs produce so many Chickens more, and so on. Thus 'twas most certainly true, That if the People of the Old World cou'd have Built a House up to Heaven, they shou'd never be Drown'd again on Earth, and they only had forgot to Measure the Heighth, *that is*, as in other Projects, it only Miscarri'd, or else 'twou'd have Succeeded.

And yet when all's done, that very Building, and the incredible Heighth it was carri'd, is a Demonstration of the vast Knowledge of that Infant-

Age of the World, who had no advantage of the Experiments or Invention of any before themselves.

> *Thus when our Fathers touch'd with Guilt,*
> *That* Huge stupendious Stair-Case *Built;*
> *We Mock indeed the fruitless Enterprize,*
> *For fruitless Actions seldom pass for Wise;*
> *But were the* Mighty Ruins *left, they'd show,*
> *To what Degree that Untaught Age did Know.*[31]

I believe a very diverting Account might be given of this, but I shall not attempt it. Some are apt to say with *Solomon,*[32] *No new thing happens under the Sun, but what is, has been*; yet I make no question but some considerable Discovery has been made in these latter Ages, and Inventions of Human Original produc'd, which the World was ever without before, either in whole, or in part; and I refer only to two Cardinal Points, the use of the Load-stone at Sea, and the use of Gunpowder and Guns; both which, as to the Inventing-part, I believe the World owes as absolutely to those particular Ages, as it does the Working in Brass and Iron to *Tubal Cain,*[33] or the Inventing of Musick to *Jubal* his Brother.[34] As to Engines and Instruments for Handycraft-Men, this Age, I dare say, can show such as never were so much as thought of, much less imitated before; for I do not call that a real Invention which has something before done like it, I account that more properly an Improvement. For Handycraft Instruments, I know none owes more to true genuine Contrivance, without borrowing from any former use, than a Mechanick Engine contriv'd in our time, call'd, *A Knitting Frame,*[35] which built with admirable Symetry, works really with a very happy Success, and may be observ'd by the Curious to have a more than ordinary Composition; for which I refer to the Engine it self, to be seen in every Stocking-Weaver's Garret.

I shall trace the Original of the Projecting Humour that now reigns, no farther back than the Year 1680, dating its Birth as a Monster then, tho' by times it had indeed something of life in the time of the late Civil War. I allow, no Age has been altogether without something of this nature; and some very happy Projects are left to us as a taste of their Success; as the Water-houses[36] for supplying of the City of *London* with Water; and since that, the *New-River,*[37] both very Considerable Undertakings, and Perfect Projects, adventur'd on the risque of Success. In the Reign of King *Charles* the First, infinite Projects were set on foot for Raising Money without a Parliament; Oppressing by Monopolies, and

Privy Seals; but these are excluded our Scheme, as Irregularities; for thus the *French* are as fruitful in Projects as we; and these are rather Stratagems than Projects. After the Fire of *London*, the Contrivance of an Engine to Quench Fires,[38] was a Project the Author was said to get well by, and we have found to be very useful. But about the Year 1680 began the Art and Mystery of Projecting to creep into the World. Prince *Rupert*,[39] Uncle to King *Charles* the Second, gave great Encouragement to that part of it that respects Engines, and Mechanical Motions; and Bishop *Wilkins*[40] added as much of the Theory to it, as writing a Book could do: The Prince has left us a Metal call'd by his Name; and the first Project upon that was, as I remember, Casting of Guns of that Metal, and boring them; done both by a peculiar Method of his own, and which died with him, to the great loss of the Undertaker, who to that purpose had, with no small Charge, erected a Water-Mill at *Hackney-Marsh*, known by the name of the *Temple-Mill*: Which Mill very happily perform'd all parts of the Work; and I have seen of those Guns on board the Royal *Charles*, a First-rate Ship, being of a Reddish Colour, different either from Brass or Copper. I have heard some Reasons of State assign'd, why that Project was not permitted to go forward; but I omit them, because I have no good Authority for it: After this, we saw a Floating Machine, to be wrought with Horses for the Towing of Great Ships both against Wind and Tide; and another for the raising of Ballast which, as unperforming Engines, had the honour of being Made, Expos'd, Tri'd, and laid by, before the Prince died.

If thus we introduce it into the World under the Conduct of that Prince; when he died, 'twas left a hopeless Brat, and had hardly any Hand to own it, till the Wreck-Voyage before-noted, perform'd so happily by Captain *Phips*,[41] afterwards Sir *William*; whose strange Performance set a great many Heads on work to contrive something for themselves; he was immediately follow'd by my Lord *Mordant*,[42] Sir *John Narborough*,[43] and others from several Parts, whose Success made 'em soon weary of the Work.

The Project of the *Penny-Post*, so well known, and still practis'd, I cannot omit; nor the Contriver Mr. *Dockwra*,[44] who has had the honour to have the Injury done him in that Affair, repair'd in some measure by the publick Justice of the Parliament. And the Experiment proving it to be a Noble and Useful Design, the Author must be remembered, where-ever mention is made of that Affair, to his very great Reputation.

'Twas no question a great hardship for a man to be Master of so fine a Thought, that had *both* the *Essential Ends of a Project* in it, *Publick Good*, and *Private Advantage*; and that the Publick shou'd reap the benefit, and the Author be left out; the Injustice of which, no doubt, discourag'd many a Good Design: But since an Alteration in Publick Circumstances has recover'd the lost Attribute of Justice, the like is not to be fear'd. And Mr. *Dockwra* has had the satisfaction to see the former Injury disown'd, and an honourable Return made even by them who did not the Injury, in bare respect to his Ingenuity.

A while before this, several People, under the Patronage of some great Persons, had engag'd in Planting of Foreign Collonies; as *William Pen*,[45] the Lord *Shaftsbury*,[46] Dr. *Cox*,[47] and others, in *Pensilvania, Carolina, East* and *West Jersey*, and the like places; which I do not call Projects, because 'twas only prosecuting what had been formerly begun: But here began the forming of publick Joint-Stocks, which, together with the *East-India, African*, and *Hudson's-Bay* Companies, before establish'd, begot a New Trade, which we call by a new Name, *Stock-Jobbing*, which was at first only the simple Occasional Transferring of Interest and Shares from one to another, as Persons alienated their Estates; but by the Industry of the Exchange-Brokers, who got the business into their hands, it became a Trade; and one perhaps manag'd with the greatest Intriegue, Artifice, and Trick, that ever any thing that appear'd with a face of Honesty could be handl'd with; for while the Brokers held the Box, they made the whole *Exchange* the Gamesters, and rais'd and lower'd the Prices of Stocks as they pleas'd; and always had both Buyers and Sellers who stood ready innocently to commit their Money to the mercy of their Mercenary Tongues. This Upstart of a Trade having tasted the sweetness of Success which generally attends a *Novel Proposal*, introduces the Illigitimate wandring Object I speak of, as a proper Engine to find Work for the Brokers. Thus Stock-Jobbing nurs'd Projecting, and Projecting in return has very diligently pimp'd for its Foster-parent, till both are arriv'd to be Publick Grievances; and indeed are now almost grown scandalous.

Of Projectors.

MAN is the worst of all God's Creatures to shift for himself; no other Animal is ever starv'd to death; Nature without, has provided them both Food and Cloaths; and Nature within, has plac'd an Instinct that never fails to direct them to proper means for a supply; but Man must either *Work or Starve, Slave or Dye*; he has indeed Reason given him to direct him, and few who follow the Dictates of that Reason come to such unhappy Exigencies; but when by the Errors of a Man's Youth he has reduc'd himself to such a degree of Distress, as to be absolutely without Three things, *Money*, *Friends*, and *Health*, he Dies in a Ditch, or in some worse place, *an Hospital*.

Ten thousand ways there are to bring a Man to this, and but very few to bring him out again.

Death is the universal Deliverer, and therefore some who want Courage to bear what they see before 'em, *Hang themselves for fear*; for certainly Self-destruction is the effect of Cowardice in the highest extream.

Others break the Bounds of Laws to satisfy that general Law of Nature, and turn open Thieves, House-breakers, Highway-men, Clippers, Coiners, &c. till they run the length of the Gallows, and get a Deliverance the nearest way at St. *Tyburn*.

Others being masters of more Cunning than their neighbours, turn their Thoughts to Private Methods of Trick and Cheat, a Modern way of Thieveing, every jot as Criminal, and in some degree worse than the other, by which honest men are gull'd with fair pretences to part from their Money, and then left to take their Course with the Author, who sculks behind the curtain of a Protection, or in the *Mint*[48] or *Friars*,[49] and bids defiance as well to Honesty as the Law.

Others yet urg'd by the same necessity, turn their thoughts to Honest Invention, founded upon the Platform of Ingenuity and Integrity.

These two last sorts are those we call *Projectors*; and as there was always *more Geese than Swans*, the number of the latter are very inconsiderable in comparison of the former; and as the greater number denominates the less, the just Contempt we have of the former sort, bespatters the other, who like Cuckolds bear the reproach of other Peoples Crimes.

A meer Projector then is a Contemptible thing, driven by his own desperate Fortune to such a Streight, that he must be deliver'd by a Miracle, or Starve; and when he has beat his Brains for some such Miracle in vain, he finds no remedy but to paint up some Bauble or other, *as Players make Puppets talk big*, to show like a strange thing, and then cry it up for a New Invention, gets a Patent for it, divides it into Shares, and *they must be Sold*; ways and means are not wanting to Swell the new Whim to a vast Magnitude; Thousands, and Hundreds of thousands are the least of his discourse, and sometimes Millions; till the Ambition of some honest Coxcomb is wheedl'd to part with his Money for it, and then

—Nascitur ridiculus mus.[50]

the Adventurer is left to carry on the Project, and the Projector laughs at him. The *Diver* shall walk at the bottom of the *Thames*; the *Saltpeter-Maker* shall Build *Tom T—ds* Pond[51] into Houses; the Engineers Build Models and Windmills to draw Water, till Funds are rais'd to carry it on, by Men who have more Money than Brains, and then *good night Patent and Invention*; the Projector has done his business, and is gone.

But the Honest Projector is he, who having by fair and plain principles of Sense, Honesty, and Ingenuity, brought any Contrivance to a suitable Perfection, makes out what he pretends to, picks no body's pocket, puts his Project in Execution, and contents himself with the real Produce, as the profit of his Invention.

Of Banks.

BANKS, without question, if rightly manag'd, are, or may be, of great Advantage, especially to a Trading People, as the *English* are; and among many others, this is one particular case in which that Benefit appears, That they bring down the Interest of Money, and take from the Goldsmiths, Scriveners, and others, who have command of running Cash, their most delicious Trade of making advantage of the necessities of the Merchant, in extravagant Discounts, and Premio's[52] for advance of Money, when either large Customs or Foreign Remittances, call for Disbursements beyond his common Ability; for by the easiness of Terms on which the Merchant may have Money, he is encourag'd to venture further in Trade than otherwise he would do; not but that there are other great advantages a *Royal Bank* might procure in this Kingdom, as has been seen in part by this, As advancing Money to the *Exchequer* upon Parliamentary Funds and Securities, by which in time of a War our Preparations for any Expedition need not be in danger of Miscarriage for want of Money, though the Taxes rais'd be not speedily paid, nor the *Exchequer* burthen'd with the excessive Interests paid in former Reigns upon Anticipations of the Revenue; Landed Men might be supplied with Moneys upon Securities on easier Terms, which would prevent the Loss of multitudes of Estates, now ruin'd and devour'd by insolent and merciless Mortgagees and the like. But now we unhappily see a *Royal Bank* Establish'd[53] by Act of Parliament, and another with a large Fund upon the *Orphans* Stock;[54] and yet these Advantages, or others, which we expected, not answer'd, tho' the pretensions in Both have not been wanting at such time as they found it needful to introduce themselves into publick Esteem, by giving out Prints of what they were rather able to do, than really intended to practice. So that our having Two Banks at this time settl'd, and more Erecting, has not yet been able to reduce the Interest of Money; not because the Nature and Foundation of their Constitution does not tend towards it; but because, finding their Hands full of better business, they are wiser than by being slaves to old obselete Proposals, to lose the advantage of the great Improvement they can make of their Stock.

This however, does not at all reflect on the Nature of a Bank, nor of the Benefit it would be to the publick Trading-part of the Kingdom, whatever it may seem to do on the practice of the present. We find Four or Five Banks[55] now in view to be settl'd; I confess I expect no more from those to come, than we have found from the past; and I think I make no breach on either my Charity or *good Manners*, in saying so; and I reflect not upon any of the Banks that are or shall be Establish'd for not doing what I mention, but for making such publications of what they would do. I cannot think any Man had expected the *Royal Bank* shou'd Lend Money on Mortgages at 4 *per Cent.* nor was it much the better for them to make publication they wou'd do so, from the beginning of *January* next after their Settlement; since to this day, as I am inform'd, they have not Lent one Farthing in that manner.

Our Banks are indeed nothing but so many Goldsmiths Shops, where the Credit being high (and the Directors as high) People lodge their Money; and They, the Directors I mean, make their advantage of it; if you lay it at Demand, they allow you nothing; if at Time, 3 *per Cent.* and so wou'd any Goldsmith in *Lombardstreet* have done before; but the very Banks themselves are so aukward in Lending; so strict, so tedious, so inquisitive, and withal so publick in their taking Securities, that Men who are any thing tender, won't go to them; and so the easiness of Borrowing Money, so much design'd, is defeated; for here is a private Interest to be made, tho' it be a publick one; and, in short, 'tis only a great Trade carri'd on for the private Gain of a few concern'd in the Original Stock; and tho' we are to hope for great things, because they have promis'd them; yet they are all Future that we know of.

And yet all this while a Bank might be very beneficial to this Kingdom; and This might be so, if either their own Ingenuity, or Publick Authority, would oblige them to take the Publick Good into equal Concern with their Private Interest.

To explain what I mean;

Banks being establish'd by Publick Authority, ought also, as all Publick things are, to be under Limitations and Restrictions from that Authority; and those Limitations being regulated with a proper regard to the Ease of Trade in General, and the Improvement of the Stock in Particular, would make a Bank a Useful, Profitable Thing indeed.

First, A Bank ought to be of a Magnitude proportion'd to the Trade of the Countrey it is in; which this Bank is so far from, that 'tis no more to the Whole, than the least Goldsmith's Cash in *Lombardstreet* is to the Bank: From whence it comes to pass, that already more Banks are contriving; and I question not but Banks in *London* will e're long be as frequent as Lotteries:[56] The Consequence of which in all Probability will be, the diminishing their Reputation, or a Civil War with one another. 'Tis true, the Bank of *England* has a Capital Stock; but yet was that Stock wholly clear of the Publick Concern of the Government, it is not above a Fifth Part of what would be necessary to manage the whole Business of the Town; which it ought, tho' not to do, at least to be Able to do: And I suppose I may venture to say, Above one half of the Stock of the present Bank is taken up in the Affairs of the Exchequer.

I suppose no body will take this Discourse for an Invective against the Bank of *England*; I believe it is a very Good Fund, a very Useful one, and a very Profitable one: It has been Useful to the Government, and it is Profitable to the Proprietors; and the establishing it at such a Juncture, when our Enemies were making great boasts of our Poverty and Want of Money, was a particular Glory to our Nation, and the City in particular. That when the *Paris Gazette* inform'd the World, That the Parliament had indeed given the King Grants for raising Money in Funds to be paid in remote Years; but Money was so scarce, that no Anticipations could be procured: That just then, besides Three Millions paid into the Exchequer that Spring on other Taxes by way of Advance, there was an Overplus-Stock to be found of 1,200,000 Pounds *sterling* or (to make it speak *French*) of above Fifteen Millions, which was all paid Voluntarily into the Exchequer, in less than   [57] Besides this, I believe the present Bank of *England* has been very useful to the Exchequer, and to supply the King with Remittances for the Payment of the Army in *Flanders*; which has also, by the way, been very profitable to it self. But still this Bank is not of that Bulk that the Business done here requires; nor is it able, with all the Stock it has, to procure the great propos'd Benefit, the low'ring the Interest of Money: Whereas all Foreign Banks absolutely govern the Interest, both at *Amsterdam, Genoa,* and other places. And this Defect I conceive the Multiplicity of Banks cannot supply, unless a perfect Understanding could be secur'd between them.

To remedy this Defect, several Methods might be propos'd: Some I shall take the Freedom to hint at.

First, That the present Bank increase their Stock to at least Five Millions *sterling*, to be settled as they are already, with some small Limitations to make the Methods more beneficial.

Five Millions *sterling* is an immense Sum; to which add the Credit of their Cash, which would supply them with all the Overplus-Money in the Town, and probably might amount to half as much more; and then the Credit of Running-Bills, which by circulating would no question be an Equivalent to the other half: So that in Stock, Credit, and Bank-bills, the Balance of their Cash would be always Ten Millions *sterling*: A sum that every body who can talk of, does not understand.

But then to find Business for all this Stock; which though it be a strange thing to think of, is nevertheless easy when it comes to be examin'd. And first for the Business; This Bank shou'd enlarge the Number of their Directors as they do of their Stock; and should then establish several Sub-Committees, compos'd of their own Members, who shou'd have the directing of several Offices relating to the distinct sorts of Business they referr'd to; to be over-rul'd and govern'd by the Governor and Directors in a Body, but to have a Conclusive Power as to Contracts. Of these there should be

One Office for Loan of Money for Customs of Goods; which by a plain Method might be so order'd, that the Merchant might with ease pay the highest Customs down; and so by allowing the Bank 4 *per Cent.* Advance, be first sure to secure the 10 *l. per Cent.* which the King allows for Prompt Payment at the *Custom-house*; and be also freed from the troublesome work of finding *Bonds-Men*, and Securities for the Money; which has expos'd many a Man to the Tyranny of Extents either for himself or his Friend, to his utter Ruin; who under a more moderate Prosecution, had been able to pay all his Debts; and by this Method has been torn to pieces, and disabled from making any tolerable Proposal to his Creditors. This is a Scene of Large Business, and would in proportion employ a Large Cash: And 'tis the easiest thing in the world to make the Bank the Paymaster of all the Large Customs, and yet the Merchant have so honourable a Possession of his Goods, as may be neither any Diminution to his Reputation, or any Hindrance to their Sale.

As for Example:

Suppose I have 100 Hogsheads of Tobacco to Import, whose Customs by several Duties comes to 1000 *l.* and want Cash to clear them; I go with my Bill of Loading to the Bank, who appoint their Officer to Enter the Goods, and pay the Duties; which Goods so entred by the Bank, shall give them Title enough to any part, or the whole, without the trouble of Bills of Sale, or Conveyances, Defeazances, and the like. The Goods are carried to a Warehouse at the Waterside, where the Merchant has a Free and Publick Access to them, as if in his own Warehouse, and as honourable Liberty to sell and deliver either the Whole (paying their Disburse) or a Part without it, leaving but sufficient for the Payment; and out of that Part delivered, either by Notes under the Hand of the Purchaser, or any other way, he may clear the same, without any Exactions, but of 4 *l. per Cent.* and the rest are his own.

The ease this wou'd bring to Trade, the deliverance it wou'd bring to the Merchants from the insults of Goldsmiths, *&c.* and the honour it wou'd give to our management of Publick Imposts, with the advantages to the Custom-House it self, and the utter destruction of Extortion, wou'd be such as wou'd give a due value to the Bank, and make all Mankind acknowledge it to be a publick good. The Grievance of Exactions upon Merchants in this case is very great; and when I lay the blame on the Goldsmiths, because they are the principal People made use of in such occasions, I include a great many other sorts of Brokers, and Money-jobbing Artists, who all get a snip out of the Merchant. I my self have known a Goldsmith in *Lumbardstreet* Lend a Man 700 *l.* to pay the Customs of a Hundred Pipes of *Spanish* Wines; the Wines were made over to him for Security by Bill of Sale, and put into a Cellar, of which the Goldsmith kept the Key; the Merchant was to pay *6 l. per Cent.* Interest on the Bond, and to allow 10 *l. per Cent.* Premio for advancing the Money: When he had the Wines in Possession, the Owner cou'd not send his Cooper to look after them, but the Goldsmith's Man must attend all the while, for which he wou'd be paid 5 *s.* a day. If he brought a Customer to see them, the Goldsmith's Man must show them; the Money was Lent for Two Months; he cou'd not be admitted to Sell or Deliver a Pipe of Wine out single, or Two or Three at a time, as he might have Sold them; but on a word or two spoken amiss to the Goldsmith, *or which he was pleased to take so,* he wou'd have none Sold, but the whole Parcel together; by this usage the Goods lay on hand, and every Month the Money remain'd, the Goldsmith demanded a Guinea *per Cent.* forbearance, besides the Interest, till at last by Leakage, Decay, and other Accidents, the Wines began to lessen: Then the Goldsmith begins to tell the Merchant, he is afraid the Wines are not worth the Money he was Lent, and demands further Security; and in a little while growing higher and rougher, he tells him, he must have his Money; the Merchant too much at his Mercy, because he cannot provide the Money, is forc'd to consent to the Sale, and the Goods being reduc'd to Seventy Pipes sound Wine, and Four unsound (the rest being sunk for filling up) were Sold for 13 *l. per* Pipe the Sound, and 3 *l.* the Unsound, which amounted to 922 *l.* together:

	l.	*s.*	*d.*
The Coopers Bill came to	30	0	0
The Cellerage a Year and Half to	18	0	0
Interests on the Bond to	63	0	0
The Goldsmith's Men for Attendance	08	0	0
Allowance for Advance of the Money, and Forbearance	74	0	0
	193	0	0
Principal Money Borrow'd	700	0	0
	893	0	0
Due to the Merchant	29	0	0
	922	0	0

By the moderatest Computation that can be, these Wines Cost the Merchant as follows:

	l.	*s.*	*d.*
First Cost with Charges on Board			
In Lisbon 15 Mille Reis *per Pipe is* 1500 Mill.			
Re. *Exchange,* at 6 *s.* 4 *d. per* Mille Rei	475	0	0
Freight to London – *then* at 3 *l. per* Ton	150	0	0
Assurance on 500 *l.* at 2 per C.	10	0	0
Petty Charges	05	0	0
	640	0	0

So that 'tis manifest by the Extortion of this Banker, the poor Man lost the whole Capital with Freight and Charges, and made but 29 *l.* produce of a Hunder'd Pipes of Wine.

One other Office of this Bank, and which wou'd take up a considerable branch of the Stock, is for Lending Money upon Pledges, which shou'd have annex'd to it a Warehouse and Factory, where all sorts of Goods might publickly be Sold by the Consent of the Owners, to the great Advantage of the Owner, the Bank receiving 4 *l. per Cent.* Interest, and 2 *per Cent.* Commission for Sale of the Goods.

A Third Office shou'd be appointed for Discounting Bills, Tallies,[58] and Notes, by which all Tallies of the *Exchequer*, and any part of the Revenue, shou'd at stated Allowances be ready Money to any Person, to the great Advantage of the Government, and ease of all such as are any ways concern'd in publick Undertakings.

A Fourth Office for Lending Money upon Land-Securities at 4 *per Cent.* Interest; by which the Cruelty and Injustice of Mortgagees wou'd be wholly restrain'd, and a Register of Mortgages might be very well kept, to prevent Frauds.

A Fifth Office for Exchanges and Foreign Correspondences.

A Sixth for Inland Exchanges, where a very large Field of Business lies before them.

Under this Head 'twill not be improper to consider, that this Method will most effectually answer all the Notions and Proposals of County-Banks; for by this Office they wou'd be all render'd useless and unprofitable; since One Bank, of the Magnitude I mention, with a Branch of its Office set apart for that Business, might with ease Manage all the Inland-Exchange of the Kingdom.

By which such a Correspondence with all the Trading-Towns in *England* might be maintain'd, as that the whole Kingdom shou'd Trade with the Bank. Under the Direction of this Office a Publick Cashier shou'd be appointed in every County, to reside in the Capital Town as to Trade, and in some Counties more, through whose Hands all the Cash of the Revenue of the Gentry, and of Trade, shou'd be return'd on the Bank in *London*, and from the Bank again on their Cashier in every respective County or Town, at the small Exchange of ¼ *per Cent.* by which means all loss of Money carri'd upon the Road, to the encouragement of Robbers, and Ruining of the Countrey, who are Su'd for those Robberies, wou'd be more effectually prevented, than by all the Statutes against Highway-Men that are or can be made.

As to Publick Advancings of Money to the Government, they may be left to the Directors in a Body, as all other Disputes and Contingent cases are; and whoever examines these Heads of Business apart, and has any Judgment in the Particulars, will, I suppose, allow, that a Stock of Ten Millions may find Employment in them, though it be indeed a very great Sum.

I cou'd offer some very good Reasons, why this way of Management by particular Offices for every particular sort of Business, is not only the easiest, but the safest way of executing an Affair of such variety and consequence; also I cou'd state a Method for the Proceedings of those private Offices, their Conjunction with, and Dependance on the General Court of the Directors, and how the various Accompts shou'd Center in one General Capital account of Stock, with Regulations and Appeals; but I believe them to be needless, at least in this place.

If it be Objected here, That it is impossible for One Joint Stock to go thorough the whole Business of the Kingdom. I Answer, I believe it is not either impossible or impracticable, particularly on this one account, that almost all the Country Business wou'd be Manag'd by running-Bills, and those the longest abroad of any, their distance keeping them out, to the Increasing the Credit, and consequently the Stock of the Bank.

Of the Multiplicity of Banks.

What is touch'd at in the foregoing part of this Chapter, refers to *One Bank-Royal*, to Preside, as it were, over the whole Cash of the Kingdom: But because some People do suppose this Work fitter for many Banks than for One; I must a little consider that Head: And first, allowing those many Banks cou'd without clashing maintain a constant Correspondence with one another, in passing each others Bills as Current from one to another, I know not but it might be better perform'd by Many, than by One; for as Harmony makes Musick in Sound, so it produces Success in Business.

A *Civil War* among Merchants is always the Ruin of Trade: I cannot think a Multitude of Banks cou'd so consist with one another in *England*, as to join Interests, and uphold one another's Credit, without joining Stocks too; I confess, if it cou'd be done, the Convenience to Trade wou'd be Visible.

If I were to Propose which way these Banks shou'd be Establish'd; I answer, Allowing a due regard to some Gentlemen who have had thoughts of the same,[59] whose Methods I shall not so much as touch upon, much less discover; My thoughts run upon quite different Methods, both for the Fund, and the Establishment.

Every principal Town in *England* is a Corporation, upon which the Fund may be settled; which will sufficiently answer the difficult and chargeable work of Suing for a Corporation by Patent or Act of Parliament.

A general Subscription of Stock being made, and by Deeds of Settlement plac'd in the Mayor and Aldermen of the City or Corporation for the time being, in Trust, to be declared by Deeds of Uses, some of the Directors being always made Members of the said Corporation, and join'd in the Trust, the Bank hereby becomes the Publick Stock of the Town, something like what they call the *Rents of the Town-House* in *France*,[60] and is Manag'd in the Name of the said Corporation, to whom the Directors are Accountable, and they back again to the General Court.

For Example:

Suppose the Gentlemen, or Tradesmen, of the County of *Norfolk*, by a Subscription of Cash, design to Establish a Bank: The Subscriptions being made, the Stock is paid into the Chamber of the City of *Norwich*, and manag'd by a Court of Directors, as all Banks are, and chosen out of the Subscribers, the Mayor only of the City to be always one; to be managed in the Name of the Corporation of the City of *Norwich*, but for the Uses in a Deed of Trust to be made by the Subscribers, and Mayor and Aldermen, at large mentioned. I make no question but a Bank thus settled, wou'd have as firm a Foundation as any Bank need to have, and every way answer the Ends of a Corporation.

Of these sorts of Banks *England* might very well establish Fifteen, at the several Towns hereafter mention'd. Some of which, tho they are not the Capital Towns of the Counties, yet are more the Center of Trade, which in *England* runs in Veins, like Mines of Metal in the Earth.

Canterbury.	*Leeds,* or *Halifax,* or *York.*
Salisbury.	*Nottingham.*
Exeter.	*Warwick,* or *Birmingham*
Bristol.	*Oxford,* or *Reading*
Worcester.	*Bedford.*
Shrewsbury.	*Norwich.*
Manchester.	*Colchester.*
Newcastle upon Tyne.	

Every one of these Banks to have a Cashier in *London*, unless they cou'd all have a general Correspondence and Credit with the Bank-Royal.

These Banks in their respective Counties should be a General Staple and Factory for the Manufactures of the said County; where every man that had Goods made, might have Money at a small Interest for Advance;

the Goods in the mean time being sent forward to Market, to a Warehouse for that purpose erected in *London*, where they shou'd be dispos'd of to all the Advantages the Owner cou'd expect, paying only 1 *per Cent.* Commission. Or if the Maker wanted Credit in *London* either for *Spanish* Wool, Cotton, Oyl, or any Goods, while his Goods were in the Warehouse of the said Bank, his Bill shou'd be paid by the Bank to the full Value of his Goods, or at least within a small matter. These Banks, either by Correspondence with each other, or an Order to their Cashier in *London*, might with ease so pass each other's Bills, that a man who has Cash at *Plymouth*, and wants Money at *Berwick*, may transfer his Cash at *Plymouth* to *Newcastle* in half an hours time, without either Hazard, or Charge, or Time, allowing only ½ *per Cent.* Exchange; and so of all the most distant parts of the Kingdom. Or if he wants Money at *Newcastle*, and has Goods at *Worcester*, or at any other Cloathing-Town, sending his Goods to be sold by the Factory of the Bank of *Worcester*, he may remit by the Bank to *Newcastle*, or any where else, as readily as if his Goods were sold and paid for; and no Exactions made upon him for the Convenience he enjoys.

This Discourse of Banks the Reader is to understand to have no relation to the present Posture of Affairs, with respect to the Scarcity of Currant Money, which seems to have put a stop to that part of a Stock we call Credit; which always is, and indeed must be the most essential part of a Bank, and without which no Bank can pretend to subsist, at least to Advantage.

A Bank is only a Great Stock of Money put together, to be employ'd by some of the Subscribers, in the name of the rest, for the Benefit of the Whole. This Stock of Money subsists not barely on the Profits of its own Stock, for that wou'd be inconsiderable, but upon the Contingences and Accidents which Multiplicity of Business occasions: As for Instance; A man that comes for Money, and knows he may have it To-morrow, perhaps he is in haste, and won't take it to day: Only that he may be sure of it to morrow, he takes a *Memorandum* under the Hand of the Officer, That he shall have it whenever he calls for it; and this *Memorandum* we call a Bill. To morrow when he Intended to fetch his Money, comes a Man to him for Money; and to save himself the labour of Telling, he gives him the *Memorandum* or Bill aforesaid for his Money; this Second Man does as the First, and a Third does as he did, and so the Bill runs about a Month, Two or Three; and this is that we call *Credit*; for by the Circulation of a quantity of these Bills, the Bank enjoys the full Benefit of as much Stock in real Value, as the supposititious

Value of the Bills amounts to; and where-ever this Credit fails, this Advantage fails; for immediately all men come for their Money, and the Bank must die of itself; for I am sure no Bank by the simple Improvement of their single Stock, can ever make any considerable Advantage.

I confess a Bank who can lay a Fund for the Security of their Bills, which shall produce, first an Annual Profit to the Owner, and yet make good the Passant-Bill, may stand, and be advantageous too, because there is a Real and a Supposititious Value both, and the Real always ready to make good the Supposititious; and this I know no way to bring to pass, but by Land, which at the same time that it lies Transferr'd to secure the Value of every Bill given out, brings in a separate Profit to the Owner; and this way no question but the whole Kingdom might be a Bank to it self, tho' no ready Money were to be found in it.

I had gone on in some Sheets with my Notion of Land, being the best bottom for Publick Banks, and the easiness of bringing it to answer all the Ends of Money deposited, with double Advantage; but I find my self happily prevented by a Gentleman, who has publish'd the very same, tho' since this was Wrote; and I was always Master of so much Wit, as to hold my Tongue while they spoke who understood the thing better than my self.

Mr. *John Asgill* of *Lincolns-Inn*,[61] in a small Tract, Entituled, *Several Assertions prov'd, in Order to Create another Species of Money than Gold and Silver*, has so distinctly handled this very Case, with such strength of Argument, such clearness of Reason, such a Judgment, and such a Stile, as all the Ingenious part of the World must acknowledge themselves extremely Oblig'd to him for that Piece.

At the sight of which Book I laid by all that had been written by me on that Subject; for I had much rather confess my self incapable of handling that Point like him, than have convinc'd the World of it by my impertinence.

Of the High-Ways.

IT is a prodigious Charge the whole Nation groans under for the Repair of High-Ways, which, after all, lie in a very ill Posture too; I make no question but if it was taken into Consideration by those who have the Power to Direct it, the Kingdom might be wholly eas'd of that Burthen, and the High-Ways be kept in good condition, which now lie in a most shameful manner in most parts of the Kingdom, and in many places wholly unpassable; from whence arise Tolls and Impositions upon Passengers and Travellers; and on the other hand, Trespasses and Incroachments upon Lands adjacent, to the great Damage of the Owners.

The Rate for the High-Ways is the most Arbitrary and Unequal Tax in the Kingdom; in some places two or three Rates of 6 *d. per l.* in the year, in others the whole Parish cannot raise wherewith to defray the Charge, either by the very bad condition of the Road, or distance of Materials; in others the Surveyors raise what they never Expend; and the Abuses, Exactions, Connivances, Frauds, and Embezlements, are innumerable.

The *Romans*, while they Govern'd this Island, made it one of their principal cares to Make and Repair the High-Ways of the Kingdom, and the Chief Roads we now use, are of their Marking out; the Consequence of maintaining them was such, or at least so esteem'd, that they thought it not below them to Employ their *Legionary Troops* in the Work; and it was sometimes the Business of whole Armies, either when in Winter-quarters, or in the intervals of Truce or Peace with the Natives. Nor have the *Romans* left us any greater tokens of their Grandeur and Magnificence, than the ruins of those Causways and Street-ways which are at this day to be seen in many parts of the Kingdom; some of which has by the visible Remains been discover'd to traverse the whole Kingdom; and others for more than an Hundred Miles are to be trac'd from Colony to Colony, as they had particular occasion. The famous High-Way, or Street, call'd *Watling-Street*, which some will tell you began at *London-Stone*,[62] and passing that very Street in the City, which we to this day call by that Name, went on *West* to that spot where *Tyburn* now stands, and then turn'd *North-West* in so straight a line to St. *Albans*, that 'tis now the exactest Road (in one Line for Twenty Miles) in the Kingdom; and tho' disus'd now as the Chief, yet is as good, and I believe the best Road to St. *Albans*, and is still call'd the *Street-way*: From whence it is trac'd into *Shropshire* above an Hundred and sixty Miles, with a multitude of visible Antiquities upon it, Discover'd and Describ'd very Accurately by Mr. *Cambden*:[63] The *Fosse*,[64] another *Roman* Work, lies at this day as visible, and as plain a high Causway, of above Thirty Foot broad, Ditch'd on either side, and Cop'd and Pav'd where need is, as exact and every jot as beautiful as the King's new Road through *Hide-Park*;[65] in which figure it now lies from near *Marshfield* to *Cirencester*, and again from *Cirencester* to the Hill Three Miles on this side *Gloucester*, which is not less than Twenty six Miles, and is made use of as the great Road to those Towns, and probably has been so for a Thousand Years with little Repairs.

If we set aside the Barbarity and Customs of the *Romans*, as *Heathens*, and take them as a Civil Government, we must allow they were the Pattern of the whole World for Improvement and Increase of Arts and Learning, Civilizing and Methodizing Nations and Countries Conquer'd by their Valour; and if this was one of their great Cares, That consideration ought to move something. But to the great Example of that Generous People, I'le add Three Arguments.

(1.) 'Tis Useful, and that as 'tis convenient for Carriages, which in a Trading Countrey is a great help to Negoce, and promotes universal Correspondence, without which our Inland Trade cou'd not be manag'd. And under this Head I cou'd name a *thousand* Conveniences of a safe, pleasant, well-Repair'd High-Way, both to the Inhabitant and the Traveller; but I think 'tis needless.

(2.) 'Tis easy. I question not to make it appear 'tis easy, to put all the High Roads, especially in *England*, in a noble Figure, Large, Dry, and Clean, well Drein'd and free from Floods, unpassable Sloughs, deep Cart-routs,[66] high Ridges, and all the Inconveniences they now are full of; and when once done, much easier still to be maintain'd so.

(3.) It may be Cheaper, and the whole Assessment for the Repairs of High-Ways for ever be Drop'd, or Appli'd to other uses for the Publick Benefit.

Here I beg the Reader's Favour for a small Digression.

I am not Proposing this as an Undertaker, or setting a Price to the Publick, for which I will perform it *like one of the Projectors I speak of*; but laying open a Project for the Performance, which whenever the Publick Affairs will admit our Governors to Consider of, will be found so feasible, that no question they may find Undertakers enough for the Performance; and in this Undertaking-Age I do not doubt but 'twou'd be easy at any time to procure Persons at their own Charge to perform it for any single County, as a Pattern and Experiment for the whole Kingdom.

The Proposal is as follows.

First, That an Act of Parliament be made, with Liberty for the Undertakers to Dig and Trench, to cut down Hedges and Trees, or whatever is needful for ditching, dreining and carrying off Water, cleaning, enlarging and levelling the Roads, with Power to lay open or inclose Lands; to incroach into Lands, dig, raise, and level Fences, plant and pull up Hedges or Trees, for the enlarging, widening, and dreining the High-Ways, with Power to turn either the Roads, or Water-Courses, Rivers and Brooks, as by the Directors of the Works shall be found needful, *always allowing* satisfaction to be first made to the Owners of such Lands, either by assigning to them equivalent Lands, or Payment in Money, the Value to be adjusted by Two indifferent Persons, to be Named by the Lord Chancellor, or Lord Keeper for the time being; and no Water-Course to be turn'd from any Water-Mill, without Satisfaction first made both to the Landlord and Tenant.

But before I proceed, I must say a word or two to this Article.

The Chief, and almost the Only Cause of the deepness and foulness of the Roads, is occasion'd by the standing Water, which for want of due care to draw it off by scouring and opening Ditches and Dreins, and other Water-Courses, and clearing of Passages, soaks into the Earth, and softens it to such a degree, that it cannot bear the weight of Horses and Carriages; to prevent which, the Power to Dig, Trench, and Cut down, &c. mention'd above, will be of absolute necessity: But because the liberty seems very large, and some may think 'tis too great a Power to be granted to any Body of Men over their Neighbours: 'Tis answer'd;

(1.) 'Tis absolutely necessary, or the Work cannot be done; and the doing of the Work is of much greater Benefit than the Damage can amount to.

(2.) Satisfaction to be made to the Owner, and that first too, before the Damage be done, is an Unquestionable Equivalent; and Both together, I think, are a very full Answer to any Objection in That case.

Besides this Act of Parliament, a Commission must be granted to Fifteen, at least, in the Name of the Undertakers, to whom every County shall have Power to join Ten, who are to Sit with the said Fifteen, so often and so long as the said Fifteen do Sit for Affairs relating to that County; which Fifteen, or any Seven of them, shall be Directors of the Works, to be advis'd by the said Ten, or any Five of them, in matters of Right and Claim; and the said Ten to adjust Differences in the Countries, and to have Right by Process to appeal in the name either of Lords of Mannors, or Privileges of Towns or Corporations, who shall be either damag'd or encroach'd upon by the said Work: All Appeals to be heard and determin'd immediately by the said Lord Chancellor, or Commission from him, that the Work may receive no Interruption.

This Commission shall give Power to the said Fifteen to press Wagons, Carts, and Horses, Oxen, and Men, and detain them to work a certain Limited Time, and within certain Limited Space of Miles from their own Dwellings, and at a certain Rate of Payment: No Men, Horses, or Carts, to be press'd against their Consent, during the times of Hay-time, or Harvest; or upon Market-days, if the Person aggriev'd will make Affidavit he is oblig'd to be with his Horses or Carts at the said Markets.

It is well known to all who have any knowledge of the Condition the High-Ways in *England* now lye in, that in most places there is a convenient distance of Land left open for travelling, either for driving of Cattel, or marching of Troops of Horse, with perhaps as few Lanes or *Defiles*, as in any Countries: The Cross-Roads, which are generally Narrow, are yet Broad enough in most places for two Carriages to pass; but on the other hand, we have on most of the High-Roads a great deal of waste-Land thrown in as it were for an Overplus to the High-Way; which though it be us'd of course by Cattle and Travellers on occasion, is indeed no Benefit at all either to the Traveller as a Road, or to the Poor as a Common, or to the Lord of the Mannor as a Waste; upon it grows neither Timber nor Grass, in any quantity answerable to the Land; but, tho to no purpose, is trodden down, poach'd, and over-run by Drifts of Cattle in the Winter, or spoil'd with the Dust in the Summer: And this I have observ'd in many parts of *England* to be as good Land as any of the Neighbouring Enclosures, as capable of Improvement, and to as good purpose.

These Lands only being enclos'd and manur'd, leaving the Roads to Dimensions without measure sufficient, are the Fund upon which I build the Prodigious Stock of Money that must do this Work. These Lands, which I shall afterwards make an Essay to value, being enclos'd, will be either saleable to raise Money, or fit to exchange with those Gentlemen who must part with some Land where the Ways are narrow: Always reserving a quantity of these Lands to be Let out to Tenants, the Rent to be paid into the Publick Stock or Bank of the Undertakers, and to be reserv'd for keeping the Ways in the same Repair; and the said Bank to forfeit the Lands if they are not so maintained.

Another Branch of the Stock must be Hands; for a Stock of Men is a Stock of Money; to which purpose every County, City, Town, and Parish, shall be Rated at a Set Price, equivalent to Eight Years Payment for the Repair of High-ways; which each County, &c. shall raise, not by Assessment in Money, but by pressing of Men, Horses, and Carriages for the Work; the Men, Horses, &c. to be employ'd by the Directors: In which case all Corporal Punishments, as of *Whippings, Stocks, Pillories, Houses of Correction*,[67] &c. might be easily transmitted to a certain Number of Days Works on the High-Ways, and in Consideration of this provision of Men, the Country shou'd for ever after be acquitted of any Contribution, either in Money or Work, for Repair of the High-Ways, Building of Bridges excepted.

There lies some Popular Objection against this Undertaking; and the first is, the great Controverted Point of *England, Enclosure of the Common*, which tends to Depopulation, and Injures the Poor.

(2.) Who shall be Judges or Surveyors of the Work, to Oblige the Undertakers to perform to a certain limited degree.

For the First; The Enclosure of the Common; A Clause that runs as far as to an Incroachment upon *Magna Charta*, and a most considerable branch of the Property of the Poor: I Answer it thus.

(1.) The Lands we Enclose, are not such as from which the Poor do indeed reap any Benefit, or at least any that is considerable.

(2.) The Bank and Publick Stock, who are to Manage this great Undertaking, will have so many little Labours to perform, and Offices to bestow, that are fit only for Labouring Poor Persons to do, as will put them in a condition to provide for the Poor who are so Injur'd, that can work; and to those who cannot, may allow Pensions for Overseeing, Supervising, and the like, which will be more than Equivalent.

(3.) For Depopulations, the contrary shou'd be secur'd, by obliging the Undertakers, at such and such certain distances, to erect Cottages, Two at least in a place, which wou'd be useful to the Work, and safety of the Traveller, to which shou'd be an Allotment of Land, always suffi-cient to invite the Poor Inhabitant, in which the Poor shou'd be Tenant for Life *Gratis*, doing Duty upon the High-Way, as shou'd be appointed; by which, and many other Methods, the Poor shou'd be great Gainers by the Proposal, instead of being Injur'd.

(4.) By this erecting of Cottages at proper distances, a Man might Travel over all *England* as though a Street, where he cou'd never want, either Rescue from Thieves, or Directions for his way.

(5.) This very Undertaking once duly settled, might in a few Years so order it, that there shou'd be no Poor for the Common; and if so, What need of a Common for the Poor? Of which in its proper place.

As to the second Objection, Who shou'd oblige the Undertakers to the Performance?

(1.) I Answer, Their Commission and Charter shou'd become Void, and all their Stock Forfeit, and the Lands Enclosed and Unsold, remain as a Pledge, which wou'd be Security sufficient.

(2.) The Ten Persons chosen out of every County, shou'd have Power to Inspect and Complain, and the Lord Chancellor upon such Complaint, to make a Survey, and to determine by a Jury, in which case on Default, they shall be oblig'd to proceed.

(3.) The Lands settled on the Bank shall be liable to be extended for the Uses mentioned, if the same at any time be not maintained in the condition at first provided, and the Bank to be amerc'd upon Complaint of the Countrey.

These and other Conditions, which on a Legal Settlement to be made by Wiser Heads than mine, might be thought on, I do believe wou'd form a Constitution so firm, so fair, and so equally Advantageous to the Country, to the Poor, and to the Publick, as has not been put in practice in these latter Ages of the World. To Discourse of this a little in general, and to instance in a Place, perhaps, that has not its fellow in the Kingdom, the Parish of *Islington* in *Middlesex*; there lies through this large Parish the greatest Road in *England*, and the most frequented, especially by Cattle for *Smithfield*-Market; this great Road has so many Branches, and lies for so long a way through the Parish, and withal has the inconvenience of a Clayey Ground, and no Gravel at hand, that, modestly speaking, the Parish is not able to keep it in Repair, by which means several Cross-Roads in the Parish lie wholly Unpassable, and Carts and Horses, and Men too, have been almost Buried in Holes and Sloughs, and the main Road it self has for many Years lain in a very ordinary condition, which occasion'd several Motions in Parliament to Raise a Toll at *Highgate*, for the performance of what it was impossible the Parish shou'd do, and yet was of so absolute necessity to be done; And is it not very probable the Parish of *Islington* wou'd part with all the waste Land upon their Roads, to be eas'd of the intolerable Assessment for Repair of the High-Way, and answer the Poor, who reap but a small Benefit from it, some other way? And yet I am free to affirm, That for a Grant of Waste, and almost useless Land, lying open to the High-Way, those Lands to be improv'd, as they might easily be, together with the Eight Years Assessment to be provided in Workmen, a noble Magnificent Causeway might be Erected, with Ditches on either side deep enough to receive the Water, and Dreins sufficient to carry it off, which Causway shou'd be Four Foot High at least, and from Thirty to Forty Foot Broad, to reach from *London* to *Barnet*, Pav'd in the middle, to keep it Cop'd, and so suppli'd with Gravel, and other proper Materials, as shou'd secure it from Decay with small Repairing.

I hope no Man wou'd be so weak now, as to imagine that by Lands lying open to the Road, to be Assign'd to the Undertakers, I shou'd mean that all *Finchly*-Common shou'd be Enclos'd and Sold for this Work; but least somebody shou'd start such a preposterous Objection, I think 'tis not improper to mention, That where-ever a High-Way is to be carri'd over a Large Common, Forest, or Waste without a Hedge on either hand for a certain distance, there the several Parishes shall allot the Directors a certain quantity of the Common to lie Parallel with the Road, at a proportioned number of Feet to the Length and Breadth of the said Road; consideration also to be had to the Nature of the Ground, or else giving them only room for the Road directly, shall suffer them to Enclose in any one Spot so much of the said Common, as shall be equivalent to the like quantity of Land lying by the Road; thus where the Land is good, and the Materials for erecting a Causway near, the less Land may serve; and on the contrary the more; but in general, allowing them the quantity of Land proportioned to the length of the Causway, and Forty Rod[68] in Breadth, tho' where the Land is poor, as on Downs and Plains, the Proportion must be consider'd to be adjusted by the Country.

Another Point for the Dimensions of Roads, shou'd be adjusted; and the Breadth of them, I think, cannot be less than thus:

From *London* every way 10 Miles the High Post-Road to be Built full 40 Foot in Breadth, and 4 Foot High, the Ditches 8 Foot Broad, and 6 Foot Deep, and from thence onward 30 Foot, and so in Proportion.

Cross Roads to be 20 Foot Broad, and Ditches Proportion'd; no Lanes and Passes less than 9 Foot without Ditches.

The Middle of the High Causeways to be Pav'd with Stone, Chalk, or Gravel, and kept always Two Foot Higher than the Sides, that the Water might have a free course into the Ditches, and Persons kept in constant Employ to fill up Holes, let out Water, open Dreins, and the like, as there shou'd be occasion: A proper Work for Highwaymen, and such Malefactors, as might on those Services be exempt'd from the Gallows.

It may here be Objected, That Eight Years Assessment to be demanded down, is too much in reason to expect any of the Poorer sort can pay; as for Instance; If a Farmer who keeps a Team of Horse be at the common Assessment, to Work a Week, it must not be put so hard upon any Man, as to Work Eight Weeks together. 'Tis easy to Answer this Objection.

So many as are wanted, must be had; if a Farmer's Team cannot be spar'd without prejudice to him so long together, he may spare it at sundry times, or agree to be Assess'd, and pay the Assessment at sundry Payments; and the Bank may make it as easy to them as they please.

Another Method, however, might be found to fix this Work at once; As suppose a Bank be settled for the High-ways of the County of *Middlesex*, which as they are, without doubt, the most us'd of any in the Kingdom, so also they require the more Charge, and in some Parts lie in the worst Condition of any in the Kingdom.

If the Parliament fix the Charge of the Survey of the High-Ways upon a Bank to be Appointed for that Purpose, for a certain term of Years, the Bank Undertaking to do the Work, or to Forfeit the said Settlement.

As thus:

Suppose the Tax on Land, and Tenements for the whole County of *Middlesex*, does, or shou'd be so order'd, as it might amount to 20000 *l. per Ann.* more or less, which it now does, and much more, including the Work of the Farmer's Teams, which must be accounted as Money, and is equivalent to it, with some Allowance to be Rated for the City of *London, &c.* who do enjoy the Benefit, and make the most use of the said Roads, both for carrying of Goods, and bringing Provisions to the City, and therefore in reason ought to Contribute towards the High-ways; for it is a most unequal thing, that the Road from *Highgate* to *Smithfield*-Market, by which the whole City is, in a manner, suppli'd with Live Cattel, and the Road by those Cattel horribly spoil'd, shou'd lie all upon that one Parish of *Islington* to Repair; wherefore I'le suppose a Rate for the High-ways to be gather'd through the City of *London* of 10000 *l. per Ann.* more; which may be Appointed to be paid by Carriers, Drovers, and all such as keep Teams, Horses, or Coaches, and the like, or many ways, as is most Equal and Reasonable; the waste Lands in the said County, which by the Consent of the Parishes, Lords of the Mannors, and Proprietors, shall be allow'd to the Undertakers when Enclos'd and Let out, may (the Land in *Middlesex* generally Letting high) amount to 5000 *l. per Ann.* more. If then an Act of Parliament be procur'd to settle the Tax of 30,000 *l. per Ann.* for Eight Years, most of which will be Levi'd in Workmen, and not in Money, and the Waste Lands for ever: I dare be bold to offer, That the High-Ways for the whole County of *Middlesex* shou'd be put into the following Form, and the 5000 *l. per Ann.* Land be bound to remain as a Security to maintain them so, and the County be never Burthen'd with any further Tax for the Repair of the High-Ways.

And that I may not Propose a Matter in General, like begging the Question, without Demonstration, I shall enter into the Particulars, How it may be perform'd, and that under these following Heads of Articles.

(1.) *What I Propose to do to the High-Ways.*
(2.) *What the Charge will be.*
(3.) *How to be Rais'd.*
(4.) *What Security for Performance.*
(5.) *What Profit to the Undertaker.*

(1.) What I Propose to do to the High-Ways.

I Answer First, Not Repair them; And yet Secondly, Not alter them, *that is*, not alter the Course they run.

But perfectly Build them as a Fabrick. And to descend to the Particulars, 'tis first necessary to Note, which are the Roads I mean, and their Dimensions.

First, The *High Post-Roads*, and they are for the County of *Middlesex* as follows.

		Miles
	Stanes, which is	15
	Colebrook is from *Hounslow*	05
	Uxbridge	15
From *London* to	*Bushy* the Old Street-way	10
	Barnet, or near it	09
	Waltham-Cross in *Ware* Road	10
	Bow	02
		—
		67

Besides these, there are Cross-Roads, By-Roads, and Lanes, which must also be look'd after, and that some of them may be put into Condition, others may be wholly slighted and shut up, or made *Drift-ways*,[69] *Bridle-ways* or *Foot-ways*, as may be thought convenient by the Countries.

The Cross-Roads of most Repute are as follows:

			Miles
	London		*Hackney, Old Ford*, and *Bow*	05
	Hackney		*Dalston* and *Islington*	02
	Ditto		*Hornsy, Muzzle-Hill*, to *Whetston*	08
	Tottenham		The *Chase, South-Gate*, &c. call'd	06
From		to	*Greenlanes*	
	Enfield-Wash		*Enfield-Town, Whetston, Totteridge*, to	10
			Egworth	
	London		*Hamstead, Hendon*, and *Edgworth*	08
	Edgworth		*Stanmore*, to *Pinner*, to *Uxbridge*	08

| From | { | London
London
Brantford
Kingston
Ditto | } | to | { | *Harrow* and *Pinner-Green*
Chelsea, Fullham
Thistleworth, Twittenham, and *Kingston*
Stanes, Colebrook and *Uxbridge*
Chersey-Bridge | 11
04
06
17
05 |

	90
Overplus Miles	50
	140

And because there may be many Parts of the Cross-Roads which cannot be accounted in the Number above-mention'd, or may slip my knowledge or memory, I allow an overplus of 50 Miles, to be added to the 90 Miles above, which together makes the Cross-Roads of *Middlesex* to be 140 Miles.

For the By-Lanes, such as may be slighted need nothing but to be ditch'd up; such as are for private use of Lands, for carrying off Corn, and driving Cattle, are to be look'd after by private hands.

But of the last sort, not to be accounted by Particulars, in the small County of *Middlesex,* we cannot allow less in Cross By-lanes, from Village to Village, and from Dwelling-Houses which stand out of the way to the Roads, than 1000 Miles.

So in the whole County I reckon up,

	Miles
Of the High Post-Road	0067
Of Cross-Roads less Publick	0140
Of By-Lanes and Passes	1000
	1207

These are the Roads I mean, and thus divided under their several denominations.

To the Question, What I wou'd do to them? I Answer,

(1.) For the 67 Miles of High Post-Road, I Propose to throw up a firm strong Causway well bottom'd, 6 Foot high in the middle, and 4 Foot on the side, fac'd with Brick or Stone, and crown'd with Gravel, Chalk, or Stone, as the several Countries they are made through will afford, being 44 Foot in Breadth, with Ditches on either side 8 Foot Broad and 4 Foot Deep; so the whole Breadth will be 60 Foot, if the Ground will permit.

At the end of every Two Miles, or such like convenient distances, shall be a Cottage Erected, with Half an Acre of Ground allow'd, which shall be given *Gratis*, with 1 *s. per* Week Wages, to such Poor Man of the Parish, as shall be approv'd, who shall Once, at least, every day, view his Walk, to open Passages for the Water to run into the Ditches, to fill up Holes or soft Places.

Two Riders shall be allow'd to be always moving the Rounds, to view every thing out of Repair, and make Report to the Directors, and to see that the Cottagers do their Duty.

(2.) For the 140 Miles of Cross-Road, a like Causway to be made, but of different Dimensions, the Breadth 20 Foot, if the Ground will allow it, the Ditches 4 Foot Broad, 3 Foot Deep, the Heighth in the middle 3 Foot, and on the sides 1 Foot, or 2 where it may be needful; to be also crown'd with Gravel, and 1 *s. per* Week to be allow'd to the Poor of every Parish, the Constables to be Bound to find a Man to Walk on the High-Way every Division, for the same Purpose as the Cottagers do on the Greater Roads.

Posts to be set up at every turning to Note whither it goes, for the Direction of Strangers, and how many Miles distant.

(3.) For a 1000 Miles By-Lanes, only good and sufficient Care to keep them in Repair as they are, and to carry the Water off by clearing and cutting the Ditches, and laying Materials where it is wanted.

This is what I Propose to do to them; and what if once perform'd, I suppose all People wou'd own to be an Undertaking both Useful and Honourable.

(2.) The Second Question I propose to give an Account of, is, What the Charge will be.

Which I account thus;

The Work of the great Causway I Propose, shall not Cost less than 10 *s. per* Foot, supposing Materials to be Bought, Carriage and Mens Labour to be all Hir'd, which for 67 Miles in Length, is no less than the Sum of 176,880 Pounds; as thus,

Every Mile accounted at 1760 Yards, and 3 Foot to the Yard, is 5280 Foot, which at 10 *s. per* Foot, is 2640 *l. per* Mile, and that again Multiplied by 67, makes the sum of 176,880, into which I include the Charge of Water-Courses, Mills to throw off Water where needful, Dreins, *&c.*

To this Charge must be added, Ditching to Enclose Land for 30 Cottages, and Building 30 Cottages at 40 *l.* each, which is 1200 *l.*

The Work of the smaller Causway I Propose to finish at the Rate of

12 *d. per* Foot, which being for 140 Miles in Length, at 5280 Foot *per* Mile, amounts to 36,960 *l.*

Ditching, Dreining, and Repairing 1000 Miles, suppos'd at 3 *s. per* Rod, as for 320,000 Rod, is 48,000 *l.* which added to the Two former Accounts, is thus,

	l.
The High Post-Roads, or the Great Cawsey	178080
The small Cawsey	036960
By Lanes, &c.	048000
	263040

If I were to Propose some Measures for the easing this Charge, I cou'd, perhaps, lay a Scheme down how it may be perform'd for less than one half of this Charge.

As first, By a grant of the Court at the *Old-Baily*, whereby all such Criminals as are Condemn'd to Die for smaller Crimes, may instead of Transportation be Order'd a Year's Work on the High-Ways; others instead of Whippings, a proportion'd Time, and the like; which wou'd, by a moderate computation, provide us generally a supply of 200 Workmen, and coming in as fast as they go off; and let the Overseers alone to make them Work.

Secondly, By an Agreement with the *Guinea*-Company[70] to furnish 200 *Negroes*, who are generally Persons that do a great deal of Work; and all these are Subsisted very reasonably out of a Publick Store-house.

Thirdly, By Carts and Horses to be Bought, not Hir'd, with a few Able Carters; and to the other a few Workmen that have Judgment to Direct the rest; and thus I question not the Great Causway shall be done for 4 *s. per* Foot Charge; but of this by the by.

Fourthly, A Liberty to ask Charities and Benevolences to the Work.

(3.) To the Question, How this Money shall be Rais'd? I think if the Parliament settle the Tax on the County for Eight Years, at 30,000 *l. per Ann.* no Man need ask, how it shall be Rais'd, – It will be easy enough to Raise the Money; and no Parish can grudge to pay a little larger Rate for such a Term, on condition never to be Tax'd for the High-Ways any more.

Eight Years Assessment at 30,000 *l. per Ann.* is enough to afford to Borrow the Money by way of Anticipation, if need be, the Fund being secur'd by Parliament, and appropriated to that Use and no other.

As to what Security for Performance:

The Lands which are Enclos'd may be appropriated by the same Act of Parliament to the Bank and Undertakers, upon condition of Performance, and to be Forfeit to the use of the several Parishes to which they belong, in case upon Presentation by the Grand Juries, and reasonable Time given, any part of the Roads in such and such Parishes, be not kept and maintain'd in that Posture they are Propos'd to be. Now the Lands thus settled are an eternal Security to the Country, for the keeping the Roads in Repair; because they will always be of so much Value over the needful Charge, as will make it worth while to the Undertakers to preserve their Title to them; and the Tenure of them being so precarious, as to be liable to Forfeiture on Default, they will always be careful to uphold the Causways.

Lastly, What Profit to the Undertakers? For we must allow them to Gain, and that considerably, or no Man wou'd undertake such a Work.

To this I propose, First,

During the Work allow them out of the Stock 3000 *l. per Ann.* for Management.

After the Work is finish'd, so much of the 5000 *l. per Ann.* as can be sav'd, and the Roads kept in good Repair, let be their own; and if the Lands Secur'd be not of the Value of 5000 *l.* a Year, let so much of the Eight Years Tax be set apart as may Purchase Land to make them up; if they come to more, let the Benefit be to the Adventurers.

It may be Objected here, That a Tax of 30,000 *l.* for Eight Years will come in as fast as it can well be laid out, and so no Anticipations will be requisite; for the whole Work Propos'd cannot be probably finished in less Time; and if so,

	l.
The Charge of the Country amounts to	240000
The Lands sav'd Eight Years Revenue	040000
	280000

which is 13,000 *l.* more than the Charge; and if the Work be done so much Cheaper, as is mentioned, the Profit to the Undertaker will be Unreasonable.

To this I say, I wou'd have the Undertakers bound to accept the Sallary of 3000 *l. per Ann.* for Management, and if a whole Years Tax can be spar'd, either leave it Unrais'd upon the Country, or put it in Bank to be improv'd against any occasion, of Building, perhaps, a great *Bridge*; or some very wet Season, or Frost, may so Damnify the Works, as to make them require more than ordinary Repair. But the Undertakers shou'd make no private Advantage of such an Overplus, there might be ways enough found for it.

Another Objection lies against the Possibility of Enclosing the Lands upon the Waste, which generally belongs to some Mannor, whose different Tenures may be so cross, and so otherwise encumbred, that even the Lord of those Mannors, though they were willing, cou'd not Convey them.

This may be Answer'd in General, That an Act of Parliament is *Omnipotent* with respect to Titles and Tenures of Land, and can Empower Lords and Tenants to Consent to what else they cou'd not; as to Particulars, they cannot be Answer'd till they are Propos'd; but there is no doubt but an Act of Parliament may adjust it all in one Head.

What a Kingdom wou'd *England* be if this were perform'd in all the Counties of it! and yet I believe it is feasible, even in the worst. I have narrowly observ'd all the Considerable Ways in that unpassable County of *Sussex*, which especially in some parts in the *Wild*, as they very properly call it, of the County, hardly admits the Countrey People to Travel to Markets in Winter, and makes Corn dear at Market because it can't be brought, and cheap at the Farmer's House because he can't carry it to Market; yet even in that County wou'd I undertake to carry on this Proposal, and that to great Advantage, if back'd with the Authority of an Act of Parliament.

I have seen in that horrible Country the Road 60 to 100 Yards Broad, lie from side to side all Poach'd with Cattel, the Land of no manner of Benefit, and yet no going with a Horse, but at every step up to the Shoulders, full of Sloughs and Holes, and covered with standing-water. It costs them incredible Sums of Money to Repair them; and the very Places that are mended, wou'd fright a young Traveller to go over them: The *Romans* Master'd this Work, and by a firm Causeway made a High-way quite through this deep Country, through *Darkin* in *Surry* to *Stansted*, and thence to *Okeley*, and so on to *Arundel*; its Name tells us what it was made of; for it was call'd *Stone-street*,[71] and many visible parts of it remain to this day.

Now would any Lord of a Mannor refuse to allow 40 Yards in breadth out of that Road I mention'd, to have the other 20 made into a Firm, Fair, and Pleasant Causeway over that Wilderness of a Countrey?

Or would not any man acknowledge, That putting this Country into a condition for Carriages and Travellers to pass, would be a great Work? The Gentlemen would find the Benefit of it in the Rent of their Land,

and Price of their Timber; the Countrey People would find the difference in the Sale of their Goods, which now they cannot carry beyond the first Market-Town, and hardly thither; and the whole County would reap an Advantage an hundred to one greater than the Charge of it. And since the Want we feel of any Convenience is generally the first Motive to Contrivance for a Remedy, I wonder no man ever thought of some Expedient for so considerable a Defect.

Of Assurances.

ASSURANCES among Merchants I believe may plead Prescription,[72] and has been of use time out of mind in Trade; tho perhaps never so much a Trade as now.

'Tis a Compact among Merchants. Its beginning being an Accident to Trade, and arose from the *Disease of Mens Tempers*, who having run larger Adventures in a single Bottom than afterwards they found convenient, grew fearful and uneasy; and discovering their uneasiness to others, who, perhaps, had no Effects in the same Vessel, they offer to bear part of the Hazard for part of the Profit; Convenience made this a Custom, and Custom brought it into a Method, till at last it becomes a Trade.

I cannot question the Lawfulness of it, since all Risque in Trade is for Gain; and when I am necessitated to have a greater Cargo of Goods in such or such a Bottom, than my Stock can afford to lose, another may *surely* offer to go a Part with me; and as 'tis just if I give another part of the Gain, he shou'd run part of the Risque, so it is as just, that if he runs part of my Risque, he shou'd have part of the Gain. Some Object the disparity of the Premio to the Hazard, when the Ensurer runs the Risque of 100 *l.* on the Seas from *Jamaica* to *London* for 40 *s.* which, say they, is preposterous and unequal. Though this Objection is hardly worth Answering to Men of Business, yet it looks something fair to them that know no better; and for the Information of such, I trouble the Reader with a few Heads.

First, They must consider the Ensurer is out no Stock.

Secondly, It is but one Risque the Ensurer runs, whereas the Assured has had a Risque out, a Risque of Debts abroad, a Risque of a Market, and a Risque of his Factor, and has a Risque of a Market to come, and therefore ought to have an answerable Profit.

Thirdly, If it has been a Trading Voyage, perhaps, the Adventurer has Paid Three or Four such Premio's, which sometimes make the

Ensurer clear more by a Voyage, than the Merchant; I my self have Paid
100 *l*. Ensurances in those small Premio's on a Voyage I have not gotten
50 *l*. by; and I suppose I am not the first that has done so neither.

This way of Assuring has also, as other Arts of Trade have, suffer'd
some Improvement (if I may be allow'd that Term) in our Age; and the
first step upon it, was an *Ensurance-Office for Houses to Ensure them from
Fire*; Common Fame gives the Project to Dr. *Barebone*;[73] a Man, I suppose,
better known as a Builder than a Physician. Whether it were his, or
whose it was, I do not enquire; it was settled on a Fund of Ground-
Rents, to Answer in case of Loss, and met with very good Acceptance.

But it was soon follow'd by another, by way of *Friendly Society*;[74] where
every one who Subscribe, pay their *Quota* to Build up any Man's House
who is a Contributor, if it shall happen to be Burnt. I won't decide which
is the Best, or which Succeeded best, but I believe the latter brings in
most Money to the Contriver.

Only one Benefit I cannot omit which they reap from these Two
Societies who are not concern'd in either, That if any Fire happen,
whether in Houses Ensur'd or not Ensur'd, they have each of them a
set of Lusty Fellows, generally Water-men, who being immediately call'd
up, where-ever they live, by Watchmen Appointed, are, it must be
confess'd, very Active and Diligent in helping to put out the Fire.

As to any further Improvement to be made upon Assurances in Trade,
no question there may, and I doubt not but on Payment of a small Duty
to the Government, the King might be made the General Ensurer of all
Foreign Trade: Of which more under another Head.

I am of the Opinion also, that an Office of Ensurance Erected to Ensure
the Titles of Lands, in an Age where they are so precarious as now, might
be a Project not unlikely to succeed, if Establish'd on a good Fund. But I
shall say no more to that, because it seems to be a Design in hand[75] by
some Persons in Town, and is indeed no Thought of my own.

Ensuring of Life I cannot admire; I shall say nothing to it; but that
in *Italy* where *Stabbing* and *Poysoning* is so much in Vogue, something
may be said for it, and on contingent Annuities; and yet I never knew
the thing much approv'd of on any account.

Of Friendly-Societies.

ANother Branch of Ensurance, is by Contribution, or (to borrow the
Term from that before-mention'd) *Friendly-Societies*; which is, in short,

a Number of People entring into a Mutual Compact to Help one another, in case any Disaster or Distress fall upon them.

If Mankind cou'd agree, as these might be Regulated, all things which have Casualty in them, might be Secur'd. But one thing is Particularly requir'd in this way of Assurances; None can be admitted, but such whose Circumstances are, at least in some degree, alike, and so Mankind must be *sorted* into Classes; and as their Contingences differ, every different Sort may be a Society upon even Terms; for the Circumstances of People, as to Life, differ extremely by the Age and Constitution of their Bodies, and difference of Employment; as he that lives on shore, against him that goes to Sea, or a Young Man against an Old Man; or a Shopkeeper against a Soldier, are unequal; I don't pretend to determine the Controverted Point of Predestination, the Foreknowledge and Decrees of Providence; perhaps, if a Man be Decreed to be Kill'd in the Trenches, the same Foreknowledge Order'd him to List himself a Soldier that it might come to pass; and the like of a Seaman; but this I am sure, speaking of Second Causes, a Seaman or a Soldier is subject to more contingent hazards than other Men, and therefore are not upon equal Terms to form such a Society; nor is an Annuity on the Life of such a Man worth so much as it is upon other Men; therefore if a Society shou'd agree together to Pay the Executor of every Member so much after the Decease of the said Member, the Seamens Executors wou'd most certainly have an Advantage, and receive more than they Pay. So that 'tis necessary to sort the World into Parcels, Seamen with Seamen, Soldiers with Soldiers, and the like.

Nor is this a new thing; the *Friendly Society* must not pretend to assume to themselves the Contrivance of the Method, or think us guilty of borrowing from them, when we draw this into other Branches; for I know nothing is taken from them but the bare word, *Friendly-Society*, which they cannot pretend to be any considerable piece of Invention neither.

I can refer them to the very individual Practice in other things, which claims prescription beyond the beginning of the last Age, and that is in our Marshes and Fens in *Essex, Kent,* and the *Isle of Ely*; where great Quantities of Land being with much Pains and a vast Charge recovered out of the Seas and Rivers, and maintain'd with Banks (which they call Walls) the Owners of those Lands agree to Contribute to the keeping up those Walls, and keeping out the Sea, which is all one with a *Friendly-Society*; and if I have a Piece of Land in any Level or Marsh, tho' it bounds no where on the Sea or River, yet I pay my Proportion to the

Maintenance of the said Wall or Bank; and if at any time the Sea breaks in, the Damage is not laid upon the Man in whose Land the Breach happened, unless it was by his neglect, but it lies on the whole Land, and is called a *Level-Lot*.

Again, I have known it practised in Troops of Horse, especially when it was so order'd that the Troopers Mounted themselves; where every private Trooper has agreed to Pay, perhaps, 2*d. per diem* out of his Pay into a Publick Stock, which Stock was employed to Remount any of the Troop who by Accident shou'd lose his Horse.

Again, The Sailors Contribution to the Chest at *Chatham*,[76] is another *Friendly-Society*; and more might be nam'd.

To argue against the Lawfulness of this, wou'd be to cry down common Equity, as well as Charity; for as 'tis kind that my Neighbour shou'd Relieve me if I fall into Distress or Decay; so 'tis but Equal he shou'd do so if I agreed to have done the same for him; and if God Almighty has Commanded us to Relieve and Help one another in Distress, sure it must be commendable to bind our selves by Agreement to Obey that Command; nay, it seems to be a Project that we are led to by the Divine Rule, and has such a Latitude in it, that, for ought I know, as I said, all the Disasters in the World might be prevented by it, and Mankind be secur'd from all the Miseries, Indigences, and Distresses that happen in the World. In which I crave leave to be a little Particular.

First, General Peace might be secur'd all over the World by it, if all the Powers agreed to suppress him that Usurp'd or Encroach'd upon his Neighbour. All the Contingences of Life might be fenc'd against by this Method, (as Fire is already) as Thieves, Floods by Land, Storms by Sea, Losses of all Sorts, and Death it self, in a manner, by making it up to the Survivor.

I shall begin with the Seamen; for as their Lives are subject to more hazards than others, they seem to come first in view.

Of Seamen.

Sailors are *Les Enfans Perdue*,[77] the *Forlorn hope*[78] *of the World*; they are Fellows that bid Defiance to Terror, and maintain a constant War with the Elements; who by the Magick of their Art, Trade in the very confines of Death, and are always posted within shot, as I may say, of the Grave: 'Tis true, their familiarity with Danger makes them despise it, for which, I hope, no body will say they are the wiser; and Custom has so harden'd them, that we find them the worst of Men, tho' always in view of their last Moment.

I have observ'd one great Error in the Custom of *England*, relating to these sort of People, and which this way of *Friendly-Society* wou'd be a Remedy for.

If a Seaman who Enters himself, or is Press'd into the King's Service, be by any Accident Wounded or Disabled, to Recompence him for the Loss, he receives a Pension during Life, which the Sailors call *Smart-Money*, and is proportioned to their Hurt, as for the Loss of an Eye, Arm, Leg, or Finger, and the like; and as 'tis a very Honourable thing, so 'tis but reasonable, That a Poor Man who Loses his Limbs (which are his Estate) in the Service of the Government, and is thereby disabled from his Labour to get his Bread, shou'd be provided for, and not suffer'd to Beg or Starve for want of those Limbs he lost in the Service of his Country.

But if you come to the Seamen in the Merchants Service, not the least Provision is made; which has been the Loss of many a good Ship, with many a Rich Cargo, which wou'd otherwise have been Sav'd.

And the Sailors are in the Right of it too: *For Instance*; A Merchant Ship coming home from the *Indies*, perhaps very Rich, meets with a Privateer (not so Strong but that She might Fight him, and perhaps get off); the Captain calls up his Crew, tells them, *Gentlemen, You see how 'tis, I don't question but we may Clear our selves of this Caper, if you will Stand by Me.* One of the Crew, as willing to Fight as the rest, and as far from a Coward as the Captain, but endow'd with a little more Wit than his Fellows, Replies, *Noble Captain, We are all willing to Fight, and don't question but to Beat him off; but here is the Case, If we are Taken, we shall be set on Shore, and then sent Home, and Lose, perhaps, our Cloaths, and a little Pay; but if we Fight and Beat the Privateer, perhaps Half a Score of us may be Wounded and Lose our Limbs, and then we are Undone and our Families; if you will Sign an Obligation to us, That the Owners, or Merchants, shall allow a Pension to such as are Maim'd, that we may not Fight for the Ship, and go a Begging our selves, we will bring off the Ship, or Sink by her side, otherwise I am not willing to Fight, for my part.* The Captain cannot do this; so they Strike, and the Ship and Cargo is Lost.

If I shou'd turn this suppos'd Example into a real History, and Name the Ship and the Captain that did so, it wou'd be too plain to be contradicted.

Wherefore, for the Encouragement of Sailors in the Service of the Merchant, I wou'd have a *Friendly-Society* Erected for Seamen; wherein all Sailors, or Seafaring-men, Entring their Names, Places of Abode, and the Voyages they go upon, at an *Office of Ensurance for Seamen*, and Paying there a certain small Quarteridge, of 1 *s. per* Quarter, shou'd have a Seal'd Certificate from the Governors of the said Office, for the Articles hereafter mentioned.

(1.) If any such Seaman, either in Fight, or by any other Accident at Sea, come to be disabled, he shou'd receive from the said Office the following Sums of Money, either in Pension for Life, or Ready Money, as he pleas'd.

		l.		*l.*	
	An Eye	25		2	
	Both Eyes	100		8	
	One Leg	50		4	
	Both Legs	80		6	
For the	Right Hand	80	or	6	*Per Ann.*
loss of	Left Hand	50		4	for Life.
	Right Arm	100		8	
	Left Arm	80		6	
	Both Hands	160		12	
	Both Arms	200		16	

Any Broken Arm, or Leg, or Thigh, towards the Cure – 10 *l.*
If taken by the *Turks*, 50 *l.* towards his Ransom.
If he become Infirm and Unable to go to Sea, or
   Maintain himself, by Age or Sickness,   6 *l. per Ann.*
To their Wives if they are Kill'd or Drown'd,   50 *l.*

In Consideration of this, every Seaman Subscribing to the Society, shall Agree to Pay to the Receipt of the said Office, his *Quota* of the Sum to be Paid, whenever, and as often as such Claims are made; the Claims to be Enter'd into the Office, and upon sufficient Proof made, the Governors to Regulate the Division, and Publish it in Print.

For Example:

Suppose 4000 Seamen Subscribe to this Society, and after Six Months, for no Man shou'd Claim sooner than Six Months, a Merchant's Ship having Engag'd a Privateer, there comes several Claims together: As thus;

		l.
A	*Was Wounded and Lost one Leg*	50
B	*Blown up with Powder, and has Lost an Eye*	25
C	*Had a Great Shot took off his Arm*	100

D	*With a Splinter had an Eye struck out*	25
		200
E	*Was Kill'd with a Great Shot, to be paid to his Wife*	50
		250

The Governors hereupon settle the Claim of these Persons, and make Publication, *That whereas such and such Seamen, Members of the Society, have in an Engagement with a* French *Privateer, been so and so Hurt, their Claims upon the Office, by the Rules and Agreements of the said Office, being adjusted by the Governors, amounts to* 250 l. *which being equally divided among the Subscribers, comes to* 1 s. 3 d. *each; which all Persons that are Subscribers to the said Office are desired to Pay in, for their respective Subscriptions, that the said Wounded Persons may be Reliev'd accordingly, as they expect to be Reliev'd, if the same, or the like Casualty shou'd befall them.*

'Tis but a small matter for a Man to Contribute, if he gave 1 s. 3 d. out of his Wages to Relieve Five Wounded Men of his own Fraternity, but at the same time to be assur'd that if he is Hurt or Maim'd he shall have the same Relief, it is a thing so rational, that hardly any thing but a Hare-brain'd Fellow that thinks of nothing, wou'd omit Entring himself into such an Office.

I shall not enter further into this Affair, because, perhaps, I may give the Proposal to some Persons who may set it on foot; and then the World may see the Benefit of it by the Execution.

II. For Widows.

The same Method of *Friendly-Society* I conceive wou'd be a very proper Proposal for Widows.

We have abundance of Women who have been Bred well, and Liv'd well, Ruin'd in a few Years, and, perhaps, left Young, with a House full of Children, and nothing to Support them; which falls generally upon the Wives of the Inferior Clergy, or of Shopkeepers and Artificers.

They Marry Wives with perhaps 300 *l.* to 1000 *l.* Portion, and can settle no Jointure upon them; either they are Extravagant and Idle, and Waste it, or Trade Decays, or Losses, or a thousand Contingences happen to bring a Tradesman to Poverty, and he Breaks; the Poor Young Woman, it may be, has Three or Four Children, and is driven to a thousand shifts, while he lies in the *Mint* or *Friars* under the *Dilemma* of a Statute of

Bankrupt; but if he Dies, then she is absolutely Undone, unless she has Friends to go to.

Suppose an Office to be Erected, to be call'd *An Office of Ensurance for Widows*, upon the following Conditions:

Two thousand Women, or their Husbands for them, Enter their Names into a Register to be kept for that purpose, with the Names, Age, and Trade of their Husbands, with the Place of their Abode, Paying at the time of their Entring 5 *s.* down with 1. *s.* 4 *d. per* Quarter, which is to the setting up and support of an Office with Clerks, and all proper Officers for the same; *for there is no maintaining such without Charge*; they receive every one of them a Certificate, Seal'd by the Secretary of the Office, and Sign'd by the Governors, for the Articles hereafter mentioned.

If any one of the Women become a Widow at any time after Six Months from the Date of her Subscription, upon due Notice given, and Claim made at the Office in form, as shall be directed, she shall receive within Six Months after such Claim made, the Sum of 500 *l.* in Money, without any Deductions, saving some small Fees to the Officers, which the Trustees must settle, that they may be known.

In Consideration of this, every Woman so Subscribing, Obliges her self to Pay as often as any Member of the Society becomes a Widow, the due Proportion or Share allotted to her to Pay, towards the 500 *l.* for the said Widow, provided her Share does not exceed the Sum of 5 *s.*

No Seaman or Soldiers Wives to be accepted into such a Proposal as this, on the account before-mention'd, because the Contingences of their Lives are not equal to others, unless they will admit this general Exception, supposing they do not Die out of the Kingdom.

It might also be an Exception, That if the Widow, that Claim'd, had really, *bona fide*, left her by her Husband to her own use, clear of all Debts and Legacies, 2000 *l.* she shou'd have no Claim; the Intent being to Aid the Poor, not add to the Rich. But there lies a great many Objections against such an Article: As

(1.) It may tempt some to For-swear themselves.

(2.) People will Order their Wills so as to Defraud the Exception.

One Exception must be made; and that is, Either very Unequal Matches, as when a Woman of Nineteen Marries an Old Man of Seventy; or Women who have Infirm Husbands, I mean known and publickly so. To remedy which, Two things are to be done.

(1.) The Office must have moving Officers without doors, who shall inform themselves of such matters, and if any such Circumstances appear, the Office shou'd have 14 days time to return their Money, and declare their Subscriptions Void.

(2.) No Woman whose Husband had any visible Distemper, shou'd claim under a Year after her Subscription.

One grand Objection against this Proposal, is, How you will oblige People to Pay either their Subscription, or their Quarteridge.

To this I Answer, *By no compulsion* (tho' that might be perform'd too) but altogether voluntary; only with this Argument to move it, that if they do not continue their Payments, they lose the Benefit of their past Contributions.

I know it lies as a fair Objection against such a Project as this, That the number of Claims are so uncertain, That no Body knows what they engage in, when they Subscribe, for so many may Die Annually out of Two thousand, as may make my Payment 20 or 25 *l. per Ann.* and if a Woman happen to Pay that for Twenty Years, though she receives the 500 *l.* at last she is a great Loser; but if she dies before her Husband, she has lessened his Estate considerably, and brought a great Loss upon him.

First, I say to this, That I wou'd have such a Proposal as this be so fair and so easy, that if any Person who had Subscrib'd, found the Payments too high, and the Claims fall too often, it shou'd be at their liberty at any time, upon Notice given, to be Released, and stand Oblig'd no longer; and if so, *Volenti non fit injuria;*[79] every one knows best what their own Circumstances will bear.

In the next Place, because Death is a Contingency, no Man can directly calculate, and all that Subscribe must take the hazard; yet that a Prejudice against this Notion may not be built on wrong grounds, let's examine a little the probable hazard, and see how many shall die Annually out of 2000 Subscribers, accounting by the common proportion of Burials, to the number of the Living.

Sir *William Petty*[80] in his *Political Arithmetick*, by a very Ingenious Calculation, brings the account of Burials in *London*, to be 1 in 40 Annually, and proves it by all the proper Rules of proportion'd Computation; and I'le take my Scheme from thence.

If then One in Forty of all the People in *England* Die, that supposes Fifty to Die every Year out of our Two Thousand Subscribers; and for a Woman to Contribute 5 *s.* to every one, wou'd certainly be to Agree to Pay 12 *l.* 10 *s. per Ann.* upon her Husband's Life, to receive 500 *l.* when he Di'd, and lose it if she Di'd first; and yet this wou'd not be a Hazard beyond reason too great for the Gain.

But I shall offer some Reasons to prove this to be impossible in our Case; First, Sir *William Petty* allows the City of *London* to contain about a Million of People,[81] and our Yearly Bill of Mortality never yet amounted to 25,000 in the most Sickly Years we have had; Plague Years excepted, sometimes but to 20,000, which is but One in Fifty: Now it is to be consider'd here, that Children and Ancient People make up, one time with another, at least one third of our Bills of Mortality; and our *Assurances* lies upon none but the Midling Age of the People, which is the only Age wherein Life is any thing steady; and if that be allow'd, there cannot Die by his Computation, above One in Eighty of such People every Year; but because I wou'd be sure to leave room for Casualty, I'le allow One in Fifty shall Die out of our Number Subscrib'd.

Secondly, It must be allow'd, that our Payments falling due only on the Death of Husbands, this One in Fifty must not be reckoned upon the Two thousand; for 'tis to be suppos'd at least as many Women shall Die as Men, and then there is nothing to Pay; so that One in Fifty upon One Thousand, is the most that I can suppose shall Claim the Contribution in a Year, which is Twenty Claims a Year, at 5 *s.* each, and is 5 *l. per Ann.* and if a Woman Pays this for Twenty Year, and Claims at last, she is Gainer enough, and no extraordinary Loser if she never Claims at all: And I verily believe any Office might Undertake to Demand at all Adventures not above 6 *l. per Ann.* and secure the Subscriber 500 *l.* in case she come to Claim as a Widow.

I forbear being more particular on this Thought, having occasion to be larger in other Prints; the Experiment being resolv'd upon by some Friends, who are pleas'd to think this too useful a Project not to be put in execution; and therefore I refer the Reader to the Publick Practice of it.

I have nam'd these two Cases as special Experiments of what might be done by Assurances in way of *Friendly Society*; and I believe I might without Arrogance affirm, That the same Thought might be improv'd into Methods that shou'd prevent the General Misery and Poverty of Mankind, and at once secure us against Beggars, Parish-Poor, Alms-Houses, and Hospitals; and by which, not a Creature so Miserable, or so Poor, but should claim Subsistence as their Due, and not ask it of Charity.

I cannot believe any Creature so wretchedly base, as to Beg of mere choice, but either it must proceed from Want, or sordid prodigious Covetousness; and thence I affirm, There can be no *Beggar*, but he ought to be either Reliev'd, or Punish'd, or both. If a man begs for mere Covetousness, without Want, 'tis a baseness of Soul so extremely sordid, as ought to be us'd with the utmost Contempt, and punish'd with the Correction due to a Dog. If he begs for Want, that Want is procur'd by Slothfulness and Idleness, or by Accident; if the latter, he ought to be reliev'd; if the former, he ought to be punish'd for the Cause, but at the same time reliev'd also; for no man ought to starve, let his Crime be what it will.

I shall proceed therefore to a Scheme, by which all Mankind, be he never so mean, so poor, so unable, shall gain for himself a Just Claim to a comfortable Subsistence, whensoever Age or Casualty shall reduce him to a necessity of making use of it. There is a Poverty so far from being Despicable, that 'tis Honourable, when a man by direct Casualty, sudden Providence, and without any procuring of his own, is reduc'd to want Relief from others, as by Fire, Shipwreck, Loss of Limbs, and the like.

These are sometimes so apparent, that they command the Charity of others; but there are also many Families reduc'd to Decay, whose Conditions are not so publick, and yet their Necessities as great. Innumerable Circumstances reduce men to want; and pressing Poverty oblige some people to make their Cases publick, or starve; and from thence came the Custom of Begging, which Sloth and Idleness has improv'd into a Trade. But the Method I propose, thoroughly put in practice, would remove the Cause, and the Effect wou'd cease of course.

Want of Consideration is the great reason why People do not provide in their Youth and Strength for Old Age and Sickness; and the ensuing Proposal is, in short, only this, That all Persons in the time of their Health and Youth, while they are able to Work and spare it, shou'd lay up some small inconsiderable part of their gettings as a deposit in safe hands, to lie as a Store in bank to relieve them, if by Age or Accident they come to be disabled, or uncapable to Provide for themselves; and that if God so Bless them, that they nor theirs never come to need it, the overplus may be employ'd to relieve such as shall.

If an Office in the same nature with this, were appointed in every County in *England*, I doubt not but Poverty might easily be prevented, and Begging wholly suppress'd.

The Proposal is for a Pension-Office.

THAT an Office be erected in some convenient place, where shall be a Secretary, a Clerk, and a Searcher, always attending.

That all Sorts of People, who are Labouring People, and of Honest Repute, of what Calling or Condition soever, Men or Women, *Beggars and Soldiers excepted*, who being sound of their Limbs, and under Fifty Years of Age, shall come to the said Office, and enter their Names, Trades, and Places of Abode, into a Register to be kept for that purpose, and shall pay down at the time of the said Entering, the Sum of Sixpence, and from thence One Shilling *per* Quarter; shall every one have an Assurance under the Seal of the said Office, for these following Conditions.

(1.) Every such Subscriber, if by any Casualty (*Drunkenness and Quarrels excepted*) they break their Limbs, dislocate Joints, or are dangerously Maim'd or Bruis'd, able Surgeons appointed for that purpose shall take them into their care, and endeavour their Cure *Gratis*.

(2.) If they are at any time dangerously Sick, on notice given to the said Office, able Physicians shall be appointed to Visit them, and give their Prescriptions *Gratis*.

(3.) If by Sickness or Accident, as aforesaid, they lose their Limbs or Eyes, so as to be visibly disabled to Work, and are otherwise Poor and unable to provide for themselves, they shall either be Cur'd at the Charge of the Office, or be allow'd a Pension for Subsistence during Life.

(4.) If they become Lame, Aged, Bedrid, or by real Infirmity of Body (*the Pox excepted*) are unable to Work, and otherwise uncapable to provide for themselves, on proof made that it is really and honestly so, they shall be taken into a *Colledge or Hospital* provided for that purpose, and be decently maintain'd during life.

(5.) If they are Seamen, and die abroad on board the Merchants Ships they were employ'd in, or are cast away and drown'd, or taken and die in slavery, their Widows shall receive a Pension during their *Widowhood*.

(6.) If they were Tradesmen, and paid the Parish Rates, if by decay and failure of Trade they Break and are put in Prison for Debt, they shall receive a Pension for Subsistence during *close Imprisonment*.

(7.) If by Sickness or Accidents they are reduc'd to extremities of Poverty for a season, on a true representation to the Office, they shall be Reliev'd as the Governors shall see cause.

It is to be Noted, That in the 4th. *Article such as by Sickness and Age are
disabled from Work, and Poor, shall be taken into the House and provided
for; whereas in the* 3d. *Article, they who are Blind, or have lost Limbs,
&c. shall have Pensions allow'd them.*

The reason of this difference is this:

A Poor Man or Woman that has lost his Hand, or Leg, or Sight, is
visibly disabled, and we cannot be deceiv'd, whereas other Infirmities are
not so easily judg'd of, and every body wou'd be claiming a Pension,
when but few will demand being taken into an Hospital but such as are
really in want.

And that this might be manag'd with such Care and Candor as a
Design which carries so good a face ought to be, I Propose the following
Method for putting it in Practice.

I suppose every Undertaking of such a magnitude must have some
principal Agent to push it forward, who must manage and direct every
thing *always* with direction of the Governors.

And First, I'le suppose One General Office erected for the great
Parishes of *Stepney* and *Whitechappel*; and as I'le lay down afterwards some
Methods to oblige all People to come in and Subscribe, so I may be
allow'd to suppose here, That all the Inhabitants of those Two large
Parishes (the meaner Labouring sort I mean) shou'd Enter their Names,
and that the number of them shou'd be a 100,000, as I believe they wou'd
be at least.

First, There shou'd be Nam'd 50 of the principal Inhabitants of the
said Parishes (of which the Church-Wardens for the time being, and all
the Justices of the Peace dwelling in the bounds of the said Parish, and
the Ministers resident for the time being, to be part) to be Governors
of the said Office.

The said 50 to be first Nominated by the Lord-Mayor of *London* for
the time being, and every Vacancy to be suppli'd in 10 days at farthest,
by the Majority of Voices of the rest.

The 50 to chuse a Committee of 11, to sit twice a week, of whom 3
to be a *Quorum*; with a Chief Governor, a Deputy-Governor, and a
Treasurer.

In the Office, a Secretary with Clerks of his own, a Register, and 2
Clerks, 4 Searchers, a Messenger, one in daily attendance under Salary,
a Physician, a Surgeon, and 4 Visitors.

In the Hospital, more or less, according to the Number of People
entertain'd, a Housekeeper, a Steward, Nurses, a Porter, and a Chaplain.

For the Support of this Office, and that the deposite Money might go to none but the Persons and Uses for whom it is paid, and that it might not be said Officers and Salaries was the chief end of the Undertaking, *as in many a Project it has been*; I propose, That the Manager, or Undertaker, who I mention'd before, be the Secretary, who shall have a Clerk allow'd him, whose business it shall be to keep the Register, take the Entries and give out the Tickets Seal'd by the Governors, and Sign'd by himself, and to Enter always the Payment of Quarteridge of every Subscriber. And that there may be no Fraud or Connivance, and too great Trust be not repos'd in the said Secretary, every Subscriber who brings his Quarteridge, is to put it into a great Chest, lockt up with 11 Locks, every Member of the Committee to keep a Key, so that it cannot be open'd but in the Presence of them all; and every time a Subscriber pays his Quarteridge, the Secretary shall give him a Seal'd Ticket, thus $\boxed{\textit{Christmas 96}}$ which shall be allow'd as the Receipt of Quarteridge for that Quarter.

> *Note, The reason why every Subscriber shall take a Receipt or Ticket for his Quarteridge, is because this must be the standing Law of the Office, that if any Subscriber fail to pay their Quarteridge, they shall never Claim after it, until double so much be paid, nor not at all that Quarter, whatever befalls them.*

The Secretary shou'd be allow'd to have 2 *d.* for every Ticket of Entry he gives out, and 1 *d.* for every Receipt he gives for Quarteridge, to be accounted for as follows:

One Third to himself in Lieu of Salary, he being to Pay Three Clerks out of it.

One Third to the Clerks, and other Officers among them.

And One Third to defray the incident Charge of the Office.

Thus Calculated.[82]	*Per Ann.*		
	l.	*s.*	*d.*
100,000 Subscribers paying 1 *d.* each every Quarter is	1666	3	4
One Third { To the Secretary *per Ann.* and Three Clerks	555	7	9

83

		l.		Per Ann.		
				l.	*s.*	*d.*
One Third	To a Register	100				
	To a Clerk	50				
	To 4 Searchers	100		550	0	0
	To a Physician	100				
	To a Surgeon	100				
	To Four Visitors	100				
One Third To Incident Charges, such as	To Ten Committee-Men, 5 *s.* each sitting, twice *per* Week is	260				
	To a Clerk of Committees	50				
	To a Messenger	40		560	15	7
	A House for the Office	40				
	A House for the Hospital	100				
	Contingencies	70				

15 *s.* 7 *d.*

| | | 1666 | 3 | 4 |

All the Charge being thus paid out of such a Trifle as 1 *d. per* Quarter, the next Consideration is to examine what the Incomes of this Subscription may be, and in time what may be the Demands upon it.

	l.	*s.*	*d.*
If 100,000 persons subscribe, they pay down at their entring, each 6 *d.* which is	2500	00	00
And the first year's Payment is in Stock at 1 *s. per* Quarter	20000	00	00
It must be allow'd, that under Three Months the Subscriptions will not be well compleat; so the Payment of Quarteridge shall not begin but from the Day after the Books are full, or shut up; and from thence one year is to pass before any Claim can be made; and the Money coming in at separate times, I suppose no Improvement upon it for the first year, except of the 2500, which lent to the King on some good Fund, at 7 *l. per Cent.* Interest, advances the first year,	175	00	00
The Quarteridge of the Second year, abating for 1000 Claims,	19800	00	00
And the Interest of the first year's Money, at the end of the second year, lent to the King, as aforesaid, at 7 *per Cent.* Interest, is	1774	10	00

The Quarteridge of the Third year, abating for Claims,	19400	00	00
The Interest of former Cash, to the end of the Third Year,	3284	08	00
Income of Three Years	66933	18	00

Note, *Any person may pay 2 s. up to 5 s. Quarterly, if they please, and upon a Claim, will be allow'd in proportion.*

To assign what shall be the Charge upon this, where Contingency has so great a share, is not to be done; but by way of Political Arithmetick a probable Guess may be made.

'Tis to be noted, That the Pensions I propose to be paid to Persons claiming by the Third, Fifth, and Sixth Articles, are thus; Every Person who paid 1 s. Quarterly, shall receive 12 d. Weekly, and so in proportion, every 12 d. paid Quarterly by any one Person, to receive so many Shillings Weekly, if they come to claim a Pension.

The first Year no Claim is allow'd; so the Bank has in Stock compleatly 22,500 *l.* From thence we are to consider the Number of Claims.

Sir *William Petty*,[83] in his Political Arithmetick, supposes not above one in 40 to dye *per Ann.* out of the whole numbers of people; and I can by no means allow, that the Circumstances of our Claims will be as frequent as Death; for these Reasons:

(1.) Our Subscriptions respect all persons grown, and in the Prime of their Age; past the first, and providing against the last part of Danger. Sir *William*'s Account including Children and Old People, which always makes up One Third of the Bills of Mortality.

(2.) Our Claims will fall thin at first, for several Years; and let but the Money increase for Ten Years, as it does in the Account for Three Years, 'twould be almost sufficient to maintain the whole Number.

(3.) Allow that Casualty and Poverty are our Debtor-side; Health, Prosperity, and Death, are the Creditor-side of the Account; and in all probable Accounts, those Three Articles will carry off Three Fourth Parts of the Number, as follows: If 1 in 40 shall dye Annually, as no doubt they shall, and more, that is 2500 a year, which in 20 Years is 50,000 of the Number, I hope I may be allow'd One Third to be out of condition to claim, apparently living without the help of Charity; and One Third in Health of Body, and able to work; which put together, makes 83,332; so it leaves 16,668 to make Claims of Charity and Pensions in the first 20 years, and One half of them must, according to Sir *William Petty*, Die on our hands in 20 years; so there remains but 8334.

But to put it out of doubt, beyond the proportion to be guess'd at, I'le allow they shall fall thus;

> *The First Year, we are to note, none can claim, and the Second Year the Number must be very few, but increasing; wherefore I suppose,*

	l.
One in every 500 shall claim the second year, which is 200, The Charge whereof is	500
One in every 100 the third year, is 1000; the Charge,	2500
Together with the former 200,	500
	————
	3000

To carry on the Calculation.

	l.	*s.*	*d.*
We find the Stock at the end of the 3*d* year,	66933	18	0
The Quarteridge of the 4*th* year, abating as before,	19000	00	0
Interest of the Stock,	4882	17	6
The Quarteridge of the 5*th* year,	18600	00	0
Interest of the Stock,	6473	00	0
	————	——	—
	115879	15	6

	l.	*s.*	*d.*
The Charge	3000	00	0
2000 to fall the 4*th* Year	5000	00	0
And the Old continued	3000	00	0
2000 the 5*th* Year	5000	00	0
The Old continued	11000	00	0
	————	——	—
	27000	00	0

By this computation the Stock is increased above the Charge in Five years 89,379 *l.* 15 *s.* 6 *d.* and yet here are sundry Articles to be considered on both sides of the Account, that will necessarily increase the Stock and diminish the Charge.

	l.	*s.*	*d.*
First, In the Five years time 6200 having claim'd Charity, the Number being abated for in the reckoning above for Stock, it may be allow'd New Subscriptions will be taken in to keep the Number full, which in Five years amounts to	3400	00	0
Their Sixpences is	155	00	0
	3555	00	0
Which added to 115879 *l.* 15 *s.* 6 *d.* Augments the Stock to	119434	15	6
Six thousand two hundred persons claiming help, which falls to be sure, on the Aged and Infirm, I think, at a modest computation, in Five years time 500 of them may be dead, which, without allowing annually, we take at an Abatement of 4000 *l.* out of the Charge	4000	00	0
Which reduces the Charge to	23000	00	0

Besides this, the Interest of the Quarteridge, which is supposed in the former Account to lie dead till the Year is out, which cast up from Quarter to Quarter, allowing it to be put out Quarterly, as it may well be, amounts to by computation for Five Year, 5250 *l.*

From the 5*th* year, as near as can be computed, the Number of Pensioners being so great I make no doubt but they shall Die off of the hands of the Undertaker as fast as they shall fall in, excepting so much difference as the Payment of every Year, which the Interest of the Stock shall supply.

For Example:

	l.	*s.*	*d.*
At the end of the Fifth Year the Stock in hand	94629	15	6
The Payment of the Sixth Year	20000	00	0
Interest of the Stock	5408	04	0
	120037	19	6
Allow an over-plus Charge for keeping in the House, which will be dearer than Pensions, 10000 *l. per Ann.*	10000	00	0
Charge of the 6*th* Year	22500	00	0
Balance in Cash	87537	19	6
	120037	19	6

This also is to be allow'd, That all those Persons who are kept by the Office in the House shall have Employment provided for them, whereby no Persons shall be kept Idle, the Works to be suited to every one's Capacity without Rigour, only some distinction to those who are most willing to Work; the Profits of the said Work to the Stock of the House.

Besides this there may be great and very profitable Methods be found out to improve the Stock beyond the settled Interest of 7 *per Cent.* which perhaps may not always be to be had, for the *Exchequer* is not always borrowing Money; but a Bank of 80000 *l.* employ'd by faithful hands, need not want opportunities of great and very considerable Improvement.

Also it wou'd be a very good Object for Persons who Die Rich to *leave Legacies to*, which in time might be very well suppos'd to raise a standing Revenue to it.

I won't say but various Contingencies may alter the Charge of this Undertaking, and swell the Claims beyond proportion, further than I extend it; but all that, and much more, is sufficiently answer'd in the Calculations, by above 80,000 *l.* in Stock to Provide for it.

As to the Calculation being made on a vast Number of Subscribers, and more than, perhaps, will be allow'd likely to Subscribe, I think the proportion may hold good in a few, as well as in a great many; and, perhaps, if 20,000 Subscrib'd, it might be as effectual; I am indeed willing to think all Men shou'd have sense enough to see the usefulness of such a Design, and be perswaded by their Interest to engage in it; but some Men have less Prudence than Brutes, and will make no provision against Age till it comes; and to deal with such, Two[84] ways might be us'd by Authority to Compel them.

(1.) The Church-Wardens and Justices of Peace shou'd send the Beadle of the Parish, with an Officer belonging to this Office, about to the Poorer Parishioners to tell them, That since such Honourable Provision is made for them to secure themselves in Old Age from Poverty and Distress, they shou'd expect no Relief from the Parish, if they refus'd to Enter themselves, and by sparing so small a part of their Earnings to prevent future Misery.

(2.) The Church-Wardens of every Parish might refuse the removal of Persons and Families into their Parish but upon their having Entred into this Office.

(3.) All Persons shou'd be publickly desir'd to forbear giving any thing to Beggars; and all common Beggars suppress'd after a certain time; for this wou'd effectually suppress Beggery at last.

And to oblige the Parishes to do this on behalf of such a Project, the Governor of the House shou'd secure the Parish against all Charges coming upon them from any Person who did Subscribe and pay the Quarteridge, and that wou'd most certainly oblige any Parish to endeavour that all the Labouring Meaner People in the Parish shou'd enter their Names; for in time 'twou'd most certainly take all the Poor in the Parish off of their hands.

I know that by Law no Parish can refuse to Relieve any Person or Family fallen into Distress, and therefore to send them word they must expect no Relief, wou'd seem a vain threatning; but thus far the Parish may do, they shall be esteem'd as Persons who deserve no Relief, and shall be us'd accordingly; For who, indeed, wou'd ever pity that Man in his Distress, who at the expence of *Two Pots of Beer a Month*, might have prevented it, and wou'd not spare it?

As to my Calculations, on which I do not depend neither, I say this, if they are probable, and that in Five years time a Subscription of a Hundred thousand Persons wou'd have 87,537 *l.* 19 *s.* 6 *d.* in Cash, all Charges paid, I desire any one but to reflect what will not such a Sum do; *for instance*, were it laid out in the Million Lottery Tickets,[85] which are now Sold at 6 *l.* each, and bring in 1 *l. per Ann.* for Fifteen Years, every 1000 *l.* so laid out, pays back in time 2500 *l.* and that time wou'd be as fast as it wou'd be wanted, and therefore be as good as Money; or if laid out in improving Rents, as Ground-Rents with Buildings to devolve in time, there is no question but a Revenue wou'd be rais'd in time to Maintain One third part of the Number of Subscribers if they shou'd come to Claim Charity.

And I desire any Man to consider the present State of this Kingdom, and tell me, if all the People of *England*, Old and Young, Rich and Poor, were to Pay into one common Bank, 4 *s. per Ann.* a Head, and that 4 *s.* duly and honestly manag'd, Whether the overplus paid by those who Die off, and by those who never come to Want, wou'd not in all probability Maintain all that shou'd be Poor, and for ever Banish Beggery and Poverty out of the Kingdom.

Of Wagering.

WAGERING, as now practis'd by Polities and Contracts, is become a Branch of *Assurances*; it was before more properly a part of Gaming, and as it deserv'd, had but a very low esteem; but shifting sides, and the War providing proper subjects, as the contingences of Sieges, Battels, Treaties, and Campaigns, is encreas'd to an extraordinary Reputation, and Offices were erected on purpose which manag'd it to a strange degree and with great Advantage, especially to the Office-keepers; so that as has been computed, there was not less Gaged[86] on one side and other upon the second Siege of *Limerick*,[87] than Two hundred thousand Pound.

How 'tis manag'd, and by what trick and artifice it became a Trade, and how insensibly Men were drawn into it, an easy Account may be given.

I believe *Novelty* was the first wheel that set it on work, and I need make no reflection upon the power of that Charm: It was wholly a new thing, at least upon the *Exchange* of *London*; and the first occasion that gave it a room among publick Discourse, was some Persons forming Wagers on the Return and Success of King *James*, for which the Government took occasion to use them as they deserv'd.[88]

I *have* heard a Bookseller in King *James*'s time say, *That if he wou'd have a Book sell, he wou'd have it Burnt by the hand of the Common Hangman*; the Man, no doubt, valu'd his Profit above his Reputation; but People are so addicted to prosecute a thing that seems forbid, that this very practice seem'd to be encourag'd by its being *Contraband*.

The Trade encreas'd, and first on the *Exchange* and then in Coffee-houses it got life, till the Brokers, *those Vermin of Trade*, got hold of it, and then particular Offices were set apart for it, and an incredible resort thither was to be seen every day.

These Offices had not been long in being, but they were throng'd with *Sharpers* and *Setters* as much as the Groom-Porter's,[89] or any Gaming-Ordinary[90] in Town, where a Man had nothing to do, but to make a good Figure and prepare the Keeper of the Office to give him a Credit as a good Man, and though he had not a Groat to pay, he shou'd take Guineas and sign Polities,[91] till he had receiv'd, perhaps 3 or 400 *l.* in Money on condition to pay great Odds, and then Success tries the Man; if he Wins, his Fortune is made; if not, he's a better Man than he was before, by just so much Money, for as to the Debt, he is your Humble Servant[92] in the *Temple* or *Whitehall*.

But besides those who are but the Thieves of the Trade, there is a Method as effectual to get Money as possible, manag'd with more appearing Honesty, but no less Art, by which the Wagerer, in Confederacy with the Office-keeper, shall lay vast Sums, great Odds, and yet be always sure to Win.

For Example:

A Town in *Flanders*, or elsewhere, during the War is besieg'd; perhaps at the beginning of the Siege the Defence is vigorous, and Relief probable, and it is the opinion of most people, the Town will hold out *so long*, or perhaps not be taken at all: The Wagerer has two or three more of his sort in conjunction, of which always the Office-keeper is one; and they run down all discourse of the taking the Town, and offer great Odds it shall not be taken by such a day: Perhaps this goes on a Week, and then the Scale turns; and tho' they seem to hold the same opinion still, yet underhand the Office-keeper has Orders to Take all the Odds which by their Example was before given, against the taking the Town; and so all their first-given Odds are easily secur'd, and yet the people brought into a vein of Betting against the Siege of the Town too. Then they order all the Odds to be Taken as long as they will run, while they themselves openly give Odds, and sign Polities, *and often-times take their own Money*, till they have receiv'd perhaps double what they at first laid. Then they turn the Scale at once, and cry down the Town, and lay that it shall be taken, till the length of the first Odds is fully run; and by this Manage, if the Town be taken they win perhaps Two or Three Thousand Pounds, and if it be not taken, they are no Losers neither.

'Tis visible by experience, not one Town in ten is besieg'd, but 'tis taken. The Art of War is so improv'd, and our Generals are so wary, that an Army seldom attempts a Siege, but when they are almost sure to go on with it; and no Town can hold out, if a Relief cannot be had from abroad.

Now if I can by first laying 500 *l.* to 200 *l.* with *A*, that the Town shall not be taken, wheedle in *B* to lay me 5000 *l.* to 2000 *l.* of the same; and after that, by bringing down the Vogue of the Siege, reduce the Wagers to Even-hand, and lay 2000 *l.* with *C* that the Town shall not be taken; by this Method, 'tis plain,

If the Town be not Taken, I win 2200 *l.* and lose 2000 *l.*
If the Town be Taken, I win 5000 *l.* and lose 2500 *l.*

This is Gaming by Rule, and in such a Knot[93] 'tis impossible to lose; for if it is in any Man's or Company of Men's power, by any Artifice to alter the Odds, 'tis in their power to command the Money out of every man's Pocket, who has no more Wit than to venture.

Of Fools.

OF all Persons who are Objects of our Charity, none move my Compassion, like those whom it has pleas'd God to leave in a full state of Health and Strength, but depriv'd of Reason to act for themselves. And it is, in my opinion, one of the greatest Scandals upon the *Understanding* of others, to mock at those who want *it*. Upon this account I think the Hospital we call *Bedlam*,[94] to be a Noble Foundation; a visible Instance of the sense our Ancestors had of the greatest Unhappiness which can befal Human Kind: Since as the Soul in Man distinguishes him from a Brute, so where the Soul is dead (for so it is as to acting) *no Brute so much a Beast as a Man*.[95] But since *never to have* it, and to have *lost* it, are synonimous in the Effect, I wonder how it came to pass, that in the Settlement of that Hospital they made no Provision for Persons born without the use of their Reason, such as we call *Fools*, or, more properly, *Naturals*.

We use such in *England* with the last Contempt, which I think is a strange Error, since tho' they are useless to the Commonwealth, they are only so by God's direct providence, and no previous Fault.

I think 'twould very well become this Wise Age to take care of such: And perhaps they are a particular Rent-Charge on the *Great Family of Mankind*, left by the Maker of us all; like a Younger Brother, who tho' the Estate be given from him, yet his Father expected the Heir should take some care of him.

If I were to be ask'd, Who ought in particular to be charg'd with this Work? I would answer in general, Those who have a Portion of Understanding extraordinary: Not that I would lay a Tax upon any man's Brains, *or discourage Wit, by appointing Wise Men to maintain Fools*: But some Tribute is due to God's Goodness for bestowing extraordinary Gifts; and who can it be better paid to, than such as suffer for want of the same Bounty?

For the providing therefore some Subsistence for such, that Natural Defects may not be expos'd:

It is Propos'd,

That a *Fool-House* be Erected, either by Publick Authority, or by the City, or by an Act of Parliament; into which, all that are *Naturals*, or born Fools, without Respect or Distinction, should be admitted and maintain'd.

For the Maintenance of this, a small stated Contribution, settl'd by the Authority of an Act of Parliament, without any Damage to the Persons paying the same, might be very easily rais'd, by a Tax upon Learning, to be paid by the Authors of Books.

Every Book that shall be Printed in Folio, *from*
    40 *sheets and upwards, to pay at the Licensing,*
    (for the whole Impression.)
	5 *l.*

Under 40 *sheets,*	40 *s.*
Every Quarto,	20 *s.*
Every Octavo *of* 10 *sheets and upward,*	20 *s.*
Every Octavo *under* 10 *sheets, and every* *Bound Book in* 12ˢ.	10 *s.*
Every stitch'd Pamphlet,	2 *s.*

Reprinted Copies the same Rates.

This Tax to be paid into the Chamber of *London*[96] for the space of Twenty Years, would without question raise a Fund sufficient to Build and Purchase a Settlement for this House.

I suppose this little Tax being to be rais'd at so few places as the Printing-Presses, or the Licensers of Books, and consequently the Charge but very small in gathering, might bring in about 1500 *l. per Annum,* for the term of Twenty Years, which would perform the Work to the degree following.

The House should be Plain and Decent, (for I don't think the Ostentation of Buildings necessary or suitable to Works of Charity); and be built somewhere out of Town, for the sake of the Air.

The Building to cost about 1000 *l.* or if the Revenue exceed, to cost 2000 *l.* at most, and the Salaries mean[97] in proportion.

In the House,

A Steward,	30	*l. per Ann.*
A Purveyor,	20	
A Cook,	20	
A Butler,	20	
Six Women to assist the Cook, and clean the House, 4 *l.* each,	24	
Six Nurses to Tend the People 3 *l.* each,	18	
A Chaplain,	20	
	152	

A Hundred Alms-People, at 8 *l. per Ann.* Dyet, &c.	}	800

		952	*l. per Ann.*
The Table for the Officers, and Contingences, and Cloaths for the Alms-People, and Firing, put together,	}	500	*l. per Ann.*

An Auditor of the Accounts, a Committee of the
Governors, and Two Clerks.

Here I suppose 1500 Pounds *per Ann.* Revenue, to be settl'd upon the House, which 'tis very probable might be rais'd from the Tax aforesaid. But since an Act of Parliament is necessary to be had for the Collecting this Duty, *and that Taxes for keeping of Fools would be difficultly obtain'd, while they are so much wanted for Wise Men*; I would propose to raise the Money by voluntary Charity, which wou'd be a Work would leave more Honour to the Undertakers, than Feasts and great Shows, which our Publick Bodies too much diminish their Stocks with.

But to pass all suppositious ways, which are easily thought of, but hardly procur'd; I propose to maintain Fools out of our own Folly: And whereas a great deal of Money has been thrown about in Lotteries, the following Proposal would very easily perfect our Work.

A Charity-Lottery.

That a Lottery be set up by the Authority of the Lord-Mayor and Court of Aldermen, for a Hundred thousand Tickets, at Twenty Shillings each, to be drawn by the known Way and Method of drawing Lotteries, as the Million-Lottery[98] was drawn; in which no Allowance to be made to any body; but the Fortunate to receive the full Sum of One hundred thousand Pounds put in, without Discount; and yet this double Advantage to follow:

(1.) That an immediate Sum of One hundred thousand Pounds shall be rais'd and paid into the *Exchequer* for the Publick Use.

(2.) A sum of above Twenty thousand Pounds be gain'd, to be put into the hands of known Trustees, to be laid out in a Charity for the Maintenance of the Poor.

That as soon as the Money shall be come in, it shall be paid into the *Exchequer*, either on some good Fund, if any suitable, or on the Credit of *Exchequer*; and that when the Lottery is drawn, the Fortunate to receive

Tallies[99] or Bills from the *Exchequer* for their Money, payable at Four Years.

The *Exchequer* receives this Money, and gives out Tallies according to the Prizes, when 'tis drawn, all payable at Four Years; and the Interest of this Money for Four Years is struck in Tallies proportion'd to the time, and given to the Trustees; which is the Profit I propose for the Work.

Thus the Fortunate have an immediate Title to their Prizes, at Four Years, without Interest; and the Hospital will have also an immediate Title to 6000 *l. per Ann.* for Four Years, which is the Interest at 6 *per Cent. per Ann.*

If any should object against the Time of staying for their Prizes, it should be answer'd thus, That whoever did not like to stay the Time for the Money, upon discounting Four Years Interest at 8 *per Cent.* should have their Money down.

I think this Specimen will inform any body what might be done by Lotteries, were they not hackney'd about in Private Hands, who by Fraud and Ill Management put them out of Repute, and so neither gain themselves, nor suffer any useful handsome Design to succeed.

'Twould be needless, I suppose, to mention, That such a Proposal as this ought to be set on foot by Publick Approbation, and by Men of known Integrity and Estates, that there may be no room left for a suspicion of private advantage.

If this or any equivalent Proposal succeeded to raise the Money, I would have the House establish'd as aforesaid, with larger or smaller Revenues, as necessity oblig'd; then the Persons to be receiv'd should be without distinction or respect, but principally such as were really Poor and Friendless; and any that were kept already by any Parish-Collection, the said Parish should allow Forty Shillings Yearly towards their Maintenance; which no Parish would refuse that subsisted them wholly before.

I make no question but that if such an Hospital was erected within a Mile or two of the City, one great Circumstance would happen, (*viz.*) That the common sort of people, who are very much addicted to rambling in the Fields, would make this House the customary Walk, to divert themselves with the Objects to be seen there, and to make what they call Sport with the Calamity of others; as is now shamefully allow'd in *Bedlam.*[100]

To prevent this, and that the condition of such, which deserves Pity, not Contempt, might not be the more expos'd by this Charity, it should be order'd, That the Steward of the House be in Commission of the Peace[101] within the Precincts of the House only, and authoriz'd to punish by limited Fines, or otherwise, any person that shall offer any Abuse to the poor Alms-people, or shall offer to make Sport at their Condition.

If any person at Reading of this, shou'd be so impertinent as to ask, To what purpose I wou'd appoint a Chaplain in an Hospital of *Fools*? I could answer him very well, by saying, For the use of the other Persons, Officers and Attendants in the House.

But besides that, Pray, *Why not a Chaplain for Fools, as well as for Knaves*, since both, tho' in a different manner, are uncapable of reaping any benefit by Religion, unless by some invisible Influence they are made docible; and since the same Secret Power can restore these to their Reason, as must make the other Sensible; Pray, Why not a Chaplain? Ideots indeed were denied the Communion in the Primitive Churches, but I never read they were not to be pray'd for, or were not admitted to hear.

If we allow any Religion, and a Divine Supreme Power, whose Influence works invisibly on the hearts of men (*as he must be worse than the people we talk of, who denies it*), we must allow at the same time, *that Power* can restore the Reasoning-Faculty to an Ideot; and 'tis our part to use the proper means of supplicating Heaven to that end, leaving the disposing-part to the Issue of unalterable Providence.

The Wisdom of Providence has not left us without Examples of some of the most stupid Natural Ideots in the world, who have been restor'd to their Reason, or as one would think, had Reason infus'd after a long Life of *Ideotism*; Perhaps, among other wise ends, to confute that sordid Supposition, That Ideots have no Souls.

Of Bankrupts.

THis Chapter[102] has some Right to stand next to that of Fools; for besides the common acceptation of late, which makes *every Unfortunate Man a Fool*, I think no man so much made a Fool of as a *Bankrupt*.

If I may be allow'd so much liberty with our Laws, which are generally good, and above all things are temper'd with Mercy, Lenity, and Freedom, This has something in it of Barbarity; it gives a loose to the Malice and Revenge of the Creditor, as well as a Power to right himself, while it leaves the Debtor no way to show himself honest: It contrives all the ways possible to drive the Debtor to despair, and encourages no

new Industry, for it makes him perfectly uncapable of any thing but
starving.

This Law, especially as it is now frequently executed, tends wholly to
the Destruction of the Debtor, and yet very little to the Advantage of
the Creditor.

(1.) The Severities to the Debtor are unreasonable, and, if I may so
say, a little inhuman; for it not only strips him of all in a moment, but
renders him for ever incapable of helping himself, or relieving his Family
by future Industry. If he 'scapes from Prison, which is hardly done too,
if he has nothing left, he must starve, or live on Charity; if he goes to
work, no man dare pay him his Wages, but he shall pay it again to the
Creditors; if he has any private Stock left for a Subsistence, he can put
it no where; every man is bound to be a Thief, and take it from him: If
he trusts it in the hands of a Friend, he must receive it again as a great
Courtesy, for that Friend is liable to account for it. I have known a poor
man prosecuted by a Statute[103] to that degree, that all he had left was a
little Money, which he knew not where to hide; at last, that he might
not starve, he gives it to his Brother, who had entertain'd him; the
Brother, after he had his Money, quarrels with him to get him out of
his House; and when he desires him to let him have the Money lent
him, gives him this for Answer, *I cannot pay you safely, for there is a Statute
against you*; which run the poor man to such Extremities, that he destroy'd
himself. Nothing is more frequent, than for men who are reduc'd by
Miscarriage in Trade, to Compound and Set up again, and get good
Estates; but a *Statute*, as we call it, for ever shuts up all doors to the
Debtor's Recovery; as if Breaking were a Crime so Capital, that he ought
to be cast out of Human Society, and expos'd to Extremities worse than
Death. And, which will further expose the fruitless Severity of this Law,
'tis easy to make it appear, That all this Cruelty to the Debtor is so far
(generally speaking) from advantaging the Creditors, that it destroys the
Estate, consumes it in extravagant Charges, and unless the Debtor be
consenting, seldom makes any considerable Dividends. And I am bold
to say, There is no Advantage made by the prosecuting of a Statute with
Severity, but what might be doubly made by Methods more merciful.
And tho' I am not to prescribe to the Legislators of the Nation, yet by
way of Essay I take leave to give my Opinion and my Experience in the
Methods, Consequences, and Remedies of this Law.

All people know, who remember any thing of the Times when that
Law was made, that the Evil it was pointed at, was grown very rank, and
Breaking to defraud Creditors so much a Trade, that the Parliament had

good reason to set up a Fury to deal with it; and I am far from reflecting on the Makers of that Law, who, no question, saw 'twas necessary at that time: But as Laws, tho' in themselves good, are more or less so, as they are more or less seasonable, squar'd, and adapted to the Circumstances and Time of the Evil they are made against; so 'twere worth while (with Submission) for the same Authority to examine:

(1.) Whether the Length of Time since that Act was made, has not given opportunity to Debtors,

1. To evade the Force of the Act by Ways and Shifts to avoid the Power of it, and secure their Estates out of the reach of it?

2. To turn the Point of it against those whom it was made to relieve? Since we see frequently now, that Bankrupts desire Statutes, and procure them to be taken out against themselves.

(2.) Whether the Extremities of this Law are not often carried on beyond the true Intent and Meaning of the Act it self, by Persons, who besides being Creditors, are also Malicious, and gratify their private Revenge, by prosecuting the Offender, to the Ruin of his Family.

If these Two Points are to be prov'd, then I am sure 'twill follow, That this Act is now a Publick Grievance to the Nation; and I doubt not but will be one time or other repeal'd by the same Wise Authority which made it.

(1.) Time and Experience has furnish'd the Debtors with Ways and Means to evade the Force of this Statute, and to secure their Estate against the reach of it; which renders it often insignificant, and consequently, the Knave, against whom the Law was particularly bent, gets off; while he only who fails of mere Necessity, and whose honest Principle will not permit him to practice those Methods, is expos'd to the Fury of this Act: And as things are now order'd, nothing is more easy, than for a man to order his Estate so, that a Statute shall have no power over it, or at least but a little.

If the Bankrupt be a Merchant, no Statute can reach his Effects beyond the Seas; so that he has nothing to secure but his Books, and away he goes into the *Friars*.[104] If a Shopkeeper, he has more difficulty; but that is made easy, for there are Men (and Carts) to be had, *whose Trade it is*, and who in One Night shall remove the greatest Warehouse of Goods, or Cellar of Wines in the Town, and carry them off into those Nurseries of Rogues, the *Mint*[105] and *Friars*; and our Constables and Watch, who are the allow'd-Magistrates of the Night, and who shall stop a poor little lurking Thief, that it may be has stole a bundle of old Cloaths, worth 5 *s.* shall let them all pass without any disturbance, and see a hundred honest men robb'd of their Estates before their faces, to the Eternal Infamy of the Justice of the Nation.

And were a man but to hear the Discourse among the Inhabitants of those Dens of Thieves, when they first swarm about a New Comer, to comfort him; for they are not all harden'd to a like degree at once. – *Well*, says the first, *Come, don't be concern'd, you have got a good Parcel of Goods away, I promise you; you need not value all the World. Ah! wou'd I had done so*, says another, *I'de a laugh'd at all my Creditors. Ay*, says the young Proficient in the harden'd Trade, *but my Creditors! Damn the Creditors*, says a Third, *Why, there's such a one and such a one, they have Creditors too, and they won't agree with them, and here they live like Gentlemen, and care not a farthing for them. Offer your Creditors Half a Crown in the Pound, and pay it them in Old Debts, and if they won't take it, let them alone, they'll come after you, never fear it. O! But a Statute*, says he again. *O! But the Devil*, cries the Minter. *Why, 'tis the Statutes we live by*, say they: *Why, if 'twere not for Statutes, Creditors would comply, and Debtors wou'd compound, and We Honest Fellows here of the Mint wou'd be starv'd. Prithee, What need you care for a Statute? A Thousand Statutes can't reach you here.* This is the *Language of the Countrey*, and the New Comer soon learns to speak it; (for I think I may say, without wronging any man, I have known many a man go in among them Honest, that is, without Ill Design, but I never knew one come away so again.) – Then comes a Graver Sort among this Black Crew, (for here, as in Hell, are Fiends of Degrees; and different Magnitude), and he falls into Discourse with the New Comer, and gives him more solid Advice. *Look you, Sir, I am concern'd to see you melancholly, I am in your Circumstance too, and if you'll accept of it, I'le give you the best Advice I can*; and so begins the Grave Discourse.

The man is in too much trouble, not to want Counsel, so he thanks him, and he goes on: *Send a Summons to your Creditors, and offer them what you can propose in the Pound* (always reserving a good Stock to begin the World again), *which if they will take, you are a Freeman, and better than you were before; if they won't take it, you know the worst of it, you are on the better side of the hedge with them: If they will not take it, but will proceed to a Statute, you have nothing to do, but to oppose Force with Force; for the Laws of Nature tell you, you must not starve; and a Statute is so barbarous, so unjust, so malicious a way of proceeding against a man, that I do not think any Debtor oblig'd to consider any thing but his own Preservation, when once they go on with that.* – For why, says the old studi'd Wretch, *should the Creditors spend your Estate in the Commission, and then demand the Debt of you too? Do you owe any thing to the Commission of the Statute?*

(No, says he); *Why then,* says he, *I warrant their Charges will come to* 200 l. *out of your Estate, and they must have* 10 s. *a day for starving you and your Family. I cannot see why any man should think I am bound in Conscience to pay the Extravagance of other men. If my Creditors spend* 500 l. *in getting in my Estate by a Statute, which I offer'd to surrender without it, I'le reckon that* 500 l. *paid them, let them take it among them; for Equity is due to a Bankrupt as well as to any man; and if the Laws do not give it us, we must take it.*

This is too rational Discourse not to please him, and he proceeds by this Advice; the Creditors cannot agree, but take out a Statute; and the man that offer'd at first, it may be, 10 s. in the Pound, is kept in that cursed place till he has spent it all, and can offer nothing, and then gets away beyond Sea, or after a long Consumption gets off by an Act of Relief to poor Debtors, and all the Charges of the Statute falls among the Creditors. Thus I knew a Statute taken out against a Shopkeeper in the Countrey, and a considerable Parcel of Goods too seiz'd, and yet the Creditors, what with Charges, and two or three Suits at Law, lost their whole Debts, and 8 s. per Pound Contribution-Money for Charges; and the poor Debtor like a man under the Surgeon's hand, died in the Operation.

(2.) Another Evil that Time and Experience has brought to light from this Act, is, when the Debtor himself shall confederate with some particular Creditor to take out a Statute; and this is a Master-piece of *Plot* and Intriegue: For perhaps some Creditor honestly receiv'd in the way of Trade a large Sum of Money of the Debtor for Goods sold him when he was *sui juris;*[106] and he by consent shall own himself a Bankrupt before that time, and the Statute shall reach back to bring in an Honest Man's Estate, to help pay a Rogue's Debt. Or a man shall go and borrow a sum of Money upon a Parcel of Goods, and lay them to Pledge; he keeps the Money, and the Statute shall fetch away the Goods to help forward the Composition. These are Tricks I can give too good an account of, having more than once suffer'd by the Experiment. I could give a Scheme of more ways, but I think 'tis needless to prove the Necessity of laying aside that Law, which is pernicious to both Debtor and Creditor, and chiefly hurtful to the Honest Man who it was made to preserve.

The next Enquiry is, Whether the Extremities of this Law are not often carried on beyond the true Intent and Meaning of the Act it self, for Malicious and Private Ends, to gratify Passion and Revenge?

I remember the Answer a Person gave me, who had taken out Statutes against several Persons, and some his near Relations, who had fail'd in his Debt; and when I was one time dissuading him from prosecuting a man who ow'd me Money as well as him, I us'd this Argument with him; *You know the man has nothing left to pay. That's true*, says he, *I know that well enough. To what purpose then*, said I, *will you prosecute him? Why, Revenge is sweet*, said he. – Now a man that will prosecute a Debtor, not as a Debtor, but by way of Revenge, such a man is, I think, not intentionally within the benefit of our Law.

In order to state the Case right, there are four Sorts of People to be consider'd in this Discourse; and the true Case is how to distinguish them.

(1.) There is the Honest Debtor, who fails by visible Necessity, Losses, Sickness, Decay of Trade, or the like.

(2.) The Knavish, Designing, or Idle, Extravagant Debtor, who fails because either he has run out his Estate in Excesses, or on purpose to cheat and abuse his Creditors.

(3.) There is the moderate Creditor, who seeks but his own, but will omit no lawful Means to gain it, and yet will hear reasonable and just Arguments and Proposals.

(4.) There is the Rigorous Severe Creditor, that values not whether the Debtor be Honest Man or Knave, Able, or Unable; but will have his Debt, *whether it be to be had or no*; without Mercy, without Compassion, full of Ill Language, Passion, and Revenge.

How to make a Law to suit to all these, is the Case: *That a necessary Favour might be shown to the first*, in Pity and Compassion to the Unfortunate, in Commiseration of Casualty and Poverty, which no man is exempt from the danger of. *That a due Rigor and Restraint be laid upon the second*, that Villany and Knavery might not be encourag'd by a Law. *That a due Care be taken of the third*, that mens Estates may, as far as can be, secur'd to them. *And due Limits set to the last*, that no man may have an unlimited Power over his Fellow-Subjects, to the Ruin of both Life and Estate.

All which I humbly conceive might be brought to pass by the following Method; to which I give the Title of

A Court of Enquiries.

This Court should consist of a select Number of Persons, to be chosen Yearly out of the several Wards of the City, by the Lord-Mayor and

Court of Aldermen; and out of the several Inns of Court, by the Lord Chancellor, or Lord Keeper, for the time being, and to consist of,

> *A President,*
> *A Secretary,*　} 　*To be chosen by the rest,*
> *A Treasurer,*　 　*and nam'd every year also.*
>
> *A Judge of Causes for the Proof of Debts.*
> *Fifty two Citizens, out of every Ward two; of which number to be Twelve Merchants.*
>
> *Two Lawyers (Baristers at least) out of each of the Inns of Court.*

That a Commission of Enquiry into Bankrupts Estates be given to these, confirm'd and settl'd by Act of Parliament, with Power to Hear, Try, and Determine Causes as to Proof of Debts, and Disputes in Accounts between Debtor and Creditor, without Appeal.

The Office for this Court to be at *Guildhall*, where Clerks shou'd be always attending, and a *Quorum* of the Commissioners to sit *de Die in Diem*,[107] from Three to Six a Clock in the Afternoon.

To this Court every man who finds himself press'd by his Affairs, so that he cannot carry on his Business, shall apply himself as follows:

He shall go to the Secretary's Office, and give in his Name, with this short Petition:

> To the Honourable the President and Commissioners of His Majesty's
> 　　Court of Enquiries. The humble Petition of *A. B.* of the Parish of
> 　　　　in the　　　　Haberdasher.
>
> 　*Sheweth,*
> 　*THat your Petitioner being unable to carry on his Business, by reason of great Losses and Decay of Trade, and being ready and willing to make a full and entire Discovery of his whole Estate, and to deliver up the same to your Honours upon Oath, as the Law directs for the satisfaction of his Creditors, and having to that purpose entred his Name into the Books of your Office on the　　　of this Instant:*
> 　*Your Petitioner humbly prays the Protection of this Honourable Court.*
> 　　　　　　　　　　　　　　　　*And shall ever Pray, &c.*

The Secretary is to lay this Petition before the Commissioners, who shall sign it of course; and the Petitioner shall have an Officer sent home with him immediately, who shall take Possession of his House and Goods, and an exact Inventory of every thing therein shall be taken at his Entrance by other Officers also, appointed by the Court; according to which Inventory the first Officer and the Bankrupt also shall be accountable.

This Officer shall supersede even the Sheriff in Possession, excepting by an Extent for the King; only with this Provision;

That if the Sheriff be in Possession by Warrant on Judgment, obtain'd by due Course of Law, and without Fraud or Deceit, and, *bona fide*, in Possession before the Debtor entred his Name in the Office, in such case the Plaintiff to have a double Dividend allotted to his Debt; for it was the fault of the Debtor to let Execution come upon his Goods before he sought for Protection; but this not to be allow'd upon Judgment confess'd.

If the Sheriff be in Possession by *fieri facias*[108] for Debt immediately due to the King, the Officer however shall quit his Possession to the Commissioners, and they shall see the King's Debt fully satisfied, before any Division be made to the Creditors.

The Officers in this case to take no Fee from the Bankrupt, nor to use any indecent or uncivil Behaviour to the Family (which is a most notorious Abuse now permitted to the Sheriffs Officers), whose Fees I have known, on small Executions, *on pretence of Civility*, amount to as much as the Debt, and yet behave themselves with unsufferable Insolence all the while.

This Officer being in Possession, the Goods may be remov'd, or not remov'd, the Shop shut up, or not shut up, as the Bankrupt upon his Reasons given to the Commissioners may desire.

The Inventory being taken, the Bankrupt shall have Fourteen Days time, and more if desir'd, upon showing good Reasons to the Commissioners, to settle his Books, and draw up his Accounts; and then shall deliver up all his Books, together with a full and true Account of his whole Estate, Real and Personal; to which Account he shall make Oath, and afterwards to any particular of it, if the Commissioners require.

After this Account given in, the Commissioners shall have Power to examine upon Oath all his Servants, or any other Person; and if it appears that he has conceal'd any thing, in breach of his Oath, to Punish him, as is hereafter specified.

Upon a fair and just Surrender of all his Estate and Effects, *bona fide*, according to the true Intent and Meaning of the Act, the Commissioners shall return to him in Money, or such of his Goods as he shall chuse, at a value by a just Appraisement, 5 *l. per Cent.* of all the Estate he surrender'd to him, together with a full and free Discharge from all his Creditors.

The Remainder of the Estate of the Debtor to be fairly and equally divided among the Creditors, who are to apply themselves to the Commissioners. The Commissioners to make a necessary Enquiry into the Nature and Circumstances of the Debts demanded, that no pretended Debt be claim'd for the private Account of the Debtor: In order to which Enquiry, they shall administer the following Oath to the Creditor, for the Proof of the Debt.

I A. B. do solemnly swear and attest, That the Account hereto annex'd is true and right, and every Article therein rightly and truly stated and charg'd in the Names of the Persons to whom they belong: And that there is no Person or Name nam'd, conceal'd, or alter'd in the said Account by me, or by my Knowledge, Order, or Consent: And that the said   does really and bona fide owe and stand indebted to me for my own proper account, the full Sum of   mention'd in the said Account, and that for a fair and just Value made good to him, as by the said Account express'd; and also that I have not made or known of any Private Contract, Promise, or Agreement between him the said   (or any body for him) and me, or any Person whatsoever.

So help me God.

Upon this Oath, and no Circumstances to render the Person suspected, the Creditor shall have an unquestion'd Right to his Dividend, which shall be made without the Delays and Charges that attend the Commissions of Bankrupts. For,

(1.) The Goods of the Debtor shall upon the first meeting of the Creditors, be either sold in Parcels,[109] as they shall agree, or divided among them in due proportion to their Debts.

(2.) What Debts are standing out, the Debtors shall receive Summons's from the Commissioners, to pay by a certain time limited; and in the mean time the Secretary is to transmit Accounts to the Persons owing it, appointing them a reasonable time to consent or disprove the Account.

And every Six Months a just Dividend shall be made among the Creditors of the Money receiv'd: And so if the Effects lye abroad, Authentick Procurations shall be sign'd by the Bankrupt to the Commissioners, who thereupon correspond with the Persons abroad, in whose hands such Effects are, who are to remit the same as the Commissioners order; the Dividend to be made, as before, every Six Months, or oftner, if the Court see cause.

If any man thinks the Bankrupt has so much favour by these Articles, that those who can dispense with an Oath have an opportunity to cheat their Creditors, and that hereby too much Encouragement is given to men to turn Bankrupt; let them consider the Easiness of the Discovery, the Difficulty of a Concealment, and the Penalty on the Offender.

(1.) I would have a Reward of 30 *per Cent.* be provided to be paid to any person who should make discovery of any part of the Bankrupt's Estate conceal'd by him; which would make Discoveries easy and frequent.

(2.) Any person who should claim any Debt among the Creditors, for the account of the Bankrupt, or his Wife or Children, or with design to relieve them out of it, other or more than is, *bona fide*, due to him for Value receiv'd and to be made out; or any person who shall receive in Trust, or by Deed of Gift, any part of the Goods or other Estate of the Bankrupt, with design to preserve them for the use of the said Bankrupt, or his Wife or Children, or with design to conceal them from the Creditors, shall forfeit for every such Act 500 *l.* and have his Name publish'd as a Cheat, and a Person not fit to be credited by any man. This would make it very difficult for the Bankrupt to conceal any thing.

(3.) The Bankrupt having given his Name, and put the Officer into Possession, shall not remove out of the House any of his Books; but during the Fourteen days time which he shall have to settle the Accounts, shall every night deliver the Books into the hands of the Officer; and the Commissioners shall have liberty, if they please, to take the Books the first day, and cause Duplicates to be made, and then to give them back to the Bankrupt to settle the Accounts.

(4.) If it shall appear that the Bankrupt has given in a false Account, has conceal'd any part of his Goods or Debts, in breach of his Oath, he shall be set in the Pillory at his own door, and be imprison'd during Life, without Bail.

(5.) To prevent the Bankrupt concealing any Debts abroad, it should be enacted, That the Name of the Bankrupt being entred at the Office, where every man might search *gratis*, should be Publication enough; and that after such Entry, no Discharge from the Bankrupt shou'd be allow'd in Account to any man, but whoever wou'd adventure to pay any Money to the said Bankrupt or his Order, shou'd be still Debtor to the Estate, and pay it again to the Commissioners.

And whereas Wiser Heads than mine must be employ'd to compose this Law, if ever it be made, they will have time to consider of more ways to secure the Estate for the Creditors, and, if possible, to tye the hands of the Bankrupt yet faster.

This Law, if ever such a Happiness shou'd arise to this Kingdom, would be a present Remedy for a multitude of Evils which now we feel, and which are a sensible detriment to the Trade of this Nation.

(1.) With submission, I question not but it wou'd prevent a great number of Bankrupts, which now fall by divers Causes: For,

1. It wou'd effectually remove all crafty design'd Breakings, by which many Honest Men are ruin'd. And

2. Of course 'twou'd prevent the Fall of those Tradesmen who are forc'd to break by the Knavery of such.

(2.) It wou'd effectually suppress all those Sanctuaries and Refuges of Thieves, the *Mint, Friars, Savoy,*[110] *Rules,*[111] and the like; and that these two ways;

1. Honest Men wou'd have no need of it, here being a more Safe, Easy, and more Honourable Way to get out of Trouble.

2. Knaves shou'd have no Protection from those Places, and the Act be fortified against those Places by the following Clauses, which I have on purpose reserv'd to this Head.

Since the Provision this Court of Enquiries makes for the ease and deliverance of every Debtor who is honest, is so considerable, 'tis most certain that no man, but he who has a design to Cheat his Creditors, will refuse to accept of the Favour; and therefore it shou'd be Enacted,

That if any man who is a Tradesman or Merchant shall break or fail, or shut up Shop, or leave off Trade, and shall not either pay or secure to his Creditors their full and whole Debts, Twenty Shillings in the Pound, without Abatement or Deduction; or shall convey away their Books or Goods, in order to bring their Creditors to any Composition; or shall not apply to this Office as aforesaid, shall be guilty of Felony, and upon Conviction of the same, shall suffer as a Felon, without Benefit of Clergy.

And if any such person shall take Sanctuary either in the *Mint, Friars,* or other pretended Priviledge-Place, or shall convey thither any of their Goods as aforesaid, to secure them from their Creditors, upon Complaint thereof made to any of His Majesty's Justices of the Peace, they shall immediately grant Warrants to the Constable, &c. to search for the said Persons and Goods, who shall be aided and assisted by the Train'd-Bands,[112] if need be, without any Charge to the Creditors, to search for and discover the said Persons and Goods; and whoever were aiding in the carrying in the said Goods, or whoever knowingly receiv'd either the Goods or the Person, shou'd be also guilty of Felony.

For as the Indigent Debtor is a branch of the Commonwealth, which deserves its Care, so the wilful Bankrupt is one of the *worst sort of Thieves.* And it seems a little unequal, that a poor Fellow, who for mere Want steals from his Neighbour some Trifle, shall be sent out of the Kingdom, *and sometimes out of the World*; while a sort of people who defye Justice, and violently resist the Law, shall be suffer'd to carry mens Estates away before their faces, and no Officers to be found who dare execute the Law upon them.

Any man wou'd be concern'd to hear with what Scandal and Reproach Foreigners do speak of the Impotence of our Constitution in this Point: That in a Civiliz'd Government, as ours is, the strangest Contempt of Authority is shown, that can be instanc'd in the world.

I may be a little the warmer on this Head, on account that I have been a larger Sufferer by such means than ordinary: But I appeal to all the world as to the Equity of the Case; What the difference is between having my House broken up in the Night to be robb'd, and a man coming in good Credit, and with a Proffer of Ready Money in the middle of the Day, and buying 500 *l.* of Goods, and carry them directly from my Warehouse into the *Mint*, and the next day laugh at me, and bid me defiance; yet this I have seen done: I think 'tis the justest thing in the world, that the last shou'd be esteem'd the greater Thief, and deserves most to be hang'd.

I have seen a Creditor come with his Wife and Children, and beg of the Debtor only to let him have part of his own Goods again, which he had bought, knowing and designing to break: I have seen him with Tears and Intreaties petition for his own, or but some of it, and be taunted and swore at, and denied by a sawcy insolent Bankrupt: That the poor man has been wholly ruin'd by the Cheat. 'Tis by the Villany of such, many an Honest man is undone, Families starv'd and sent a begging, and yet no Punishment prescrib'd by our Laws for it.

By the aforesaid *Commission of Enquiry*, all this might be most effectually prevented, an Honest, Indigent Tradesman preserv'd, Knavery detected, and punish'd; *Mints, Friars,* and Privilege-Places suppress'd and without doubt a great number of Insolencies avoided and prevented; of which many more Particulars might be insisted upon, but I think these may be sufficient to lead any body into the Thought; and for the Method, I leave it to the wise Heads of the Nation, who know better than I how to state the Law to the Circumstances of the Crime.

Of Academies.

WE have in *England* fewer of these than in any part of the World, at least where Learning is in so much esteem. But to make amends, the two great Seminaries[113] we have, are without comparison the *Greatest*, I won't say the *Best* in the World; and tho' much might be said here concerning Universities in general, and Foreign Academies in particular, I content my self with noting that part in which we seem defective. The *French*, who justly value themselves upon erecting the most Celebrated Academy of *Europe*, owe the Lustre of it very much to the great Encouragement the Kings of *France* have given to it. And one of the Members making a Speech at his Entrance, tells you, *That 'tis not the least of the Glories of their Invincible Monarch, to have engross'd all the Learning of the World in that Sublime Body.*

The peculiar Study of the Academy of *Paris*,[114] has been to Refine and Correct their own Language; which they have done to that happy degree, that we see it now spoken in all the Courts of *Christendom*, as the Language allow'd to be most universal.

I had the Honour once to be a Member of a small Society, who seem'd to offer at this Noble Design in *England*. But the Greatness of the Work, and the Modesty of the Gentlemen concern'd, prevail'd with them to desist an Enterprize which appear'd too great for Private Hands to undertake. We want indeed a *Richlieu*[115] to commence such a Work: For I am persuaded, were there such a *Genius* in our Kingdom to lead the way, there wou'd not want Capacities who cou'd carry on the Work to a Glory equal to all that has gone before them. The *English* Tongue is a Subject not at all less worthy the Labour of such a Society than the *French*, and capable of a much greater Perfection. The Learned among the *French* will own, That the Comprehensiveness of Expression is a Glory in which the *English* Tongue not only Equals but Excels its Neighbours; *Rapin*,[116] St. *Evremont*,[117] and the most Eminent *French* Authors have acknowledg'd it: And my Lord *Roscommon*,[118] who is allow'd to be a good Judge of *English*, because he wrote it as exactly as any ever did, expresses what I mean, in these Lines;

> 'For who did ever in French *Authors see*
> *The Comprehensive* English *Energy?*
> *The weighty* Bullion *of one* Sterling *Line,*
> *Drawn to* French Wire *wou'd through whole Pages shine.*

'And if our Neighbours will yield us, as their greatest Critick has done, the Preference for Sublimity and Nobleness of Stile, we will willingly quit all Pretensions to their Insignificant Gaiety.'

'Tis great pity that a Subject so Noble shou'd not have some as Noble to attempt it: And for a Method, what greater can be set before us, than the Academy of *Paris*? Which, to give the *French* their due, stands foremost among all the Great Attempts in the Learned Part of the World.

The present King of *England*,[119] of whom we have seen the whole World writing *Panegyricks* and *Encomiums*, and whom his Enemies, when their Interest does not silence them, are apt to say more of than our selves; as in the War he has given surprizing Instances of a Greatness of Spirit more than common; so in Peace, I dare say, with Submission, he shall never have an Opportunity to illustrate his Memory more, than by such a Foundation: By which he shall have Opportunity to darken the Glory of the *French* King in Peace, as he has by his daring Attempts in the War.

Nothing but Pride loves to be flatter'd, and that only as 'tis a Vice which blinds us to our own Imperfections. I think Princes as particularly unhappy in having their Good Actions magnify'd, as their Evil Actions cover'd: But King *William*, who has already won Praise by the Steps of dangerous Virtue, seems reserv'd for some Actions which are above the Touch of Flattery, whose Praise is in themselves.

And such wou'd this be: And because I am speaking of a Work which seems to be proper only for the Hand of the King himself, I shall not presume to carry on this Chapter to the Model, as I have done in other Subjects. Only thus far;

That a Society be erected by the King himself, *if his Majesty thought fit*, and composed of none but Persons of the first Figure in Learning; and 'twere to be wish'd our Gentry were so much Lovers of Learning, that Birth might always be join'd with Capacity.

The Work of this Society shou'd be to encourage Polite Learning, to polish and refine the *English* Tongue, and advance the so much neglected Faculty of Correct Language, to establish Purity and Propriety of Stile, and to purge it from all the Irregular Additions that Ignorance and Affectation have introduc'd; and all those Innovations in Speech, if I may call them such, which some Dogmatic Writers have the Confidence to foster upon their Native Language, as if their Authority were sufficient to make their own Fancy legitimate.

By such a Society I dare say the true Glory of our *English* Stile wou'd appear; and among all the Learned Part of the World, be esteem'd, as it really is, the Noblest and most Comprehensive of all the Vulgar Languages in the World.

Into this Society should be admitted none but Persons Eminent for Learning, and yet none, or but very few, whose Business or Trade was Learning: For I may be allow'd, I suppose, to say, We have seen many great Scholars, meer Learned Men, and Graduates in the last Degree of Study, whose *English* has been far from Polite, full of Stiffness and Affectation, hard Words, and long unusual Coupling of *Syllables* and Sentences, which sound harsh and untuneable to the Ear, and shock the Reader both in Expression and Understanding.

In short, There should be room in this Society for neither *Clergyman*, *Physician*, or *Lawyer*. Not that I wou'd put an Affront upon the Learning of any of those Honourable Employments, much less upon their Persons: But if I do think that their several Professions do naturally and sever-ally prescribe Habits of Speech to them peculiar to their Practice, and prejudicial to the Study I speak of, I believe I do them no wrong. Nor do I deny but there may be, and now are among some of all those Professions, Men of Stile and Language, great Masters of *English*, whom few men will undertake to Correct; and where such do at any time appear, their extraordinary Merit shou'd find them a Place in this Society; but it shou'd be rare, and upon very extraordinary Occasions, that such be admitted.

I wou'd therefore have this Society wholly compos'd of Gentlemen; whereof Twelve to be of the Nobility, if possible, and Twelve Private Gentlemen, and a Class of Twelve to be left open for meer Merit, let it be found in who or what sort it would, which should lye as the Crown of their Study, who have done something eminent to deserve it. The Voice of this Society should be sufficient Authority for the Usage of Words, and sufficient also to expose the Innovations of other mens Fancies; they shou'd preside with a Sort of Judicature over the Learning of the Age, and have liberty to Correct and Censure the Exorbitance of Writers, especially of Translators. The Reputation of this Society wou'd be enough to make them the allow'd Judges of Stile and Language; and no Author wou'd have the Impudence to Coin without their Authority. *Custom*, which is now our best Authority for Words, wou'd always have its Original here, and not be allow'd without it. There shou'd be no more occasion to search for Derivations and Constructions, and 'twou'd be as Criminal then to *Coin Words*, *as Money*.

The Exercises of this Society wou'd be Lectures on the *English* Tongue, Essays on the Nature, Original, Usage, Authorities and Differences of

Words, on the Propriety, Purity, and *Cadence of Stile*, and of the Politeness and *Manner* in Writing; Reflections upon Irregular Usages, and Corrections of Erroneous Customs in Words; and in short, every thing that wou'd appear necessary to the bringing our *English* Tongue to a due Perfection, and our Gentlemen to a Capacity of Writing like themselves; to banish Pride and Pedantry, and silence the Impudence and Impertinence of Young Authors, whose Ambition is to be known, tho' it be by their Folly.

I ask leave here for a Thought or two about that Inundation Custom has made upon our Language and Discourse by *Familiar Swearing*; and I place it here, because Custom has so far prevail'd in this foolish Vice, that a man's Discourse is hardly agreeable without it; and some have taken upon them to say, *It is pity it shou'd not be lawful, 'tis such a Grace in a man's Speech, and adds so much Vigour to his Language.*

I desire to be understood right, and that by Swearing I mean all those Cursory Oaths, Curses, Execrations, Imprecations, Asseverations, and by whatsoever other Names they are distinguish'd, which are us'd in Vehemence of Discourse, in the Mouths almost of all men more or less, of what sort soever.

I am not about to argue any thing of their being sinful and unlawful, as forbid by Divine Rules; *let the Parson alone to tell you that*, who has, no question, said as much to as little purpose in this Case as in any other: But I am of the opinion, that there is nothing so Impertinent, so Insignificant, so Senseless and Foolish, as our vulgar way of Discourse, when mix'd with Oaths and Curses; and I wou'd only recommend a little Consideration to our Gentlemen, who have Sense and Wit enough, and wou'd be asham'd to speak Nonsense in other things, but value themselves upon their Parts; I wou'd but ask them to put into Writing the Common-Places of their Discourse, and read them over again, and examine the *English*, the *Cadence*, the *Grammar* of them; then let them turn them into *Latin*, or translate them into any other Language, and but see what a *Jargon* and Confusion of Speech they make together.

Swearing, that Lewdness of the Tongue, that Scum and Excrement of the Mouth, is of all Vices the most foolish and senseless; it makes a man's Conversation *unpleasant*, his Discourse *fruitless*, and his Language *Nonsense*.

It makes Conversation unpleasant, at least to those who do not use the same foolish way of Discourse; and indeed, is an Affront to all the Company who swear not as he does; for if I swear and Curse in Company, I either presume all the Company likes it, or affront them who do not.

Then 'tis *fruitless*; for no man is believ'd a jot the more for all the Asseverations, *Damnings* and Swearings he makes: Those who are us'd to it themselves, do not believe a man the more, because they know they are so customary, that they signify little to bind a man's Intention; and they who practise them not, have so mean an opinion of those that do, as makes them think they deserve no belief.

Then, they are the Spoilers and Destroyers of a man's Discourse, and turn it into perfect *Nonsense*; and to make it out, I must descend a little to Particulars, and desire the Reader a little to foul his Mouth with the Bruitish, Sordid, Sensless Expressions, which some Gentlemen call Polite *English*, and speaking with a Grace.

Some part of them indeed, tho' they are foolish enough, as Effects of a mad, inconsiderate Rage, are yet *English*; as when a man swears he will do this or that, and it may be adds, *God damn him he will*; that is, *God damn him if he don't*: This, tho' it be horrid in another sense, yet may be read in writing, and is *English*: But what Language is this?

Jack, *God damn me* Jack, *How do'st do, thou little dear Son of a Whore? How hast thou done this long time, by God?* – And then they kiss; and the t'other, as lewd as himself, goes on;

Dear Tom, *I am glad to see thee with all my heart, let me dye. Come, let us go take a Bottle, we must not part so; prithee let's go and be drunk by God.* –

This is some of our new florid Language, and the Graces and Delicacies of Stile, which if it were put into *Latin*, I wou'd fain know which is the principal Verb.

But for a little further remembrance of this Impertinence, go among the Gamesters, and there nothing is more frequent than, *God damn the Dice*, or *God damn the Bowls*.

Among the Sportsmen 'tis, *God damn the Hounds*, when they are at a Fault; or *God damn the Horse*, if he bau'ks a Leap: They call men *Sons of Bitches*, and *Dogs*, *Sons of Whores*: And innumerable Instances may be given of the like Gallantry of Language, grown now so much a *Custom*.

'Tis true, Custom is allow'd to be our best Authority for Words, and 'tis fit it should be so; but Reason must be the Judge of Sense in Language, and Custom can never prevail over it. *Words*, indeed, like Ceremonies in Religion, may be submitted to the Magistrate; but *Sense*, like the Essentials, is positive, unalterable, and cannot be submitted to any Jurisdiction; 'tis a Law to it self, 'tis ever the same, even an Act of Parliament cannot alter it.

Words, and even Usages in Stile, may be alter'd by Custom, and Proprieties in Speech differ according to the several Dialects of the Countrey, and according to the different manner in which several Languages do severally express themselves.

But there is a direct Signification of Words, or a *Cadence in Expression*, which we call speaking *Sense*; this, like Truth, is sullen and the same, ever was and will be so, in what manner, and in what Language soever 'tis express'd. *Words* without it, are only Noise, which any Brute can make as well as we, and Birds much better; for *Words* without *Sense* make but dull Musick. Thus a man may speak in *Words*, but perfectly unintelligible as to *Meaning*; he may *talk* a great deal, but *say* nothing. But 'tis the proper Position of *Words*, adapted to their Significations, which makes them intelligible, and conveys the Meaning of the Speaker to the Understanding of the Hearer; the contrary to which we call *Nonsense*; and there is a superfluous crowding in of insignificant Words, more than are needful to express the thing intended, and this is *Impertinence*; and that again carry'd to an extreme, is *ridiculous*.

Thus when our Discourse is interlin'd with needless Oaths, Curses, and long *Parentheses* of Imprecations, and with some of very indirect signification, they become very *Impertinent*; and these being run to the extravagant degree instanc'd in before, become perfectly *ridiculous* and *Nonsense*; and without forming it into an Argument, it appears to be *Nonsense* by the Contradictoriness; and it appears *Impertinent*, by the Insignificancy of the Expression.

After all, how little it becomes a Gentleman to debauch his Mouth with Foul Language, I refer to themselves in a few Particulars.

This Vicious Custom has prevail'd upon Good Manners too far; but yet there are some degrees to which it is not yet arriv'd.

As first, The worst Slaves to this Folly will neither teach it *to*, nor approve of it *in* their Children: Some of the most careless will indeed negatively teach it, by not reproving them for it; but sure no man ever order'd his Children to be taught to curse or swear.

2. The Grace of Swearing has not obtain'd to be a Mode yet among the Women; *God damn ye*, does not sit well upon a Female Tongue; it seems to be a Masculine Vice, which the Women are not arriv'd to yet; and I wou'd only desire those Gentlemen who practice it themselves, to hear a Woman swear: It has no Musick at all there, I am sure; and just as little does it become any Gentleman, if he wou'd suffer himself to be judg'd by all the Laws of Sense or Good Manners in the world.

'Tis a sensless, foolish, ridiculous Practice; 'tis a Mean to no manner of End; 'tis Words spoken which signify nothing; 'tis Folly acted for the sake of Folly, which is a thing even the Devil himself don't practice: The Devil does evil, we say, but it is for some design, either to seduce others, or, as some Divines say, from a Principle of Enmity to his Maker: Men Steal for Gain, and Murther to gratify their Avarice or Revenge; Whoredoms and Ravishments, Adulteries and Sodomy, are committed to please a vicious Appetite, and have always alluring Objects; and generally all Vices have some previous Cause, and some visible Tendency; but this, of all Vicious Practices, seems the most Nonsensical and Ridiculous; there is neither Pleasure nor Profit; no Design pursued, no Lust gratified, but is a mere Frenzy of the Tongue, a Vomit of the Brain, which works by putting a Contrary upon the Course of Nature.

Again, other Vices men find some Reason or other to give for, or Excuses to palliate; men plead Want, to extenuate Theft; and strong Provocations, to excuse Murthers; *and many a lame Excuse they will bring for Whoring*; but this sordid Habit, even those that practise it will own to be a Crime, and make no Excuse for it; and the most I cou'd ever hear a man say for it, was, That *he cou'd not help it*.

Besides, as 'tis an inexcusable Impertinence, so 'tis a Breach upon Good Manners and Conversation, for a man to impose the Clamour of his Oaths upon the Company he converses with; if there be any one person in the Company that does not approve the way, 'tis an imposing upon him with a freedom beyond Civility; as if a man shou'd *Fart* before a Justice, or *talk Bawdy* before the Queen, or the like.

To suppress this, Laws, Acts of Parliaments,[120] and Proclamations, are Bawbles and Banters, the Laughter of the Lewd Party, and never had, as I cou'd perceive, any Influence upon the Practice; nor are any of our Magistrates fond or forward of putting them in execution.

It must be Example, not Penalties, must sink this Crime; and if the Gentlemen of *England* wou'd once drop it as a Mode, the Vice is so foolish and ridiculous in it self, 'twou'd soon grow odious and out of fashion.

This Work such an Academy might begin; and I believe nothing wou'd so soon explode the Practice, as the Publick Discouragement of it by such a Society. Where all our Customs and Habits both in Speech and Behaviour, shou'd receive an Authority. All the Disputes about Precedency of Wit, with the Manners, Customs, and Usages of the Theatre wou'd be decided here; Plays shou'd pass here before they were Acted, and the Criticks might give their Censures, and damn at their pleasure; nothing wou'd ever dye which once receiv'd Life at this Original: The Two Theatres[121] might end their Jangle, and dispute for Priority no more; Wit and Real Worth shou'd decide the Controversy, and here shou'd be the *Infallible Judge.*

> *The Strife wou'd then be only to do well,*
> *And he alone be crown'd who did excell.*
> *Ye call them* Whigs, *who from the Church withdrew,*
> *But now we have our* Stage-Dissenters *too;*
> *Who* scruple Ceremonies *of Pit and Box,*
> *And very few are Sound and Orthodox:*
> *But love Disorder so, and are so nice,*
> *They hate* Conformity, *tho' 'tis in Vice.*
> *Some are for* Patent-Hierarchy; *and some,*
> *Like the old* Gauls, *seek out for Elbow-room;*
> *Their Arbitrary Governors disown,*
> *And build a* Conventicle-Stage o' *their own.*
> *Phanatick* Beaus *make up the gawdy Show,*
> *And Wit alone appears* Incognito.
> *Wit and Religion suffer equal Fate;*
> *Neglect of both attends the warm Debate.*
> *For while the Parties strive and countermine,*
> *Wit will as well as Piety decline.*

Next to this, which I esteem as the most Noble and most Useful Proposal in this Book, I proceed to Academies for Military Studies; and because I design rather to express my meaning, than make a large Book, I bring them all into one Chapter.

I allow the War is the best Academy in the World, where men study by Necessity, and practise by Force, and both to some purpose, with Duty in the Action, and a Reward in the End; and 'tis evident to any man who knows the World, or has made any Observations on things, what an Improvement the *English* Nation has made, during this Seven Years War.

But should you ask how dear it first cost, and what a condition *England* was in for a War at first on this account; how almost all our Engineers and Great Officers were Foreigners, it may put us in mind how necessary it is to have our people so practis'd in the Arts of War, that they may not be Novices when they come to the Experiment.

I have heard some, who were no great Friends to the Government, take advantage to reflect upon the King in the beginning of his Wars in *Ireland,* That he did not care to trust the *English,* but all his Great Officers, his Generals, and Engineers were Foreigners. And tho' the Case was so plain as to need no Answer, and the Persons such as deserv'd none, yet this must be observ'd tho' twas very strange, That when the present King took Possession of this Kingdom, and seeing himself entring upon the bloodiest War this Age has known, began to regulate his Army, he found but very few among the whole Martial Part of the Nation fit to make use of for General Officers; and was forced to employ Strangers, and make them *Englishmen*; as the Counts *Schomberg, Ginkel, Solms, Ruvigny*,[122] and others: And yet it is to be observ'd also, that all the Encouragement imaginable was given to the *English* Gentlemen, to qualify themselves, by giving no less than Sixteen Regiments to Gentlemen of Good Families, who had never been in any Service, and knew but very little how to command them: Of these several are now in the Army, and have the Rewards suitable to their Merit, being Major-Generals, Brigadeers, and the like.

If then a long Peace had so reduc'd us to a degree of Ignorance that might have been dangerous to us, had we not a King, who is always follow'd by the greatest Masters in the World, Who knows what Peace and different Governors may bring us to again?

The manner of making War differs perhaps as much as any thing in the world; and if we look no further back than our Civil Wars; 'tis plain a General *then* wou'd hardly be fit to be a Collonel now, saving his Capacity of Improvement. The Defensive Art always follows the Offensive; and tho' the latter has extremely got the start of the former in this Age, yet the other is mightily improving also.

We saw in *England* a bloody Civil War, where, according to the old Temper of the *English*, fighting was the Business. To have an Army lying in such a Post, as not to be able to come at them, was a thing never heard of in that War; even the weakest Party would always come out and fight; *Dunbar* Fight,[123] for instance; and they that were beaten to day, would fight again to morrow, and seek one another out with such Eagerness, as if they had been in haste to have their Brains knock'd out. Encampments, Intrenchments, Batteries, Counter-marchings, fortifying of Camps, and Cannonadings, were strange, and almost unknown things, and whole Campaigns were past over, and hardly any Tents made use of. Battels, Surprizes, Storming of Towns, Skirmishes, Sieges, Ambuscades, and Beating up Quarters, was the News of every day. Now 'tis frequent to have Armies of Fifty thousand men of a side stand at Bay within view of one another, and spend a whole Campaign in Dodging, or as 'tis genteely call'd, *Observing one another*, and then march off into Winter-Quarters. The difference is in the Maxims of War, which now differ as much from what they were formerly, as Long Perukes do from Piqued Beards;[124] or as the Habits of the People do now, from what they then wore. The present Maxims of the War are;

Never Fight without a manifest Advantage.
And always Encamp so as not to be forc'd to it.

And if two opposite Generals nicely observe both these Rules, it is impossible they shou'd ever come to fight.

I grant that this way of making War spends generally more Money and less Blood than former Wars did; but then it spins Wars out to a greater Length; and I almost question whether if this had been the way of Fighting of old, our Civil War had not lasted till this day. Their Maxim was,

Whereever you meet your Enemy, fight him.

But the Case is quite different now, and I think 'tis plain in the present War, that 'tis not he who has the longest Sword, so much as he who has the *longest Purse*, will hold the War out best. *Europe* is all engag'd in the War, and the Men will never be exhausted while either Party can find Money; but he who finds himself poorest, must give out first; and this is evident in the *French* King, who now inclines to Peace, and owns it, while at the same time his Armies are numerous and whole; but the Sinews fail, he finds his Exchequer fail, his Kingdom drain'd, and Money hard to come at: Not that I believe half the Reports we have had of the Misery and Poverty of the *French* are true; but 'tis manifest the King of *France* finds, whatever his Armies may do, his Money won't hold out so long as the *Confederates*; and therefore he uses all the means possible to procure a Peace, while he may do it with the most advantage.

There is no question but the *French* may hold the War out several Years longer; but their King is too wise to let things run to extremity; he will rather condescend to Peace upon hard terms now, than stay longer, if he finds himself in danger to be forc'd to worse.

This being the only Digression I design to be guilty of, I hope I shall be excus'd it.

The Sum of all is this, That since 'tis so necessary to be in a condition for War in a time of Peace, our People shou'd be inur'd to it. 'Tis strange that every thing shou'd be ready but the Soldier: Ships are ready, and our Trade keeps the Seamen always taught, and breeds up more; but Soldiers, Horsemen, Engineers, Gunners, and the like, must be bred and taught; men are not born with Muskets on their Shoulders, nor Fortifications in their Heads; 'tis not natural to shoot Bombs, and undermine Towns: For which purpose I propose,

A Royal Academy for Military Exercises.

The Founder the King himself; the Charge to be paid by the Publick, and settled by a Revenue from the Crown, to be paid Yearly.

I propose this to consist of Four Parts.

(1.) A Colledge for breeding up of Artists[125] in the useful Practice of all Military Exercises; the Scholars to be taken in Young, and be maintain'd, and afterwards under the King's Care for Preferment, as their Merit and His Majesty's Favour shall recommend them; from whence His Majesty wou'd at all times be furnish'd with able Engineers, Gunners, Fire-masters, Bombardiers, Miners, and the like.

The Second College for Voluntary Students in the same Exercises; who shou'd all upon certain limited Conditions be entertain'd, and have all the advantages of the Lectures, Experiments, and Learning of the College, and be also capable of several Titles, Profits, and Settlements in the said College, answerable to the Fellows in the Universities.

The Third College for Temporary Study, into which any Person who is a Gentleman, and an *Englishman*, entring his Name, and conforming to the Orders of the House, shall be entertain'd like a Gentleman for one whole Year *gratis*, and taught by Masters appointed out of the Second College.

The Fourth College, of Schools only, where all Persons whatsoever for a small Allowance shall be taught and entred in all the particular Exercises they desire; and this to be suppli'd by the Proficients of the first College.

> *I cou'd lay out the Dimensions, and necessary Incidents of all this Work; but since the Method of such a Foundation is easy and regular from the Model of other Colleges, I shall only state the Oeconomy of the House.*

The Building must be very Large, and shou'd rather be Stately and Magnificent in Figure, than Gay and Costly in Ornament: And I think such a House as *Chelsea-College*,[126] only about four times as big, wou'd answer it; and yet I believe might be finish'd for as little Charge as has been laid out in that *Palace-like Hospital*.

The First College should consist of,

One General.
Five Collonels.
Twenty Captains.

Being such as Graduates by Preferment, at first nam'd by the Founder; and after the first Settlement to be chosen out of the First or Second College; with Apartments in the College, and Salaries.

The General	300 l. per Ann.
The Collonels	100
The Captains	60

2000 *Scholars*; among whom shall be the following Degrees;

Governors	100	*Allow'd*	10 l. *per An.*
Directors	200		5.
Exempts[127]	200		5.
Proficients	500		
Juniors	1000		

The *General* to be nam'd by the Founder, out of the *Collonels*; the *Collonels* to be nam'd by the *General*, out of the *Captains*; the *Captains* out of the *Governors*; the *Governors* from the *Directors*, and the *Directors* from the *Exempts*, and so on.

The *Juniors* to be divided into Ten Schools; the Schools to be thus govern'd: Every School has

100 *Juniors*, in 10 *Classes*.
Every *Class* to have 2 *Directors*.

100 *Classes* of *Juniors*, is	1000
Each *Class* 2 *Directors*,	200
	────
	1200

The *Proficients* to be divided into Five *Schools*:
Every *School* to have 10 *Classes* of 10 each.
Every *Class* 2 *Governors*.

50 *Classes* of *Proficients*, is	500
Each *Class* 2 *Governors*, is	100
	────
	600

The *Exempts* to be Supernumerary, having a small Allowance, and maintain'd in the College till Preferment offer.

The Second College to consist of *Voluntary Students*, to be taken in after a certain Degree of Learning, from among the *Proficients* of the First, or from any other Schools, after such and such Limitations of Learning; who study at their own Charge, being allow'd certain Privileges; as,

> *Chambers Rent-free, on condition of Residence.*
> *Commons* gratis, *for certain fix'd terms.*
> *Preferment, on condition of a Term of Years Residence.*
> *Use of Libraries, Instruments, and Lectures of the College.*

This College should have the following Preferments, with Salaries.

A Governor,	200 l. per Ann.
A President,	100
50 *College-Majors,*	50
200 *Proficients,*	10
500 *Voluntary Students,* without Allowance.	

The Third and Fourth Colleges, consisting only of Schools for Temporary Study, may be thus;

The Third being for Gentlemen to learn the necessary Arts and Exercises, to qualify them for the Service of their Countrey, and entertaining them one whole year at the Publick Charge, may be suppos'd to have always One thousand Persons on its hands, and cannot have less than 100 *Teachers*; who I wou'd thus order;

> *Every Teacher shall continue at least One year, but by allowance Two years at most; shall have* 20 l. *per Ann. Extraordinary Allowance; shall be bound to give their constant Attendance, and shall have always* 5 *College-Majors of the Second College to supervise them, who shall command a Month, and then be succeeded by* 5 *others, and so on;* 10 l. *per Ann. extraordinary to be paid them for their Attendance.*

The Gentlemen who practise, to be put to no manner of Charge, but to be oblig'd strictly to the following Articles:

(1.) *To constant Residence, not to lye out of the House without leave of the College-Major.*

(2.) *To perform all the College-Exercises, as appointed by the Masters, without dispute.*

(3.) *To submit to the Orders of the House.*

To quarrel, or give Ill Language, shou'd be a Crime to be punish'd by way of Fine only, the College-Major to be Judge, and the Offender be put into Custody till he ask Pardon of the Person wrong'd; by which means every Gentleman who has been affronted, has sufficient satisfaction.

But to Strike, Challenge, Draw, or fight, shou'd be more severely punish'd; the Offender to be declar'd no Gentleman, his Name posted up at the College-Gate, his Person expell'd the House, and to be pump'd[128] as *a Rake* if ever he is taken within the College-Walls.

The Teachers of this College to be chosen, one half out of the Exempts *of the First College, and the other out of the* Proficients *of the second.*

The Fourth College being only of Schools, will be neither Chargeable nor Troublesome, but may consist of as many as shall offer themselves to be taught, and suppli'd with Teachers from the other Schools.

The Proposal being of so large an Extent, must have a proportionable Settlement for its Maintenance; and the Benefit being to the whole Kingdom, the Charge will naturally lye upon the Publick, and cannot well be less, considering the Number of Persons to be maintain'd, than as follows;

First College.

		l. per An.
The General,		300
5 *Collonels*	at 100 l. per Ann. *each,*	500
20 *Captains,*	at 60.	1200
100 *Governors,*	at 10.	1000
200 *Directors,*	at 5.	1000
200 *Exempts,*	at 5.	1000
2000 *Heads for Subsistence, at* 20 l. per *Head, per Ann.* *Including Provision, and all the Officers Salaries in the House, as Butlers, Cooks, Purveyors, Nurses, Maids, Laundresses, Stewards, Clerks, Servants, Chaplains, Porters, and Attendants, which are numerous,*		40000

Second College.

		l. per An.
A Governor,		200
A President,		100
50 *College-Majors,*	*at* 50 l. per An.	2500
200 *Proficients,*	*at* 10 l.	2000

Commons for 500 *Students, during times of Exercises,* | *at* 5 l. per An. *each,* ∫	2500
200 *Proficients Subsistence, reckoning as above,*	4000

Third College.

The Gentlemen here are maintain'd as Gentlemen, and are to | *have good Tables, who shall therefore have an Allowance at the* ⎬ *Rate of* 25 l. per *Head, all Officers to be maintain'd out of it;* | *which is,* ∫	25000
100 *Teachers, Salary and Subsistence* ditto,	4500
50 *College-Majors at* 10 l. per Ann. *is*	500
	———
Annual Charge	86300
The Building to cost	50000
Furniture, Beds, Tables, Chairs, Linnen, &c.	10000
Books, Instruments, and Utensils for Experiments,	2000
	———
So the Immediate Charge would be	62000
	l. per An.
The Annual Charge,	86300
To which add the Charges of Exercises and Experiments,	3700
	———
	90000

The King's Magazines to furnish them with 500 *Barrels of Gunpowder* per An. *for the Publick Uses of Exercises and Experiments.*

In the first of these Colleges should remain the Governing-Part, and all the Preferments be made from thence, to be suppli'd in course from the other; the General of the first to give Orders to the other, and be subject only to the Founder.

The Government shou'd be all Military, with a Constitution for the same regulated for that purpose, and a Council to hear and determine the Differences and Trespasses by the College-Laws.

The Publick Exercises likewise Military, and all the Schools be disciplin'd under proper Officers, who are so in turn, or by Order of the General, and continue but for the Day.

The several Classes to perform several Studies, and but one Study to a distinct Class, and the Persons as they remove from one Study to another, to change their Classes, but so as that in the General Exercises all the Scholars may be qualified to act all the several Parts, as they may be order'd.

The proper Studies of this College should be the following:

Geometry	*Bombarding*
Astronomy	*Gunnery*
History	*Fortification*
Navigation	*Encamping*
Decimal Arithmetick	*Entrenching*
Trigonometry	*Approaching, Attacking*
Dialing[129]	*Delineation*
Gauging	*Architecture*
Mining	*Surveying.*
Fireworking	

And all Arts or Sciences Appendixes to such as these.

With Exercises for the Body, to which all should be oblig'd, as their Genius and Capacities led them. As,

(1.) *Swimming*; which no Soldier, and indeed no Man whatever ought to be without.

(2.) *Handling all sorts of Fire-Arms.*

(3.) *Marching and Countermarching in Form.*

(4.) *Fencing, and the Long Staff.*

(5.) *Riding and Managing, or Horsemanship.*

(6.) *Running, Leaping, and Wrestling.*

And herewith shou'd also be preserv'd and carefully taught all the Customs, Usages, *Terms of War*, and *Terms of Art*, us'd in Sieges, Marches of Armies, and Encampments; that so a Gentleman taught in this College, shou'd be no Novice when he comes into the King's Armies, tho' he has seen no Service abroad. I remember the Story of an *English* Gentleman, an Officer at the Siege of *Limerick*[130] in *Ireland*, who tho' he was Brave enough upon Action, yet for the only matter of being ignorant in the Terms of Art, and knowing not how to talk *Camp-Language*, was expos'd to be laugh'd at by the whole Army, for mistaking the opening of the Trenches, which he thought had been a Mine against the Town.

The Experiments of these Colleges wou'd be as well worth publishing, as the Acts of the *Royal Society*. To which purpose the House must be built where they may have Ground to cast Bombs, to raise Regular Works, as Batteries, Bastions, Half-Moons, Redoubts, Horn-works, Forts, and the Like; with the convenience of Water to draw round such Works, to exercise the Engineers in all the necessary Experiments of Dreining, and Mining, under Ditches. There must be room to fire Great Shot at a distance, to Canonade a Camp, to throw all sorts of Fire-works and Machines, that are or shall be invented; to open Trenches, form Camps, *&c.*

Their Publick Exercises will be also very diverting, and more worth while for any Gentlemen to see, than the Sights or Shews which our people in *England* are so fond of.

I believe, as a Constitution might be form'd from these Generals, this wou'd be the Greatest, the Gallantest, and the most Useful Foundation in the World. The *English* Gentry wou'd be the best qualifi'd, and consequently, best accepted abroad, and most useful at home of any people in the world; and His Majesty shou'd never more be expos'd to the necessity of employing Foreigners in the Posts of Trust and Service in His Armies.

And that the whole Kingdom might in some degree be better qualifi'd for Service, I think the following Project wou'd be very useful.

When our Military Weapon was the *Long-Bow*, at which our *English* Nation in some measure excell'd the whole World, the meanest Countreyman was a good Archer; and that which qualifi'd them so much for Service in the War, was their Diversion in Times of Peace; which also had this good Effect, That when an Army was to be rais'd, they needed no disciplining: And for the Encouragement of the People to an Exercise so publickly Profitable, an Act of Parliament was made, to oblige every Parish to maintain Buts[131] for the Youth in the Countrey to shoot at.

Since our way of fighting is now alter'd; and this destructive Engine, the *Musquet*, is the proper Arms for the Soldier, I could wish the Diversion also of the *English* would change too, that our Pleasures and Profit might correspond. 'Tis a great Hindrance to this Nation, especially where Standing-Armies are a Grievance, that if ever a War commence, men must have at least a Year before they are thought fit to face an Enemy, to instruct them how to handle their Arms; and new-rais'd men are call'd *Raw Soldiers*. To help this, at least in some measure, I wou'd propose, That the Publick Exercises of our Youth shou'd by some Publick Encouragement, (*for Penalties won't do it*) be drawn off from the foolish Boyish Sports of Cocking,[132] and Cricketing, and from Tipling, to shooting with a Firelock,[133] an Exercise as Pleasant, as 'tis Manly and Generous; and *Swimming*, which is a thing so many ways profitable, besides its being a great Preservative of Health, that methinks no Man ought to be without it.

(1.) For *Shooting*; the Colleges I have mention'd above, having provided for the instructing the Gentry at the King's Charge; the Gentry in return of that Favour shou'd introduce it among the Countrey-people; which might easily be done thus:

If every Countrey-Gentleman, according to his degree, wou'd contribute to set up a Prize, to be shot for by the Town he lives in, or the Neighbourhood, about once a year, or twice a year, or oftner, as they think fit; which Prize not single only to him who shoots nearest, but according to the Custom of Shooting:

This wou'd certainly set all the Young Men in *England* a shooting, and make them Marks-men; for they wou'd be always practising and making Matches among themselves too, and the advantage wou'd be found in a War; for no doubt if all the Soldiers in a Battalion took a true Level at their Enemy, there wou'd be much more Execution done at a distance than there is; whereas it has been known now, that a Battalion of men has receiv'd the Fire of another Battalion, and not lost above 30 or 40 men; and I suppose it will not easily be forgot how at the Battel of *Agrim*,[134] a Battalion of the *English* Army receiv'd the whole Fire of an *Irish* Regiment of Dragoons, but never knew to this day whether they had any Bullets or no; and I need appeal no further than to any Officer that serv'd in the *Irish* War, what advantages the *English* Armies made of the *Irish* being such wonderful Marks-men.

Under this Head of *Academies*, I might bring in a Project for

An Academy for Women.

I Have often thought of it as one of the most barbarous Customs in the world, considering us as a Civilized and a Christian Countrey, that we deny the advantages of Learning to Women. We reproach the Sex every day with Folly and Impertinence, while I am confident, had they the advantages of Education equal to us, they wou'd be guilty of less than our selves.

One wou'd wonder indeed how it shou'd happen that Women are conversible at all, since they are only beholding to Natural Parts for all their Knowledge. Their Youth is spent to teach them to Stitch and Sow, or make Bawbles: They are taught to Read indeed, and perhaps to Write their Names, or so; and that is the heighth of a Woman's Education. And I wou'd but ask any who slight the Sex for their Understanding, What is a Man (a Gentleman, I mean) good for, that is taught no more?

I need not give Instances, or examine the Character of a Gentleman with a good Estate, and of a good Family, and with tolerable Parts, and examine what Figure he makes for want of Education.

The Soul is plac'd in the Body like a rough Diamond, and must be polish'd, or the Lustre of it will never appear: And 'tis manifest, that as the Rational Soul distinguishes us from Brutes, so Education carries on the distinction, and makes some less brutish than others: This is too evident to need any demonstration. But why then shou'd Women be deni'd the benefit of Instruction? If Knowledge and Understanding had been useless additions to the Sex, God Almighty wou'd never have given them Capacities; for he made nothing needless: Besides, I wou'd ask such, What they can see in Ignorance, that they shou'd think it a necessary Ornament to a Woman? Or how much worse is a Wise Woman than a Fool? Or what has the Woman done to forfeit the Privilege of being taught? Does she plague us with her Pride and Impertinence? Why did we not let her learn, that she might have had more Wit? Shall we upbraid Women with Folly, when 'tis only the Error of this inhuman Custom, that hindred them being made wiser?

The Capacities of Women are suppos'd to be greater, and their Senses quicker than those of the Men; and what they might be capable of being bred to, is plain from some Instances of Female-Wit, which this Age is not without; which upbraids us with Injustice, and looks as if we deni'd Women the advantages of Education, for fear they shou'd *vye* with the Men in their Improvements.

To remove this Objection, and that Women might have at least a needful Opportunity of Education in all sorts of Useful Learning, I propose the Draught of an Academy for that purpose.

I know 'tis dangerous to make Publick Appearances of the Sex; they are not either to be *confin'd* or *expos'd*; the first will disagree with their Inclinations, and the last with their Reputations; and therefore it is somewhat difficult; and I doubt a Method propos'd by an Ingenious Lady, in a little Book, call'd *Advice to the Ladies*,[135] would be found impracticable. For, saving my Respect to the Sex, the Levity, which perhaps is a little peculiar to them, at least in their Youth, will not bear the Restraint; and I am satisfi'd, nothing but the heighth of Bigotry can keep up a Nunnery: Women are extravagantly desirous of going to Heaven, and will punish their *Pretty Bodies* to get thither; but nothing else will do it; and even in that case sometimes it falls out that *Nature will prevail*.

When I talk therefore of an Academy for Women, I mean both the Model, the Teaching, and the Government, different from what is propos'd by that Ingenious Lady, for whose Proposal I have a very great Esteem, and also a great Opinion of her Wit; different too from all sorts of Religious Confinement, and above all, from *Vows of Celibacy*.

Wherefore the Academy I propose should differ but little from Publick Schools, wherein such Ladies as were willing to study, shou'd have all the advantages of Learning suitable to their Genius.

But since some Severities of Discipline more than ordinary wou'd be absolutely necessary to preserve the Reputation of the House, that Persons of Quality and Fortune might not be afraid to venture their Children thither, I shall venture to make a small Scheme by way of Essay.

The House I wou'd have built in a Form by it self, as well as in a Place by it self.

The Building shou'd be of Three plain Fronts, without any Jettings,[136] or Bearing-Work,[137] that the Eye might at a Glance see from one Coin[138] to the other; the Gardens wall'd in the same Triangular Figure, with a large Moat, and but one Entrance.

When thus every part of the Situation was contriv'd as well as might be for discovery, and to render *Intrieguing* dangerous, I wou'd have no Guards, no Eyes, no Spies set over the Ladies, but shall expect them to be try'd by the Principles of Honour and strict Virtue.

And if I am ask'd, *Why?* I must ask Pardon of my own Sex for giving this reason for it:

I am so much in Charity with Women, and so well acquainted with Men, that 'tis my opinion, There needs no other Care to prevent Intrieguing, than to keep the men effectually away: For tho' *Inclination*, which we prettily call *Love*, does sometimes move a little too visibly in the Sex, and Frailty often follows; yet I think verily, *Custom*, which we miscall *Modesty*, has so far the Ascendant over the Sex, that *Solicitation* always goes before it.

> *Custom with Women 'stead of Virtue rules;*
> *It leads the Wisest, and commands the Fools:*
> *For this alone, when Inclinations reign,*
> *Tho' Virtue's fled, will Acts of Vice restrain.*
> *Only by Custom 'tis that Virtue lives,*
> *And Love requires to be ask'd, before it gives.*
> *For that which we call* Modesty, *is* Pride:
> *They scorn to ask, and hate to be deni'd.*
> *'Tis Custom thus prevails upon their Want;*

> *They'll never beg, what askt they eas'ly grant.*
> *And when the needless Ceremony's over,*
> *Themselves the Weakness of the Sex discover.*
> *If then Desires are strong, and Nature free,*
> *Keep from her Men, and Opportunity.*
> *Else 'twill be vain to curb her by Restraint;*
> *But keep the Question off, you keep the Saint.*

In short, let a Woman have never such a Common-Principle, she will let you ask before she complies, at least if she be a Woman of any Honour.

Upon this ground I am persuaded such Measures might be taken, that the Ladies might have all the Freedom in the world within their own Walls, and yet no Intrieguing, no Indecencies, nor Scandalous Affairs happen; and in order to this, the following Customs and Laws shou'd be observ'd in the Colleges; of which I wou'd propose One at least in every County in *England*, and about Ten for the City of *London*.

After the Regulation of the Form of the Building as before;

(1.) All the Ladies who enter into the House, shou'd set their Hands to the Orders of the House, to signify their Consent to submit to them.

(2.) As no Woman shou'd be receiv'd, but who declar'd her self willing, and that it was the Act of her Choice to enter her self, so no Person shou'd be confin'd to continue there a moment longer than the same voluntary Choice inclin'd her.

(3.) The Charges of the House being to be paid by the Ladies, every one that entred shou'd have only this Incumbrance, That she shou'd pay for the whole Year, tho' her mind shou'd change as to her continuance.

(4.) An Act of Parliament shou'd make it Felony without Clergy,[139] for any man to enter by Force or Fraud into the House, or to solicit any Woman, *tho' it were to Marry*, while she was in the House. And this Law wou'd by no means be severe; because any Woman who was willing to receive the Addresses of a Man, might discharge her self of the House when she pleas'd; and on the contrary, any Woman who had occasion, might discharge her self of the Impertinent Addresses of any Person she had an Aversion to, by entring into the House.

In this House,

The Persons who Enter, shou'd be taught all sorts of Breeding suitable to both their Genius and their Quality; and in particular, *Musick* and *Dancing*, which it wou'd be cruelty to bar the Sex of, because they are their Darlings: But besides this, they shou'd be taught Languages, as particularly *French* and *Italian*; and I wou'd venture the Injury of giving a Woman more Tongues than one.

They shou'd, as a particular Study, be taught all the Graces of Speech, and all the necessary Air of Conversation; which our common Education is so defective in, that I need not expose it: They shou'd be brought to read Books, and especially History, and so to read as to make them understand the World, and be able to know and judge of things when they hear of them.

To such whose Genius wou'd lead them to it, I wou'd deny no sort of Learning; but the chief thing in general is to cultivate the Understandings of the Sex, that they may be capable of all sorts of Conversation; that their Parts and Judgments being improv'd they may be as Profitable in their Conversation as they are Pleasant.

Women, in my observation, have little or no difference in them, but as they are, or are not distinguish'd by Education. Tempers indeed may in some degree influence them, but the main distinguishing part is their Breeding.

The whole Sex are generally Quick and Sharp: I believe I may be allow'd to say generally so; for you rarely see them lumpish and heavy when they are Children, as Boys will often be. If a Woman be well-bred, and taught the proper Management of her Natural Wit, she proves generally very sensible and retentive: And without partiality, a Woman of Sense and Manners is the Finest and most Delicate Part of God's Creation; the Glory of her Maker, and the great Instance of his singular regard to Man, his Darling Creature, to whom he gave the best Gift either God could bestow, or man receive: And 'tis the sordid'st Piece of Folly and Ingratitude in the world, to withhold from the Sex the due Lustre which the advantages of Education gives to the Natural Beauty of their Minds.

A Woman well Bred and well Taught, furnish'd with the additional Accomplishments of Knowledge and Behaviour, *is a Creature without comparison*; her Society is the Emblem of sublimer Enjoyments; her Person is Angelick, and her Conversation heavenly; she is all Softness and Sweetness, Peace, Love, Wit, and Delight: She is every way suitable to the sublimest Wish; and the man that has such a one to his Portion, has nothing to do but to rejoice in her, and be thankful.

On the other hand, Suppose her to be the *very same* Woman, and rob her of the Benefit of Education, and it follows thus;

If her Temper be Good, want of Education makes her Soft and Easy.

Her Wit, for want of Teaching, makes her Impertinent and Talkative.

Her Knowledge, for want of Judgment and Experience, makes her Fanciful and Whimsical.

If her Temper be Bad, want of Breeding makes her worse, and she grows Haughty, Insolent, and Loud.

If she be Passionate, want of Manners makes her Termagant, and a Scold, *which is much at one with Lunatick.*

If she be Proud, want of Discretion (which still is Breeding) makes her Conceited, Fantastick, and Ridiculous.

And from these she degenerates to be Turbulent, Clamorous, Noisy, Nasty, *and the Devil.*

Methinks Mankind for their own sakes, since say what we will of the Women, we all think fit one time or other to be concern'd with 'em, shou'd take some care to breed them up to be *suitable* and *serviceable*, if they expected no such thing as *Delight* from 'em. Bless us! What Care do we take to Breed up a good Horse, and to Break him well! and what a Value do we put upon him when it is done, and all because he shou'd be fit for our use! and why not a Woman? Since all her Ornaments and Beauty, without suitable Behaviour, is a Cheat in Nature, like the false Tradesman, who puts the best of his Goods uppermost, that the Buyer may think the rest are of the same Goodness.

Beauty of the Body, which is the Womens Glory, seems to be now unequally bestow'd, and Nature, or rather Providence, to lye under some Scandal about it, as if 'twas given a Woman for a Snare to Men, and so make a kind of a *She-Devil* of her: Because they say Exquisite Beauty is *rarely* given with Wit; *more rarely* with Goodness of Temper, and *never at all* with Modesty. And some, pretending to justify the Equity of such a Distribution, will tell us 'tis the Effect of the Justice of Providence in dividing particular Excellencies among all his Creatures, *share and share alike, as it were,* that all might for something or other be acceptable to one another, else some wou'd be despis'd.

I think both these Notions false, and yet the last, which has the shew of Respect to Providence, is the worst; for it supposes Providence to be Indigent and Empty; as if it had not wherewith to furnish all the Creatures it had made, but was fain to be parcimonious in its Gifts, and distribute them by *piece-meal*, for fear of being exhausted.

If I might venture my Opinion against an almost universal Notion, I wou'd say, Most men mistake the Proceedings of Providence in this case, and all the world at this day are mistaken in their Practice about it. And because the Assertion is very bold, I desire to explain my self.

That Almighty First Cause which made us all, is certainly the Fountain of Excellence, as it is of Being, and by an Invisible Influence could have diffused Equal Qualities and Perfections to all the Creatures it has made, as the Sun does its Light, without the least Ebb or Diminution to himself; and has given indeed to every individual sufficient to the Figure his Providence had design'd him in the world.

I believe it might be defended, if I should say, That I do suppose God has given to all Mankind equal Gifts and Capacities, in that he has given them all *Souls* equally capable; and that the whole difference in Mankind proceeds either from Accidental Difference in the Make of their Bodies, or from the *foolish Difference* of Education.[140]

1. *From Accidental Difference in Bodies.* I wou'd avoid discoursing here of the Philosophical Position of the Soul in the Body: But if it be true as Philosophers do affirm, That the Understanding and Memory is dilated or contracted according to the accidental Dimensions of the Organ through which 'tis convey'd; then tho' God has given a Soul as capable to me as another, yet if I have any Natural Defect in those Parts of the Body by which the Soul shou'd act, I may have the same Soul infus'd as another man, and yet he be a Wise Man, and I a very Fool. *For example*, If a Child naturally have a Defect in the Organ of Hearing, so that he cou'd never distinguish any Sound, that Child shall never be able to speak or read, tho' it have a Soul capable of all the Accomplishments in the world. The Brain is the Centre of the Souls actings, where all the distinguishing Faculties of it reside; and 'tis observable, A man who has a narrow contracted Head, in which there is not room for the due and necessary Operations of Nature by the Brain, is never a man of very great Judgment; and that Proverb, *A Great Head and Little Wit*, is not meant by Nature, but is a Reproof upon Sloth; as if one shou'd, by way of wonder, say, *Fye, fye, you that have a Great Head, have but Little Wit, that's strange! that must certainly be your own fault.* From this Notion I do believe there is a great matter in the Breed of Men and Women; not that Wise Men shall always get Wise Children; but I believe Strong and Healthy Bodies have the Wisest Children; and Sickly Weakly Bodies affect the Wits as well as the Bodies of their Children. We are easily persuaded to believe this in the Breeds of Horses, Cocks, Dogs, and other Creatures; and I believe 'tis as visible in Men.

But to come closer to the business; the great distinguishing difference which is seen in the world between Men and Women, is in their Education; and this is manifested by comparing it with the difference between one Man or Woman, and another.

And herein it is that I take upon me to make such a bold Assertion, That all the World are mistaken in their Practice about Women: For I cannot think that God Almighty ever made them so delicate, so glorious Creatures, and furnish'd them with such Charms, so Agreeable and so Delightful to Mankind, with Souls capable of the same Accomplishments with Men, and all to be only Stewards of our Houses, *Cooks and Slaves*.

Not that I am for exalting the Female Government in the least: But, in short, *I wou'd have Men take Women for Companions, and Educate them to be fit for it*. A Woman of Sense and Breeding will scorn as much to encroach upon the Prerogative of the Man, as a Man of Sense will scorn to oppress the *Weakness* of the Woman. But if the Womens Souls were refin'd and improv'd by Teaching, that word wou'd be lost; to say *The Weakness of the Sex*, as to Judgment, wou'd be Nonsense; for Ignorance and Folly wou'd be no more to be found among Women than Men. I remember a Passage which I heard from a very Fine Woman, she had Wit and Capacity enough, an Extraordinary Shape and Face, and a Great Fortune, but had been cloyster'd up all her time, and for fear of being stoll'n had not had the liberty of being taught the common necessary knowledge of Womens Affairs; and when she came to converse in the world, her Natural Wit made her so sensible of the want of Education, that she gave this short Reflection on her self:

I am asham'd to talk with my very Maids, says she, *for I don't know when they do right or wrong: I had more need go to School, than be Married*.

I need not enlarge on the Loss the Defect of Education is to the Sex, nor argue the Benefit of the contrary Practice; 'tis a thing will be more easily granted than remedied: This Chapter is but an Essay at the thing, and I refer the Practice to those Happy Days, if ever they shall be, when men shall be wise enough to mend it.

Of a Court-merchant.[141]

I Ask Pardon of the Learned Gentlemen of the *Long Robe*, if I do 'em any wrong in this Chapter, having no design to affront 'em; when I say, That in Matters of Debate among Merchants, when they come to be argued by Lawyers at the Bar, they are strangely handled. I my self have heard very famous Lawyers make sorry Work of a Cause between the Merchant and his Factor; and when they come to argue about *Exchanges, Discounts, Protests, Demorages, Charter-Parties, Fraights, Port-*

Charges, Assurances, Barratries, Bottomries, Accounts Current, Accounts in Commission, and *Accounts in Company*, and the like, the Sollicitor has not been able to draw a Brief, nor the Council to understand it: Never was Young Parson more put to it to make out his Text when he's got into the Pulpit without his Notes, than I have seen a Council at the Bar, when he wou'd make out a Cause between two Merchants: And I remember a pretty History of a particular Case, by way of Instance, When two Merchants contending about a long Factorage-Account,[142] that had all the Niceties of Merchandizing in it, and labouring on both sides to instruct their Council, and to put them in when they were out; at last they found them make such ridiculous stuff off it, that they both threw up the Cause, and agreed to a Reference; which Reference in one Week, without any Charge, ended all the Dispute, which they had spent a great deal of Money in before to no purpose.

Nay, the very Judges themselves (no Reflection upon their Learning) have been very much at a loss in giving Instructions to a Jury, and Juries much more to understand them; for when all is done, Juries, which are not always, nor often indeed of the Wisest Men, are to be sure ill Umpires in Causes so nice, that the very Lawyer and Judge can hardly understand them.

The Affairs of Merchants are accompanied with such variety of Circumstances, such new and unusual Contingences, which change and differ in every Age, with a multitude of Niceties and Punctilio's, and those again altering as the Customs and Usages of Countries and States do alter; that it has been found impracticable to make any Laws that could extend to all Cases: And our Law it self does tacitly acknowledge its own Imperfection in this Case, by allowing the *Custom of Merchants* to pass as a kind of Law, in cases of Difficulty.

Wherefore it seems to me a most Natural Proceeding, That such Affairs shou'd be heard before, and judg'd by such as by known Experience and long Practice in the Customs and Usages of Foreign Negoce, are of course the most capable to determine the same.

Besides the Reasonableness of the Argument, there are some Cases in our Laws in which it is impossible for a Plaintiff to make out his Case, or a Defendant to make out his Plea; as in particular, when his Proofs are beyond Seas, for no Protests, Certifications, or Procurations are allow'd in our Courts as Evidence; and the Damages are Infinite and Irretrievable by any of the Proceedings of our Laws.

For the answering all these Circumstances, a Court might be erected by Authority of Parliament, to be compos'd of Six Judges Commissioners, who shou'd have Power to Hear and Decide as a Court of Equity, under the Title of, *A Court-Merchant*.

The Proceedings of this Court shou'd be short, the Trials speedy, the Fees easy, that every man might have immediate Remedy where Wrong is done: For in Trials at Law about Merchants Affairs, the Circumstances of the Case are often such, as the long Proceedings of Courts of Equity are more pernicious than in other Cases; because the matters to which they are generally relating, are under greater Contingences than in other cases, as Effects in hands abroad, which want Orders, Ships and Seamen lying at Demoreage,[143] and in Pay, and the like.

These Six Judges shou'd be chosen of the most Eminent Merchants of the Kingdom, to reside in *London*, and to have Power by Commission to summon a Council of Merchants, who shou'd decide all Cases on the Hearing of both Parties, with Appeal to the said Judges.

Also to delegate by Commission Petty Councils of Merchants in the most considerable Ports of the Kingdom for the same purpose.

The Six Judges themselves to be only Judges of Appeal; all Trials to be heard before the Council of Merchants, by Methods and Proceedings Singular and Concise.

The Council to be sworn to do Justice, and to be chosen annually out of the principal Merchants of the City.

The Proceedings here shou'd be without Delay; the Plaintiff to exhibit his Grievance by way of Brief, and the Defendant to give in his Answer, and a time of Hearing to be appointed immediately.

The Defendant by Motion shall have liberty to put off Hearing, upon showing good Cause; not otherwise.

At Hearing, every man to argue his own Cause, if he pleases, or introduce any person to do it for him.

Attestations and Protests from Foreign Parts, regularly procur'd, and authentickly signifi'd in due Form, to pass in Evidence; Affidavits in due Form likewise attested and done before proper Magistrates within the King's Dominions, to be allow'd as Evidence.

The Party griev'd may appeal to the Six Judges, before whom they shall plead by Council, and from their Judgment to have no Appeal.

By this Method Infinite Controversies wou'd be avoided, and Disputes amicably ended, a multitude of present Inconveniences avoided; and Merchandizing-Matters wou'd in a Merchant-like manner be decided, by the known Customs and Methods of Trade.

Of Seamen.

IT is observable, That whenever this Kingdom is engaged in a War with any of its Neighbours, two great Inconveniences constantly follow; one to the *King*, and one to *Trade*.

(1.) That to the *King* is, That he is forced to press Seamen for the Manning of his Navy, and force them involuntarily into the Service: Which way of violent dragging men into the Fleet, is attended with sundry ill circumstances: As,

1. Our Naval Preparations are retarded, and our Fleets always late, for want of Men; which has expos'd them not a little, and been the ruin of many a good and well-laid Expedition.

2. Several Irregularities follow, as the Officers taking Money to dismiss Able Seamen, and filling up their Complement with raw and improper Persons.

3. Oppressions, Quarrelings, and oftentimes Murthers, by the rashness of Press-masters, and the obstinacy of some unwilling to go.

4. A secret Aversion to the Service, from a Natural Principle, common to the *English* Nation, to hate Compulsion.

5. Kidnapping people out of the Kingdom, robbing Houses, and picking Pockets, frequently practised under pretence of Pressing; as has been very much used of late.

With various Abuses of the like nature, some to the King, and some to the Subject.

(2.) To *Trade*. By the extravagant Price set on Wages for Seamen, which they impose on the Merchant with a sort of Authority, and he is obliged to give by reason of the Scarcity of Men; and that not from a real want of Men; for in the heighth of a Press, if a Merchant-man wanted Men, and could get a Protection for them, he might have any number immediately, and none without it; so shye were they of the Publick Service.

The First of these things has cost the King above Three Millions *Sterling*, since the War, in these Three Particulars:

1. Charge of Pressing on Sea, and on Shore, and in small Craft employed for that purpose.

2. Ships lying in Harbour for want of Men, at a vast Charge of Pay and Victuals for those they had.

3. Keeping the whole Navy in constant Pay and Provisions all the Winter, for fear of losing the Men against Summer, which has now been done several Years, besides Bounty-Money and other Expences, to court and oblige the Seamen.

The Second of these, (*viz.*) the great Wages paid by the Merchant, has cost Trade, since the War, above Twenty Millions *Sterling*. The Coal-Trade gives a Specimen of it, who for the first Three Years of the War gave 9 *l.* a Voyage to Common Seamen, who before sailed for 36 *s.* which computing the number of Ships and Men used in the Coal-Trade, and of Voyages made, at 8 hands to a Vessel, does modestly accounting make 89600 *l.* difference in one year, in Wages to Seamen in the Coal-Trade only.

For other Voyages, the difference of Sailors Wages is 50 *s. per* Month, and 55 *s. per* Month, to Foremast-men, who before went for 26 *s. per* Month; besides subjecting the Merchant to the Insolence of the Seamen, who are not now to be pleased with any Provisions, will admit no Half-Pay, and command of the Captains even what they please; nay, the King himself can hardly please them.

For Cure of these Inconveniences it is, the following Project is propos'd; with which the Seamen can have no reason to be dissatisfied, nor are not at all injur'd; and yet the Damage sustain'd will be prevented, and an immense sum of Money spar'd, which is now squander'd away by the Profuseness and Luxury of the Seamen: For if Prodigality weakens the Publick Wealth of the Kingdom in general, then are the Seamen but ill Commonwealths-men, who are not visibly the Richer for the prodigious Sums of Money paid them either by the King or the Merchant.

The Project is this;

That by an Act of Parliament an Office or Court be erected, within the Jurisdiction of the Court of Admiralty, and subject to the Lord High Admiral; or otherwise Independent, and subject only to a Parliamentary Authority; as the Commission for taking and stating the Publick Accounts.

In this Court or Office, or the several branches of it (which to that end shall be subdivided, and plac'd in every Sea-Port in the Kingdom) shall be listed and entred into immediate Pay all the Seamen in the Kingdom, who shall be divided into Colleges or Chambers of sundry degrees, suitable to their several Capacities, with Pay in proportion to their Qualities; as *Boys, Youths, Servants, Men Able, and Raw, Midship-men, Officers, Pilots, Old Men,* and *Pensioners.*

The Circumstantials of this Office;

1. No Captain or Master of any Ship or Vessel shou'd dare to hire or carry to Sea with him any Seaman, but such as he shall receive from the Office aforesaid.

2. No man whatsoever, Seaman or other, but applying himself to the said Office to be employ'd as a Sailor, shou'd immediately enter into Pay, and receive for every Able Seaman 24 *s. per* Month, and Juniors in proportion; to receive Half-Pay while unemploy'd, and liberty to work for themselves, only to be at Call of the Office, and leave an account where to be found.

3. No Sailor cou'd desert, because no Employment wou'd be to be had elsewhere.

4. All Ships at their clearing at the Custom-house, shou'd receive a Ticket to the Office for Men, where wou'd be always Choice rather than Scarcity; who shou'd be deliver'd over by the Office to the Captain or Master, without any Trouble or Delay; all liberty of Choice to be allow'd both to Master and Men, only so as to give up all Disputes to the Officers appointed to decide.

> Note, *By this wou'd be avoided the great Charge Captains and Owners are at to keep Men on Board before they are ready to go; whereas now the care of getting Men will be over, and all come on board in one day; for the Captain carrying the Ticket to the Office, he may go and chuse his Men, if he will; otherwise they will be sent on board him, by Tickets sent to their Dwellings, to repair on board such a Ship.*

5. For all these Men that the Captain or Master of the Ship takes, he shall pay the Office, not the Seamen, 28 *s. per* Month, (which 4 *s. per* Month Overplus of Wages, will be employ'd to pay the Half-Pay to the men out of Employ), and so in proportion of Wages for Juniors.

6. All Disputes concerning the mutinying of Mariners, or other matters of Debate between the Captains and Men, to be tri'd by way of Appeal, in a Court for that purpose to be erected as aforesaid.

7. All discounting of Wages, and Time, all Damages of Goods, Avarages,[144] stopping of Pay, and the like, to be adjusted by stated and Publick Rules, and Laws in Print, establish'd by the same Act of Parliament; by which means all litigious Suits in the Court of Admiralty (which are Infinite) would be prevented.

8. No Ship that is permitted to enter at the Custom-House, and take in Goods, should ever be refus'd Men, or delay'd in the delivering them above five days after a Demand made, and a Ticket from the Custom-house deliver'd; general Cases, as Arrests and Embargoes, excepted.

The Consequences of this Method.

1. By this means the Publick wou'd have no want of Seamen, and all the Charges and other Inconveniences of Pressing Men would be prevented.

2. The intolerable Oppression upon Trade, from the Exorbitance of Wages, and Insolence of Mariners, wou'd be taken off.

3. The following Sums of Money shou'd be paid to the Office, to lye in Bank as a Publick Fund for the Service of the Nation, to be dispos'd of by Order of Parliament, and not otherwise; a Committee being always substituted in the Intervals of the Session, to audit the Accounts, and a Treasury for the Money, to be compos'd of Members of the House, and to be chang'd every Session of Parliament.

1. Four Shillings *per* Month Wages advanc'd by the Merchants to the Office for the Men, more than the Office pays them.

2. In consideration of the reducing Mens Wages, and consequently Fraights to the former Prices or near them, *the Owners of Ships*, or Merchants, shall pay at the Importation of all Goods, 40 *s. per Ton* Freight, to be stated upon all Goods and Ports[145] in proportion; reckoning it on Wine Tonnage[146] from *Canaries*, as the Standard, and on special Freights in proportion to the Freight formerly paid, and half the said Price in times of Peace.

> Note, *This may well be done, and no Burthen; for if Freights are reduced to their former Prices (or near it) as they will be if Wages are so too, then the Merchant may well pay it: As for Instance; Freight from* Jamaica *to* London, *formerly at* 6 *l.* 10 *s.* per Ton, *now at* 18 *and* 20 *l. From* Virginia, *at* 5 *l. to* 6 *l.* 10 *s. now at* 14, 16, *and* 17 *l. From* Barbadoes, *at* 6 *l. now at* 16 *l. From* Oporto, *at* 2 *l. now at* 6 *l. and the like.*

The Payment of the abovesaid Sums being a large Bank for a Fund, and it being supposed to be in fair hands, and currently managed, the Merchants shall further pay upon all Goods shipp'd out, and shipp'd on board from abroad, for and from any Port of this Kingdom, 4 *l. per Cent.* on the real Value, *bona fide*, to be sworn to, if demanded: In consideration whereof, the said Office shall be obliged to pay and make good all Losses, Damages, Avarages, and Casualities whatsoever, as fully as by the Custom of Assurances now is done, without any Discounts, Rebates or Delays whatsoever; the said 4 *l. per Cent.* to be stated on the Voyage to the *Barbadoes*, and enlarged or taken off, in proportion to the Voyage, by Rules and Laws, to be Printed and publickly known.

Reserving only, That then, as reason good, the said Office shall have Power to direct Ships of all sorts, how, and in what manner, and how long they shall sail, with, or wait for Convoys; and shall have Power (with Limitations) to lay Embargoes on Ships, in order to compose Fleets for the benefit of Convoys.

These Rules, formerly noted, to extend to all Trading by Sea, the Coasting and Home-Fishing Trade excepted; and for them it should be order'd;

First, For Coals; the Colliers being provided with Men at 28 *s. per* Month, and Convoys in sufficient number, and proper Stations from *Tinmouth-Bar* to the River[147] so as they need not go in Fleets, but as Wind and Weather presents, run all the way under the Protection of the Men of War, who shou'd be continually cruising from Station to Station; they would be able to perform their Voyage in as short time as formerly, and at as cheap Pay, and consequently cou'd afford to sell their Coals at 17 *s. per* Chaldron,[148] as well as formerly at 15 *s.*

Wherefore there shou'd be paid into the Treasury appointed at *Newcastle*, by Bond to be paid where they deliver, 10 *s. per* Chaldron, *Newcastle* Measure; and the stated Price at *London* to be 27 *s. per* Chaldron in the *Pool*,[149] which is 30 *s.* at the Buyers House; and is so far from being dear, at a^a time of War especially, as it is cheaper than ever was known in a War; and the Officers shou'd by Proclamation confine the Seller to that Price.

In consideration also of the Charge of Convoys, the Ships bringing Coals shall all pay 1 *l. per Cent.* on the Value of the Ship, to be agreed on at the Office; and all Convoy-Money exacted by Commanders of Ships, shall be relinquish'd, and the Office to make good all Losses of Ships, *not Goods*, that shall be lost by Enemies only.

These Heads indeed are such as wou'd need some Explication, if the Experiment were to be made; and, with submission, wou'd reduce the Seamen to better Circumstances, at least 'twou'd have them in readiness for any Publick Service much easier than by all the late methods of Encouragement by registring Seamen,[150] &c.

For by this Method all the Seamen in the Kingdom shou'd be the King's hired Servants, and receive their Wages from him, *whoever employ'd them*; and no man cou'd hire or employ them, but from him: The Merchant shou'd hire them of the King, and pay the King for them; nor wou'd there be a Seaman in *England* out of Employ, *which, by the way, wou'd prevent their seeking Service abroad*: If they were not actually at Sea, they wou'd receive Half-Pay, and might be employ'd in Works about the Yards, Stores, and Navy, to keep all things in Repair.

If a Fleet or Squadron was to be fitted out, they wou'd be mann'd in a Week's time, for all the Seamen in *England* wou'd be ready: Nor wou'd they be shye of the Service; for *it is not* an Aversion to the King's Service; nor *'tis not* that the Duty is harder in the Men of War than the Merchantmen; nor *'tis not* fear of Danger which makes our Seamen lurk, and hide, and hang back in a time of War; but 'tis *Wages* is the matter: 24 *s. per* Month in the King's Service, and 40 to 50 *s. per* Month from the Merchant, is the true cause; and the Seaman is in the right of it too; for who wou'd serve his King and Countrey, and fight, and be knock'd o' the head at 24 *s. per* Month that can have 50 *s.* without that hazard: And till this be remedied, in vain are all the Encouragements which can be given to Seamen; for they tend but to make them Insolent, and encourage their Extravagance.

Nor wou'd this Proceeding be any damage to the Seamen in general; for 24 *s. per* Month Wages, and to be kept in constant Service, or Half-Pay when idle, is really better to the Seamen than 45 *s. per* Month, as they now take it, considering how long they often lye idle on shore, out of Pay: For the extravagant Price of Seamens Wages, tho' it has been an Intolerable Burthen to Trade, has not visibly enrich'd the Sailors; and they may as well be content with 24 *s. per* Month now as formerly.

On the other hand, Trade wou'd be sensibly reviv'd by it, the intolerable Price of Freights wou'd be reduced, and the Publick wou'd reap an immense Benefit by the Payments mention'd in the Proposal; as,

(1.) 4 *s. per* Month upon the Wages of all the Seamen employ'd by the Merchant; which if we allow 200000 Seamen always in Employ, as there cannot be less in all the Ships belonging to *England*, is 40000 l. *per* Month.

(2.) 40 *s. per* Ton Freight upon all Goods imported.

(3.) 4 *per Cent.* on the Value of all Goods exported or imported.

(4.) 10 *s. per* Chaldron upon all the Coals shipp'd at *Newcastle*; and 1 *per Cent.* on the Ships which carry them.

What these Four Articles wou'd pay to the *Exchequer* yearly, 'twou'd be very difficult to calculate, and I am too near the End of this Book to attempt it: But I believe no Tax ever given since this War, has come near it.

'Tis true, out of this the Publick wou'd be to pay Half-Pay to the Seamen who shall be out of Employ, and all the Losses and Damages on Goods and Ships; which tho' it might be considerable, wou'd be small, compar'd to the Payment aforesaid; for as the *Premio* of 4 *per Cent.* is but small, so the Safety lies upon all men being bound to Insure: For I believe any one will grant me this, 'tis not the smallness of a Premio Ruins the Ensurer, but 'tis the smallness of the Quantity he Insures; and I am not at all asham'd to affirm, That let but a Premio of 4 *l. per Cent.* be paid into one Man's hand for all Goods Imported and Exported, and any Man may be the General Ensurer of the Kingdom, and yet that Premio can never hurt the Merchant neither.

So that the vast Revenue this wou'd raise, wou'd be felt no where, neither Poor nor Rich wou'd Pay the more for Coals; Foreign Goods wou'd be brought home cheaper, and our own Goods carri'd to Market cheaper; Owners wou'd get more by Ships, Merchants by Goods, and Losses by Sea wou'd be no Loss at all to any Body, because Repaid by the Publick Stock.

Another unseen Advantage wou'd arise by it, we shou'd be able to outwork all our Neighbours, even the *Dutch* themselves, by Sailing as cheap, and carrying Goods as cheap in a time of War as in Peace, an Advantage which has more in it, than is easily thought of, and wou'd have a noble influence upon all our Foreign Trade. For what cou'd the *Dutch* do in Trade, if we cou'd carry our Goods to *Cadiz* at 50s. *per Ton* Freight, and they give 8 or 10 *l.* and the like in other Places? Whereby we cou'd be able to Sell cheaper or get more than our Neighbours.

There are several considerable clauses might be added to this Proposal, some of great advantage to the General Trade of the Kingdom, some to particular Trades, and more to the Publick; but I avoid being too Particular in things which are but the Product of my own private Opinion.

If the Government shou'd ever proceed to the Experiment, no question but much more than has been hinted at wou'd appear; nor do I see any great difficulty in the Attempt, or who wou'd be aggriev'd at it; and there I leave it, rather wishing than expecting to see it undertaken.

The Conclusion.

UPon a Review of the several Chapters of this Book, I find that instead of being able to go further, some things may have suffer'd for want of being fully express'd; which if any person object against, I only say, I cannot now avoid it: I have endeavour'd to keep to my Title, and offer'd but at an *Essay*; which any one is at liberty to go on with as they please; for I can promise no Supplement. As to Errors of Opinion, tho' I am not yet convinc'd of any, yet I no where pretend to Infallibility: However, I do not willingly assert any thing which I have not good Grounds for. If I am mistaken, let him that finds the Error, inform the World better, and never trouble himself to animadvert upon this, since I assure him I shall not enter into any Pen and Ink Contest on the matter.

As to Objections which may lye against any of the Proposals made in this Book, I have in some places mention'd such as occurr'd to my Thoughts. I shall never assume that Arrogance to pretend no other or further Objections may be rais'd; but I do really believe no such Objection can be rais'd, as will overthrow any Scheme here laid down, so as to render the thing impracticable: Neither do I think but that all men will acknowledge most of the Proposals in this Book would be of as great, and perhaps greater Advantage to the Publick, than I have pretended to.

As for such who read Books only to find out the Author's *faux Pas*, who will quarrel at the Meanness of Stile, Errors of Pointing, Dulness of Expression, or the like, I have but little to say to them; I thought I had corrected it very carefully, and yet some Mispointings and small Errors have slipt me, which 'tis too late to help: As to Language, I have been rather careful to make it speak *English* suitable to the Manner of the Story, than to dress it up with Exactness of Stile; chusing rather to have it Free and Familiar, according to the Nature of *Essays*, than to strain at a Perfection of Language, which I rather wish for, than pretend to be Master of.

AN

ESSAY

ON THE

REGULATION

OF THE

PRESS.

LONDON,
Printed in the Year, 1704.

Some Persons think that laying a Tax upon Printed News, may be of Service: but in my Opinion, it will only give Encouragement to the News Writers to vent their own Opinions thro'out *England*: besides the small Sum that can be raised by it is not worth mentioning.

AN ESSAY, &c.

ALL Men pretend the Licentiousness of the Press to be a publick Grievance, but it is much easier to say it is so, than to prove it, or prescribe a proper Remedy; nor is it the easiest Grievance to Cure.

To put a general stop to publick Printing, would be a check to Learning, a Prohibition of Knowledge, and make Instruction Contraband: And as Printing has been own'd to be the most useful Invention ever found out, in order to polish the Learned World, make Men Polite, and encrease the Knowledge of Letters, and thereby all useful Arts and Sciences; so the high Perfection of Human Knowledge must be at a stand, Improvements stop, and the Knowledge of Letters decay in the Kingdom, if a general Interruption should be put to the Press.

To Restrain the Licentious Extravagance of Authors therefore, and bring the Press under Regulations, is the Case before us, and this is for that Reason call'd, *An Essay on the Regulation of the Press.*

'Twould be endless to examine the Liberty taken by the Men of Wit in the World, the loose they give themselves in Print, at Religion, at Government, at Scandal; the prodigious looseness of the Pen, in broaching new Opinions in Religion, as well as in Politicks, are real Scandals to the Nation, and well deserve a Regulation.

No Nation in the Christian World, but ours, would have suffered such Books as *Asgill* upon Death; *Coward* against the Immortality of the Soul; — on Poligamy; — against the Trinity; *B—t's* Theory;[1] and abundance more tending to Atheism, Heresie, and Irreligion, without a publick Censure, nor should the Authors have gone without Censure and Punishment, in any place in *Europe*, but here.

On these accounts, I cannot but agree that a Regulation, or due Restraint of the Press, is a good work. But the next and most material Enquiry is, how shall it be obtain'd?

By a License Office, says a Messenger of the Press,[2] that I may be employ'd to make work in the Town, as has been done in the days of yore.

That this is the hopes of a forward Party upon that head, is very plain to make out, but I shall avoid charging any Body, and only proceed to examine what are the proper Consequences of a License to the Press.

First, It makes the Press a slave to a Party; let it be which Party it will, I meddle not with that; but whatever Party of Men obtain the Reins of Management, and have power to name the Person who shall License the Press, that Party of Men have the whole power of keeping the World in Ignorance, in all matters relating to Religion or Policy, since the Writers of that Party shall have full liberty to impose their Notions upon the World, and if any Man offers to reply, the Licenser shall refuse the Copy.

This has been accounted Arbitrary, and not the least Grievance in former Reigns; for indeed an absolute submitting the Press to the will of a Licenser, is bringing the whole Trade of Books, and the whole Body of Learning, under the Arbitrary Power of Mercenary Men.

The Labours of the most capable Scholar, the Elaborate Works of the most exquisite Artist, the most Practical Discourse on the Divinest Subject, Dissertations and Transactions in all Sciences shall fall to the Ground, and the Student lose his Years of Labour, and the World the Advantage of his Learning and Parts, unless a sum of Mony can be rais'd to bribe a Mercenary Licenser, and a Hackney Messenger.

'Twould be endless to reckon up the many Volumes on all needful Subjects, which were absolutely rejected in the days of the Press's Restriction, when the most Orthodox Divinity was suppress'd, because the Man was not approv'd that wrote it, and a Book was Damn'd for the Author, not the Author for the Book.

This was a branch of Arbitrary Power in the Government; for in Rightful Governments they do not Tyrannize themselves, but if the Officers are allow'd to impose upon them, Under-spur-leathers[3] are always the Tyrants; a Government regulated by such Laws, and Govern'd according to such Regulations never willingly put it into the power of any Inferiour Officer to Tyrannize over his fellow Subjects.

I observe there are sorts of people who are willing to promote a general License, and very studious to defend it; but 'tis plain they are such as promote Principles in Argument, which they can but very sorrily defend; and flattering themselves, from what Grounds I believe they themselves hardly know; that they may obtain a Licenser to their Advantage, they suppose from thence a liberty to obtrude their preposterous Notions upon the World, and by favour of a Law and an Arbitrary Licenser, partial to their own Factions, suppress the possibility of a reply.

These people are in the right to desire such a thing, as a Licenser; for false and designing Reasoning, requires the support of Power to defend it from the invincible force of Truth and Demonstration.

But methinks they should be able to see that the present Government is not so suited to those Principles, as that they should expect so Arbitrary and unjustifiable an Office should be erected, after so many Years being laid side.

The People of *England* do not believe the Parliament will make a Law to abridge them of that Liberty they should protect, for tho' it were more true than it is, that the Exorbitances of the Press ought to be restrain'd, yet I cannot see how the supervising, and passing all the Works of the Learned part of the World by one or a few Men, and giving them an absolute Negative on the Press, can possibly be reconcil'd to the liberty of the *English Nation*.

Laws are often made against Facts not in themselves unlawful, but as Convenience and Reason of State requires, and Circumstances may make a thing unfit to be allow'd in a Country, which would otherwise be no Crime; but in these Cases such Laws are enforc'd by a Penalty, and he that will suffer the Penalty, is always at Liberty to commit the Crime.

But in this case a Man is abridg'd of his Liberty, and must not do this or that, whether it Transgresses the Law or no. For Example, a person having Writ a Book, brings it to one or other Licenser, the Law is not express that such a Book shall not appear in the World, there is no Crime committed, but the Book shall be Damn'd in its Womb, not because any thing in it is offensive to the Government, Irreligious, Blasphemous, or any other way Criminal, not because 'tis a Book unfit to appear, but because Mr. *Licenser* does not please to like it.

I know no Nation in the World, whose Government is not perfectly Despotick, that ever makes preventive Laws, 'tis enough to make Laws to punish Crimes when they are committed, and not to put it in the power of any single Man, on pretence of preventing Offences to commit worse.

Even the Laws against Theft and Murther, do not say they shall not commit the Crime, but if they do, they shall be so and so punish'd. 'Tis for the Commands of God to say, *Thou shalt not do this or that, Kill, Steal, commit Adultery,* and the like; but Man can only say, if any Man shall wilfully do this, or that, commit this or that Crime, he shall suffer such or such Pains, and Penalties; and some are of opinion, all men have a Negative right, *as to Human Liberty,* to commit any Fact, if they submit to the penalty which the Law inflicts; for as to its being a sin against

God, the Laws have nothing to say to that, and as to a sin against Civil Government, there can be no such thing as a Crime till the Fact is committed, and therefore to anticipate the Man by laws, before the Crime, is to abridge him of his Liberty without a Crime, and so make a Punishment without a Transgression, which is illegal in its own Nature, and Arbitrary in the most intense degree.

It might not be improper here to Examine what particular Inconveniences attend such a Law in our present Case, and upon what just Grounds I except against.

1. I object against it as the first step to restore Arbitrary Power in this Nation, and the worst way of restoring it, *viz.* by a Law. For to go back again to that which we once complain'd of as Arbitrary, is a tacit acknowledging the former Complaint to be groundless, and giving us cause to think that there's more steps of that Nature to be introduc'd.

'Tis ill making Precedents in cases so dangerous, where the Liberty of a Nation is concern'd; and I cannot doubt but our wise Legislators will consider what the Consequences of yielding in the least point of the Subjects Priviledges are, and we have always found them very tender of the very least punctilio's of that great Fundamental, the Peoples Liberty. 'Tis needless to quote Cases, the general practice of the House of Commons, ever since the liberty of the Subject, was to secure the *English* freedom, and carefully to watch against all Encroachments of any sort, either from without or from any Parties among themselves.

2. 'Tis a Foundation of Frauds, Briberies, and all the ill practices possible; the absolute conduct of so considerable an Article, being committed to the Breast of a few Men, every part of their proceedings are Arbitrary and Unreasonable: Nay, even when he passes a Book that ought to be pass'd, yet 'tis Arbitrary in him, because he passes it not because it ought so to be pass'd, but because he has receiv'd some Perquisite, Gratuity, or other Argument to prevail upon him to do it.

Take this Licenser without a Fee, and fancy an Author brings a Copy to him, suppose of Divinity, and where is the Book against which he can find no excuse, tho' Penn'd with never so much caution? here it reflects upon the Church, there upon the Government; this seems to look asquint on such an Article of the Church of *England*, that at too much a Ceremony in the Liturgy and Rubrick, and he cannot allow it to be Publish'd; but send him the next morning two or three *Guineas*, and you have the *Imprimatur* at first word. Suppose it be a Book of Politicks, then this Sentence is a reflection on this great Man, that on another, this may signifie the Parliament, that the King or Queen, but still the Guineas sets it all to right again, the Gold makes the Book Orthodox and Loyal, and private Constructive Objections vanish in the Mist raised before his Eyes by the Mony.

Then suppose this or that Licenser, a Party-Man, that is, One put in, and upheld by a Party; suppose him of any Party, which you please, and a Man of the opposite Kidney, brings him a Book, he views the Character of the Man, *O*, says he, *I know the Author, he is a damn'd* Whig, *or a rank* Jacobite, *I'll License none of his Writings*; here is Bribery on one Hand, partiality to Parties on the other; but get a Man of his own Kidney to own the very same Book, and as he refus'd it without opening before, he is as easie to pass it now, not for the Good or Ill in the Book, but on both Hands for the Character of the Author.

There is another Engine of Fraud comes in to make up this Complication of Frauds, and ill Practices, and that is the Messenger of the Press, and this serves for the Receiver, while the t'other is the Th—f, and he takes the Fees, and the Licenser does the Work, and so casting up together they bring all to an Account of Profit and Loss. This is the Broker of the Press, the Stock-Jobber of the License-Office; he Talks with you, and Treats with any Body to get a Book Licensed, and Rates his Fees as he finds the Person more or less Obnoxious to his Master, or his Party.

This is a New Mouse Trap, and he that will come into the Press must expect to be catch'd in it, and then in a little Time all the force of the Law, so far as design'd against the Exorbitance of the Pen, is Evaded and Eluded, all revolves in the Bribery and Villainy of Officers and Licensers, the Law looks like a Phantome of the Brain, made for one Man in an Age to raise a Fortune by, and he must turn Round to perform it.

These Things have often been consider'd in Parliament, and have been the true Reasons why our Wise Representers, tho' willing enough to Restrain any undue Liberty, yet have always avoided this Pernitious Remedy, as a thing of much worse Consequence to the Constitution and Privileges of *Englishmen*, than the Licentiousness of the Press can be to the Government.

To Cure the ill Use of Liberty, with a Deprivation of Liberty, is like cutting off the Leg to cure the Gout in the Toe, like expelling Poison with too Rank a Poison, where both may struggle which Poison shall prevail, but which soever prevails, the Patient suffers.

If the Exorbitance of some few People in Printing Seditious and Dangerous Books, must Abridge all the Men of Learning in the Nation of their Liberty in Printing, what after exceeding toil and unwearied Pains they are willing to Communicate to Posterity, then who will Study, who will breed up their Children to Letters, when all the Fruits of their Labours are liable to the Blast of the Arbitrary Breath of Mercenary Men.

By such a Law, a Fellow of no Letters, of Knowledge too little to fit him for a Ballad-Singer, shall be Capable of Tyrannizing over the whole World of Learning, and no Book can see the Light without his leave, when after a Man has wrote enough to have all the World acknowledge him, and such a Work, which in some Countries he would have suffi-cient Gratification for, here he shall not bestow it on the World, without putting himself to the Charge of Bribing the Licenser, and so cannot give them his Labour, but he must give them his Money too.

In this very thing the King of *France*[4] out does all the Princes of *Europe*, where such Encouragement is given to Learning, that all useful Books in the World now speak *French*, and a Man may be an Universal Schollar, read *Virgil, Horace, Ovid,* and all the Antient Poets; *Cicero, Plato, Epictetus, Aristotle,* and all the Antient Philosophers; St. *Athanasius,* St. *Augustine,* and all the Primitive Fathers; *Plutarch, Livy,* and all the Antient Historians, and yet neither understand a Word of *Greek* or *Latin,* and pray let us Examine if ever the Press has been Restrain'd to the Absolute Power of a Licenser or Reviser, on the contrary all the Liberty and Encouragement imaginable has been given to the Press, all the Abbies, and publick Libraries in the Kingdom are oblig'd to take One, and when any Author has publish'd an Extraordinary Piece, the King himself has thought fit to reward him with a Magnificence, peculiar to the Pride and State of the *French* Court.

But this Liberty has been the Life of Learning, and ever since Cardinal *Richlieu* Erected the Royal Academy, no Nation in the World ever flour-ish'd in Learning like them.

The *English* Nation has always carried a figure equal to their Neighbours, as to all sorts of Learning, and in some very much superior, and tho' without all those Encouragements, have not yet sunk their Character that way. But we cannot say that Learning is grown to such a height that it needs a Check, that it wants a Tyrant of the Press to govern it: Knowledge is much Improv'd, 'tis confess'd, but the World is not so over-run with Letters, that it should be Tax'd as a Vice, and Laws made to Suppress the little Degrees of it, that are attain'd to.

What those Gentlemen propose to themselves who are so forward to procure, or at least so eagerly plead for this Padlock to the Press, I cannot imagine, unless it be that they have some grounds to hope they shall keep the Key.

And what can the design of that Power be? If it be that they would have the Advantage to Print what they please, and that the adverse Party should not have the liberty of the Press to Reply, is a sign the Cause they Embark in is not to be Defended, and will not bear an Answer, and if it be that they would have no Writing at all, but such points as they are doubtful in, 'tis an Unquestionable Argument that their Cause won't bear Canvasing, and that the less 'tis Examined into, the better for them.

Some People have an Arrogance peculiar to themselves, and can venture things into the World upon the Reputation of a bold Expression, presuming, no Man will venture Examination after the positive Assertion of their Pen. If these Gentlemen are so full of Assurance, *Anglicè,*[5] Impudence, as to affirm things without Ground, when other Men as well Read as themselves, are at their Elbows to Confute them, to Examine their Authorities and reprove them when they Act without Authority; what work would such Men as these make in the World with their Cause, if this Padlock of the Press was set on by the Laws, and they were to keep the Key, that is, in short, if they had a full License to vent their Notions, and the Law should place a Sentinel of their own at the Door of the Press, that no Man but he that had the Word should come there.

We should have more *Wise Nations* quoted upon us for things no Nation ever did, and Precedents brought in by Wholesale, without any other Authority than the *Imprimatur* of the Party.

New and Old Association-Men might then cry out of Rebellion in *Scotland,* from the *Presbyterian,* and make the World believe the *Cameronians* were up in Arms there to restore *Episcopacy.* Boys may beat Men if their Hands were Ty'd; if the Hands of a Party are ever Ty'd up by a Law of Licensing, 'tis not then who talks Sense, or Matter of Fact, nor who has the best of the Argument, nor who can say most to the purpose, but who shall be Licensed to speak what he has to say, and who not, who shall Talk, and who shall hold his Tongue.

This I take to be the true state of the Case, and if it be so, I leave it to any body to judge, whether a *License of the Press* can be consistent either with the Encouragement due to Learning, the Liberty of this Nation, the Reason of the thing, or the Reputation of any Party who desire it.

It remains to Enquire,

First, Is it then fit the Licentiousness of the Press should be Unrestrain'd? And Secondly, How shall it be done?

To the First I reply. Licentiousness of all sorts ought to be Restrain'd, whether of the Tongue, the Pen, the Press, or any thing else, and it were well if all sorts of Licentiousness were as easy to Govern as this; but to Regulate this Evil by an Evil ten times more pernicious, is doing us no service at all.

'Tis apparent the Injury done to the whole Nation, by severely Punishing small things, and letting more substantial Grievances alone, is what there has been Cause to Complain of.

There are Parties in all our Justice and Crimes have, or have not been Punish'd, as *Parties* and *Sides* have Govern'd. But I am not going to write a Satyr on Government, several has paid Dear enough for that; to give me Notice what is to be expected from such a Liberty; as 'tis in all the World so it has too much been here, where there are *Powers* and *Parties* always struggling, there must be a Byass of Justice as this or that *Side* prevails.

But 'tis pitty the Press should come into a Party-strife: This is like two Parties going to War, and one depriving the other of all their Powder and Shot. Ammunition stands always Neuter, or rather, *Jack a both Sides*, every body has it, and then they get the Victory who have most Courage to use it, and Conduct to manage it.

And thus 'tis in the Press, with submission to Powers, this I think is a just Consequence from Reason, that since this Nation is unhappily Divided into Parties, every Side ought to have an equal Advantage in the use of the Press, and this can never be in Case of Licensing; for whatsoever Party assumes the Power of placing this Paper Magistrate, will, in effect, have an Exclusive Power over the Press, to give their Friends a full liberty of *Affirming*, and to refuse the other Side the liberty of *Replying*.

Now, as our Legislation cannot be said to be of any Party, because they are Whole; so they cannot make a Law which can be equal to the Whole, while it gives the Power to any one Party.

It cannot be prov'd, that any one Party has more Right, *as a Party*, to Publish any thing than another, and therefore cannot in Justice have more liberty given them to do it: For no Man can justly Demand an Exclusive Power, where he had no precedent Right.

Besides, 'tis a Scandal both to the Merit of a Cause, and the Wit of the Managers, that any Party shou'd fly to the Law to suppress his Adversary's Pen. If two Men fall Out, and one having struck the other, the Person who receiv'd the Blow instead of Fighting him goes to Law with him for the Assault. 'Tis a natural Consequence for all Men to believe such a Man was afraid to Fight; either he was a Coward in his Nature, or he thought himself over-matcht, and his Enemy would be too hard for him.

So where a Party flies to the Engine of the Law to prevent their Opponent's appearing in Print, it looks like a Confession that they would have the Advantage, if the *Liberty* was not Restrain'd by the Law.

But then to have a Law which should be so Circumstanc'd, as that one Party shall Write and Print, and the other shall not, this has a further Scandal in it, it not only Confesses superiority in the Enemy Suppressor, but seems to have something base in the Party, like getting two Men to hold a Man while I Beat him.

The Grand Question then seems thus,

You own the Liberty of the Press ought to be restrain'd, but you are of the Opinion a Licence is Arbitrary and Unequal. How then would you have the end Answered?

'Tis not for me to direct the Legislative Authority, nor do these Sheets pretend to it, but to me the properest Methods seem to be such as follow.

1. To make an Act that no Man shall, by Writing or by Printing, Argue, Dispute, Reflect upon, or pretend to Vindicate such and such Points, Persons, Bodies, Members, &c. of the State or[a] the Church, or of any other Matter or Thing as the law shall mention, and they will be such as the Law-makers see proper to insert.

2. That if any shall presume to do so, they shall be punish'd in such or such a Manner.

By the first, all Men will know when they Transgress, which at present they do not; for as the Case now stands, 'tis in the Breast of the Courts of Justice to make any Book a Scandalous and Seditious Libel, and nothing is more ridiculous than the Letter of an Indictment in such Cases, and the Jury being accounted only Judges of Evidence, Judges of Fact, and not of the Nature of it, the Judges are thereby Unlimited.

In the Case of Mr. *Delaun*,[6] who was Indicted at the *Old Bailey*, for Writing a Book, call'd, *A Plea for the Nonconformists*, says the Indictment, *and the said* Delaun *did then, and there by Force and Arms write the aforesaid Scandalous and Seditious Book, against the Peace of our Sovereign Lord the King, his Crown and Dignity*, which are the actual Words in most Indictments of that nature.

All these Evils would be Obviated, and Men might know when they Transgress, and when they do not.

Laws in their Original Design are not made to draw Men into Crimes, but to prevent Crimes; *Laws are Buoys* set upon dangerous Places under

Water, to warn Mankind, that such Sands or Rocks are there, and the Language of them is, *Come here at your Peril.*

The Crime of an Author is not known; and I think verily no Book can be wrote so warily, but that if the Author be brought on his Tryal, it shall be easy for a cunning Lawyer, ay for a Lawyer of no great Cunning, to put an *Innuendo* upon his Meaning, and make some Part of it Criminal. Thus it was in the Case of *Baxter's Comment upon the New Testament; Algernon Sidney's Answer to Sir* Robert Filmer; *De Laun's Plea for the Nonconformists;* Anderton's *two Books;*[7] and so it may be with this Book, or the best in the World.

Now since there are Dangers thus conceal'd in the Law, and no Man can tell when he offends, 'twould be a wholsome Piece of Justice to all the Nation, to place a *Buoy* on the Rock, and whoever splits on it afterwards would deserve no pity.

Such a Law would be a sufficient Restraint to the Exorbitance of the Press, for then the Crime would be plain, and Men would be afraid of committing it. Whereas the present uncertainty of the Crime seems to be the greatest Occasion of the Crime, for Men are apt to be bold in a Thing which they cannot find expressly Condemn'd by the Letter of the Law.

Secondly, As the Crime may be stated, so may the Punishment, and then no Man can be at the Mercy of arbitrary Men; no *Sidneys* will be found to have Sentence revers'd, and Attainders taken off; no *De Launs* die in Prison under Exorbitant Fines; no *post Factum's,*[8] no Complaint can be made by the Person offending, because they know what they were to trust to.

And above all, the End of restraining the Press would be obtain'd by it; for when Men know both the Crime and the Punishment, they would be much more wary of the one for fear of the other.

I humbly conceive, the uncertainty of both at present, is the real, if not the only Ground of the Licentiousness of the Press. When I am told the present Liberty of the Press is a Grievance, I must say, the reason is plain, 'tis because there is a Liberty, and no Law to ascertain the Fact. But let the Law adjust the Crime, and tie it to the Penalty, that Authors may know what to trust to; there needs no Licenser to pick Men's Pockets, permit Crimes when he is paid for them, and refuse useful and valuable Books if he is not fee'd.

But here remains a Question unanswer'd, that in other Cases is not usual. There are many ways to commit this Crime, and lie conceal'd; the Crime may be committed, and the Malefactor hard to be found, and therefore the Licensing the Press was thought necessary to prevent the Fact, because when committed, the Offender is not easily brought to Justice.

This is easily answered, and the Parliament has thought fit, in two Cases, to make a Precedent that exactly reaches the Case, and they are, *first*, in the Case of buying stolen Goods; and the other is, in putting off, or exchanging counterfeit Money; both which, tho' Accessaries to the Crime, are now made equally Criminal with the Principal, if knowingly done.

If in the Case of the Press, a Law be made to make the last Seller the Author, unless the Name of Author, Printer, or Bookseller, be affix'd to the Book, then no Book can be published, but there will be some body found to answer for it. Whoever puts a false Name, to forfeit . . . *&c.*

Nor can this be thought hard upon the Seller of the Book, because as he knows the Consequence, no Bookseller will be so foolish as to sell any Book that has not the Name of some Printer, Bookseller, or Author affix'd to the Title; and so this Law will answer two Ends together; be a means to prevent the Crime, and fix the Offender if it be committed.

If the Name of the Author, or of the Printer, or of the Bookseller, for whom it is printed, be affix'd, every Man is safe that sells a Book; but if not, then no Man will sell it, but he that hath some private Reason for propagating what the Book treats of, and such a Man has some Title to pass for the Author.

I place the Excellency of a Law very much, as before, in the Power and Efficacy it has to prevent the Crime; and the Justice of that Law can never be plainer, than when the Fact is ascertain'd, the Penalty settled, and the Criminal describ'd: No Man can then be Guilty but he that is wilfully and knowingly so, and whoever is so, *let him suffer*, no Man will be concern'd for him.

All the Excuse that ever I could meet with for a Licenser, was built upon the Difficulty of discovering the true Author of a Book, and the Difficulty being such that no Laws could easily be made effectual to fix the Writer of any thing, they found room for the Stratagem of a Licenser. I call it an Excuse for it, because 'tis plain, the Licenser was not found out as a Remedy for the Evil: But the Design of a Licenser being first resolv'd on, the pretended Difficulty was made a Handle to introduce the new Engine into the World, and place this Monarch of the Press, as a Tyrant to exercise his absolute Authority over the World of Letters, and so suppress one Mischief by another.

But leaving the Press in the full Enjoyment of all its just Liberties, and answer all these Ends, while 'tis yet fenc'd about with due Restriction of Laws, every Man may have a full Freedom of promoting the Extent of Learning, exercising his Parts, defending his Arguments, and answering his Adversary, and yet at the same time will know how far he may go, with safety, and when he transgresses: If any Man then gives offence, he knows it, and what he must expect; if any Man does thus offend, the Law knows the Offender, and how to punish him: All things would run in the open free Course of Laws. Criminals and Laws, Offences and Punishment are due Opposites, and ought always to stand in view of one another. If the Punishment or the Law is conceal'd from the Offender, he is trapann'd[9] into the Crime to his Destruction, when he knows nothing of the Matter, and the Law is made a Gin or Snare to hook him into Punishment, which is contrary to the Nature of Laws, and the Practice of all just Governments.

A Law therefore to settle what an Author may or may not do, to bring the Offences of the Pen to a Regulation, and then to annex the Punishment to the Crime, would bring all this Matter to a Square.

Authors would be known as soon as the Book, because this Law would oblige the Printer or Bookseller to place the Author's Name in the Title, or himself.

Nor is it the small Advantage of this Law, to have the Punishment of Authors adjusted; for I know nothing in which our Laws have been executed with a greater Irregularity, no Crime has been punish'd with such improper Punishments, such arbitrary Latitude, or such inconsistent Variety. In other Cases we have Crimes and Punishments link'd together; if a Man robs a House, counterfeits the Coin, or kills a Man, he knows what he has to trust to, but Authors have never known their Punishment: We have had the very same Crime punish'd with trifling Fines of Twenty Shillings, and exorbitant Fines of a Thousand Marks,[10] and yet the Twenty-Shilling-Man hath the greatest Guilt; writing of a Book has been punish'd with *Fines, Whippings, Pillories, Imprisonment for Life, Halters and Axes*: How 'tis possible the Guilt of the Pen can extend to merit all these several Penalties, is a thing I never met with a Lawyer yet that could resolve.

There must be something else than Law in the Case; when I shall commit an Offence, and be fined 20 Mark, or perhaps less; another, for the same Crime, shall not be prosecuted at all; another hang'd or beheaded.

All the World cannot shew me a Crime punished by such unequal Variety, where the Crime is the same in Kind, and can only differ in

Circumstances; nor is it possible those Circumstances can have so much Variety, such unusual Distance in their Nature, as there has been in the Punishments; but all this comes from the Law having left the Punishment unsettled, and plac'd it in the unlimited Judgements of Men.

This Law would also put a Stop to a certain sort of Thieving which is now in full practice in *England*, and which no Law extends to punish, *viz.* some Printers and Booksellers printing Copies none of their own.

This is really a most injurious piece of Violence, and a Grievance to all Mankind; for it not only robs their Neighbour of their just Right, but it robs Men of the due Reward of Industry, the Prize of Learning, and the Benefit of their Studies; in the next Place, it robs the Reader, by printing Copies of other Men uncorrect and imperfect, making surreptitious and spurious Collections, and innumerable Errors, by which the Design of the Author is often inverted, conceal'd, or destroy'd, and the Information the World would reap by a curious and well studied Discourse, is dwindled into Confusion and Nonsense.

'Twere endless to instance in[11] the Mischiefs which have been done of this kind. An Author prints a Book, whether on a Civil or Religious Subject, Philosophy, History, or any Subject, if it be a large Volume, it shall be immediately *abridg'd* by some mercenary Book-seller, employing a Hackney-writer, who shall give such a contrary Turn to the Sense, such a false Idea of the Design, and so huddle Matters of the greatest Consequence together in abrupt Generals, that no greater Wrong can be done to the Subject; thus the sale of a Volume of twenty Shillings is spoil'd, by perswading People that the Substance of the Book is contain'd in the Summary of 4 *s.* price, the Undertaker is ruin'd, the Reader impos'd upon, and the Author's perhaps 20 Years Labour is lost and undervalued: I refer my Reader, for the Truth of this, to the several Abridgments of the *Turkish* History, *Josephus*, *Baxter*'s Life,[12] and the like.

I think in Justice, no Man has a Right to make any Abridgement of a Book, but the Proprietor of the Book; and I am sure no Man can be so well qualified for the doing it, as the Author, if alive, because no Man can be capable of knowing the true Sense of the Design, or of giving it a due Turn like him that compos'd it.

This is the first Sort of the Press-Piracy, the next is pirating Books in smaller Print, and meaner Paper, in order to sell them lower than the first Impression. Thus as soon as a Book is publish'd by the Author, a raskally Fellow buys it, and immediately falls to work upon it, and if it was a Book of a Crown, he will contract it so as to sell it for two Shillings, a Book of three Shillings for one Shilling, a Pamphlet of a Shilling for

2d. a Six-penny Book in a penny Sheet, and the like. This is down-right robbing on the High-way, or cutting a Purse, (were they not afraid of their Deserts) is a Ruin to Trade, a Discouragement to Learning, and the Shame of a well mannag'd Government.

The Law we are upon, effectually suppresses this most villainous Practice, for every Author being oblig'd to set his Name to the Book he writes, has, by this Law, an undoubted exclusive Right to the Property of it. The Clause in the Law is a Patent to the Author, and settles the Propriety of the Work wholly in himself, or in such to whom he shall assign it; and 'tis reasonable it should be so: For if an Author has not the right of a Book, after he has made it, and the benefit be not his own, and the Law will not protect him in that Benefit, 'twould be very hard the Law should pretend to punish him for it.

'Twould be unaccountably severe, to make a Man answerable for the Miscarriages of a thing which he shall not reap the benefit of if well perform'd; there is no Law so much wanting in the Nation, relating to Trade and Civil Property, as this, nor is there a greater Abuse in any Civil Employment, than the printing of other Mens Copies, every jot as unjust as lying with their Wives, and breaking-up their Houses.

This Grievance a Licenser will never remedy; nay these People who act them in secret, and without Principles, are out of the reach of a Licenser, for they value not the Law, are *unaccountable themselves*, and have their Hawkers and Mannagers under them.

But if an Author has a Right of Action given him by Law, not against him only who shall print his Copy, but against the Publisher of it also; and this Law being made full and express, the Evil will die, for no body will dare to sell the Book, when the villainous Pirate has finish'd the Impression.

It has been objected against such a Regulation of the Press, That it will fill the Town with scandalous Lampoons and *Pasquinadoes*,[13] which will be handed about in manuscript, and do as much harm as Printing. To this I must answer, A Restraint upon the Press will do so, and always did; and I appeal to any Man's Judgment, to shew me a time when ever the Town swarm'd with things of that Nature, as it did in King *Charles* the Second's Time, King *James*'s, and some part of King *William*'s, when the Press was under the Government of a Licenser, and therefore this Law can no way be more instrumental to it than that was, nor I think will not be so much.

I can see no further Objection against my Opinion, and shall be very willing to consider it when I meet with it; in the mean time, if any one can propose a better Method, more agreeable to the Justice of the Nation, and more effectual to all the Ends that are needful to be consider'd, I hope he will not be discourag'd by this Essay, from making the Proposal.

To the Honourable
the C—s of England
Assembled in P—t.
[1704]

TO THE HONOURABLE THE C—S OF ENGLAND ASSEMBLED IN P—T. THE HUMBLE PETITION AND REPRESENTATION OF THE TRUE LOYAL AND ALWAYS OBEDIENT CHURCH OF ENGLAND, RELATING TO THE BILL FOR RESTRAINING THE PRESS.

Humbly Praying and Representing,

THat whereas Divers Worthy M—s of this Honourable House, being sensible of the present Necessity, and great Advantages of a B— for Restraining the Licentiousness of the Press; particularly in the present Circumstances of the Church; and looking upon this as the Only Opportunity they have, or are like to have, of bringing the Church to Triumph over her Enemies. Have for these and divers other good Considerations brought in and presented to this Honourable House a Bill to restrain the Press, and to place the just Privilege of Judging what is fit to be Printed in the World, in the hands of the Church of *England* – And whereas this Bill, so much for our Advantage, has, to our great Sorrow of Heart, been now a long Time under your Honours Consideration, and our Hearts are fill'd with Grief, from the just Apprehensions we have least the said Bill, having been so long depending, should at last be dropt, and should not be brought to perfection during this Session of Parliament now drawing too near a conclusion.

In order therefore to Quicken your Honours in your Just Apprehensions of the Churches danger, and to make you more sensible of the great Reason there is for, and the High and Extraordinary need the CHURCH of *England* is in of this wholsome Law; we humbly crave leave to Represent to your Honours, our most Cogent Reasons why such a Bill is at present absolutely necessary for the Safety of the Church.

First, Because at present the Whigs and Moderate Church-men, *a worse sort of Enemies than the Fanaticks*, are continually Affronting us, and Bullying the CHURCH of *England* in their Pamphlets and Writings about Law, Liberty, Property and Conscience, things we find it absolutely necessary, our present Circumstances Considered, not to be so much concern'd about as we use to be, and which perhaps we may be oblig'd a little to entrench upon, and when your Honours for weighty Reasons find it necessary to Support the Church, tho' some few Incroachments are made on those Trifles call'd Liberty of Conscience, *&c.* it is absolutely necessary we should suppress the Clamours of the Party.

Secondly, Because the Press being under the Superintendency of a Loyal and True Church Licencer, we may with the greater freedom Write what we please without the hazard of being replyed to, and this is more particularly Necessary at this time for these following Reasons:

1st, To prevent the absolute Necessity of Answering Arguments by Fines *Ultra Tenementum*,[1] *Pillories*, *Railery* and the like, which are things make too much Noise.

2dly, Because we do find that these Damn'd Whigs are a little too hard for us, when we come to Down Right Arguments, Demonstration, *&c.*

3dly, To prevent our Designs of being Lampoon'd, and Expos'd by way of Irony *Shortest Ways*,[2] *Golden Ages*,[3] *Auctions of Books*,[4] &c.

Thirdly, Because Freedom of Speech ought not to be allow'd to any body except the Members of your Honourable House and *us of the Pulpit*: And since the just Law of speaking Treason was Unhappily Expir'd, 'tis absolutely necessary to lock up the Pen of the Party since we cannot otherwise stop their Mouths.

Fourthly, Because they Unhappily Write some Truths which it is not convenient the World should hear, at least till we have brought our Resolutions for their Destruction a little further on.

Fifthly, Because we cannot Answer them so well by Argument and Writing as we can by Effects, Management, Acts of Parliament, *&c.*

Sixthly, Because we may have the freedom under a Church Licenser to impose any thing upon the World, and to Forge as many Histories of *New Associations*[5] and the like, as we find convenient, we may then challenge them without Answers, and Defend such Occasional Bills[6] we find convenient without being bantered and laught at, and if they attempt to Print, we shall take care to smother the Impressions at the Printers, and fright the Authors from appearing.

Seventhly, As things are to go, 'tis absolutely necessary the World should be a little Imposed upon, and we must prevent too plain English, least it open their Eyes.

Having thus represented to your Honours the Reasons which make it necessary for the present Prosperity of the Church, that the Bill now depending in your House should be pass'd with all possible speed, We further Humbly Petition your Honours in your abundant Tenderness for the Poor CHURCH of *England*, compast about with *Dissenters, Phanaticks, and Shismaticks*, and betray'd by Whiggish Members and *Presbiterian* B—s,[7] that you would be pleased not[a] only to pass the said Bill, but so to furnish it with needful Clauses, that the Press may for the time to come be wholly in the Power of the Church, and that nothing be Printed and Published but what the Loyal Zealous Members of the Church may License and Approve, and to that end the Superintendency of the Press, and of all things belonging to Books and Letters may be in the Hands of the Church, that we may meet with no more Interruption in our Proceeding with all the Churches Enemies than *the Shortest Way*.

Further, we humbly Petition your Honours, that whereas 'tis the Duty of the Church and the Members thereof, to Instruct Mankind, and consequently 'tis rational they should judge what Persons are fit to be Entrusted with the Publick Instruction. We are therefore your Honours Humble Petitioners, that you would be pleas'd in your great Wisdom, to provide such a Clause in the said Bill, as may more fully provide for the Licensing such as keep Schools, and instruct Youth, that under the Favour and Protection of such a Bill we may effectually suppress all the Seminaries of Sedition in this Nation, as the most effectual and at present *the Shortest Way*, to prevent the Growth and Encrease of Schism and Faction, which too eminently prevails in this Kingdom by reason of the too many private Academys[8] set up, where the Youth are Debauchd from their Loyalty, and Instructed to Study the Ruin of our Holy Mother the CHURCH of *ENGLAND*: According to a Laudable Legend of such needful Truths, as were lately Wrote by the Reverend Dr. *Renegado Westly*,[9] which Book we are very much afraid will be Expos'd, before this Blessed Bill will be pass'd.

We also humbly pray your Honours, that the Licenser for the Press may not receive his Commission from the Crown, Her Majesty having lately left us in the Lurch, *as a Worthy Member has it*; and the uncertainty of Humane Affairs being such, with relation to Succession, that we fear may in process of time, deprive us of the Good and Pious purposes for which which wholesome Law is design'd.

Nor in the Hands of the most Reverend and Right Reverend the Bishops, because the present Lights and Fathers of the Church, to our great Affliction, being too much tainted and infected with Presbyterian, Factious, Moderate, low Church Principles; and thereby unfit to be Trusted with so Weighty and Extraordinary a Concern, we cannot think the Church safe under their Conduct.

But we humbly desire your Honours, either to cause such a Licenser to be Named and Commissioned by the Lower House of Convocation,[10] or by your Honours in Parliament, or by such other Body of the Pious and Learned Clergy, as shall from time to time seem to meet your Honours.

So shall the Mouth of Faction and Sedition be effectually stop'd, and your Petitioners be enabled to attest and defend the Doctrines and Practices of the Famous *High-Exalted* Church of *England*: So shall our dearly Beloved *Lesly*, alias *White*,[11] defend the present Government, tho' he never lov'd it well enough to Swear Allegiance to it. *Toland*[12] shall then be a safe Advocate for the Trinity, which he does not believe Dr. B—[13] shall advocate for the Queen, and perswade the World She may keep her Promise, and yet Dissolve the Toleration Act: Then we may depose our Kings and call in Forreign Forces, and yet defend our Non-Resisting Principles: *Sachaverel* may hoist his Bloody Flag[14] against the Dissenters, and not be Scandaliz'd for contriving the *Shortest Way*.

Your Honours will be no more Bully'd with Legion Papers,[15] Thirty Seven Articles *Kentish* Petitions,[16] Observators,[17] and the like; nor we, your Petitioners, be Insulted and Expos'd with *Shortest Ways*,[18] *Challenges to Peace*,[19] *Hymns*,[20] *Ballads*,[21] &c. To the Reproach of our Church and the discouragement of those True *Packingtonian*[22] Principles Publish'd to the World by the Learned and Reverend Mr. *Stubbs*,[23] Sir *H. M.*[24] Mr. *D.*[25] Mr. *S.*[26] and the rest of the Champions of the True Church of *England*, as by Law we would have it Established.

And your Petitioners (as in Duty bound) shall ever Plot and Pray, &c.

Giving Alms no Charity,

And Employing the

POOR

A Grievance to the

NATION,

Being an

ESSAY

Upon This

𝔊𝔯𝔢𝔞𝔱 ℚ𝔲𝔢𝔰𝔱𝔦𝔬𝔫,

Whether Work-houses, Corporations,[1] and Houses of Correction for Employing the Poor, as now practis'd in *England*; or Parish-Stocks,[2] as propos'd in a late Pamphlet,[3] Entituled, *A Bill for the better Relief, Imployment and Settlement of the Poor*, &c. Are not mischievous to the Nation, tending to the Destruction of our Trade, and to Encrease the Number and Misery of the Poor.

Addressed to the Parliament of England.

LONDON:
Printed, and Sold by the Booksellers of *London* and *Westminster*. MDCCIV.

TO THE KNIGHTS, CITIZENS AND BURGESSES IN PARLIAMENT ASSEMBLED.

Gentlemen,

HE that has Truth and Justice, and the Interest of *England* in his Design, can have nothing to fear from an *English* Parliament.

This makes the Author of these Sheets, however Despicable in himself, apply to this Honourable House, without any Apology for the Presumption.

Truth, *Gentlemen*, however meanly dress'd, and in whatsoever bad Company she happens to come, was always entertain'd at your Bar; and the Commons of *England* must cease to act like themselves, or which is worse, like their Ancestors, when they cease to entertain any Proposal, that offers it self at their Door, for the general Good and Advantage of the People they Represent.

I willingly grant, That 'tis a Crime in good Manners to interrupt your more weighty Councils, and disturb your Debates; with empty nauseous Trifles in Value, or mistaken Schemes, and whoever ventures to Address You, ought to be well assur'd he is in the right, and that the Matter suits the Intent of your meeting, *viz. To dispatch the weighty Affairs of the Kingdom.*

And as I have premis'd this, so I freely submit to any Censure this Honourable Assembly shall think I deserve, if I have broke in upon either of these Particulars.

I have but one Petition to make with respect to the Author, and that is, That no freedom of Expression, which the Arguments may oblige him to, may be constru'd as a want of Respect, and a breach of the due Deference every *English* Man owes to the representing Power of the Nation.

It would be hard, that while I am honestly offering to your Consideration something of Moment for the general Good, Prejudice should lay

Snares for the Author, and private Pique make him an Offender for a Word.

Without entring upon other Parts of my Character, 'tis enough to acquaint this Assembly, that I am an *English* Freeholder, and have by that a Title to be concern'd in the good of that Community of which I am an unworthy Member.

This Honourable House is the Representative of all the Freeholders of *England*; you are Assembl'd for their Good, you study their Interest, you possess their Hearts, and you hold the Strings of the general Purse.

To you they have Recourse for the Redress of all their Wrongs, and if at any time one of their Body can offer to your Assistance, any fair, legal, honest and rational Proposal for the publick Benefit, it was never known that such a Man was either rejected or discourag'd.

And on this Account I crave the Liberty to assure you, That the Author of this seeks no Reward; to him it shall always be Reward enough to have been capable of serving his native Country, and Honour enough to have offer'd something for the publick Good worthy of Consideration in your Honourable Assembly.

Pauper Ubique jacet,[4] said our famous Queen *Elizabeth*, when in her Progress thro' the Kingdom she saw the vast Throngs of the Poor, flocking to see and bless her; and the Thought put her Majesty upon a continu'd study how to recover her People from that Poverty, and make their Labour more profitable to themselves in Particular, and the Nation in General.

This was easie then to propose, for that many useful Manufactures were made in foreign Parts, which our People bought with *English* Money, and Imported for their use.

The Queen, who knew the Wealth and vast Numbers of People which the said Manufactures had brought to the neighbouring Countries then under the King of *Spain*, the *Dutch* being not yet Revolted,[5] never left off endeavouring what she happily brought to pass, *viz.* the transplanting into *England* those Springs of Riches and People.

She saw the *Flemings* prodigiously Numerous, their Cities stood thicker than her Peoples Villages in some parts; all sorts of useful Manufactures were found in their Towns, and all their People were rich and busie, no Beggars, no Idleness, and consequently no want was to be seen among them.

She saw the Fountain of all this Wealth and Workmanship, I mean the Wool, was in her own Hands, and *Flanders* became the Seat of all these Manufactures, not because it was naturally Richer and more Populous than other Countries, but because it lay near *England*, and the Staple[6] of the *English* Wool which was the Foundation of all their Wealth, was at *Antwerp* in the Heart of that Country.

From hence, it may be said of *Flanders*, it was not the Riches and the number of People brought the Manufactures into the *Low Countries*, but it was the Manufactures brought the People thither, and Multitudes of People make Trade, Trade makes Wealth, Wealth builds Cities, Cities Enrich the Land round them, Land Enrich'd rises in Value, and the Value of Lands Enriches the Government.

Many Projects were set on foot in *England* to Erect the Woollen Manufacturer here, and in some Places it had found Encouragement, before the Days of this Queen, especially as to making of Cloath, but Stuffs,[7] Bays,[8] Says,[9] Serges,[10] and such like Wares were yet wholly the Work of the *Flemings*.

At last an Opportunity offer'd perfectly unlook'd for, *viz.* The Persecution of the Protestants, and introducing the *Spanish* Inquisition into *Flanders*, with the Tyranny of the Duke *D'Alva*.[11]

It cannot be an ungrateful Observation, here to take notice how Tyranny and Persecution, the one an Oppression of Property, the other of Conscience, always Ruine Trade, Impoverish Nations, Depopulate Countries, Dethrone Princes, and Destroy Peace.

When an *English* Man reflects on it, he cannot without infinite Satisfaction look up to Heaven, and to this Honourable House, *that* as the spring, *this* as the Stream *from* and *by* which the Felicity of this Nation has obtain'd a Pitch of Glory, Superior to all the People in the World.

Your Councils especially, when blest from Heaven, *as now we trust they are*, with Principles of Unanimity and Concord, can never fail to make Trade Flourish, War Successful, Peace certain, Wealth flowing, Blessings probable, the Queen Glorious, and the People Happy.

Our unhappy Neighbours of the *Low Countries* were the very Reverse of what we *bless our selves for in You*.

Their Kings were Tyrants, their Governours Persecutors, their Armies Thieves and Blood-hounds.

Their People Divided, their Councils Confus'd, and their Miseries Innumerable.

D'Alva the *Spanish* Governor, Besieg'd their Cities, Decimated the Inhabitants, Murther'd their Nobility, Proscrib'd their Princes and Executed 18000 Men by the Hand of the Hang-man.

Conscience was trampl'd under foot, Religion and Reformation hunted like a Hare upon the Mountains, the Inquisition threatned, and Foreign Armies introduc'd.

Property fell a Sacrifice to Absolute Power, the Countrey was Ravag'd, the Towns Plunder'd, the Rich Confiscated, the Poor Starv'd, Trade Interrupted, and the 10th. Penny[12] demanded.

The Consequence of this was, *as in all Tyrannies and Persecutions it is,* the People fled and scatter'd themselves in their Neighbouring Countries, Trade languish'd, Manufactures went abroad, and never return'd, Confusion reign'd, and Poverty succeeded.

The Multitude that remain'd, push'd to all Extremities, were forc'd to obey the Voice of Nature, and in their own just Defence to take Arms against their Governours.

Destruction it self has its uses in the World, the Ashes of one City Rebuilds another, and God Almighty, who never acts in vain, brought the Wealth of *England,* and the Power of *Holland* into the World from the Ruine of the *Flemish Liberty.*

The *Dutch* in defence of their Liberty revolted, renounc'd their Tyrant Prince, and prosper'd by Heaven and the Assistance of *England,* erected the greatest Common-wealth in the World.

Innumerable Observations would flow from this part of the present Subject, but Brevity is my study; I am not teaching; for I know who I speak to, but relating and observing the Connexion of Causes, and the wonderous Births which *lay then* in the Womb of Providence, and are since come to life.

Particularly how Heaven directed the Oppression and Tyranny of the Poor should be the Wheel to turn over the great Machine of Trade from *Flanders* into *England.*

And how the Persecution and Cruelty of the *Spaniards* against Religion should be directed by the secret Over-ruling Hand, to be the Foundation of a People, and a Body that should in Ages then to come, be one of the chief Bulwarks of that very Liberty and Religion they sought to destroy.

To this general Ruine of Trade and Liberty, *England* made a Gain of what she never yet lost, and of what she has since encreas'd to an inconceivible Magnitude.

As *D'Alva* worried the poor *Flemings,* the Queen of *England* entertain'd them, cherish'd them, invited them, encourag'd them.

Thousands of innocent People fled from all Parts from the Fury of this Merciless Man, and as *England, to her Honour* has always been the

Sanctuary of her distress'd Neighbours, so now she was so to her special and particular Profit.

The Queen who saw the Opportunity put into her hands which she had so long wish'd for, not only receiv'd kindly the Exil'd *Flemings*, but invited over all that would come, promising them all possible Encouragement, Priviledges and Freedom of her Ports, and the like.

This brought over a vast multitude of *Flemings, Walloons,* and *Dutch*, who with their whole Families settled at *Norwich*, at *Ipswich, Colchester, Canterbury, Exeter,* and the like. From these came the *Walloon* Church at *Canterbury*, and the *Dutch* Churches *Norwich, Colchester* and *Yarmouth*; from hence came the True born *English* Families[13] at those Places with Foreign Names; as the *De Vinks* at *Norwich*, the *Rebows* at *Colchester*, the *Papilons*, &c. at *Canterbury*, Families to whom this Nation are much in debt for the first planting those Manufactures, from which we have since rais'd the greatest Trades in the World.

This wise Queen knew that number of Inhabitants are the Wealth and Strength of a Nation, she was far from that Opinion, we have of late shown too much of in complaining that Foreigners came to take the Bread out of our Mouths, and ill treating on that account the *French* Protestants who fled hither for Refuge in the late Persecution.[14]

Some have said that above 50,000 of them settled here, and would have made it a Grievance, tho' without doubt 'tis easie to make it appear that 500,000 more would be both useful and profitable to this Nation.

Upon the setling of these Forreigners, the Scale of Trade visibly turn'd both here and in *Flanders*.

The *Flemings* taught our Women and Children to Spin, the Youth to Weave, the Men entred the Loom to labour instead of going abroad to seek their Fortunes by the War, the several Trades of *Bayes* at *Colchester, Sayes* and *Perpets*,[15] at *Sudbury, Ipswich,* &c. Stuffs at *Norwich, Serges* at *Exeter, Silks* at *Canterbury,* and the like, began to flourish. All the Counties round felt the Profit, the Poor were set to Work, the Traders gain'd Wealth, and Multitudes of People flock'd to the several Parts where these Manufactures were erected for Employment, and the Growth of *England*, both in Trade, Wealth and People since that time, as it is well known to this Honourable House; so the Causes of it appear to be plainly the Introducing of these Manufactures, and nothing else.

Nor was the Gain made here by it more visible than the loss to the *Flemings*, from hence, and not as is vainly suggested from the building the *Dutch* Fort of *Lillo* on the *Scheld*, came the Decay of that flourishing

City of *Antwerp*. From hence it is plain the *Flemings*, an Industrious Nation, finding their Trade ruin'd at once, turn'd their Hands to other things, as making of *Lace, Linnen,* and the like, and the *Dutch* to the Sea Affairs and Fishing.

From hence they become *Poor*, thin of People, and *weak* in Trade, the Flux both of their Wealth and Trade, running wholly into *England*.

I humbly crave leave to say, this long Introduction shall not be thought useless, when I shall bring it home by the Process of these Papers to the Subject now in hand, *viz. The Providing for and Employing the Poor.*

Since the Times of *Queen Elizabeth* this Nation has gone on to a Prodigy of Trade, of which the Encrease of our Customs from 400,000 Crowns to two Millions of Pounds Sterling, *per Ann.* is a Demonstration beyond the Power of Argument; and that this whole Encrease depends upon, and is principally occasion'd by the encrease of our Manufacturers is so plain, I shall not take up any room here to make it out.

Having thus given an Account how we came to be a rich, flourishing and populous Nation, I crave leave as concisely as I can to examine how we came to be Poor again, if it must be granted that we are so.

By Poor here, I humbly desire to be understood, not that we are a poor Nation in general; I should undervalue the bounty of Heaven to *England*, and act with less Understanding than most Men are Masters of, if I should not own, that in general we are *as Rich a Nation* as any in the World; but by Poor I mean burthen'd with a crowd of clamouring, unimploy'd, unprovided for poor People, who make the Nation uneasie, burthen the Rich, clog our Parishes, and make themselves worthy of Laws, and peculiar Management to dispose of and direct them how these came to be thus is the Question.

And first I humbly crave leave to lay these Heads down as fundamental Maxims, which I am ready at any time to Defend and make out.

1. *There is in* England *more Labour than Hands to perform it, and consequently a want of People, not of Employment.*
2. *No Man in* England, *of sound Limbs and Senses, can be Poor meerly for want of Work.*
3. *All our Work-houses, Corporations*[16] *and Charities for employing the Poor, and setting them to Work, as now they are employ'd, or any Acts of Parliament to empower Overseers of Parishes, or Parishes themselves, to employ the Poor, except as shall be hereafter excepted, are, and will be publick Nusiances, Mischiefs to the Nation which serve to the Ruin of Families, and the Encrease of the Poor.*

4. *That 'tis a Regulation of the Poor that is wanted in* England, *not a setting them to Work.*

If after these things are made out, I am enquir'd of what this Regulation should be, I am no more at a loss to lay it down than I am to affirm what is above; and shall always be ready, when call'd to it, to make such a Proposal to this Honourable House, as with their Concurrence shall for ever put a stop to Poverty and Beggery, Parish Charges, Assessments[17] and the like, in this Nation.

If such offers as these shall be slighted and rejected, I have the Satisfaction of having discharg'd my Duty, and the Consequence must be, that complaining will be continued in our Streets.

'Tis my Misfortune, that while I study to make every Head so concise, as becomes me in things to be brought before so Honourable and August an Assembly, I am oblig'd to be short upon Heads that in their own Nature would very well admit of particular Volumes to explain them.

1. I affirm, *That in* England *there is more Labour than Hands to perform it.* This I prove,

1*st.* From the dearness of Wages, which in *England* out goes all Nations in the World; and I *know no greater Demonstration in Trade.* Wages, like Exchanges, Rise and Fall as the Remitters and Drawers, the Employers and the Work-men, Ballance one another.

The Employers are the Remitters, the Work-men are the Drawers, if there are more Employers than Work-men, the price of Wages must Rise, because the Employer wants that Work to be done more than the Poor Man wants to do it, if there are more Work-men than Employers the price of Labour falls, because the Poor Man wants his Wages more than the Employer wants to have his Business done.

Trade, like all Nature, most obsequiously obeys the great Law of Cause and Consequence; and this is the occasion why even all the greatest Articles of Trade follow, and as it were pay Homage to this seemingly Minute and Inconsiderable Thing, *The poor Man's Labour.*

I omit, with some pain, the many very useful Thoughts that occur on this Head, to preserve the Brevity I owe to the Dignity of that Assembly I am writing to. But I cannot but Note how from hence it appears, that the Glory, the Strength, the Riches, the Trade, and all that's valuable in a Nation, as to its Figure in the World, depends upon the Number of its People, be they never so mean or poor; the consumption of Manufactures encreases the Manufacturers; the number of Manufacturers encreases the Consumption; Provisions are consum'd to feed them, Land

Improv'd, and more Hands employ'd to furnish Provision: All the Wealth of the Nation, and all the Trade is produc'd by Numbers of People; but of this by the way.

The price of Wages not only determines the Difference between the Employer and the Work-man, but it rules the Rates of every Market. If Wages grows high, Provisions rise in Proportion, and I humbly conceive it to be a mistake in those People, who say Labour in such parts of *England* is cheap because Provisions are cheap, but 'tis plain, Provisions are cheap there because Labour is cheap, and Labour is cheaper in those Parts than in others; because being remoter from *London* there is not that extraordinary Disproportion between the Work and the Number of Hands; there are more Hands, and consequently Labour cheaper.

'Tis plain to any observing Eye, that there is an equal plenty of Provisions in several of our South and Western Counties, as in *Yorkshire*, and rather a greater, and I believe I could make it out, that a poor labouring Man may live as cheap in *Kent* or *Sussex* as in the Bishoprick of *Durham*; and yet in *Kent* a poor Man shall earn 7s. 10s. 9s. a Week, and in the North 4s. or perhaps less; the difference is plain in this, that in *Kent* there is a greater want of People, in Proportion to the Work there, than in the North.

And this on the other hand makes the People of our northen Countries spread themselves so much to the South, where Trade, War and the Sea carrying off so many, there is a greater want of Hands.

And yet 'tis plain there is Labour for the Hands which remain in the North, or else the Country would be depopulated, and the People come all away to the South to seek Work; and even in *Yorkshire*, where Labour is cheapest, the People can gain more by their Labour than in any of the Manufacturing Countries of *Germany*, *Italy* or *France*, and live much better.

If there was one poor Man in *England* more than there was Work to employ, either somebody else must stand still for him, or he must be starv'd; if another Man stands still for him he wants a days Work, and goes to seek it, and by consequence supplants another, and this a third, and this Contention brings it to this; no says the poor Man, *That is like to be put out of his Work*, rather than that Man shall come in I'll do it cheaper; nay, says the other, but I'll do it cheaper than you; and thus one poor Man wanting but a Days work would bring down the price of Labour in a whole Nation, for the Man cannot starve, and will work for any thing rather than want it.

It may be Objected here, This is contradicted by our Number of Beggars.

I am sorry to say I am oblig'd here to call begging an Employment, since 'tis plain, if there is more Work than Hands to perform it, no Man that has his *Limbs* and his *Senses* need to beg, and those that *have not* ought to be put into a Condition not to want it.

So that begging is a meer scandal in the General, *in the Able* 'tis a scandal upon their Industry, and *in the Impotent* 'tis a scandal upon the Country.

Nay, the begging, as now practic'd, is a scandal upon our Charity, and perhaps the foundation of all our present Grievance – How can it be possible that any Man or Woman, who being sound in Body and Mind, may as 'tis apparent they may, have Wages for their Work, should be so base, so meanly spirited, as to beg an Alms for God-sake – Truly the scandal lies on our Charity; and People have such a Notion in *England* of being pittiful and charitable, that they encourage Vagrants, and by a mistaken Zeal do more harm than good.

This is a large Scene, and much might be said upon it; I shall abridge it as much as possible – . The Poverty of *England* does not lye among the craving Beggars but among poor Families, where the Children are numerous, and where Death or Sickness has depriv'd them of the Labour of the Father; these are the Houses that the Sons and Daughters of Charity, if they would order it well, should seek out and relieve; an Alms ill directed may be Charity to the particular Person, but becomes an Injury to the Publick, and no Charity to the Nation. As for the craving Poor, I am perswaded I do them no wrong when I say, that if they were Incorporated they would be the richest Society in the Nation; and the reason why so many pretend to want Work is, that they can live so well with the pretence of wanting Work, they would be mad to leave it and Work in earnest; and I affirm of my own knowledge, when I have wanted a Man for labouring work, and offer'd 9s. *per* Week to strouling Fellows at my Door, they have frequently told me to my Face, they could get more a begging, and I once set a lusty Fellow in the Stocks for making the Experiment.

I shall, in its proper place, bring this to a Method of Tryal, since nothing but Demonstration will affect us, 'tis an easie matter to prevent begging in *England*, and yet to maintain all our Impotent Poor at far less charge to the Parishes than they now are oblig'd to be at.

When Queen *Elizabeth* had gain'd her Point as to Manufactories in *England*, she had fairly laid the Foundation, she thereby found out the way how every Family might live upon their own Labour, like a wise Princess she knew 'twould be hard to force People to Work when there was nothing for them to turn their Hands to; but assoon as she had brought the matter to bear, and there was Work for every body that had no mind to starve, then she apply'd her self to make Laws to oblige the People to do this Work, and to punish Vagrants, and make every one live by their own Labour; all her Successors followed this laudable Example, and from hence came all those Laws against sturdy Beggars,[18] Vagabonds, Stroulers, &c. which had they been severely put in Execution by our Magistrates, 'tis presum'd these Vagrant Poor had not so encreas'd upon us as they have.

And it seems strange to me, from what just Ground we proceed now upon other Methods, and fancy that 'tis now our Business to find them Work, and to Employ them rather than to oblige them to find themselves Work and go about it.

From this mistaken Notion come all our Work-houses and Corporations, and the same Error, with submission, I presume was the birth of this Bill now depending, which enables every Parish to erect the Woollen Manufacture within it self, for the employing their own Poor.

'Tis the mistake of this part of the Bill only which I am enquiring into, and which I endeavour to set in a true light.

In all the Parliaments since the Revolution, this Matter has been before them, and I am justified in this attempt by the House of Commons having frequently appointed Committees to receive Proposals upon this Head.

As my Proposal is General, I presume to offer it to the General Body of the House; if I am commanded to explain any part of it, I am ready to do any thing that may be serviceable to this great and noble Design.

As the former Houses of Commons gave all possible Encouragement to such as could offer, or but pretend to offer at this needful thing, so the imperfect Essays of several, whether for private or publick Benefit. I do not attempt to determine which have since been made, and which have obtain'd the Powers and Conditions they have desir'd, have by all their Effects demonstrated the weakness of their Design; and that they either understood not the Disease, or know not the proper Cure for it.

The Imperfection of all these Attempts is acknowledg'd, not only in the Preamble of this new Act of Parliament, but even in the thing, in that there is yet occasion for any new Law.

And having survey'd, not the necessity of a new Act, but the Contents of the Act which has been propos'd as a Remedy in this Case; I cannot but offer my Objections against the Sufficiency of the Proposal, and leave it to the Consideration of this Wise Assembly, and of the whole Nation.

I humbly hope the Learned Gentleman, under whose Direction this Law is now to proceed, and by whose Order it has been Printed,[19] will not think himself personally concern'd in this Case, his Endeavours to promote so good a Work, as the Relief, Employment, and Settlement of the Poor merit the Thanks and Acknowledgment of the whole Nation, and no Man shall be more ready to pay his share of that Debt to him than my self. But if his Scheme happen to be something superficial, if he comes in among the number of those who have not search'd this Wound to the bottom, if the Methods propos'd are not such as will either answer his own Designs or the Nations, I cannot think my self oblig'd to dispense with my Duty to the Publick Good, to preserve a Personal Value for his Judgment, tho' the Gentleman's Merit be extraordinary.

Wherefore, as in all the Schemes I have seen laid for the Poor, and in this Act now before your Honourable House; the general Thought of the Proposers runs upon the Employing the Poor by Work-houses, Corporations, Houses of Correction, and the like, and that I think it plain to be seen, that those Proposals come vastly short of the main Design. These Sheets are humbly laid before you, as well to make good what is alledg'd, *viz.* That all these Work-houses, *&c.* Tend to the Encrease, and not the Relief of the Poor, as to make an humble Tender of mean plain, but I hope, rational Proposals for the more effectual Cure of this grand Disease.

In order to proceed to this great Challenge, I humbly desire the Bills already pass'd may be review'd, the Practice of our Corporation Work-houses, and the Contents of this proposed Act examin'd.

In all these it will appear that the Method chiefly proposed for the Employment of our Poor, is by setting them to Work on the several Manufactures before mention'd; as *Spinning, Weaving,* and Manufacturing our *English Wool.*

All our Work-houses, lately Erected in *England,* are in general thus Employ'd, for which without enumerating Particulars, I humbly appeal to the Knowledge of the several Members of this Honourable House in their respective Towns where such Corporations have been erected.

In the present Act now preparing, as Printed by Direction of a Member of this Honourable House, it appears, *that in order to set the Poor to Work, it shall be Lawful for the Overseers*[20] *of* every Town, *or of one or more* Towns joyn'd together to *occupy any Trade, Mystery, &c. And raise Stocks*[21] *for the carrying them on for the setting the Poor at Work, and for the purchasing Wool, Iron, Hemp, Flax, Thread, or other Materials for that Purpose. Vide the Act Publish'd by Sir* Humphry Mackworth.

And that Charities given so and so, and not exceeding 200*l. per Annum* for this Purpose, shall be Incorporated of Course for these Ends.

In order now to come to the Case in hand, *it is necessary to premise*, that the thing now in debate is not the Poor of this or that particular Town. The House of Commons are acting like themselves, as they are the Representatives of all the Commons of *England*, 'tis the Care of all the Poor of *England* which lies before them, not of this or that particular Body of the Poor.

In proportion to this great Work, I am to be understood that these Work-houses, Houses of Correction, and Stocks to Employ the Poor may be granted to lessen the Poor in this or that particular part of *England*; and we are particularly told of that at *Bristol*, that it has been such a Terror to the Beggars that none of the stouling Crew will come near the City. But all this allow'd, in general, 'twill be felt in the main, and the end will be an Encrease of our Poor.

1. The Manufactures that these Gentlemen Employ the Poor upon, are all such as are before exercis'd in *England*.

2. They are all such as are manag'd to a full Extent, and the present Accidents of War and Forreign Interruption of Trade consider'd rather beyond the vent of them than under it.

Suppose now a Work-house for Employment of Poor Children, sets them to spinning of Worsted. – For every Skein of Worsted these Poor Children Spin, there must be a Skein the less Spun by some poor Family or Person that spun it before; suppose the Manufacture of making Bays to be erected in *Bishopsgate-street*, unless the Makers of these Bays can at the same time find out a Trade or Consumption for more Bays than were made before: For every piece of Bays so made in *London* there must be a Piece the less made at *Colchester*.

I humbly appeal to the Honourable House of Commons what this may be call'd, and with submission, I think it is nothing at all to Employing the Poor, since 'tis only the transposing the Manufacture from *Colchester* to *London*, and taking the Bread out of the Mouths of the Poor of *Essex* to put it into the Mouths of the Poor of *Middlesex*.

If these worthy Gentlemen, who show themselves so commendably forward to Relieve and Employ the Poor, will find out some new Trade, some new Market, where the Goods they make shall be sold, where none of the same Goods were sold before; if they will send them to any place where they shall not interfere with the rest of that Manufacture, or with some other made in *England*, then indeed they will do something worthy of themselves, and may employ the Poor to the same glorious Advantage as Queen *Elizabeth* did, to whom this Nation, as a trading Country, owes its peculiar Greatness.

If these Gentlemen could establish a Trade to *Muscovy* for *English* Serges, or obtain an Order from the *Czar*, that all his Subjects should wear Stockings who wore none before, every poor Child's Labour in Spining and Knitting those Stockings, and all the Wool in them would be clear gain to the Nation, and the general Stock would be improved by it, because all the growth of our Country, and all the Labour of a Person who was Idle before, is so much clear Gain to the General Stock.

If they will Employ the Poor in some Manufacture which was not made in *England* before, or not bought with some Manufacture made here before, then they offer at something extraordinary.

But to set Poor People at Work, on the same thing which other poor People were employ'd on before, and at the same time not encrease the Consumption, is giving to one what you take away from another; enriching one poor Man to starve another, putting a Vagabond into an honest Man's Employment, and putting his Diligence on the Tenters[22] to find out some other Work to maintain his Family.

As this is not at all profitable, so *with Submission for the Expression*, I cannot say 'tis honest, because 'tis transplanting and carrying the poor Peoples Lawful Employment from the Place where was their Lawful Settlement, and the hardship of this *our Law consider'd* is intolerable. For Example.

The Manufacture of making Bays is now Establish'd at *Colchester* in *Essex*, suppose it should be attempted to be Erected in *Middlesex*, as a certain Worthy and Wealthy Gentleman near *Hackney* once propos'd, it may be suppose'd if you will grant the Skill in Working the same, and the Wages the same, that they must be made cheaper in *Middlesex* than in *Essex*, and cheapness certainly will make the Merchant buy here rather than there, and so in time all the Bay making at *Colchester* Dyes, and the Staple for that Commodity is remov'd to *London*.

What must the Poor of *Colchester* do, there they have[a] a Parochial Settlement, those that have numerous Families cannot follow the Manufacture and come up to *London*, for our Parochial Laws Impower the Church wardens to refuse them a Settlement, so that they are confin'd to their own Countrey, and the Bread taken out of their Mouths, and all this to feed Vagabonds, and to set them to Work, who by their choice would be idle, and who merit the Correction of the Law.

There is another Grievance which I shall endeavour to touch at, which every Man that wishes well to the Poor does not foresee, and which, with humble Submission to the Gentlemen that contriv'd this Act, I see no notice taken of.

There are Arcanas[23] in Trade, which though they are the Natural Consequences of Time and casual Circumstances, are yet become now so Essential to the Publick Benefit, that to alter or disorder them would be an irreparable Damage to the Publick.

I shall explain my self as concisely as I can.

The Manufactures of *England* are happily settled in different Corners of the Kingdom, from whence they are mutually convey'd by a Circulation of Trade to *London* by Wholesale, like the Blood to the Heart, and from thence disperse in lesser quantities to the other parts of the Kingdom by Retail. For Example.

Serges are made at *Exeter, Taunton,* &c. Stuffs at *Norwich; Bays Sayes, Shaloons,*[24] &c. at *Colchester, Bocking, Sudbury,* and Parts adjacent, Fine Cloath in *Somerset, Wilts, Gloucester* and *Worcestershire,* Course Cloath in *Yorkshire, Kent, Surry,* &c. Druggets[25] at *Farnham, Newbury,* &c. All these send up the Gross of their Quantity to *London,* and receive each others Sorts in Retail for their own use again. *Norwich* Buys *Exeter* Serges, *Exeter* buys *Norwich* Stuffs, all at *London; Yorkshire* Buys Fine Cloths, and *Gloucester* Course, still at *London*; and the like, of a vast Variety of our Manufactures.

By this Exchange of Manufactures abundance of Trading Families are maintain'd by the Carriage and Re-carriage of Goods, vast number of Men and Cattle are employed, and numbers of Inholders, Victuallers, and their Dependencies subsisted.

And on this account I cannot but observe to your Honours, and 'tis well worth your Consideration, that the already Transposing a vast Woollen Manufacture from several Parts of *England* to *London,* is a manifest detriment to Trade in general, the several Woollen Goods now made in *Spittlefields,* where within this few Years were none at all made, has already visibly affected the several Parts, where they were before made, as *Norwich, Sudbury, Farnham,* and other Towns, many of whose Principal Tradesmen are now remov'd hither, employ their Stocks here, employ the Poor here, and leave the Poor of those Countries to shift for Work.

This Breach of the Circulation of Trade must necessarily Distemper the Body, and I crave leave to give an Example or two. I'll presume to give an Example in Trade, which perhaps the Gentlemen concern'd in this Bill may, without Reflection upon their knowledge, be ignorant of.

The City of *Norwich*, and parts adjacent, were for some Ages employ'd in the Manufactures of Stuffs and Stockings.

The Latter Trade, which was once considerable, is in a manner wholly transpos'd into *London*, by the vast quanties of worsted Hose Wove by the Frame,[26] which is a Trade within this 20 Years almost wholly new.

Now as the knitting Frame perform that in a Day which would otherwise employ a poor Woman eight or ten Days, by consequence a few Frames perform'd the Work of many Thousand poor People; and the Consumption being not increased, the Effect immediately appear'd; so many Stockings as were made in *London* so many the fewer were demanded from *Norwich*, till in a few Years the Manufacture there wholly sunk; the Masters there turn'd their hands to other Business; and whereas the Hose Trade from *Norfolk* once return'd at least 5000 *s. per* Week, and as some say twice that Sum, 'tis not now worth naming.

'Tis in fewer Years, and near our Memory, that of *Spittle-fields* Men have fallen into another branch of the *Norwich* Trade, *viz.* making of Stuffs, Drugets, *&c.*

If any Man say the People of *Norfolk* are yet full of Employ, and do not Work; and some have been so weak as to make that Reply, avoiding the many other Demonstrations which could be given, this is past answering, *viz.* That the Combers of Wool in *Norfolk* and *Suffolk*, who formerly had all, or ten Parts in eleven of their Yarn Manufactur'd in the Country, now comb their Wool indeed, and spin the Yarn in the Country, but send vast Quantities of it to *London* to be woven; will any Man question whether this be not a Loss to *Norwich*; Can there be as many Weavers as before? And are there not abundance of Work-men and Masters too remov'd to *London*?

If it be so at *Norwich*, *Canterbury* is yet more a melancholy Instance of it, where the Houses stand empty, and the People go off, and the Trade dye, because the Weavers are follow'd the Manufacture to *London*; and whereas there was within few Years 200 broad Looms at Work, I am well assur'd there are not 50 now Employ'd in that City.

These are the Effects of transposing Manufactures, and interrupting the Circulation of Trade.

All Methods to bring our Trade to be manag'd by fewer hands than it was before, are in themselves pernicious to *England* in general, as it lessens the Employment of the Poor, unhinges their Hands from the Labour, and tends to bring our Hands to be superior to our Employ, which as yet it is not.

In *Dorsetshire* and *Somersetshire* there always has been a very considerable Manufacture for Stockings, at *Colchester* and *Sudbury* for Bayes,

Sayes, &c. most of the Wool these Countries use is bought at *London* and carried down into those Counties, and then the Goods being Manufactur'd are brought back to *London* by Market; upon transposing the Manufacture as before, all the poor People and all the Cattel who hitherto were Employ'd in that *Voiture*,[27] are immediately disbanded by their Country, the Inkeepers on the Roads must Decay, so much Land lye for other uses, as the Cattle Employ'd, Houses and Tenement on the Roads, and all their Dependencies sink in Value.

'Tis hard to calculate what a blow it would be to Trade in general, should every County but Manufacture all the several sorts of Goods they use, it would throw our Inland Trade into strange Convulsions, which at present is perhaps, or has been, in the greatest Regularity of any in the World.

What strange Work must it then make when every Town shall have a Manufacture, and every Parish be a Ware-house; Trade will be burthen'd with Corporations,[28] which are generally equally destructive as Monopolies, and by this Method will easily be made so.

Parish Stocks, under the Direction of Justices of Peace, may soon come to set up petty Manufactures, and here shall all useful things be made, and all the poorer sort of People shall be aw'd or byass'd to Trade there only. Thus the Shop-keepers, who pay Taxes, and are the Support of our inland Circulation, will immediately be ruin'd, and thus we shall beggar the Nation to provide for the Poor.

As this will make every Parish a Market Town, and every Hospital a Store-house, so in *London*, and the adjacent Parts, to which vast quantities of the Woollen Manufacture will be thus transplanted thither, will in time too great and disproportion'd Numbers of the People assemble.

Tho' the settled Poor can't remove, yet single People will stroul about and follow the Manufacturer; and thus in time such vast numbers will be drawn about *London*, as may be inconvenient to the Government, and especially Depopulating to those Countries where the numbers of People, by reason of these Manufactures are very considerable.

An eminent Instance of this we have in the present Trade to *Muscovy*,[29] which however design'd for an Improvement to the *English* Nation, and boasted of as such, appears to be Converted into a Monopoly, and proves Injurious and Destructive to the Nation. The Persons concern'd removing and carrying out our People to teach that unpolish'd Nation the Improvements they are capable of.

If the bringing the *Flemings* to *England* brought with them their Manufacture and Trade, carrying our People abroad, especially to a Country where the People work for little or nothing, what may it not do towards Instructing that populous Nation in such Manufactures as may in time tend to the destruction of our Trade, or the reducing our Manufacture to an Abatement in Value, which will be felt at home by an abatement of Wages, and that in Provisions, and that in Rent of Land; and so the general Stock sinks of Course.

But as this is preparing, by eminent Hands, to be laid before this House as a Grievance meriting your Care and Concern, I omit insisting on it here.

And this removing of People is attended with many Inconveniences which are not easily perceived, as

1. The immediate fall of the Value of all Lands in those Countries where the Manufactures were before; for as the numbers of People, by the Consumption of Provisions, must where ever they encrease make Rents rise, and Lands valuable; so those People removing, tho' the Provisions would, if possible, follow them, yet the Price of them must fall by all that Charge they are at for Carriage, and consequently Lands must fall in Proportion.

2. This Transplanting of Families, in time, would introduce great and new Alterations in the Countries they removed to, which as they would be to the Profit of some Places, would be to the Detriment of others, and can by no means be just any more than it is convenient; so no wise Government studies to put any Branch of their Country to any particular Disadvantages, tho' it may be found in the general Account in another Place.

If it be said here will be Manufactures in every Parish, and that will keep the People at home,

I humbly represent what strange Confusion and particular Detriment to the general Circulation of Trade *mention'd before* it must be, to have every Parish make its own Manufactures.

1. It will make our Towns and Counties independent of one another, and put a damp to Correspondence, which all will allow to be a great Motive of Trade in general.

2. It will fill us with various sorts and kinds of Manufactures, by which our stated sorts of Goods will in time dwindle away in Reputation, and Foreigners not know them one from another. Our several Manufactures are known by their respective Names; and our Serges, Bayes and other Goods, are bought abroad by the Character and Reputation of the Places where they are made; when there shall come new and unheard of Kinds to Market, some better, some worse, as to besure new Undertakers will vary in kinds, the Dignity and Reputation of the *English* Goods abroad

will be lost, and so many Confusions in Trade must follow, as are too many to repeat.

3. Either our Parish-stock must sell by Wholesale or by Retail, or both; If the first, 'tis doubted they will make sorry work of it, and having other Business of their own make but poor Merchants; if by Retail, then they turn Pedlars, will be a publick nuisance to Trade; and at last quite ruin it.

4. This will ruin all the Carriers in *England*, the Wool will be all Manufactured where it is sheer'd, every body will make their own Cloaths, and the Trade which now lives by running thro' a multitude of Hands, will go then through so few, that thousands of Families will want Employment, and this is the only way to reduce us to the Condition spoken of, to have more Hands than Work.

'Tis the excellence of our *English* Manufacture, that it is so planted as to go thro' as many Hands as 'tis possible; he that contrives to have it go thro' fewer, ought at the same time to provide Work for the rest – As it is it Employs a great multitude of People, and can employ more; but if a considerable number of these People be unhing'd from their Employment, it cannot but be detrimental to the whole.

When I say we could employ more People in *England*, I do not mean that we cannot do our Work with those we have, but I mean thus:

First, It should be more People brought over from foreign Parts. I do not mean that those we have should be taken from all common Employments and put to our Manufacture; we may unequally dispose of our Hands, and so have too many for some Works, and too few for others; and 'tis plain that in some parts of *England* it is so, what else can be the reason, why in our Southern Parts of *England*, *Kent* in particular, borrows 20,000 People of other Counties to get in her Harvest.

But if more Forreigners came among us, if it were 2 Millions it could do us no harm, because they would consume our Provisions, and we have Land enough to produce much more than we do, and they would consume our Manufactures, and we have Wool enough for any Quantity.

I think therefore, with submission, to erect Manufactures in every Town to transpose the Manufactures from the settled places into private Parishes and Corporations, to parcel out our Trade to every Door, it must be ruinous to the Manufacturers themselves, will turn thousands of Families out of their Employments, and take the Bread out of the Mouths of diligent and industrious Families to feed Vagrants, Thieves and Beggars, who ought much rather to be compell'd, by Legal Methods, to seek that Work which it is plain is to be had; and thus this Act will instead of settling and relieving the Poor, encrease their Number, and starve the best of them.

It remains now, according to my first Proposal Page [174] to consider from whence proceeds the Poverty of our People, what Accident, what Decay of Trade, what want of Employment, what strange Revolution of Circumstances makes our People Poor, and consequently Burthensom, and our Laws Deficient, so as to make more and other Laws Requisite, and the Nation concerned to apply a Remedy to this growing Disease. I Answer.

1. Not for want of Work; and besides what has been said on that Head, I humbly desire these two things may be consider'd.

First, 'Tis apparent, That if one Man, Woman, or Child, can by his, or her Labour, earn more Money than will subsist one body, there must consequently be no want of Work, since any Man would Work for just as much as would supply himself rather than starve – What a vast difference then must there be between the Work and the Work-men, when 'tis now known that in *Spittle-fields*, and other adjacent parts of the City, there is nothing more frequent than for a journey-man Weaver, of many sorts, to gain from 15 *s.* to 30 *s. per* Week Wages, and I appeal to the Silk Throwsters,[30] whether they do not give 8 *s.* 9 *s.* and 10 *s. per* Week to blind Men and Cripples, to turn Wheels, and do the meanest and most ordinary Works.

Cur Moriatur Homo,[31] *&c.*

Why are the Families of these Men starv'd, and their Children in Work-houses, and brought up by Charity: I am ready to produce to this Honourable House the Man who for several Years has gain'd of me by his handy Labour at the mean scoundrel Employment of Tile making[32] from 16 *s.* to 20 *s. per* Week Wages, and all that time would hardly have a pair of Shoes to his Feet, or Cloaths to cover his Nakedness, and had his Wife and Children kept by the Parish.

The meanest Labours in this Nation afford the Work-men sufficient to provide for himself and his Family, and that could never be if there was a want of Work.

2. I humbly desire this Honourable House to consider the present Difficulty of Raising Soldiers in this Kingdom; the vast Charge the Kingdom is at to the Officers to procure Men; the many little and *not over honest Methods* made use of to bring them into the Service, the Laws made to compel them; Why are Goals rumag'd for Malefactors; and the Mint and Prisons for Debtors, the War is an Employment of Honour

and suffers from scandal in having Men taken from the Gallows, and immediately from Villains and House-breakers made Gentlemen Soldiers. If Men wanted Employment, and consequently Bread, this could never be, any Man would carry a Musquet rather than starve, and wear the Queen's Cloth, or any Bodies Cloth, rather than go Naked, and live in Rags and want; 'tis plain the Nation is full of People, and 'tis as plain our People have no particular aversion to the War, but they are not poor enough to go abroad; 'tis Poverty makes Men Soldiers, and drives crowds into the Armies, and the Difficulties to get *English*-men to List[33] is, because they live in Plenty and Ease, and he that can earn 20 *s. per* Week at an easie, steady Employment, must be Drunk or Mad when he Lists for a Soldier, to be knock'd o' th' Head for 3 *s. 6 d. per* Week; but if there was no Work to be had, if the Poor wanted Employment, if they had not Bread to eat, nor knew not how to earn it, thousands of young lusty Fellows would fly to the Pike and Musquet, and choose to dye like Men in the Face of the Enemy, rather than lye at home, starve, perish in Poverty and Distress.

From all these Particulars, and innumerable unhappy Instances which might be given, 'tis plain, the Poverty of our People which is so burthensome, and increases upon us so much, does not arise from want of proper Employments, and for want of Work, or Employers, and consequently,

Work-houses, Corporations, Parish-stocks, and the like, to set them to Work, as they are Pernicious to Trade, Injurious and Impoverishing to those already employ'd, so they are needless, and will come short of the End propos'd.

The Poverty and Exigence of the Poor in *England*, is plainly deriv'd from one of these two particular Causes,

Casualty or *Crime*.

By Casualty, I mean Sickness of Families, loss of Limbs or Sight, and any, either Natural or Accidental Impotence as to Labour.

These as Infirmities meerly Providential are not at all concern'd in this Debate; ever were, will, and ought to be the Charge and Care of the Respective Parishes where such unhappy People chance to live, nor is there any want of new Laws to make Provision for them, our Ancestors having been always careful to do it.

The Crimes of our People, and from whence their Poverty derives, as the visible and direct Fountains are,

1. Luxury.
2. Sloath.
3. Pride.

Good Husbandry is no *English* Vertue, it may have been brought over, and in some Places where it has been planted it has thriven well enough, but 'tis a Forreign Species, it neither loves, nor is belov'd by an *English-man*; and 'tis observ'd, nothing is so universally hated, nothing treated with such a general Contempt as a Rich Covetous Man, tho' he does no Man any Wrong, only saves his own, every Man will have an ill word for him, if a Misfortune happens to him, hang him as covetous old Rogue, 'tis no Matter, he's Rich enough, nay when a certain great Man's House was on Fire, I have heard the People say one to another, let it burn and 'twill, he's a covetous old miserly Dog, I won't trouble my head to help him, he'd be hang'd before he'd give us a bit of Bread if we wanted it.

Tho' this be a Fault, yet I observe from it something of the natural Temper and Genius of the Nation, generally speaking, they cannot save their Money.

'Tis generally said the *English* get Estates, and the *Dutch* save them; and this Observation I have made between Forreigners and *English-men*, that where an *English-man* earns 20 s. *per* Week, and *but just lives*, as we call it, a *Dutch-man* grows Rich, and leaves his Children in very good Condition; where an *English* labouring Man with his 9 s. *per* Week lives wretchedly and poor, a *Dutch-man* with that Wages will live very tolerably well, keep the Wolf from the Door, and have every thing handsome about him. In short, he will be Rich with the same Gain as makes the *English-man* poor, he'll thrive when the other goes in Rags, and he'll live when the other starves, or goes a begging.

The Reason is plain, a Man with good Husbandry, and Thought in his Head, brings home his Earnings honestly to his Family, commits it to the Management of his Wife, or otherwise disposes it for proper Subsistance, and this Man with mean Gains lives comfortably, and brings up a Family, when a single Man getting the same Wages, Drinks it away at the Ale-house, thinks not of to morrow, layes up nothing for Sickness, Age, or Disaster, and when any of these happen he's starved, and a Beggar.

This is so apparent in every place, that I think it needs no Explication; that *English* Labouring People eat and drink, but especially the latter three times as much in value as any sort of Forreigners of the same Dimensions in the World.

I am not Writing this as a Satyr on our People, 'tis a sad Truth, and Worthy the Debate and Application of the Nations Physicians Assembled in Parliament; the profuse Extravagant Humour of our poor People in eating and drinking, keeps them low, causes their Children to be left naked and starving, to the care of the Parishes, whenever either Sickness or Disaster befalls the Parent.

The next Article is their *Sloath*.

We are the most *Lazy Diligent* Nation in the World, vast Trade, Rich Manufactures, mighty Wealth, universal Correspondence and happy Success has been constant Companions of *England*, and given us the Title of an Industrious people, and so in general we are.

But there is a general Taint of Slothfulness upon our Poor, there's nothing more frequent, than for an *English-man* to Work till he has got his Pocket full of Money, and then go and be idle, *or perhaps drunk*, till 'tis all gone, and perhaps himself in Debt; and ask him in his Cups what he intends, he'll tell you honestly, he'll drink as long as it lasts, and then go to work for more.

I humbly suggest this Distemper's so General, so Epidemick, and so deep Rooted in the Nature and Genius of the *English*, that I much doubt it's being easily redress'd, and question whether it be possible to reach it by an Act of Parliament.

This is the Ruine of our Poor, the *Wife mourns*, the Children *starves*, the Husband *has Work before him*, but lies at the Ale-house, or otherwise *idles away* his time, and won't Work.

'Tis the Men that *won't work*, not the Men that *can get no work*, which makes the numbers of our Poor; all the Work-houses in *England*, all the Overseers setting up Stocks and Manufactures won't reach this Case; and I humbly presume to say, if these two Articles are remov'd, there will be no need of the other.

I make no Difficulty to promise on a short Summons, to produce above a Thousand Families in *England*, within my particular knowledge, who go in Rags, and their Children wanting Bread, whose Fathers can earn their 15 to 25 *s. per* Week, but will not work, who may have Work enough, but are too idle to seek after it, and hardly vouchsafe to earn any thing more than bare Subsistance, and Spending Money for themselves.

I can give an incredible number of Examples in my own Knowledge among our Labouring Poor. I once paid 6 or 7 Men together on a *Saturday* Night, the least 10 *s.* and some 30 *s.* for Work, and have seen them go with it directly to the Ale-house, lie there till *Monday*, spend it every Penny, and run in Debt to boot, and not give a Farthing of it to their Families, tho' all of them had Wives and Children.

From hence comes Poverty, Parish Charges, and Beggary, if ever one of these Wretches falls sick, all they would ask was a Pass to the Parish they liv'd at, and the Wife and Children to the Door a Begging.

If this Honourable House can find out a Remedy for this part of the Mischief; if such Acts of Parliament may be made as may effectually cure the Sloth and Luxury of our Poor, that shall make Drunkards take care of Wife and Children; Spendthrifts, lay up for a *wet Day*; Idle, Lazy Fellows Diligent; and Thoughtless Sottish Men, Careful and Provident.

If this can be done, I presume to say there will be no need of transposing and confounding our Manufactures, and the Circulation of our Trade; they will soon find work enough, and there will soon be less Poverty among us, and if this cannot be done, setting them to work upon Woolen Manufactures, and thereby encroaching upon those that now work at them, will but ruine our Trade, and consequently increase the number of the Poor.

I do not presume to offer the Schemes I have now drawn of Methods for the bringing much of this to pass, because I shall not presume to lead a Body so August, so Wise, and so Capable as this Honourable Assembly.

I humbly submit what is here offered, as Reasons to prove the Attempt now making insufficient; and doubt not but in your Great Wisdom, you will find out Ways and Means to set this Matter in a clearer Light, and on a right Foot.

And if this obtains on the House to examine farther into this Matter, the Author humbly recommends it to their Consideration to accept, *in behalf of all the Poor of this Nation*, a Clause in the room of this objected against, which shall answer the End without this terrible Ruin to our Trade and People.

REMARKS

ON THE

BILL

To Prevent FRAUDS

Committed by

BANKRUPTS.

WITH

Observations on the Effect it may have
upon TRADE.

LONDON:
Printed in the Year 1706.

REMARKS ON THE BILL
TO PREVENT FRAUDS COMMITTED
BY BANKRUPTS, &c.

BEFORE I come to the more immediate Subject of this Book, *viz.* the Bankrupts Bill, it cannot be amiss to enter a little into the History of its Introduction, Proposing, and Passing in the Parliament; in which, if I have had any Share, I am very willing to leave the World to censure me, as the Effects of this Bill are or are not of general Good to the Trade of *England*, and, in short, to the whole Nation.

I need not remind the Reader of the unhappy Circumstances of Trade in general, occasion'd by a long War,[1] great Losses at Sea, and a general Stop upon the *Spanish* Trade.

Nor was our Loss at Sea singly occasion'd by the War, though on that Score Trade had felt several very severe Shocks, particularly in two *Barbadoes* Fleets, one East Country Fleet, and a Multitude of other Ships which fell into the Enemies Hands; but, as if Heaven had particularly stretcht out its Hand to touch us in the most sensible Article, our Trade, has happen'd unusual Tempests which made strange Havock among our Shipping, and that more than any former History can remind us of in so short a time.

Particularly the Great Storm,[2] on the 27th of *Nov.* 1703. in which an innumerable Number of our Ships perished; and the Loss among the Merchants was incredible.

The very same time Twelve month, we had so many Storms, tho' less severe, that Abundance of Ships were cast away on every Coast of *England*, but particularly on the North.

In *August*, last Summer, a Tempest, equally violent as the Great Storm, sunk 14 *Barbadoes* Ships, just come into *Plymouth* Sound, with all their Loading, and most of their Men; and made a dreadful Havock at *Portsmouth*, and Isle of *Wight*.

In *Barbadoes*, a Hurricane destroy'd, I think, Two or Three and Twenty of our Merchants Ships.

The *Jamaica* Fleet felt the Force of it at Sea, and were terribly scattered; some came stragling home, some fell into the Enemies Hand, some perished at Sea, and the rest with their Convoy made for *New York*, and *New England*, to repair having suffered extraordinary Damage.

These, and a Multitude of Circumstances, too many to reckon up here, fell heavy upon Trade, which added to the general Obstruction of the *Spanish* Trade, and Deadness of our Manufactures, had among others this most necessary Consequence, that an unusual Number of Tradesmen, as well Merchants as others, sunk under the Calamity, and became Bankrupt.

Now, as in former times, the Liberties and Refuges Bankrupts had found became grievous and scandalous to the Nation, the Parliament at sundry times had made very severe Laws to prevent the Advantages which Insolvents took by those Retreats to injure and abuse their Creditors.

But when, as before, the Multitude of Insolvents increased to such a Degree, and many honest Families fell into the same Circumstances, the Severity of these Laws, design'd against Knaves, fell so severely on the miserable and unfortunate, tho' honest Traders, that it began to move the Nation to Compassion.

The priviledg'd Places being suppress'd, the Rules[3] of the *Fleet* and *Queen's-Bench* became so throng'd, and the Objects so melancholy, that some of the cruellest Creditors began to relent.

The *Escape Act*,[4] as it was call'd, had fill'd the Prisons with a great Number of Debtors; who being committed without Bail, had no Hopes of ever being delivered, but by the general Jayl-Delivery of the Grave.

Under this Circumstance Matters stood, when one Mr. *Pitkin*,[5] a Linnen-Draper, breaking for a very great Sum of Money, and that with all the dark Circumstances of a designed Fraud, Application was made to the Parliament by his Creditors for Relief against this notorious Cheat.

This produc'd the Form of a Bill in general against Bankrupts, but the Parliament being just coming to a Conclusion, and the Session at an end, there was no time to finish it as a Law; and so it was given over for that Year.

The Substance of this Act was very short, only to compel the Bankrupt to come in, and surrender himself, Goods, Books, and Effects to his Creditors; and to ascertain the Penalties and Punishments in Case he did not.

Upon the meeting of this present Parliament, this Bill was the first thing read in the House, and being committed to a Committee to consider of it, it lay before them a long time.

'Tis needless to recite here the Attempts made to put it forward, and by whom: The Bill was all this while a Provision only to punish; but as it seem'd a sufficient Foundation to answer both Debtor and Creditor, several Persons on both sides began to consider how to make it a compleat Act, and both to relieve the miserable but honest Debtor already fallen into Disaster, and secure Trade against the numerous Mischiefs of Bankrupts for the future.

And the Business now before me is, To propose how this Act may be rendered useful to these two happy Ends; and, if possible, to provide against and warn us of all the common Abuses of Knaves, which may pervert the End of this, and rob the publick of the Good that is so plainly design'd in it to both Parties.

But a little to persue the History of the Bill: It was a great Advantage to the good Design of making a compleat Act, that there happen'd an Absurdity in the first Contrivance, which, when it came to be examined into, made it almost impracticable, as it was; and that was this,

The Act was to compel Bankrupts to surrender themselves and Effects to the Commissioners. Now the Case was thus, When a Commission of Bankrupt is taken out against a Man, the Creditors are at Liberty to come in, or not come in; he that refuses to come in, has indeed no Share of the Bankrupt's Estate, but is left to get his Debt how he can, and has a Right of Action against the Debtor as before. – 'Tis true, if he recovers any thing, it shall be recovered again by the Commission; but he may lie still, and wait, and fall upon the poor Debtor at last.

Now to make the Debtor surrender all his Effects to the Commission, and yet leave him expos'd to all the Creditors that pleas'd to stand out, was first unjust to the Creditor, to share all among a few, and leave the rest without any thing, and barbarous to the Debtor, to force him to give up his whole Estate to a part of his Creditors, and leave him expos'd to the Mercy of the rest with nothing to pay.

From this Circumstance it seem'd so rational, either to force all the Creditors to come in, or to discharge the Debtor from them that stood out, that when such an Offer was made to the House, it was too reasonable to be opposed; and on the first Motion made in the House, it was ordered, *That the Committee be empower'd to receive a Clause for the Encouragement of such Bankrupts as shall voluntarily surrender their Effects to the use of their Creditors.*

This was the Birth of the following Law: For now it remain'd only to consider, what could encourage the Man to strip himself naked, and make an honest Surrender? – And the Answer was natural, *HIS LIBERTY*. What could you give him that would cost the Creditors less? What that he could value more? A Thousand Arguments offer'd themselves to usher this into the Bill, and little but mere Trifling was urg'd against it.

It was unanswerably argued to the faint Opposers of this Bill, That no Man could pay more than all; That to keep a Man in Prison, when you had stript him naked, was unchristian and unreasonable; That to make a Man surrender all he had, and not give him his Liberty, was to starve him, and put him to Death for Debt, which, however a Crime, was not yet made Fellony by the Law; That to force him to surrender all his Effects, and not give him leave to work for Bread, was to force Men upon Perjuries, and all sorts of Extremities, for fear of perishing; That this would be the way to make more Bankrupts, and Bankrupts more fraudulent; since Desperation would now run them upon all possible Methods to secure their Effects abroad, and afterwards themselves, and so Commissions would be able to reach nothing; That to make Men desperate, was the way to make them Knaves; and as there never was any Law but some way or other might be evaded or avoided, this would put Mens Inventions upon the rack for new Methods to defraud their Creditors; That this would farther encrease the Complaint already made of our Trades-men taking Sanctuary in foreign Countries, and robbing the Nation of its People, since now not a few only of our Bankrupts, but all Bankrupts must go beyond Sea, to avoid a Law, by the Severity of which they must be so hardly treated; and a general Depopulation must in time follow us, as far as extends to all our unfortunate Trades-men; That not our People only, but vast Riches would be thus carried out of the Nation, all our Bankrupts being thus forced to carry their Creditors Estates with them to subsist them, and enable them to trade and maintain their Families abroad; That this Law was unjust in its Nature, because 'twas all Penalty and no Reward, and had a Tendency to bring Men to a Necessity of Punishment, without any room to avoid it, since the Man was bound to Misery every way; he was to be hang'd if he did not surrender, and starv'd if he did.

There were Abundance more Arguments used of the like Nature, which were never yet answer'd, and which made the Act appear so Rational, so Necessary, and so Christian, that few People oppos'd it of any Consideration; and those that did were brought to this, that they could not object against the Bill, only they would not have had it pass'd till the next Session.

Against this was urged the present Necessity of the Bill, the Disasters of Trade having crowded us with Bankrupts, whom the Cruelty and Obstinacy of Creditors had driven to such Extremities, that they liv'd languishing in Prisons and priviledg'd Places, where they were forc'd to subsist, *and at an expensive Rate too*, upon the Estates of their Creditors, and upon those very Estate, which, upon the least reasonable Encouragement, they were willing to surrender: That this at last brought them to have nothing, either for themselves, or Creditors; and then, having no hope of Deliverance, they went abroad, and the Creditors lost all that they might have had.

And indeed these things began to be so scandalous to the whole Nation, that even the Creditors themselves seem'd eager for this Bill, and, I am forward to say, will be the greatest Gainers by it.

Nothing was more frequent than for a Bankrupt to make a good Offer, perhaps of 5 to 10 and 15 *s. per l.* to his Creditors, which all but Two or Three Men would be willing to accept:- And these Two or Three Men, either rashly, and inconsiderately obstinate, or having secret Expectations of more advantageous Offers, or from Malice, Revenge, or a hundred various Causes, absolutely reject all Composition: Now by the harden'd Cruelty of these Two or Three, the Man is kept in the Mint or Rules[6] in Misery and Distress, till in time a Wife and Family and other Circumstances waste the whole Sum; the rest of the Creditors lose the Offer they had made them, and the miserable Man has nothing at all to pay.

I could go on here to publish, *and did design it*, a melancholy Journal of the Barbarities and unheard of Cruelties of Creditors in many particular Instances, which Posterity would hardly believe could be practised in this Protestant Nation, where we pretend to generous Principles, and to practise Compassion to the miserable: I could give a dreadful List of the distresses of Families, who have really perish'd under these Barbarities; and whose Miseries his Heart must be harder than mine that can bear to relate.

I choose therefore to cover them with an universal Blank, that they may not rise up in Judgement, even in this World, against the Honour of the Protestant Religion, and the general Character of my Native Country: and since the Progress of it is stopt, I desire to have the Particulars forgotten, by which we were labouring in *England*, to recover the Name of the most barbarous Nation under the Sun.

Nor shall I record, to their Reproach, the Names and Endeavours of some Men to loose a Bill of such general Usefulness to the Nation, from their own Concern in the Cruelties abovesaid, and for the Sake of private Cases, where they had some Debtors under their Hands, who they were loth should escape them: I congratulate the poor Men that are thus delivered from the Power of unreasonable Creditors; and I congratulate those Creditors too, in their being restrain'd from being so wicked as they would be, and being forc'd to be moderate, though against their Wills.

These Men indeed made some Clamours at this Bill, upon the Lords ordering the Merchants to come up, and give their Opinions; but the Arguments were so weak, and the People appear'd so hot, and so visibly partial, that the Lords, convinc'd by the Reasonableness and Justice of the Bill, agreed to it with some Amendments; to which Amendments the Commons agreed; and the Bill obtain'd the Royal Assent the 19th of *March*, 1705.[7] The Substance of which is as follows.

THE Bill Enacts, That whosoever shall become Bankrupt after the 24th of June, *and shall not, within thirty Days after Notice given, that a Commission of Bankrupt is issued against them, surrender themselves to the Commissioners,* &c. *and submit to be examined upon Oath,* &c. *and conform to all the Statutes already in Force against Bankrupts, and discover[8] how, and in what manner, they have disposed of their Estates, and also deliver up to the said Commissioners all such Goods, Wares,* &c. *as at the time of such Examination is in their Custody,* &c. *wearing Apparel excepted; in Default, or wilful Omission thereof, upon lawful Conviction, shall suffer as a Felon.*

All Persons who shall surrender and conform as above shall be allowed 5 per Cent. *of the Net Produce of the Estate so surrendred, and shall be fully set free and discharged from all former Debts; and if arrested afterwards, shall be discharg'd on common Bail, and may plead in general the Cause of Action accrued before they became Bankrupt.*

The Allowance of 5 per Cent. *shall not exceed* 200 l. *in the whole, nor be allow'd at all, unless the Effects amount to* 8 s. *in the Pound; but the Commissioners to be left to Discretion what to allow.*

Persons who conceal any of the Bankrupts Effects, or receive any Trust for them, if within thirty Days after Notice given them, they do not discover them to the Commissioners, shall forfeit 100 l. *and double the Value concealed, but if they discover voluntarily, shall have* 3 per Cent. *for all that shall be recovered by such Discovery.*

Commissioners to have Power to state open Accompts, and shall accept the Ballance in full Payment.

No Bankrupt that has given above 100 l. *on the Marriage of any of his Children, unless they can prove upon Oath they were then worth more than the said* 100 l. *all their Debts paid; or that hath lost in one Day the Value of* 5 l. *or in the whole,* 100 l. *within a Year, before he became a Bankrupt, at any sort of Game or Play, shall have any Benefit by this Act.*

Former Bankrupts, against whom Commissions have been issued before the 10th *of* March, *have Liberty to come in till the* 24th *of* June; *and on the same Terms of Surrender shall have the Benefit of this Act.*

No Discovery upon Oath as above shall entitle the Bankrupt to the Benefit of this Act, unless the Commissioners or the major part of them certify to the Lord Chancellor or Keeper, &c. that the said Bankrupt has conform'd to this Act, and that there doth not appear any Reason to doubt the said Oath and Discovery; and unless the said Certificate shall be confirm'd by the said Lord Chancellor or Keeper, &c. or Two of the Judges, to whom such Certificate shall be referr'd, and the Creditors to be heard if they desire.

No Expence to be allowed to the Commissioners for Eating and Drinking; and if any Commissioner shall order any such Expence to be made, &c. to be for ever disabled to act as a Commissioner.

I confess I cannot but wonder why the Gentlemen that oppos'd this Law, *so universally desir'd*, should be so eager against it. I am loth to suggest *what some for want of Charity are of the Opinion is too true* that these Men, whether Drapers or others, taking large Credit themselves are loth to be depriv'd of the Opportunity when they shall find Occasion to break to their Advantage: I won't affirm, that these Gentlemen having always practised the scandalous Method of standing out in Compositions, to get collateral, clandestine Securities, are loth to venture standing upon even hand with other Men in Cases of Bankrupts; – Nor will I say they frequently set up young Men without Stocks, give them large Credits at first; under the Shadow of which Sham Beginnings they get into other Mens Debt, and pay these off with their Neighbours Estates: I won't say they all do, as one of them own'd to me he did, *viz.* stretch the Law to get a Man out of his House, and then swear him a Bankrupt, though he never had committed the least Act of Bankrupcy, but what they forc'd him to.

I won't say, (tho' I doubt 'tis too true) that they have by Cruelties and Oppressions, got already seperate Payments and private Considerations from Bankrupts, under their Power, and made them purchase their Favour at the Price of abusing the rest of their Creditors, which separate Sums *must now be refunded,* and the Knavery of it appear.

But this I will say, that unless these or such as these are the Reasons, 'tis a perfect Mystery to the World, why these Gentlemen, or any Man of Trade in *England*, should be against this Bill; and I wonder they have not attempted to show some better Reasons for it.

And this I must say, That this Act sets all Creditors on an equal foot with one another; and takes away all the Advantages obstinate designing Knaves had over honest Men: Creditors will now fare all alike; they will go Hand in Hand to make the best of the Bankrupt's Estate, and all have their Share in it.

I shall now enter a little into the probable Advantages of this Bill to the Publick, as well as in particular to both Creditor and Debtor; and then descend to the Methods proper to be taken on both Sides, in the Pursuit of this Act, to make it useful to the Publick: And, I doubt not, before I have done, the Gentlemen who seem'd to be against this Act will be very glad it has pass'd, and very sensible with how much mistaken Zeal they oppos'd their own Benefit.

I shall not in the Advantages of this Bill insist much upon the Debtor's Part; 'tis plain, his Advantage consists in obtaining his Liberty, to try his Fortune again in the World, and go to work for Bread, that he may support his Family, and live. – If he has a more than common Stock of Principle, he has room given him, if ever God in his Providence trusts him again with an Estate, he has an Opportunity put in his Hand to recover the Reputation of his Integrity, which having suffered some Scandal, he may restore by a gratuitous Payment of those Creditors, from whom he has been legally discharged. And I cannot quit this Head, without earnestly moving such Men to remember, that the Obligation of Conscience must remain as far as with corresponding Circumstances they can reasonably answer things, besides a Debt of Gratitude to such Creditors in particular, who being kind, tender, and forward to comply with reasonable Offers, have been untainted with the Cruelties that have helpt to ruin and destroy the Nation.

Again the Vicissitude of Fortunes must weigh with those Gentlemen, that have left in them any thing of a Sense of humane Misery; you Gentlemen that being delivered by this Act from the Cruelty and Fury of your Creditors. – Perhaps some of you may live to see those very Creditors reduc'd and Bankrupt, when you are free again, and flourishing.

Remember then the Condition you are in now, remember who sets up, and who pulls down, and double the Generosity of your Principle, by the timeing your Honesty to their Necessity; let your Compassion to their Misfortunes testify how well you merited Compassion in your own; and never reflect on their ill Treatment of you, if they are of the Number of your present Opposers, but heap Coles of Fire upon their Heads, by letting them see your Sence of Honour and Conscience has an absolute

Dominion over your Passions and Resentments; that you are Gentlemen enough to forget Injuries, and Christians enough to relieve your Enemies.

Perhaps some may think this Labour lost, but I cannot ask Pardon for the Digression; if it moves but one Man in Ten Thousand to act the generous and honest part, I am satisfy'd, and shall not think I have labour'd in vain.

But I must own, after all, the Advantages of this Bill seem to be vastly great and extensive, beyond what I can touch at; on the part of the Creditor, on the part of Trade in general, and on the part of the whole Nation.

The Effect it has on the present Distresses of Bankrupts already insolvent, which some merciful Men, Thanks be to their Ignorance, would have had omitted, are indeed considerable; and made so at this time by the unusual Multitude of such unhappy Cases, which now lie upon the Nation.

But these are Trifles to what's to come, and though I am very glad to see the Generality of the Trading part of the People are sensible of it; yet I cannot but a little enter into the Particulars of it, for the Sake of those who pretend to profess some Ignorance upon that Account.

1st. I think I may affirm, we shall not have so many Bankrupts as we had before, no not by a very great Number; and this I make plain from these Consequences.

1. That the Estates of Bankrupts being immediately surrendred, and fairly divided among the Creditors, the Fall of one Man will not have the same fatal Effect upon others, as it formerly had, when they lost Stock and Block; and when Dividends being postpon'd, and by the Knavery of Commissioners, perhaps wholly sunk, the Creditor has not been able to wait, but sinks under the Loss.

2. Obstinate Creditors can no longer make willing Creditors loose their Estates, and force the Debtor to live upon the Stock that should be divided among them; by which means Losses will not fall so heavy upon the Sufferer, which now is too often the Ruin of the Creditor as well as Debtor, and makes one follow the other to the End of the Chapter. But now all the vast Sums squander'd away in the Mint, Rules, Prisons, Commissions of Bankrupt, in Suits at Law, bribing of Officers, and Prison-keepers, and the like will be honestly shar'd among the Creditors, to help support them under the Loss, which of it self is often times Load enough, not to need the Addition of such destructive Articles.

3. The fraudulent Bankrupt has his way hedg'd up; he will now find it so difficult to break thro' the Bars and Bolts of the Law, that where

Ten ventur'd before to rob their Creditors, and contrive a Rupture, it is probable, and I hope rational to believe, scarce one will do it now; since whoever he is that will attempt to break by Design, has but two Doors open for him, *viz.* Perjury or Banishment. Now tho' there may be found a Villain so harden'd, such an Incendiary in Trade, that to amass an Estate will venture upon God and Man, and neither values Banishment out of the Kingdom of *England,* no nor out of the Kingdom of Heaven; that will forswear himself to stay, or purchase the Brand of Infamy, and be gone; yet all Men will allow, such Difficulties, such Hazards, and such Consequences attend both, that Men will not be so forward to venture.

He that will fly and abandon his Country and Friends, indeed has the safest Part, and may go, and even that way the Nation is well rid of him, and he can never come home again: He is banish'd for Life with that infamous Title of a common Thief; and if ever, *Pitkin* like, he should be recovered and brought back by Force, he goes directly to the Gallows, as he deserves.

He that will stay at home, mortgages Soul and Body to make a Reserve, if he has any separate Hopes, he must swear as thro' a 10 Inch Plank;[9] At the same time he is hedg'd about with Dangers; and if he has not laid his Matters very nicely together, if either for good Will or ill Will it should ever come out, he is gone, and he dyes without Benefit of Clergy: If it never comes out, he lives in a constant Dread of it, is a Slave to every one he has trusted; and besides the Trifle of the Perjury, and little regarded Terror of something hereafter, which sometime or other may come upon him hand in hand with Death, there is a settled Uneasiness least sometime or other he shall be betrayed even by himself.

Will any Man doubt whether fewer Men will venture than did before. 'Tis plain, Gentlemen, now, there will be nothing to be got by breaking, but what will be had at such a Price, that the Purchase is not worth the Repentance: No Man in his Wits will venture; he must be compleatly a Villain that will go, and he must have Walls of Brass about his Heart, and be fenc'd against all sorts of common Terrors, that dare stay here; That can look Justice and his Creditors in the Face with a Lye, and keep a steady Countenance with a Load of intollerable Guilt.

That perhaps some such Men may be found is not unlikely, but that equal Numbers of them to what were before should be seen, is highly improbable; and were there no other Advantage to Trade from this Bill, than the lessening the Numbers of Bankrupts, it is an Article worth all the rest.

2. In the next Place, there will be fewer Commissions of Bankrupt issued than usual; and, if I may guess right, I am of the Opinion not One to Five.

When Creditors know, that the Debtor, upon delivering his Effects upon Oath, shall obtain his Liberty, to what purpose should they take out a Commission? If the Debtor offers his Effects, and a voluntary Oath, and they see Reason to believe him sincere, what Occasion is there of the Commissioners?

When the Debtor knows, that upon a Commissions being taken out, he must come in, and surrender, upon Pain of Death, to what purpose should he decline making an Oath, and honestly coming in at first?

At the Beginning of a Disaster, when a Trades-man falls, he is generally tender, willing to be fair, open, and forward to make a free Offer; Retreats and Time, put Men upon Shiftings and Subterfuges, Mints, Rules, and the Society there, harden them in their Circumstances: This Act takes them into its Protection at first, upon stated Terms easy for the Creditor, and safe for the Debtor, and secures him from falling into Hands that may debauch his Principles, and prompt him to more Evil than he understood before: And, I believe, no body will dispute with me this Proposition, That were all Debtors complyed with in the first Offers to their Creditors, the Creditors would have been Gainers, and the Morals of the Debtors have been better preserv'd.

If then the Man in his first Sorrows is clos'd with his all, honestly tender'd, as frankly accepted, while the Man is sincere, and willing to be honest, all Men will allow there will be no need of Commissions; the Charges, Dilemma's, and long Croud of Inconveniences that attend Statutes, will be sav'd, and even this way this Act will be a publick Benefit to Trade.

This Bill is a kind of Truce between Debtor and Creditor; the Debtor is fallen into Decay, and coming to his Creditor, as his injur'd Friend, tells him, how willing he is to make him Satisfaction to the utmost of his Capacity, and to give up all he has in the World to that End; and the Creditor by this Act is oblig'd to accept it: The Creditor comes to the Debtor, and tells him, 'You have taken my Goods, and now you are not able to make me Satisfaction, pray be so just to me to make Satisfaction as far as you can, and give me up what you have, for 'tis all mine'; and by this Act he is bound to comply with him: And both these are consonant to the highest Reason, as well as agreeable to Humanity and Christian Dealing one with another.

3.[a] All the War of Revenge, all the Persecutions of Malice and Fury, ruining Families for the Sake of it, all cruel Imprisonments, murthering Warrants, perpetual Confinements, Perishings, and Starvings in Jayls and Rules, will be at an End by this Act.

The Cries of oppress'd Families, starving by the inexorable Cruelty of merciless Creditors, will be heard no more among us; Debtors will be no more made desperate by the Creditors refusing the sincerest Offers, and Families obliged to live and spend the Stocks of their Creditors.

Above all the Grievances, both real and pretended, of Mint, Rules, Prisoners at large, Protections, and all the long roll of Law Shams, equally mischievous both to Debtor and Creditor, will now be entirely sunk of Course: The Keepers of the Prisons Warden, Marshal, *&c.* will have no Men in their Hands, *as least upon the Article of Trade*, that either can ask them any Favour, or to whom they can give any Protection. Thirty Days the Mint may skreen a Bankrupt, but after that he shall be demanded as a Felon, and be fetch'd even from the Horns of the Altar.[10]

Pity and Compassion will now cease to be a Debt to Men in Misfortune, for who would be mov'd with the Miseries of those, who, if they will be honest, may be safe and refuse it.

Here will be no Shelterers in these Sanctuaries above the Law, this Act, with no other Coercive than that of Mens own Interest, will bring Men back; the true Sanctuary of an honest Man will be in the Arms of the Law: Instead of flying from the Law for fear of Punishment, he now will fly to the Law for Protection; instead of absconding and hiding himself from his Creditors, now he will run to seek them out, offer them all he has as their Due, and demand his Liberty as his Right, which they have no Power to abridge him of, or deny him.

It remains now to attempt two things; first, to anticipate those People, who, by the Craft and Subtilty of the times, always furnish themselves with Methods to evade the Laws.

2. To direct Men who honestly design to do what this Law obliges them to, in order both to the Satisfaction of their Creditors, and their own Liberty.

As to evading this Law, I must say this to it, that I believe no Law has been lately made less subject to the Chicane and Artifice of Men of Cunning than this; though it is not without its weak part neither: I shall endeavour to examine it strictly.

1st. This I pretend to affirm for the Satisfaction of the objecting Creditor, there is not one Flaw, not one loose Place, not one Inch of Room for the Debtor to creep out by, on your Side; if he is once a

Bankrupt, you have him fast, he must surrender himself, Books, Goods, and Effects, and swear they are all he has, you have left him nothing but the Cloths on his Back, not a Bed to lie on, not a Knife to cut his Bread with, nor a Penny to buy him any; and if he fails in the least Point, he lies at your Mercy for his Life.

I know 'tis objected, that the Felony part will never be put in Execution. – I would advise no Debtor to run the Risque, especially if any of those Gentlemen happen to be their Creditors, who have so vigorously appear'd against this Bill: I cannot question, but that Creditor, that by an Escape Warrant would put his Debtor in Prison for Life, would also take away his Life, if the Law furnish'd him with Power to do it.

If there is any weak Part in this Law, 'tis I think on the Debtor's side.

1. When a Man breaks, and has surrendred all he has in the World, it seems to leave him at the Mercy of the Commissioners, whether they will believe his Oath, and whether they will certify for him to my Lord Keeper, or no.

I confess, I press'd hard in Parliament for an Amendment to this Part, and was for adding these Words, '*Which Certificate the said Commissioners are hereby requir'd to make in — Days after the said Oath, or to shew Cause,*' &c. Which Amendment was so reasonable, that I doubt not it would have been agreed to by both Houses, had there been Time for it.

But I would have no Man discourag'd for want of this Clause, for the Nature of the thing, and the true Design of the Clause join together to shew the Commissioners their Duty in this Case; and as the Commissioners of Bankrupt are but the Lord Keeper's Servants and Deputies, he is their Judge; and it shall not be sufficient to a Commissioner to say to the Bankrupt, I will not certify that I do believe you, or I will not believe you, but he shall certify that he does, or does not, and upon his Refusal, my Lord Keeper[11] is too just not to oblige him to it.

And the Words of the Act explain this, which does not say, Unless the Commissioner shall certify that he does not doubt, but unless he shall certify that he *has no Reason to doubt;* so that the Liberty of the Bankrupt does not depend upon his *will* or *will not,* but upon the Reason he has for it; of which Reason I presume no Commissioner will pretend to say my Lord Keeper is not the Judge.

The Commissioner then is to certify, or he is not; if he certifies to the Release of the Debtor yet it is not decisive, for my Lord Keeper must confirm it, and the Creditor shall be heard; what is this but making my Lord Keeper judge of the Commissioners Certificate, in behalf of the Creditor? *On the other Hand,* if he[a] certify in the Negative, shall not the Lord Keeper be Judge of his Reasons, and the Debtor be heard, this would not be consonant to Reason or Justice at all.

Again, if the Lord Keeper shall be Judge what he shall certify, shall he not be Judge whether he ought to certify at all or no? – Our Laws are grounded upon Reason; and this would be to act contrary to Reason, and consequently against the Sense, Intent, and Meaning of the Act it self, and no Debtor need fear Relief against such an Oppression.

My Lord Chancellor, Lord Keeper, &c. has the absolute Power of naming the Commissioners to every Statute; he that should offer such an apparent Partiality, and refuse arbitrarily to certify to a Debtor's Discharge, or his Reasons against it, must have very mean Thoughts of my Lord Keeper's Justice, if ever he expected to be trusted in a Commission again, and have the Liberty of a Debtor, or the Estates of Creditors committed to him.

Nor can the Commissioners teaz the Debtor with that usual ruinous Cavil of the Creditors, we are not satisfied, and you must make a farther Discovery, we believe this is not all; for here the Surrender and Oath is actually finish'd, before the Certificate can be demanded: The Discovery is perfect, or it is not; if it is not perfect, the Commissioners[a] know it, or they do not; if they know it, the matter of a Certificate is at an End, the Man must be indicted for Perjury, and die as a Felon; if they do not know it, yet they must certify.

But they may have Grounds to suspect; these Suspicions then must be Legal Suspicions or Moral. A Legal Suspicion I do not understand, and cannot think any thing can raise justifiable Doubts in this Case, but a moral Assurance, deficient only in Form and literal Points; and of all these, my Lord Keeper shall without question be Judge.

Again, should Commissioners refuse or delay their Certificates in such Cases as these, it would quite invert the Design of this Act, which really is, to have Bankrupts surrender their Effects; and if once the Commissioners render the Debtor's Liberty precarious, we shall run back into worse Disasters than we were in before: Debtors will all fly from the Terror of the first part of the Act, being not secur'd of the Mercy of the second.

This would be, *indeed*, to make it a Law, *To banish Bankrupts, and their Effects, beyond Sea*, and not a Law to prevent their Frauds.

These Reasons, I hope, will be sufficient to move the Bankrupts to surrender without Fear, and to let the Commissioners know, that to refuse them Justice in this Case, will be but a vain Attempt to serve private Interests, and ruin the Design of the Act, in which perhaps they may find themselves overrul'd by the Lord Keeper, and used as they deserve.

I had some Thoughts here, to have answered the weak foolish Objections against this Act.

As that People will break the faster for it; that they will run on to the last Gasp, and being sure upon what foot they shall be accepted and discharg'd, will stand as long as they can; that when broke in any tolerable Circumstances, they were always well treated before, and the like.

That any Man will break *for the Sake of beginning again with* 5 per Cent. is too absurd to need an Answer; that Men will be encourag'd to run *to the last*, is just arguing against Fact; 'tis plain, this Act takes all possible Care to encourage them to surrender *in time*, by an Encouragement of 5 *per Cent. and none*, if they do not pay 8 *s*. per *l*. 'Tis as plain, Men held out to the last Gasp before, by the Terrors *of ill Usage* they expected if they fell. As to Peoples being always kind, when Debtors offer high, there are such innumerable Instances of the contrary that I refer them to Practice, particularly of a late Citizen and Draper, who perish'd in Jail, and, as some say, of meer want, under the Severity of a Statute, when one Ship brought home Effects for him but a few Days after his Death, which, added to what they had had before, was sufficient to pay all his Debts, and 5 *s*. per *l*. over; and yet they were so far from Compassion to him, that they would neither supply him with Food, or Physick, but let him dye under *their Commission Mercy*.

I could give innumerable Instances of the like Trade Lenity, sufficient to warn Debtors from throwing themselves upon the Mercy of their Creditors; but 'tis too obvious to want any such Illustration.

The remaining Question is, What must the Debtor do now, to obtain the Justice of this Law at the Hands of his Creditors?

The Answer to this is short and direct.

1st. Be very plain, genuine, and sincere on your part, and, making no Reserves or Hesitations, give such evident Demonstrations of an untainted Integrity, that no Creditor or Commissioner, without blushing, can have the least Jealousy, or the least Shadow of Suspicion, that the worst Enemy cannot have the Face to deny you the Certificate. *There is something in Truth*, something in *Native Honesty* so just, so genuine, so natural, and so free, that even Malice it self submits to the Power of it, and Envy is asham'd to appear against it.

2. If such a Behaviour gives you no Advantage with mercenary brib'd Commissioners, and it should be your Misfortune to meet with such, depend upon it, it will stand your Friend with my Lord Keeper; *the Power*

of Truth will prevail there, and Honesty will be too conspicuous not to be discern'd by a Judge so impartial, and so penetrating as his Lordship is allow'd to be, by Men of all Parties.

I know, 'tis recommended by some People to fly to politick Methods, and make, as they call it, sure Work with them; these are such as follow.

1. To those who are already Bankrupt, and who are left to their Liberty, whether they will come in or no; that they should state to the Creditors what they are able to surrender, and capitulate with them to consent to their Discharge, or not agree to the Surrender.

2. To those hereafter who are oblig'd to come in upon Pain of Death, to secure all their Effects possible at the first Rupture, and then make Conditions with the Commissioners and Creditors, during the Thirty Days, which Conditions if they will accept, they are discharg'd of course; if not, they have Thirty Days to prepare to be gone in.

As to these things, I confess, if Commissioners and Creditors appear refractory and scrupulous, and refuse Men their Liberty after fair Surrenders, it will drive People to such things, and more that I could mention; and 'tis a good Caution to Commissioners and Creditors, not to trapan their Debtors into Surrenders, and then trick them into Prisons, and refuse their Discharges; and for this end I name these things.

But that which clears up the thing to me, is, To what End should the Creditors or Commissioners deny the Man his Discharge? – If by delaying it, they could hope for farther Discovery, there was something to be said for it; but the Debtor is foreclosed in that by his Oath, and the Penalty of Felony on an imperfect Surrender.

If they can discover any thing he has reserv'd, though after the Discharge, he forfeits the Liberty they gave him, and his Life too. To what purpose then can they deny the Certificate? It must be meer naked Malice, and ungrounded Prejudice; and I believe most Commissioners will be not very forward to show themselves to my Lord Keeper in that, or to run the Risque of his Lordship's Censure.

They cannot put him off here with the Suggestion, that they do not believe him, and that he must think of a farther Discovery; for a farther Discovery is his Destruction, and lies upon them to find out, and detect him in, not for him to discover.

I cannot omit to examine here what may entitle the Bankrupt to the Honour of the Penalty of this Act, I mean the Gallows: And I think 'tis necessary to hint it, as well to warn him what will condemn him, that he may avoid it, as to prevent needless Terrors upon well meaning Men, and the needless Awe which some Creditors, I understand already, think to fix upon their Debtors, to fright them from taking the Benefit of this Act.

1. It is not every Error in Accompt, Mistake in casting up, wrong Ballance, or over or under Appraisement of things, will bring a Man in Danger of this Act; – but it is in Case of any *WILFUL OMISSION*; the Act is express in that, and no Advantage can be taken where the Omission does not appear wilful, and with Design to defraud the Creditors. – Nor, with Submission, is it the Business of the Debtor to State and Ballance his Accompts: 'Tis his Business to deliver up his Books just as they stood into the Commissioners Custody, and they to have the Stating and Ballancing the Accompts themselves; otherwise the Bankrupt Stating things in the Books may give him Opportunities to make Concealments which he could not do before.

2. Nor do any former Concealments from Creditors entitle a Bankrupt to the Penalties of this Act, provided they are fairly acknowledg'd, and laid open now; and therefore this Act seems to me exactly calculated to make Knaves honest Men, and to put an End to the former secret Clue of Frauds, which on both Sides, as well Creditor as Debtor, occasion'd many an honest Man to lose his Estate.

I do not wonder therefore to hear Men exclaim against this Act, who have got large Shares of the Estates of their Debtors in their Hands; and who by Cunning, by Force, and a hundred Pretences, have made private Bargains with Debtors, who sign Compositions for a Colour, and to draw other Men in, but get private Bonds, collateral Securities, and the like, from the poor Debtor, to bring them to that Compliance. This Act will be a Day of Judgment to such People, and honest Men will now see who rob'd them. These Men I take to be worse Cheats than the Bankrupt, because they drive a Man into a Crime, by such a Force which they know the Necessity of his Affairs will not suffer him to resist. They are Thieves of other Mens Estates; for though they seek but a just Debt, and that is their Excuse; yet they prompt the poor Man to pay them, what they know is none of his own.

The Debtor, 'tis true, is equally in Debt to every Creditor separately, and ought to pay them the whole; but after a Fraction, and he is unable to discharge the particular Obligation, he becomes then oblig'd to them all as a Body, and in Honesty must not pay one more in Proportion than another; he that does is not honest, and he that prompts him to do it to obtain any Relaxation, or Abatement of Prosecution, is a worse Knave than he; that Creditor that takes it wilfully, and in such a manner, is an accessary to one of the worst of Cheats. – And let him be who he will, he is a Destroyer of other Mens Property, and a Robber of his Neighbour.

That this Act will make Abundance of such Frauds as these publick, I make no doubt; and that the guilty must refund, I believe they do not doubt; and I question not, but this is the principal Reason, why some People fly out against the Act, and against me for my Share in it: – And let them rail, their Guilt makes them angry, but honest Men will share in the Restitution they must make, and that's my Satisfaction: I take them all to be politick Thieves, and rejoice to see them come off so well, and not fare like Thieves of less Guilt, that die only because they have the Misfortune to come within the Letter of the Law.

Let no Bankrupt therefore blush to own, what cruel Creditors have lain hard upon them to do, whom they have made wrong their other Creditors, to give them private Satisfaction. This Law is made not to punish you for the Concealment, but them for the Encroachment, and to bring them to Restitution, that honest Creditors may stand upon the same foot with them; and Compositions make a better Show than they used to do.

And I cannot omit here, what I purposely reserv'd to this Place, that this Act will produce this Benefit to Trade among the rest, that most Bankrupts will make better Compositions than before; and there are Abundance of Reasons to be given for it;

1. The tedious Expences of securing, and coming at the Effects will be shortned.
2. The Easiness of Concealments will be straightned, and the Occasion of them in part removed.
3. Clandestine, collateral, and separate Agreements with Creditors, and partial, private Payments be effectually destroyed.

All which will contribute to preserve the Estate of the Bankrupt, and consequently make the Dividend the larger.

That the Division of the Bankrupt's Estate will be sooner, is a thing I need not spend time about, because 'tis apparent it must come sooner into the Hands of the Commissioners; and the Bankrupt will be always assistant to the collecting and recovering it, which, as it has been, cannot often be had.

But to return to the Danger of the Debtor in his surrendering his Effects to his Creditor.

Every forgotten Debt, which may be really owing to the Bankrupt, and which in his Accompt he may not have given in, will not expose him to the Penalty of this Act: 'Tis true, if after such Surrender, the Bankrupt should go about to receive the Money, and apply it to his private Use, or should be put in mind of such a Debt owing to him, and should not immediately discover it, he would in either of those Cases incur the Penalty, and deservedly suffer it.

I would therefore, *in this Case*, to avoid the Censure and Misconstructions of Mankind, and to remove the Opportunity and Advantages any Man *might make* of other's Infirmity; I would, *I say*, recommend to every Bankrupt, that comes in, and claimes the Benefit of this Act, under the Account of his Affairs, which he gives, *and before his Oath*, to subscribe some short Provisio like this:

> I *A. B.* do farther declare, That if there be *any Error* in the said Accounts, or if any Debt due, or to grow due to me from any Person, *not incerted* in this Account, or any Goods or Effects of mine remaining in any Persons Hands, not mentioned and discovered *in this said Account*; it is not *wilfully* made, *omitted*, or *conceal'd*, and shall be faithfully discover'd, *rectify'd*, and *surrender'd*, as soon as it shall occur to my Knowledge and Remembrance.

I am not insensible, that Men whose Affairs are declining, are not always *the exactest People* in their Books: 'Tis a melancholy thing to be always ballancing *Accompts of Loss*; there is something unpleasant in the very Aspect of things, when *all goes to rack*; Omissions, Mistakes, and forgotten Articles are never so frequent, as when Men, knowing they are *playing a losing Game*, grow desperate, and care not which way things go; and in these Hurries it may happen, that an honest well-meaning Man may forget both a Debt or a Credit; *a great many* little Clauses may slip his Memory, and yet really design no wrong. *God forbid* Men should be hang'd *for forgetting*, while no Fraud is intended in the Design: Let such therefore not fear; the Law is not designed for a Trap to catch Men upon Advantages; Commissions[a] and Commissioners are not Ambuscades to surprise Men. – I would therefore have no Man fear, in such Cases, to make an honest Discovery, nor *to come again* if afterwards he finds any thing has slipt his Memory, and honestly discover and restore it: Such a Man will meet with Encouragement, not Reproach; and the Honesty of a second Discovery will be a Confirmation of the Sincerity of the First.

This Law is made to encourage *honest Men*, and to punish *Knaves*: 'Tis made to make *Knavish Debtors* deliver, and *Knavish Creditors* refund; and in this it seems to have in it all the parts of a perfect Law.

I have been told the lawyers are hard at work to find out *some Flaws* in this Act, and studying how they may still *hamper the Debtor* after he has done all the Act requires, and is actually discharged: – And really I would have those Gentlemen go on with their pious Endeavours; the Discovery of their Designs will only clear the way for the Parliament *another Sessions* to add such Clauses, as, *if need be*, shall farther explain and determine all the Doubts remaining, and bar all the Back-Doors and Outlets to Knavery on one Hand, and Cruelty on the other.

There may, *for ought I know*, be one publick Misfortune in this Bill; with which I shall close this Account, and, if possible, propose an equivalent.

The Mischief I speak of is, to the Manufacture of *Bumbing* and *Bullying*, which will be in great Danger of being lost, to the Ruin and impoverishing Abundance of poor industrious Families, who are now maintain'd by the laudable Employment of *Bayliffs*, Bayliffs *Followers*, *Sergeants*, *Yeomen*, *Marshal's-Men*, and all the worthy *et cetera's* of *Setters*,[12] *Spungers*, *Appraisers*,[13] *Brokers*, *Spunging Houses*,[14] private *Prisons*, and the like, who now live on the Life Blood of Trades-men, and help pull down those, that are falling fast enough of themselves.

Add to these, the Fall of Rents in the *Mint* and *Rules*, where Bills begin to be seen upon the Doors already, by the Multitude of People, who, Creditors *finding this Act will at last compel them to it*, begin to agree with, and voluntarily release; and where in time the like Desolation may be probable to ensue, as already has happen'd in *White-Fryers*.[15]

Jayls will also be Sharers in this Disaster, *Waiters*, *Tenders*, *Turnkeys*, &c. will lose their Fees; and those Nests of Cruelty and Misery be like a Cage without a Bird.

Multitudes of laborious People, call'd *Solicitors*, and *petty fogging Attorneys*, *Hackney-Bails*,[16] *Affidavit-Men*, and the like, may now be in Danger to lose their Employment, lose the Opportunity of taking large Pay for doing *no Business*, and charging double Fees for leaving People *worse that they find them*.

Now as this can no way be immediately prevented, I cannot think I am able to say any thing more to their Consolation than to propose *some Equivalent* to prevent the entire Ruin of so many *Diligent People*, and their *Dependents*.

And that this may be effectual, I shall divide it as I have done the People.

1. As to the Fraternity of the *Catchpoles*,[17] I propose to them honestly, and for the Good of their Country, to assemble together, and make a Detatchment of Ten Thousand able-body'd Men out of their Society, *a Number they can very well spare*, and offer their Service on board Her

Majesty's Fleet, to fight in Defence of the Kingdom, and make amends for the Damage they have done at Home, by ruining many Thousand honest Families they might have sav'd; and this 'tis plain, they may do, and yet leave enough of their Trade to execute all the necessary part of the Law.

2. As to the Attorneys, Sollicitors, &c. they may turn their Hands to the more Laudable Practice of picking Pockets, *according to the Letter of it*, and then in time may meet with the Reward of their *former Merit*, by a way they have often deserv'd it.

All the rest, applying to honest Livelihoods, may be pardon'd, and live to give God Thanks, with the rest of the Nation, for the Blessing of this Act of Parliament.

EVERY-BODY'S Business,

IS

NO-BODY'S Business;

OR,

Private Abuses, Publick Grievances:

EXEMPLIFIED

In the Pride, Insolence, and Exorbitant Wages of our WOMEN-SERVANTS, FOOTMEN, &c.

WITH

A PROPOSAL for amendment of the same; as also for clearing the Streets of those Vermin call'd SHOE-CLEANERS, and substituting in their stead many Thousands of Industrious Poor, now ready to starve. With divers other Hints, of great Use to the Publick.

Humbly submitted to the Consideration of our Legislature, and the careful perusal of all Masters and Mistresses of Families.

By ANDREW MORETON, *Esq;*

LONDON:
Sold by T. WARNER, *at the* Black Boy *in* Pater-Noster-Row;
A. DODD, *without* Temple Bar; *and* E. NUTT,
at the Royal-Exchange. 1725.
Price Six Pence.

The Preface

SINCE this little Book appear'd in print, it has had no less than three Answers,[1] *and fresh Attacks are daily expected from the Powers of* Grub-Street; *but should threescore Antagonists more arise (unless they say more to the purpose than the afore-mention'd) they shall not tempt me to reply.*

Nor shall I engage in a Paper-War, but leave my Book to answer for itself, having advanc'd nothing therein but evident Truths, and incontestable Matters of Fact.

The general Objection is against my Style; I do not set up for an Author, but write only to be understood, no matter how plain.

As my Intentions are good, so have they had the good Fortune to meet with Approbation from the sober and substantial Part of Mankind; as for the Vicious and Vagabond their Ill-will is my Ambition.

It is with uncommon Satisfaction I see the Magistracy begin to put the Laws against Vagabonds in force with the utmost Vigour, a great many of those Vermin, the Jappaners, having lately been taken up and sent to the several Work-Houses in and about this City; and indeed high time, for they grow every Day more and more pernicious.

My Project for putting Watermen under Commissioners, will I hope be put in practice, for it is scarce safe to go by Water unless you know your Man.

As for the Maid-Servants, if I undervalue my self to take notice of them, as they are pleas'd to say, it is because they over-value themselves so much they ought to be taken notice of.

This makes the guilty take my Subject by the wrong end, but any impartial Reader may find, I write not against Servants, but bad Servants; not against Wages, but exorbitant Wages, and am entirely of the Poet's Opinion.

> The Good should meet with Favour and Applause,
> The Wicked be restrain'd by wholsome Laws.[2]

The Reason why I did not publish this Book till the End of the last Sessions of Parliament, was because I did not care to interfere with more momentous Affairs; but leave it to the Consideration of that august Body during this Recess, against the next Sessions, when I shall exhibit another Complaint against a growing Abuse, for which I doubt not but to receive their Approbation, and the Thanks of all honest Men.

EVERY-BODY'S BUSINESS,
IS NO-BODY'S BUSINESS.

THIS is a Proverb so common in Every-body's Mouth, that I wonder No-body has yet thought it worth while to draw proper Inferences from it, and expose those little Abuses, which, tho' they seem trifling, and as it were scarce worth Consideration, yet by Insensible Degrees, they may become of injurious Consequences to the Publick; like some Diseases, whose first Symptoms are only trifling Disorders, yet by Continuance and Progression, their last Periods terminate in the Destruction of the whole Humane Fabrick.

In Contradiction therefore to this general Rule, and out of sincere Love and Well-meaning to the Publick, give me leave to enumerate the Abuses insensibly crept in among us, and the Inconveniences daily arising from the Insolence and Intrigues of our Servant Wenches, who, by their caballing together, have made their Party so considerable, that Every-body cries out against 'em; and yet, to verify the Proverb, No-body has thought of, or at least proposed a Remedy, altho' such an Undertaking (mean as it seems to be) I hope will one Day be thought worthy the Consideration of our King, Lords and Commons.

Women Servants are now so scarce, that from thirty and forty[a] Shillings a Year, their Wages[3] are increased of late to six, seven, and eight[b] Pounds *per Annum*, and upwards; insomuch, that an ordinary Tradesman cannot well keep one; but his Wife, who might be useful in his Shop, or Business, must do the Drudgery of Houshold Affairs: and all this, because our Servant Wenches are so puff'd up with Pride, now a Days, that they never think they go fine enough: It is a hard Matter now[c] to know the Mistress from the Maid by their Dress, nay very often the Maid shall be much the finer of the two. Our Woollen Manufacture suffers much by this, for nothing[d] but Silks and Sattins will go down with our Kitchen Wenches: to support which intollerable Pride, they[e] have insensibly raised their Wages to such a Heighth, as was never known in any Age or Nation but this.

Let us trace this from the beginning, and suppose a Person has a Servant Maid sent him out of the Country at fifty[a] Shillings, or three[b] Pounds a Year. The Girl has scarce been a Week, nay, a Day in her Service, but a Committee of Servant Wenches are appointed to examine her, who advise her to raise her Wages, or give warning; to encourage her to which, the Herb-Woman or Chandler-Woman,[4] or some other old Intelligencer, provides her a Place of four or five[c] Pounds a Year; this sets Madam cock-a-hoop, and she thinks of nothing now but Vails[5] and high Wages, and so gives warning from Place to Place, 'till she has got her Wages up to the tip-top.

Her Neat's Leathern[6] Shoes are now transform'd into lac'd Shoes with high Heels; her Yarn Stockings are turn'd into fine Worsted ones, with silk Clocks;[7] and her high Wooden Pattens[8] are kickt away for Leathern Clogs;[9] she must have a Hoop[10] too, as well as her Mistress; and her poor scanty Linsey-Woolsey[11] Petticoat is changed into a good Silk one, four or five[d] Yards wide at the least: Not to carry the Description farther, in short, plain Country-*Joan* is now turned into a fine *London*-Madam, can drink Tea, take Snuff, and carry her self as high as the best.

If she is tollerably handsome, and has any share of Cunning, the Apprentice or her Master's Son is entic'd away and ruin'd by her. Thus many good Families are impoverished and disgrac'd by these Pert Sluts, who, taking the Advantage of a Young Man's Simplicity and unruly Desires, draw many heedless Youths, nay, some of good Estates into their Snares; and of this we have but too many Instances.

Some more artful shall conceal their Condition, and palm themselves on Young Fellows for Gentlewomen, and great Fortunes; How many Families have been ruin'd by these Ladies? When the Father or Master of the Family, preferring the flirting Airs of a young prinkt[e] up Strumpet, to the artless sincerity of a plain, grave, and good Wife, has given his Desires a-loose, and destroy'd Soul, Body, Family and Estate. But they are very favourable if they wheedle No-body into Matrimony, but only make a Present of a small live Creature, no bigger than a Bastard to some of the Family; no matter who gets it, when a Child is born it must be kept.

Our Sessions Papers of late are crowded with Instances of Servant Maids robbing their Places, this can be only attributed to their devilish Pride; for their whole Enquiry now a Days, is how little they shall do, how much they shall have.

But all this while they make so little reserve, that if they fall sick the Parish must keep 'em, if they are out of Place, they must prostitute their Bodies, or starve; so that from chopping and changing, they generally proceed to whoring and thieving, and this is the Reason why our Streets swarm with Strumpets.

Thus many of 'em rove from Place to Place, from Bawdy-House to Service, and from Service to Bawdy-House again, ever unsettled, and never easy, nothing being more common than to find these Creatures one Week in a good Family, and the next in a Brothel: This Amphibious Life makes 'em fit for neither, for if the Bawd uses them ill, away they trip to Service, and if their Mistress gives 'em a wry Word, whip[12] they're at a Bawdy-House again, so that in Effect they neither make good Whores or good Servants.

Those who are not thus slippery in the Tail, are light of Finger, and of these the most pernicious, are those who beggar you Inch-meal.[13] If a Maid is a downright Thief, she strips you at once, and you know your Loss; but these[a] retail Pilferers waste you insensibly, and tho' you hardly miss it, yet your Substance shall decay to such a degree, that you must have a very good Bottom indeed, not to feel the ill Effects of such Moths in your Family.

Tea, Sugar, Wine, &c. or any such trifling Commodities are reckoned no Thefts, if they do not directly take your Pewter from your Shelf, or your Linnen from your Drawers, they are very Honest: What harm is there, say they, in cribbing[14] a little Matter for a Junket, or a merry Bout or so? Nay, there are those that when they are sent to Market for one Joint of Meat, shall take up two on their Master's Account, and leave one by the Way, for some of these Maids are mighty[b] charitable, and can make a shift to maintain a small Family with what they can Purloin from their Masters and Mistresses.

If you send 'em with ready Money they turn Factors,[15] and take three pence or four pence[c] in the Shilling Brokeridge.[16] And here let me take Notice of one very heinous Abuse, not to say petty Felony, which is practiced in most of the great Families about Town, and that is, when the Tradesmen gives the House-keeper, or other commanding Servant, a Penny or two Pence in the Shilling, or so much in the Pound, for every Thing they send in, which from thence is called Poundage.

This, in my Opinion, is the greatest of Villanies, and ought to incur some Punishment, yet nothing is more common, and our topping Tradesmen, who seem otherwise to stand mightily on their Credit, make this but a Matter of Course and Custom. If I don't, says one, another will, (for the Servant is sure to pick a Hole in the Persons Coat, who shall not pay Contribution:) Thus this wicked Practice is carried on and wink'd at, while receiving of stolen Goods, and confederating with Felons, which is not a jot worse, is so openly cry'd out against, and so severely punish'd, Witness *Jonathan Wild.*[a17]

And yet if a Master or Mistress enquire after any Thing missing, they must be sure to place their Words in due Form, or Madam huffs and flings about at a strange Rate, What would you make a Thief of her? Who would live with such mistrustful Folks? Thus you are obliged to hold your Tongue, and sit down quietly by your loss, for fear of offending your Maid, forsooth.

Again, if your Maid shall maintain one, two, or more Persons from your Table, whether they are her poor Relations, Country Folk, Servants out of Place, Shoe-cleaners,[b] Chare-women, Porters, or any other of her menial Servants who do their[c] Ladyships Drudgery, and go of her Errands, you must not grumble or complain at your Expence, or ask, What is become of such a Thing, or such a Thing? altho' it might never so reasonably be supposed, that it was altogether impossible to have so much expended in your Family; but hold your Tongue for Peace sake, or Madam will say, You grudge her Victuals, and expose you to the last Degree all over the Neighbourhood.

Thus have they a Salve for every Sore, cheat you to your Face, and insult you into the Bargain; nor can you help your self without exposing yourself, or putting yourself into a Passion.

Another great Abuse crept in among us, is the giving of Vails, to Servants; this was intended originally as an Incouragement to willing and handy Servants, but by Custom and Corruption it is now grown to be a Thorn in our Sides, and like other good Things, abused, does more hurt than good; for now they make it a Perquisite, a material Part of their Wages; nor must their Master give a Supper, but the Maid expects the Guests should pay for it, nay, sometimes through the Nose. Thus have they spirited People up to this unnecessary and burthensome Piece of Generosity, unknown to our Forefathers, who only gave Gifts to Servants at *Christmas*-tide, which Custom is yet kept up into the Bargain, insomuch, that a Maid shall have eight[d] Pounds *per Annum*, in a Gentleman's or Merchant's Family: And if her Master is a Man of a free Spirit, and receives much Company, she very often doubles her Wages by her Vails; thus having Meat, Drink, Washing, and Lodging for her Labour, she throws her whole Income upon her Back, and by this Means looks more like the Mistress of the Family, than the Servant-Wench.

And now we have mention'd washing, I would ask some good House-wifely Gentlewomen, If Servant-Maids wearing printed Linnens, Cottons, and other Things of that Nature, which require frequent washing, do not, by enhauncing[18] the Article of Soap, add more to House-keeping, than the Generality of People would imagine? And yet these Wenches cry out against great Washes, when their own unnecessary Dabs[19] are very often the Occasion.

But the greatest Abuse of all, is, that these Creatures are become their own Law-givers; nay, I think they are ours too, tho' No-body would imagine that such a Set of Slatterns should bamboozle a whole Nation: But it is neither better or worse, they hire themselves to you by their own Rule.

That is, a Month's Wages, or a Month's Warning; if they don't like you they will go away the next Day, help yourself how you can; if you don't like them, you must give them a Month's Wages to get rid of them.

This Custom of Warning,[20] as practis'd by our Maid-Servants, is now become a great Inconvenience to Masters and Mistresses. You must carry your Dish very upright, or Miss, forsooth, gives you Warning, and you are either left destitute, or to seek for a Servant: So that generally speaking, you are seldom or never fix'd, but always at the Mercy of every new Comer[a] to divulge your Family-Affairs, to inspect your private Life, and treasure up the Sayings of yourself and Friends. A very great Confinement, and much complain'd of in most Families.

Thus have these Wenches, by their continual Plotting and Cabals, united themselves into a formidable Body, and got the Whip-Hand of their Betters; they make their own Terms with us; and two Servants now, will scarce undertake the Work which one might perform with Ease; which,[b] notwithstanding they have rais'd their Wages to a most exorbitant Pitch; and, I doubt not, if there be not a Stop put to their Career, but they will bring Wages up to 20 *l.*[c] *per Annum* in time, for they are much about half Way already.

'Tis by these Means they run away with a great Part of our Money, which might be better employ'd in Trade; and what is worse, by their insolent Behaviour, their Pride in Dress, and their exorbitant Wages, they give Birth to the following Inconveniences.

First, They set an ill Example to our Children, our Apprentices, our Covenant-Servants, and other Dependants, by their saucy and insolent Behaviour, their pert, and sometimes abusive, Answers, their daring

Defiance of Correction, and many other Insolencies which Youth are but too apt to imitate.

2dly, By their Extravagance in Dress, they put our Wives and Daughters upon yet greater Excesses, because they will (as indeed they ought) go finer than the Maid: Thus the Maid striving to out-do the Mistress, the Tradesman's Wife to out-do the Gentleman's Wife, the Gentleman's Wife emulating the Lady, and the Ladies one another, it seems as if the whole Business of the female Sex, were nothing, but Excess of Pride, and Extravagance in Dress.

3dly, The great Height to which Women-Servants have brought their Wages, makes a Mutiny among the Men-Servants, and puts them upon raising their Wages too: So that in a little Time our Servants will become our Partners, nay, probably, run away with the better Part of our Profits, and make[a] Servants of us *vice versa*. But[b] yet with all these Inconveniences, we cannot possibly do without these Creatures; let us therefore cease to talk of the Abuses arising from 'em, and begin to think of redressing 'em. I do not set up for a Law-giver, and therefore[c] shall lay down no certain Rules, humbly submitting in all things, to the Wisdom of our Legislature. What[d] I offer shall be under Correction, and upon Conjecture, my utmost Ambition being but to give some Hint to remedy this growing Evil, and leave the Prosecution to abler Heads.

And first it would be necessary to settle and limit their Wages, from forty and fifty Shillings to four and five Pounds *per Annum*, that is to say, according to their Merits and Capacities: For Example, a young unexperienc'd Servant to have Forty Shillings[e] *per Annum* 'till she qualifies herself for a larger Sum; a Servant who can do all Houshold-Work, or, as the good Women term it, can take her Work and leave her Work, should have four Pounds *per Annum*; and those who have liv'd seven Years in one Service, should ever after demand five Pounds *per Annum*; for I would very fain have some particular Encouragements and Privileges given to such Servants, who should continue long in a Place; it would incite a Desire to please, and cause an Emulation very beneficial to the Publick.

I have heard of an ancient Charity in the Parish of St. *Clement's-Danes*, where a Sum of Money, or Estate, is left, out of the Interest or Income of which, such Maid-Servants, who have liv'd in that Parish seven Years in one Service, if they please to demand it, receive a Reward of ten Pounds a Piece.

This is a noble Benefaction, and shews the publick Spirit of the Donor; but Every-body's Business is No-body's; nor have I[f] heard that such

Reward has been paid to any Servant of late Years. A^a thousand pities that a Gift of that Nature should sink in Oblivion, and not be kept up as an Example to incite all Parishes to do the like.

The *Romans* had a Law, call'd *Jus Trium Liberorum*,²¹ by which every Man who had been Father of three Children had particular Honours and Privileges: This incited the Youth to quit a dissolute single Life, and become Fathers of Families, to the Support and Glory of the Empire.

In Imitation of this most excellent Law, I would have such Servants, who should continue many Years in one Service, meet with singular Esteem and Reward.

The Apparel of our Women-Servants should be next regulated, that we may know the Mistress from the Maid. I remember I was once put very much to the Blush, being at a Friend's House, and by him requir'd to salute the Ladies, I kiss'd the Chamber-Jade in to the bargain, for she was as well dress'd as the best. But I was soon undeceiv'd by a general Titter, which^b gave me the utmost Confusion, nor can I believe myself the only Person who has made such a Mistake.

Things of this Nature would be easily avoided, if Servant-Maids were to wear Liveries, as our Footmen do; or oblig'd^c to go in a Dress suitable to their Station. What should ail them, but a Jacket and Petticoat of good Yard-wide Stuff,²² or Callimanco²³ might keep 'em decent and Warm.

Our Charity Children are distinguish'd by their Dress, why then may not our Women Servants? Why may they not be made frugal *per* force, and not suffer'd to^d put all on their Backs, but oblig'd to^e save something against a rainy Day? I am therefore entirely against any Servants wearing of Silks, Laces, and other superfluous Finery; it sets them above themselves, and makes their Mistresses contemptible in their Eyes. I am handsomer than my Mistress, says a young prink'd up Baggage, what pity 'tis I should be her Servant; I go as well dress'd or better than she. This makes the Girl take the first Offer to be made a Whore, and there is a good Servant spoil'd; whereas were her Dress but suitable to her Condition, it would teach her Humility, and put her in Mind of her Duty.

Besides, the fear of spoiling their Cloaths makes them afraid of Houshold-Work; so that in a little Time we shall have none but Chamber-maids, and Nursery-Maids; and of this let me give one Instance: My Family is composed of my self and Sister, a Man and a Maid; and being without the last,^f a young Wench came to hire her self. The^g Man was gone out, and my Sister above Stairs, so I open'd the Door my self, and this Person presented herself to my View, dress'd compleatly, more[a] like a Visitor than a Servant-Maid; she, not knowing me, ask'd for my Sister: Pray Madam, said I, be pleas'd to walk into the Parlour, she[b] shall wait on you presently. Accordingly, I handed Madam in, who took it very cordially. After some Apology, I left her alone for a Minute or two, while I (stupid Wretch!) ran[c] up to my Sister, and told her there was a Gentlewoman below come to visit her. Dear Brother, said she, don't leave her alone, go down and entertain her while I dress my self. Accordingly, down I went, and talk'd of indifferent Affairs; mean[d] while my Sister dress'd herself all over again, not being willing to be seen in an Undress. At last she came down dress'd as clean as her Visitor: but how great was my Surprize, when I found my fine Lady a common Servant-Wench.

My Sister, understanding what she was, began to ask what Wages she expected? She modestly asked but eight Pounds a Year. The next Question was, what Work she could do to deserve such Wages? To this she answer'd, That she could clean a House, or dress a common Family-Dinner. But cannot you wash, reply'd my Sister, or get up Linnen? She answer'd in the Negative, and said, She would undertake neither, nor would she go into any Family that did not put out their Linnen to wash, and hire a Chare-woman to scour. She desir'd to see the House, and after having carefully survey'd it, said, The Work was too hard for her, nor could she undertake it. This put my Sister beyond all Patience, and me into the greatest Admiration. Young Woman, said she, you have made a Mistake, I want a House-Maid, and you are a Chamber-Maid. No Madam, reply'd she, I am not Needle-Woman enough for that. And yet you ask 8 Pounds a Year reply'd my Sister. Yes Madam, said she, nor shall I bate a Farthing. Then get you gone for a lazy impudent Baggage, said I; you want to be a Boarder, and not a Servant: Have you a Fortune, or an Estate, that you dress at that Rate? No Sir, said she, but I hope I may wear what I work for without Offence. What you work for, Interrupted my Sister, why you don't seem willing to undertake any Work:[e] You will not wash or scour; you cannot dress a Dinner for Company; you are no Needle-Woman, and our little House, of two Rooms on a Floor, is too much for you. For God's sake what can you do? Madam, reply'd she pertly, I know my Business, and don't fear a Service; there are more Places than Parish Churches; if you wash at Home, you should have a Laundry-Maid; if you give Entertainments, you must have a Cook-Maid; if you have any Needle-Work, you should have a Chamber-Maid; and such a House as this is enough for a House-Maid in all Conscience.

I was pleas'd at the Wit, and astonish'd at the Impudence of the Girl, and dismiss'd[a] her with Thanks for her Instructions; assuring her, that when I kept four Maids she should be House-Maid, if she pleas'd. Were a Servant to do my Business with chearfulness, I should not grudge at five or six Pounds *per Annum*: Nor would I be so unchristian as to put more upon any one, than they can bear; but to pray, and pay too, is the Devil. It[b] is very hard, that I must keep four Servants or none.

In great Families indeed, where many Servants are requir'd, these Distinctions of Chamber-Maid, House-Maid, Cook-Maid, Laundry-Maid, Nursery-Maid, *&c.* are requisite, to the End that each may take her particular Business, and many Hands may make the Work light: But for a private Gentleman, of a small Fortune, to be oblig'd to keep so many Idle Jades, when one might do the Business, is intollerable, and matter of great Grievance.

I cannot close this Discourse without a gentle Admonition and Reproof to some of my own Sex, I mean those Gentlemen who give themselves unnecessary Airs, and cannot go to see a Friend, but they must kiss and slop[24] the Maid; and all this is done with an Air of Gallantry, forsooth, and must not be resented: Nay, some Gentlemen are so silly, that they shall carry on an underhand Affair, with their Friend's Servant-Maid, to their own Disgrace, and the Ruin of many a young Creature. Nothing is more base and ungenerous, yet nothing more common; and withal so little taken Notice of. *D— me, Jack,* says one Friend to another, *this Maid of yours is a pretty Girl, you do so and so to her by G—d.* This makes the Creature[c] Pert, Vain and Impudent, and spoils many a good Servant.

What Gentleman will descend to this low Way of Intrigue, when he shall consider, that he has a Foot-Boy or an Apprentice for his Rival; and that he is seldom or never admitted, but when they have been his Tasters: And the Fool of Fortune, tho' he comes at the latter End of the Feast, yet pays the whole Reckoning; and so indeed would I have all such silly Cullies[25] serv'd.

If I must have an Intrigue, let it be with a Woman that shall not shame me. I would never go into the Kitchen, when the Parlour-Door was open. We are forbidden at *Highgate*, to kiss the Maid when we may kiss the Mistress: Why then will Gentlemen descend so low, by too much familiarity with these Creatures, to bring themselves into Contempt.

I have been at Places, where the Maid has been so dizzied with these idle Compliments, that she has mistook one Thing for another, and not regarded her Mistress in the least; but put on all the flirting Airs imaginable. This[a] Behaviour is no where so much complain'd of as in Taverns, Coffee-Houses, and Places of publick Resort, where there are handsome Bar-Keepers, &c. These Creatures being puff'd up with the fulsome flattery of a set of Flesh-Flies, that are continually buzzing about 'em, carry themselves with the utmost Insolence imaginable; insomuch, that you must speak to them with a great deal of Deference, or you are sure to be affronted. Being[b] at a Coffee-House t'other Day, where one of these Ladies kept the Bar, I[c] had bespoke a Dish of Rice-Tea; but Madam was so taken up with her Sparks, that she had quite forgot it. I spoke for it again, and with some Temper, but was answer'd after a most taunting Manner, not without a toss of the Head, a Contraction of the Nostrils, and other Impertinencies, too many to enumerate. Seeing my self thus publickly insulted by such an Animal, I could not chuse but shew my Resentment: Woman, said I, sternly, I want a Dish of Rice-Tea, and not what your Vanity and Impudence may imagine; therefore treat me as a Gentleman and a Customer, and serve me with what I call for, and keep your impertinent Repartees and impudent Behaviour for the Coxcombs that swarm round your Bar, and make you so vain of your blown Carcass. And indeed I believe the Insolence of this Creature will ruin her Master at last, by driving away Men of Sobriety and Business, and making the Place a Den of Vagabonds and Rake-Hells.

Gentlemen therefore ought to be very circumspect in their Behaviour, and not undervalue themselves to Servant-Wenches, who are but too apt to treat a Gentleman Ill, when ever he puts himself into their Power.

Let me now beg pardon for this Digression, and return to my Subject, by proposing some practicable Methods for regulating of Servants, which whether they are followed or not, yet if they afford Matter of Improvement and Speculation, it will answer the Heighth of my Expectation; and I will be the first who shall approve of whatever Improvements are made from this small Beginning.

The first Abuse I would have reform'd, is, that Servants should be restrain'd from throwing themselves out of Place on every idle Vagary: This might be remedied were all Contracts between Master and Servant to be made before a Justice of the Peace, or other proper Officer, and a Memorandum thereof taken in Writing: Nor should such Servant leave his or her Place (for Men and Maids might come under the same Regulation) 'till the Time agreed on be expir'd, unless such Servant be misus'd or deny'd Necessaries, or show some other reasonable Cause for their Discharge. In that Case, the Master or Mistress should be reprimanded, or fin'd: But if Servants misbehave themselves, or leave their

Places, not being regularly discharg'd, they ought to be amerc'd[26] or punish'd. But all those idle ridiculous Customs and Laws of their own making, such as, a Month's Wages or a Month's Warning, and such like, should be intirely set aside and abolish'd.

When a Servant has serv'd the limited Time duly and faithfully, they should be intitul'd to a Certificate, as is practiced at present in the Wool-Combing Trade: Nor should any Person hire a Servant without a Certificate, or other proper Security. A Servant without a Certificate should be deem'd a Vagrant: And a Master or Mistress ought to assign very good Reasons, when they object against giving a Servant his or her Certificate.

And tho' to avoid Prolixity, I have not mention'd Footmen particularly in the foregoing Discourse: Yet the Complaints alledg'd against the Maids are as well Masculine as Feminine, and very applicable to our Gentlemen's Gentlemen. I would therefore have them under the very same Regulations; and as they are Fellow Servants, would not make Fish of one and Flesh of the other, since daily Experience teaches us, that

Never a Barrel the Better Herring.[27]

The next great Abuse among us is, that under the Notion of cleaning our Shoes, above Ten Thousand Wicked, Idle, Pilfering Vagrants, are permitted to patrol about our City and Suburbs. These are call'd the *Black-Guard*, who Black your Honour's Shoes, and incorporate themselves under the Title of the *Worshipful Company of Jappanners.*

Were this all, there were no hurt in it, and the whole might terminate in a Jest: But the mischief Ends not here, they corrupt our Youth, especially our Men-Servants; Oaths and Impudence are their only Flowers of Rhetorick; Gaming and Thieving are the principal Parts of their Profession; but japanning, the Pretence. For Example, a Gentleman keeps a Servant, who, among other Things, is to clean his Masters Shoes; but our Gentlemen's Servants are above it now a-Days, and your Man's Man performs the Office; for which piece of Service you pay double and treble, especially if you keep a Table: And[a] are well off if the Jappanner has no more than his own Diet from it.[b]

I have often observ'd these Rascals sneaking from Gentlemen's Doors with Wallets, or Hats, full of good Victuals, which they either carry to their Trulls,[28] or sell for a Trifle. By this Means our Butcher's, our Baker's, our Poulterer's and Cheesemonger's Bills are monstrously exaggerated: Not to mention Candles just lighted, which sell for five Pence a Pound; many other Perquisites best known to themselves and the pilfering Villains their Confederates.

Add to this, that their continual Gaming sets Servants upon their Wits to supply this Extravagance, tho', at the same Time the Master's Pocket pays for it; and the Time, which should be spent in a Gentleman's Service, is loiter'd away among these Rake-hells: Insomuch, that half our Messages are inefectual, the Time intended being often expir'd before the Message is deliver'd.

How many and frequent Robberies are committed by these Jappanners? And to how many more are they Confederates? Silver-Spoons, Spurs, and other small Pieces of Plate, are every Day missing, and very often found upon these sort of Gentlemen. Yet are they permitted, to the shame of all our good Laws, and the Scandal of our most excellent Government, to lurk about our Streets, to debauch our Servants and Apprentices, to support an infinite Number of scandalous, shameless Trulls, yet more wicked then themselves: For not a jack among 'em, but must have his Gill.

By whom such Indecencies are daily acted even in our open Streets, as are very offensive to the Eyes and Ears of all sober Persons, and even abominable in a Christian Country.

In any Riot or other Disturbance, these Sparks are always the foremost; for most among 'em can turn their Hands to picking of Pockets; to run away with Goods from a Fire, or other publick Confusion; to snatch any Thing from a Woman, or Child; to strip a House when the Door is open; or any other Branch of a Thief's Profession.

In short, it is a Nursery for Thieves and Villains; modest Women are every Day insulted by them and their Strumpets; and such Children as run about the Streets, or those Servants who[a] go on Errands, do but too frequently bring home some Scraps of their beastly, profane Wit; insomuch, that the Conversation of our lower Rank of People runs only upon Bawdy and Blasphemy, notwithstanding our Societies for Reformation,[29] and our Laws in force against Profaness: For this lazy Life gets them many Proselites, their Numbers daily increasing by run-away Apprentices and Foot-Boys; insomuch that it is a very hard Matter for a Gentleman to get him a Servant, or for a Tradesman to find an Apprentice.

Innumerable other Mischiefs accrue, and others will spring up, from this Race of Caterpillars, who must be swept from out our Streets, or we shall be over-run with all manner of Wickedness.

But the Subject is so low, that it becomes disagreeable even to my self, give me leave therefore to propose a Way to clear the Streets of these Vermin, and to substitute as many honest industrious Persons in their stead, who are now starving for want of Bread, while these execrable Villains live (though in Rags and Nastiness, yet) in Plenty and Luxury.

I therefore humbly propose, that these Vagabonds be put immediately under the Command and Inspection of such Task-Masters[30] as the Government shall appoint, and that they be employ'd, punish'd and rewarded, according to their Capacities and Demerits, that is to say, the industrious and docible[31] to Wool-combing and other Parts of the Woollen Manufacture, where Hands are wanted; as also to Husbandry and other Parts of Agriculture.

For it is evident, that there are scarce Hands enow in the Country to carry on either of these Affairs. Now these Vagabonds might not only by this Means be kept out of Harm's Way, but be render'd serviceable to the Nation. Nor is there any need of transporting 'em beyond Seas, for if any are refractory, they should be sent to our Stannaries[32] and other Mines, to our Coal-Works and other Places, where hard Labour is requir'd. And here I must offer one Thing, never yet thought of, or proposed by any, and that is, the keeping in due Repair the Navigation of the River-*Thames*, so useful to our Trade in general: And yet of late Years such vast Hills of Sand are gathered together in several Parts of the River, as are very prejudicial to its Navigation. One of which is near *London-Bridge*, another near *White-Hall*, and another near *Battersea*. These two last in particular are of very great Hindrance to the Navigation. And indeed the Removal of them ought to be a National Concern, which I humbly propose may be thus effected.

The rebellious Part of these Vagabonds, as also other Thieves and Offenders, should be form'd in Bodies under the Command of proper Officers, and under the Guard and Awe of our Soldiery. These should every Day at low Water carry away these Sand-Hills, and remove every other Obstruction to the Navigation of this most excellent and useful River.

It may be objected, that the Ballast-Men[33] might do this; and that as fast as the Hills are taken away they would gather together again; or, that the Watermen[34] might do it. To the first I answer, that the Ballast-Men, instead of taking from these Hills, make Holes in other Places of the River, which is the Reason so many young Persons are drown'd when swiming or bathing in the River. Besides, it is a Work for many Hands, and of long Continuance, so that Ballast-Men do more harm than good. The second Objection is as silly, as if I should never wash my self because I shall be dirty again, and I think needs no other Answer. And as to the third Objection, the Watermen are not so publick spirited, they live only from Hand to Mouth, tho' not one of 'em but finds the Inconvenience of these Hills every Day, being obliged to go a great Way round about for fear of running a ground: Insomuch, that in a few Years the Navigation of that Part of the River will be intirely obstructed. Nevertheless, every one of these Gentlemen-Watermen hopes it will last his Time, and so they all cry, the Devil take the hindmost; but yet I judge it highly necessary, that this should be made a National Concern, like *Dagenham*-Breach,[35] and that these Hills be remov'd by some Means or other.

And now I have mention'd Watermen, give me leave to complain of the Insolencies and Exactions they daily commit on the River *Thames*, and in particular this one Instance which cries aloud for Justice.

A young Lady of Distinction, in Company with her Brother, a little Youth, took a Pair of Oars at or near the Temple on *April*-Day[a] last, and order'd the Men to carry them to *Pepper-Alley-Stairs*.[36] One of the Fellows (according to their usual Impertinence) ask'd the Lady where she was going? She answer'd, near St. *Olave's* Church. Upon which he said, she had better go through Bridge. The Lady reply'd, she had never gone through Bridge in her Life, nor would she venture for an Hundred Guineas; so commanded him once more to land her at *Pepper-Alley-Stairs*. Notwithstanding which, in spight of her Fears, Threats and Commands, nay, in spight of the Persuasion of his Fellow, he forc'd her through *London*-Bridge, which frighten'd her beyond Expression; and, to mend the matter, he oblig'd her to pay double Fare, and mobb'd her into the Bargain.

To resent which Abuse, Application was made to the Hall,[37] the Fellow summon'd, and the Lady order'd to attend, which she did, waiting there all the Morning, and appointed to call again in the Afternoon. She came accordingly, but they told her the Fellow had been there, but was gone, and that she must attend[b] another *Friday*. She attended again and again,[c] but to the same Purpose. Nor have they yet produc'd the Man, but tir'd out the Lady, who has spent above ten Shillings in Coach-hire, been abus'd, and baffled into the Bargain.

It is pity therefore, that there are not Commissioners for Watermen, as there are for Hackney-Coachmen; or that Justices of the Peace might not inflict bodily Penalties on Watermen thus offending. But while Watermen are Watermen's Judges, I shall laugh at those who carry their Complaints to the Hall.

The usual Plea in behalf of abusive Watermen is, that they are drunk, ignorant, or poor; but will that satisfy the Party aggriev'd, or deter[d] the

Offender from re-offending? Whereas were the Offenders sent to the House of Correction,[38] and there punish'd, or sentenc'd to work at the Sand-Hills aforemention'd for a Time, suitable to the Nature of their Crimes, the Terror of such Punishments would[a] make them fearful of offending, to the great Quiet of the Subject.

Now it may[b] be ask'd, How shall we have our Shoes clean'd, or how are these industrious Poor to be maintain'd? To this I answer, that the Places of these Vagabonds may be very well supply'd by great Numbers of ancient Persons, poor Widows and others, who have not enough from their respective Parishes to maintain 'em. These poor People I would have authoriz'd and station'd by the Justices of the Peace, or other Magistrates. Each of these should have a particular Walk or Stand, and no other Shoe-cleaner should come into that Walk unless the Person misbehave and be remov'd. Nor should any Person clean Shoes in the Streets, but these authoriz'd Shoe-cleaners, who should have some Mark of Distinction, and be under the immediate Government of the Justices of the Peace.

Thus would many Thousands of poor People be provided for, without burthening their Parishes. Some of these may earn a Shilling or two in a Day, and none less then six Pence or thereabouts. And least the old Jappanners should appear again, in the shape of Link-Boys,[39] and knock[c] down Gentlemen in Drink, or[d] lead others out of the Way into dark remote Places, where they either put out their Lights and rob 'em themselves, or run away and leave 'em to be pillag'd by others, as is daily practised, I[e] would have no Person carry a Link for Hire but some of these industrious Poor, and even such[f] not without some Ticket or Badge, to let People know who they trust. Thus would the Streets be clear'd Night and Day of these Vermin: Nor would Oaths, Skirmishes, Blasphemy, obscene Talk, or other wicked Examples be so publick and frequent. All gaming at Orange and Gingerbread-Barrows should be abolish'd, as also all Penny and half Penny Lotteries, Thimbles and Balls,[40] &c. so frequent in *Moorfields*, *Lincolns-Inn-Fields*, &c. where Idle Fellows resort, to play with Children and Apprentices, and tempt them to steal their Parents or Masters Money.

There is one admirable Custom in the City of *London*, which I could wish were imitated in the City and Liberties of *Westminster*, and Bills of Mortality,[41] which is, no Porter can carry a Burthen, or Letter, in the City unless he be a Ticket-Porter: Whereas out of the Freedom-part of *London*, any Person may take a Knot[42] and turn Porter, 'till he be intrusted with something of Value, and then you never hear of him more. This is very common and ought to be amended. I would therefore have all Porters under some such Regulation as Coachmen, Chairmen, Carmen, &c. a Man may then know whom he intrusts, and not run the Risque of losing his Goods, &c. Nay I would not have a Person carry a Basket in the Markets, who is not subject to some such Regulation; for very many Persons oftentimes lose their Dinner in sending their Meat home by Persons they know nothing of.

Thus would all our Poor be station'd, and a Man or Woman, able to perform any of these Offices, must either comply or be term'd an idle Vagrant, and so sent to a Place where they shall be forc'd to work. By this means Industry will be encourag'd, Idleness punish'd, and we shall be fam'd as well as happy, for our Tranquility and Decorum.

THE
Protestant Monastery:
OR, A
COMPLAINT
AGAINST THE
Brutality of the present AGE.

PARTICULARLY

The PERTNESS and INSOLENCE of our
YOUTH to aged PERSONS.

WITH A

CAUTION to People in Years, how they give the STAFF out of
their own Hands, and leave themselves at the Mercy of others.

CONCLUDING

With a PROPOSAL for erecting a *PROTESTANT MONASTERY*,
where Persons of small Fortunes may end their Days in Plenty,
Ease, and Credit, without burthening their Relations, or
accepting Publick Charities.

By ANDREW MORETON, Esq;
Author of *Every-Body's Business is No-Body's Business.*

LONDON:
Printed for *W. Meadows*, at the *Angel* in *Cornhill*; and sold by *J.
Roberts*, in *Warwick-Lane*; *E. Nutt*, under the *Royal Exchange*; *A. Dodd*,
without *Temple-Bar*; and *N. Blanford*, at *Charing-Cross*. 1727.
Price *6d.*

The Preface.

A COMMONWEALTH *is a Machine actuated by many Wheels, one depen-*
dant on the other, yet the Obstruction of a small Wheel may stop the Motion
of the whole: Every Man ought therefore as much as in him lies, to contribute
in his Station, to the publick Welfare, and not be afraid or ashamed of doing,
or at least meaning well.

I hope therefore the Reader will excuse the Vanity of an over officious Old
Man, *if like* Cato, *I enquire whether or not before I go hence and be no more,*
I can yet do any thing for the Service of my Country.

For if every Man should say Children are burthensome, and the Cause of
many Sorrows, therefore will not I be a Father, farewell to all Ties of Nature,
and every Blessing of human Society.

Or if every Man should say to himself, what have I to do with State Affairs?
is it my Business? are there not enough at the Helm? what need I interfere?
Let me be subject to the Higher Powers,[1] *and let Matters sink or swim, I shall*
have Neighbours Fare.

Would not this be a very churlish Resolution? would it not very much
contibute to universal Anarchy and Confusion? should every Man thus throw
the Care of the Publick from his shoulders, and acquit himself of any Concern
for the rest of Mankind.

This would be my Case, should I, knowing I am Master of a Project, which
in all probability may be of great use to Mankind, reason thus to my self; what
have I to do to divulge my Secrets? What though they are of Benefit to the
Publick, shall I reap any Advantage by them? Shall I not rather be laugh'd at
and despised as a Projector,[2] *the most contemptible Character in this Part of*
the World? May not another run away with the Profits of my Labour, and by
a little Improvement make my Project his own? is it not better for me to repose
myself, to die in Peace, and leave an ungrateful World to their own
Imaginations? Non nobis nati sumus.[3] *That Thought would quash all harsh*
Comtemplations, I could hazard with Pleasure, the publick Contumely for the
publick Good, knowing it has been the Fate of much better Men than my self,
to be despised when living, tho' rever'd when dead.

Prompted by this Reflection, I once more take Pen in Hand, as I hope for
the Service of my Country: If my Countrymen find what I advance practicable,
I hope they will not call my Integrity in question, and if they have patience to

read my well intended Thoughts, tho' digested I fear but too mildly, and in too mean a Stile, I hope they will find I have advanc'd nothing but what is practicable, beneficial, and without Self-Interest; having excluded myself from any propriety in my own Project, by thus publishing it and making it every Body's: and if any think I write for Money, let them ask my Bookseller.

Alas I have but small Health and little Leisure to turn Author, being now in my 67th Year,[4] almost worn out with Age and Sickness. The Old Man *cannot trouble you long; take then in good part his best Intentions, and impute his Defects to Age and Weakness: Look on him as a Man of more Experience than Learning; excuse his Stile for the sake of his Subject, and take the Will for the Deed. Assure your self, gentle Reader, I had not published my Project in this Pamphlet, could I have got it inserted in any of the Journals, without Feeing the Journalists or Publishers.*

I cannot but have the Vanity to think, they might as well have inserted what I sent them, Gratis, *as many Things I have since seen in their Papers. But I have not only had the Mortification to find what I sent rejected, but to lose my Originals, not having taken Copies of what I wrote.*

However, to justify my Complaints to the World, I shall, in a proper Place, let them know the Substance of what was rejected, and by whom.

In the mean time, give me leave to assure my Readers, that the Reason why this Project appears in a Pamphlet is, because I have been thus baffled and disheartened by Journalists; for if by any Means the Publick could have had it at a cheaper Rate, I had been better pleased.

THE PROTESTANT MONASTERY.

THERE is nothing on Earth more shocking, and withal more common, in but too many Families, than to see Age and Grey Hairs derided, and ill used. The OLD MAN or the OLD WOMAN, can do nothing to please; their Words are perverted, their Actions misrepresented, and themselves look'd upon as a Burthen to their Issue, and a Rent Charge upon those who came from their Loins.

This Treatment, as it is directly opposite to the Dignity and Decency of Human Nature, calls aloud for Redress; the Helpless and Innocent ought to be the care of the Healthy and able. Shall a Man or Woman toil and moil to bring up a numerous Issue? shall they rear up, thro' all the Uncertainties and Fatigues of Childhood, a Race who shall spring up but to abandon them? shall they enfeeble themselves to give Strength to those who shall one Day thrust them aside, and despise them?

Yet this is the Case of many aged Persons, who have outlived the Comforts of this World; who survive only to hear themselves wish'd out of the way, by those very Persons upon whom they have bestowed their whole Substance, and upon whom their whole Hopes have been fixed. Uncertain Hopes indeed! and far unfit for so degenerate an Age. *Honour thy Father and thy Mother* is a Commandment given by God, and ratified by our Blessed Saviour,[5] both in Precept and Example; If so, what Brutes are those who shall dare to spurn those Persons whom God has thought fit to make the Means of their Entrance into human Life?

But indeed, not only Parents, but all aged People in general, are thought to stand in the way of the present Generation: and but for some good Children, some Persons of Tenderness and Humanity, who honour the hoary Head, and comfort the Feeble; immediate Vengeance would be pulled down on those who let not their Sires live out half their Days.

The Word OLD is a standing Jest among our youthful Gentry. When they would frighten Children, they tell them *The old Man's a coming:*

Thus they inculcate an Abhorrence of Age, even in sucking Babes; which no doubt will improve with adult Age, according to the Proverb;

Quo semel est imbut a recens, servabit odorem testa diu.[6]

If any whimsical or ridiculous Story is told, 'tis of an *Old Woman*. If any Person is aukward at his Business, or any thing else, he is called an *Old Woman*,[7] forsooth; But this is no new thing, for we read in former Ages, that they made Witches of their Old Women. Those were brave Days for young People, when they could swear the old Ones out of their Lives! and get a Woman hanged or burnt only for being a little too old; as has been the Case of many a poor innocent ancient Creature. The Story of the Witch, *alias*, the poor Old Woman of *Hertford*, is yet fresh in every one's Memory; and had not the very Judges on the Bench seen through the Enthusiasm and Obstinacy of the Evidence, who swore thorough thick and thin: had not the Judges themselves, I say, represented the thing in a right Light to the *Higher Powers*, poor *Jane Wenman*[8] had certainly been truss'd up; as a Warning to all ancient Persons, who should dare to live longer than the young Ones think convenient.

It is well it has never been in the young Ones Power, to bring in a Bill for the better trimming of Mankind, *i.e.* to knock all ancient People on the Head.

But though they are suffered to live, 'tis under many Hardships and Restrictions, many Humps and Grumps; and scarce a Day, but they are ask'd, what they do out of their Graves. This is a very common, but withal, a most impious and unchristian Saying; nay, not only unchristian, but even unmahometan: For the very Infidels themselves pay more Veneration to old Age, than the Christians do; to the Shame and Scandal of our Holy Profession.

Far be it from me, to tax all Christians, or all Children with so severe a Reproach. No, I only blame those who triumph in the Strength of their Youth, and snuff up their Nostrils at *Old-Age*: Who laugh at the Groanings of the hoary Head, and have no Bowels of Compassion for the Bowels that gave them Nourishment.

Let such self-sufficient Persons consider, that it was once in their Parents Power to have abandoned them, when they were more helpless than any other Being to which God has given Life. When they must inevitably have perished, without great Care and Tenderness: and indeed the Divine Wisdom is most manifestly seen, in making Man, the Chief of all his earthly Creatures, to require so delicate a Management, and so tender a Nourishment: parental Love being encreas'd by its Care, as filial

Love ought to be, by a Gratitude for that Care it can never too much acknowledge or repay.

All Creatures whom God has ordained to quit their Sires, or indeed those whom he has not endow'd with a rational Soul, to distinguish between good and bad, or to know Duty or Obligation, are easily brought up, and can help themselves better the Hour they are born, than Man can in a whole Year, nay in Years. They perform all the necessary Functions of Life, and there is no need of Education. Far otherwise is it with Man; he in his Infancy requires a constant and careful Attendance, his Members know not their Functions, and it is a long while before he can feed himself, even then his Parents have the Care for his Food. When the Body is duly nourished, there is yet a further Care to form the Mind, and cultivate the rational Soul God has endow'd him with.

Shall such a Being, possest of a rational Soul, to distinguish between Good and Bad, between Gratitude and Ingratitude, so far debase himself, or indeed become so much a Brute, as to forsake his Parent, to spurn him who begot him? or at least, by using him ill, to elbow him as it were out of the World, to give himself the greater Scope for Luxury?

Yet how many do we see of such? how many truly compassionate Hearts daily bleed, when they see the Son curbing the Father, or the Daughter snubbing the Mother? It seems as if the Order of Nature were perverted: So shocking is it to any Soul who has the least Tincture of Humanity.

I am sure I speak by Experience: for but very lately I went to see an old School-Fellow and Acquaintance of mine, who had lately married his Daughter, and settled himself in her Family; accordingly he gave me a general Invitation to come one Day or other and take a Dinner with him; he had been a Merchant from his Youth, and always liv'd in what we call high Life, had travell'd much, and was Master of the most good Manners I ever met with.

This Gentleman being very weary, and indeed almost incapable of Business, thought it best to leave off House keeping, to marry his Daughter, and settle in her Family. Accordingly he gave her his All for her Portion, made her a Fortune of 12,000 Pounds, and match'd her to an eminent Merchant, who us'd the same Trade with himself.

During the Honey-Moon, and till the Portion was paid, the Old Gentleman liv'd in Clover; nothing was too hot or too heavy for him. 'Twas *Dear Sir! Dear Father!* at every Word; the Servants were ordered to respect him, and he was in some Share Master of the Family; but alas! he found this but a short-liv'd Dream, the Servants began to taunt at him, and he must call twenty Times for a thing, before he could have it. If he gently chid 'em, or reason'd with them, they flew to their Mistress, and made twenty Stories about it: so that his Life was in a manner a Burthen to him.

I went to my Chariot[9] to see him; and had not the little Appearance I made, commanded some respect, I had danc'd Attendance, till they should find in their Hearts to call him. However, without much Ceremony, they directed me up three pair of Stairs, into a better sort of a Garret; there might be indeed some Lodging-Rooms over Head for the Servants; but I have seen many Servants have much better Apartments: but the Room would not have so much surpriz'd me, had the Furniture been any thing tollerable. I dare swear it was as old as the House, and had no doubt pass'd from Tenant to Tenant half a score Times.

This I thought an odd Residence for my Friend, but he seem'd contented; and I saw no Reason I had to make him otherwise. He amused me till Dinner time, with shewing me his Books, and reading some of his Verses to me, as having a pretty Knack that way: he would have play'd me a lesson on his Flute, but that he said it would disturb his Daughter, who did not love Musick. I saw that all his little Arts were only to beguile the Time, lest a Whet[10] before Dinner, which I never mist at his House, should be expected; and which I believe was now out of his Power to give. At last the Bell rang, and he desired me to walk down to Dinner, but with an Air that seem'd chidingly to say, Ah! why did you not come sooner, when I had more Authority: However, with a long Apology to his Son and Daughter, he introduced me; and by pleading our long and intimate Acquaintance, and the Obligations he was under to me; he prevail'd on them at last to bid me a very ceremonious Welcome. Excusing themselves, as indeed they had need, that they had not made a proper Provision; and pleading their Ignorance of my coming, accordingly down we sate to some cold Roast-Beef, a few Herrings, and a Plate of Fritters.[11] Every thing was indeed very clean, and we had Attendance enough, but never in my Life made I a worse Dinner. Herrings are my aversion, I never eat cold Meat, judge then what a Belly full I could make of my share of the Fritters. I happened by Mistake to call for a Glass of Wine, without which I never dine, when the Gentleman told me he had none in the House; but if I pleas'd he would send for some, recommending at the same time some of his Home-brew'd Ale, which I in Complaisance could not but accept in Preference to Wine. They took me at my Word, and with much ado I got down half a Glass of the worst Potion I ever took in my Life. But had the Dinner been never so elegant, my indignation would have spoil'd my Stomach; to hear the Daughter at every turn, take up her Father in his Discourse, as if he had been an Idiot or an underling, with *Oh! fye Sir*, and *I wonder Father you should say so!* But lest the Readers, by my Recital of the Lady's Phrases, should think my Friend spake ludicrously or indecently, I beg Leave to assure them the contrary, and that he is a Man of great Wit and strict Modesty. Even the Son who was the least Severe upon him, could not refrain contradicting him every now and then, meerly for contradiction sake, with, *Pray, Sir, give me Leave*, and *indeed, Sir, you have forgot your self*; this was my whole Entertainment: For my Part I said little, but admired not only at this wondrous Frugality, but the surprizing Impertinence and Ingratitude of the young Couple. However, I was unde- ceived at last, as I hope my Readers will be when I assure them, that the Reason why *Sir* and *Madam* eat so sparingly with us was, because they had devour'd in Hugger Mugger by themselves, a good handsome Fowl, and Oyster Sauce, and dispens'd with a Bottle of Wine, though they could drink none in our Company.

Seeing this penurious Management, and the Awe my poor Friend was in, I thought it best to adjourn to the Tavern to smoak a Pipe, and withal to take a Glass to warm my Stomach, which rak'd prodigiously. I had before learn'd that the poor old Soul had been oblig'd to leave off Smoaking, because forsooth his spitting and spawling[12] turn'd *Madam's* Stomach; his smoaking she said, made the House stink, and damaged the Furniture. He had been from his Youth a great Smoaker, and this sudden Check, upon a Habit of so long standing, had very much impair'd his Health.

Accordingly to the Tavern we went; where a Pipe and a Bottle gave new Life to my old Acquaintance; he resum'd his native Gayety; and eleven of the Clock stole upon us, before we could think of Parting, and even then but with great Reluctance; so agreeably did the Time pass away in recounting our old Adventures. Indeed our sweet was intermix'd with sour, for his poor Heart was so full, he could not contain himself from lodging his Sorrows in the Bosom of his old Friend. With Tears in his Eyes, he recounted all the Indignities he daily met with, not only from his own Children, but from the very Servants. If he spake to them as to Servants, his Daughter would take him up, and tell him he domi- neer'd too much in her House: If he spake submissively, he was told he had no occasion to make himself so little; insomuch that he knew not what Medium to take.

He told me his Daughter had lately a Chamber-Maid, who was the Daughter of a decay'd Gentleman, and who having had a tolerable

Education, had imbib'd high Notions of Virtue; and amongst other things, an Abhorrence of undutifulness in Children, or indeed any disrespect for[a] old Age. This young Woman having learn'd in what Fashion my Friend had once liv'd, could not without Indignation, see how ill he was treated: and being of a good Family her self, scorn'd to take Part with the other Servants, to torment a poor old Man; but on the contrary, would do him all the Christian Offices she could, would constantly get him something warm in a Morning, and if he was out of Order at any time, would tend him, and do him a thousand little Services, for which he in Recompence, when her Lady was gone a Visiting, would read to the Girl a whole Afternoon together, while she sat at Work. And as so many good Offices must consequently engage her to him, especially when every Body else had abandon'd him, he, with an innocent Familiarity, us'd to call her his *Nanny*: This was taken in great Dudgeon, and the spiteful Servants improv'd it into an Intrigue, and never left till poor *Nanny* was turn'd away; and with her all the old Man's Comfort; for he had no warm Breakfast now, if he was Sick, there he might lie, for nobody would help him; and as for Attendance, they neglected him so much, he was scarce clean, which drew Tears from my Eyes, as knowing what a neat old Man he was us'd to be. And but for disgracing his Children, he wish'd himself a thousand Times in the *Charter-House*,[13] or some other Place of publick Charity: I dissuaded him from such Thoughts, and comforted him in the best Manner I could; and so we both parted and ended our pleasant Evening, with heavy Hearts and wet Eyes.

About a Week after, by the Penny-post,[14]
I receiv'd the following Letter.

Dear Friend,

THOUGH I shall carry to my Grave the agreeable Remembrance of our last Meeting, I believe I shall suffer to my dying Day for that Night's Pleasure. Your engaging Company, and my long Abstinence from Wine, made me, I think, drink a little too much; and tho' not to disguise my self, as you I hope might well perceive, yet more than my Age and Weakness cou'd well bear. My Daughter, who seldom or never comes Home before Midnight, took Care to be at Home that very Night before Nine a-Clock; and at Ten she sent all the Family to Bed, and sate up for me her self, out of mere Spight and pure Intention to rattle me off; which she did with a Vengeance, crying out shame of such Hours; telling me I was drunk: and when I complain'd of sickness at my Stomach, she said it was good enough for me. This you may conclude made me worse. I thought I should have died, and had not I eas'd my Stomach, I had not surviv'd that Moment.

This put her beyond all Patience, and instead of pitying her almost Dying Father, she called me (would you believe it!) she called me *Old Beast*; and used me in such a Manner as has riv'd[15] my very Heart; Nor is this all, for ever since I am become the Jest of the whole Family: they call me *Old Fool*, and *drunken old Beast* to my Face, and every Visitor that comes in, is told what a Sot I am; so that I keep my Chamber, and dare not show my Head about the House; but I thank God, who has heard my Prayers, that I hourly find my self weaker and weaker, and I doubt not but my long wished for Dissolution is near at hand; for all the Torments of a lingering Death are Trifles to the Usage I meet with. *Dear Friend*, let me see you once more before I dye, having some Manuscripts, and a few other Trifles to give you in Remembrance of our old Friendship; which alas! is all I can give to the only Friend I have left on this side the Grave.

Your Affectionate Friend.

FOR the sake of the young Lady, to whom God grant a speedy Repentance, I forbear subscribing even the initial Letters of her Father's Name; that the World may not know how good a Man she has murthered: For her Usage was such, that before I could find Opportunity to visit him according to his Desire, I was prevented by a Ticket, which invited me to hold up his Pall,[16] which more surpriz'd than afflicted me, as knowing the miserable Life he lead under his most unnatural Daughter.

Quis talia fando temperet a Lachrymis?[17]

The burying was of a Piece with the rest; and I hope the whole will be a Warning to all aged Parsons, and teach 'em to reserve at least where-withal to maintain themselves elsewhere, in Case of the like Usage from their Children or Relations.

I hope, at the same time, it will be a Looking Glass to young People, especially those guilty of the like Actions. If they see any thing ugly in this Lady's Character, let them not be so over good natured to their own Persons, as to think what is a Crime in her, may be excusable in themselves: No, the Sin is the same, let who will commit it.

To do as we would be done by, one would think a sufficient Restraint upon any, who would give themselves the least time to consider, that they in all probability may be Fathers and Mothers; and that though they are young and healthy now, they may be old and feeble hereafter. Let them therefore use the Old as they could wish to be us'd when they are so, and let them be as tender of their Parents, as they wou'd have their Posterity tender of them.

But on the contrary, we bring up our Youth, as it were to despise us; and to our shame be it spoken, make Rods for our selves: Every one indulges his own Children, and so all act with Impunity. Our Youth are not half educated, nor are they under any Restraint; we make Men and Women of them too soon, and put 'em upon a footing with ourselves, before they have well learned good Manners, or indeed any thing else.

For good Manners does not altogether consist in a formal Courtesy or Bow, in coming in and going out of a Room: No, a Man may behave himself most punctually Ceremonious at a Ball, a drawing Room, a Tea-Table, or indeed in any other fiddle faddle part of Life; and yet for all this be but a Man of Clouts,[18] a meer *Sir-courtly-Nice*. I have very often seen some of these well dress'd, well bred Gentlemen, *alias* Hobbydehoy's[19] have Assurance enough to stare a whole Coffee-Room out of Countenance; but neither Sense or Learning sufficient to give any Man of Parts a reasonable Answer.

No, the Satchel is too soon taken from the Shoulders of our young Sparks, and the Rod from their Backsides; the Tye-Wig[20] and Sword are too soon put on, and little Master is made a Man before he is a well-grown Child; our little Girls, through the Indulgence of their Mothers, are yet more forward, and put on womanly Airs even at ten Years of Age. In a Word, our Youth in general, are above Correction; without Shame, too ripe, too ignorant, and too impudent, and according to the Poet:

> *Now little Miss in Hanging-Sleeves knows more*
> *Than formerly her Grandame at three-score:*
> *And Master who was lately whipt at School,*
> *At bare thirteen sets up for Rake and Fool,*
> *Runs the whole Race of Vice with full Career,*
> *Is green and ripe and rotten in a Year.*[21]

Instead of Puerile Diversions, our Boys of 14 or 15 Years of Age go to Plays, become Members of Clubs, keep Hounds and Horses, and sometimes follow worse Game. This is owing to the over Indulgence of Parents, who let them finger Money before they know the Worth of it; and if a Stop be not put to such Practices in this Generation, the next may severely repent it.

Instead of Babies, Play-Things, and other pretty Innocencies used of old, our Girls at 10 or 11 Years of Age, keep their visiting Days, have their select Companies, and treat 'em with as much Solemnity and Expence, as their Parents do their own Acquaintance: This prevails not only at Court, but in the City; and I doubt not but the Court Airs of the Mother, and the womanly Airs of the Daughter, have made Bankrupt many an honest Man, who had not Courage enough to repel the Force of this most prevailing, most pernicious Custom.

This idle Custom is not only very Expensive, but extreamly inconvenient withal; for there is as much a Fuss made at some Houses against such a Miss or such a Miss come to visit the Daughter, as if a Dutchess was expected. The Servants are hindred from their other Business, and the whole House is in a Fluster to receive Miss's Visitors forsooth. When the Visit is return'd, she must be dress'd up to the heighth of the Mode, and some new Thing or other is always wanted: Not to mention Top-Knots,[22] Gloves, Coach-hire, and other unavoidable Expences.

This is most criminal in those who cannot afford it; Such People would therefore do well to reduce their Children to the Old Standard; that is to say, make Scholars of their Boys, and Housewives of their Girls: for the Education above complain'd of, has spoil'd many a good Tradesman's Wife, and been the Ruin of many a Family.

I cannot close this Discourse, without particularly cautioning the young Ladies of this Age, how they Laugh, Fleer, and toss up their Noses at sober matrons, and elderly Ladies. Let 'em consider, that those very Persons were once young and beautiful as themselves, if not more beautiful: For to say truth, Tea, Drams, Wine, and late Hours, have not a jot added to the Beauty of the present Generation.

Let them again consider, that their own Mothers as well as themselves, are of the same Sex: That it is a foul Bird bewrays its own Nest;[23] that the very Infirmities they deride in those Persons, are probably occasioned by the bearing and bringing up many Children; and that the Wrinkles in their Faces are occasioned by their Care to support such giddy brain'd Creatures as themselves.

But such is the Ignorance and Impudence of the present Generation, that young People look upon their Elders, as upon a different Species, an inferiour Class of People: They ascribe no Merit to the Virtue and Experience of Old Age, but assume to themselves the Preference in all things. With them a Face and a good Shape is Merit, a scornful toss of the Head, and despising every Body but their own dear selves is Wit, an everlasting Giddiness, and an eternal Grin is Affability and good Nature, fancy in Dress is Understanding, a supine Neglect of every thing commendable Gentility; and a prodigious Punctilio in the greatest Trifles, is the Heighth of good Breeding.

From this general Corruption in Education, proceeds all that may be complain'd of in this present Age, and whatever Evils may be expected in Generations to come. But above all, nothing has more contributed to this Corruption, than the disregard paid to Teachers and other Persons concern'd in the Education of Youth; for the first and chief Step to the Ruin of Youth, is when they have no Awe upon 'em and are above Correction.

Spare the Rod and spoil the Child,[24] is a Sentence of so much Weight and Truth; that no sharper a Reprimand can be given to those Parents, who have stimulated in their Children a Spirit of Pride, and taught them to look contemptibly on their Tutors. The very Word *Master* or *Mistress* implies something of Dominion; and as Youth are committed to their Care, so they ought to be subject to their Discipline.

It shocks me when I see a Tutor in a great Family, put upon a Footing with the Servants; it makes his Pupil think contemptibly of him, and is too great a Curb on his Spirits, to let him deliver his Instructions and Sentiments, in a manner suitable to the Dignity of an Instructor. And what is worse, the little Deference paid to him, begets in the young Gentleman a mean Opinion of and Indifference to Learning it self, seeing his Master reap so little Advantage and Respect from it.

It is the same Case in Schools, where the Master's or Mistress's passive and sordid Temper makes them the Slaves of the Scholars, whom they dare not correct, for fear of loosing: Nothing being more common now a days, than for Parents to make it in their Bargain, that their Children shall not be whipt, or otherwise corrected at School. Hence proceeds all that Noise and Misrule, which reigns in Schools, stunning both Master and Scholars to such a Degree, that they can hardly hear each other speak.

Parents therefore can blame none but themselves, if by these pernicious Methods, their Children grow in time to be too many for them; nor can they with any reason expect to find Duty and Humanity, where they have not been inculcated. If they have countenanc'd, or indulg'd their Children, in deriding the hoary Head, are they to be pitied when they reap seven Fold the Fruits of so ungenerous a Tillage? or to speak more plain, when it comes Home to themselves. Let every Person therefore make the Case their own, when they see Children taunting and flouncing at their Parents, Teachers, or Relations; mocking and deriding People for Age and Infirmities, or indeed any other bodily Misfortune, or Deformity; upbraiding any for their Poverty, or crowing over any Person, over whom they may pretend to claim Preheminence. This domineering way being now a days so prevalent, that Tradesmen, Servants and other Dependants, are generally more insulted by Children, than by Masters and Mistresses themselves.

To conclude, as we sow we shall reap; As we bring up our Children, so we may expect to find them: If we educate them in the Nurture and Fear of the Lord,[25] in an universal Benevolence to all Mankind, void of all personal or Party Prejudice; if we train them up to be dutiful to their Parents, respectful to their Teachers, mannerly to their Equals, and courteous to their Inferiours; if we incite in 'em an Emulation and Thirst after Knowledge and other liberal Acquirements; If we instil into 'em early Principles of Humanity, Compassion and Forbearance; and in a Word, all that may inspire to the highest Notions of Honour, and carry human Nature to its most exalted Pitch; then may we expect to have Comfort in Old Age, from our Grand Children, our Children and other Relations; then may we conclude we have laid a sure Foundation for the Happiness of succeeding Generations.

But if on the contrary, we humour and favour all their little Petulancies, and by over praising and indulging them, make our selves contemptible in their Eyes; if instead of correcting them in their Errors, we arraign the Justice of Discipline, and call it Severity; if we suffer them with Impunity to fly in the Faces of their Parents and Relations, to defy their Teachers, to outvie their Equals, and insult their Inferiours; if we permit 'em to scoff at, and turn to ridicule the Misfortunes, and Afflictions of others, and in a manner, suppress, or at least, not encourage in them any Propensity to Tenderness, but suffer their Hearts to be hardened, and to know no Pity: we must expect to have our Eyes pluck'd out by those we have brought up. We must look for nothing in Old Age, but Contempt, Oppression, and all the Insults we have but too much reason to fear from so inhuman a Generation.

A Project for erecting a Protestant-Monastery.

THAT a Joint-Stock of Twenty Thousand Pounds be raised between 50 Persons, by an equal Deposite of four Hundred Pounds each; which Stock is to be vested in themselves only. For this being no Charity, but rather a Co-partnership, there is no need of having any Governor, Treasurer, Director, or other commanding Officer, but what may be chosen among themselves; and as the Money is their own, they are the fittest Persons to keep it.

2. That after they have obtained his Majesty's Sanction, and are become a Body Corporate under what Name or Title they shall think fit, they may chuse from among themselves, one Treasurer, two Wardens,

and such other Officers they shall deem proper; which Officers shall have annual Rotation, and new ones be chosen every Year.

3. That instead of consuming all, or a great Part of the Stock in Building, which would nip the Project in the Bud, they shall rent a convenient Hall or House in Town or Country, at their own Option; which House must be equally divided into Apartments: and to save another great Expence, as well as to prevent Partiality, or Disgust, 'tis fit that every Person furnish their own Apartment, which Furniture they may bequeath to whom they please. For as all the Members of the College are to be upon an equal Footing, 'tis highly necessary there should not be the least Distinction among them in Diet, Lodging, &c. And if one Person dresses or furnishes better than another, there will be no need of Complaint, because they do it at their own Charge: Tho' to speak my Mind, it would look most lovely, to have a decent Equality and Uniformity in Dress.

4. The Kitchin, the Infirmary, and other Offices, to be furnished at the common Expence, but not to be taken out of the Joint-Stock. On the contrary, every Person to pay an equal Proportion, which cannot amount to above two Guineas a Head. But in Case the Joint-Stock encreases, the Money to be refunded.

5. That they call a Court among themselves as often as they shall think fit; at which every Member shall have an equal Vote; the Treasurer taking the Chair. At these Courts every thing shall be settled, all Bargains made, all Accounts audited, Servants hired or displac'd, the Diet, and College Hours settled; and bye Laws made or amended as Occasion, or the general Consent shall point out.

6. As all are to share the Benefit, it may readily be supposed that the best Advantage will be made of the Money; but above all that they will go on a sure Footing, and content themselves with the less Interest, upon the greater Security. Tho' I must confess I know of no safer and more profitable Method than to lend Money on proper Deposits; as Goods, Merchandises, &c. after the Manner of the Charitable Corporation in *Fenchurch-Street*. This, or some such sure Method, may bring in twenty *per Cent.* on their Money, which will considerably encrease their Capital, better their Provision, &c. and in time make them a very wealthy Body. But in case no more than five *per Cent.* Interest be produc'd from their Capital of twenty Thousand Pounds, it will amount to one Thousand Pounds *per Annum*; which may be laid out after this, or the like Manner.

	l. per An		
To a Physician	20	00	00
To a Clerk for the Treasury	20	00	00
To a Chaplain	20	00	00
To a Cook	10	00	00
To a Laundry Maid	05	00	00
To a House Maid	05	00	00
To two Nurses for the Infirmary	20	00	00
	100	00	00

These Salaries may be enlarged as the College encreases in Wealth, or the whole Subscription may be doubled at first, and every thing in proportion. But as this is only a Sketch or rough Draught, farther particulars from me would be needless: Besides I am but a poor Calculator, and only give the Hint to the Publick, as my Duty to my fellow Christians: I wish for nothing more than to see it improved, and if I don't properly explain my self, People must be so charitable to think for me: For I write even this under many bodily Infirmities, and am so impatient to have done, that I forget half I have to say. But to proceed,

The Salaries amounting to a Hundred Pounds a Year, and allowing another Hundred for a House, till there shall be Overplus enough to build one; there remains just eight Hundred Pounds per *Annum* for Provision.

If this should be deficient, it will easily be made up out of the Overplus which will accrue.

1*st*, From making better Advantage of their Money than is here proposed.

2*dly*, From the Money paid at the Admission of new Members, as the old ones dye. And,

3*dly*, From the Legacies which the old Members may leave to augment the Stock; for if but one Member die in a Year, there is four Hundred Pounds to be added to the Thousand, which will considerably augment every Article. If more should dye, or Legacies be left, the Stock will encrease, and consequently the Interest thereof will make allowance for greater Expences, and by degrees render the whole more Noble and Magnificent.

Excuse, gentle Reader! my immethodical Manner of calculating, and help me out the best you can, for I have forgot some Things which ought to have been mentioned before; but writing just as they occur,

I must leave the whole to be methodized and amended, by a clearer Head and a more able Hand.

I have mentioned Salaries without prescribing for what, give me leave therefore to assign the Officers their proper Employments.

The *Treasurer* must have care of the Cash, and be Chairman of all Committees.

The *Wardens* must look after the Provisions, agree with all Tradesmen, and superintend the Accounts.

The *Physician* must visit twice a Week, or oftner if need be, and prescribe to the sick Members: He may likewise appoint the Apothecary, inspect his Medicines, and tax his Bills.

The *Clerk* or *Book-keeper* must be constantly in the accompting House, to set down every Particular, to minute the proceeding of Committees, to keep the account of Cash, and in a word, to take the trouble of writing off the *Treasurer* and *Warden's* Hands; he must diet in the House. As also,

The *Chaplain*, some sober elderly decay'd Clergyman of good Morals, to read Prayers Morning and Evening; and every Sunday a Sermon out of Bishop *Tillotson*, Dr. *Scot*, Dr. *South*,[26] or some other sound Divine: And to further this good Work, I my self will present the College with a handsome Bible, and Common Prayer Book, and all the Sermons above-mentioned, if I live to see it finish'd; and if I dye before, I have made proper provision in my Will.

The *Cook* must dress the Victuals, keep clean the Kitchin, Pantry and Cellar.

The *Laundry-Maid* must wash and mend their Linnen, and wait at Table.

The *House-Maid* must make the Beds, sweep the Rooms and wait at Table.

The two *Nurses* must attend the Infirmary, and sit up alternately if need be; and when none are Sick, they must help, get up and mend the Linnen, and assist the other Servants, as the Treasurer and Wardens shall appoint.

As the Thing encreases, so may the Servants and their Wages. A Porter, a Butler, a Scullion, and other Servants may be added as the Members think fit.

To crown all, let the whole be independent, and among themselves; let them always keep the Staff in their own Hands, and never subject themselves to Treasurers, *&c.* out of their own Body. Let them accept of no Charities, but do as many as they are able; and in a Word, let them keep up the Grandeur of the Design, to such a Pitch, that their Friends and Relations may not be ashamed to visit them; but on the contrary, be proud they are of such a Body. Let the Election of new Members be vested only in themselves, and let them chuse only such as shall give Reputation to the College.

In a Word, I have drawn up my Scheme in general Terms, it being intended for the Benefit of either Sex. 'Tis indifferent whether the Ladies compose a College, and call themselves Sisters, or any other Name they shall think fit; or whether a College be compos'd of Gentlemen, under the Title of Brothers, Fellows, or any other Denomination; our *PROTESTANT MONASTERY* is still the same; nor can a Name alter its Property, or make it less beneficial or commendable.

Augusta Triumphans:

OR, THE

WAY

TO MAKE

LONDON

The most flourishing

CITY in the Universe.

FIRST,

By establishing an University where Gentlemen may have Academical Education under the Eye of their Friends.

II. To prevent much Murder, *&c.* by an Hospital for Foundlings.

III. By suppressing pretended Mad-Houses, where many of the fair Sex are unjustly confin'd, while their Husbands keep Mistresses, *&c.* and many Widows are lock'd up for the Sake of their Jointure.

IV. To save our Youth from Destruction, by clearing the Streets of impudent Strumpets, Suppressing Gaming-Tables, and Sunday Debauches.

V. To avoid the expensive Importation of Foreign Musicians, by forming an Academy of our own.

VI. To save our lower Class of People from utter Ruin, and render them useful, by preventing the immoderate Use of Geneva: With a frank Explosion of many other common Abuses, and incontestable Rules for Amendment.

CONCLUDING WITH
An effectual Method to prevent STREET ROBBERIES;

AND

A LETTER to Coll. *ROBINSON*, on account of the ORPHAN'S TAX.

LONDON:

Printed for *J. Roberts* in *Warwick-Lane*; and Sold by *E. Nutt* at the *Royal Exchange*; *A. Dodd* without *Temple-Bar*, *N. Blandford* at *Charing-Cross*, and *J. Stagg* in *Westminster-Hall.* 1728.
Price One Shilling.

AUGUSTA TRIUMPHANS:[1]
OR, THE WAY TO MAKE LONDON
THE MOST FLOURISHING CITY
IN THE UNIVERSE.

A Man who has the Publick Good in View, ought not in the least to be alarm'd at the tribute of Ridicule which Scoffers constantly pay to projecting Heads: It is the Business of a Writer, who means well, to go directly forward, without regard to Criticism, but to offer his Thoughts as they occur; and if in twenty Schemes, he hits but on one to the Purpose, he ought to be excused failing in the Nineteen for the Twentieth Sake. 'Tis a kind of good Action to mean well, and the Intention ought to palliate the Failure; but the *English*, of all People in the World, show least Mercy to Schemists,[2] for they treat them in the vilest manner; whereas other Nations give them fair Play for their Lives, which is the reason why we are esteem'd so bad at Invention.

I have but a short Time to live, nor would I waste my remaining Thread of Life in Vain, but having often lamented sundry Publick Abuses, and many Schemes having occur'd to my Fancy, which to me carried an Air of Benefit, I was resolv'd to commit them to Paper before my Departure, and leave, at least, a Testimony of my good Will to my Fellow Creatures.

But of all my Reflections, none was more constantly my Companion than a deep Sorrow for the present decay of Learning among us, and the manifest Corruption of Education; we have been a brave and learned People, and are insensibly dwindling into an Effeminate, Superficial Race: Our young Gentlemen are sent to the Universities 'tis true, but not under Restraint or Correction as formerly; not to study, but to drink; not for Furniture for the Head, but a Feather for the Cap, merely to say they have been at *Oxford* or *Cambridge*, as if the Air of those Places inspir'd Knowledge without Application. 'Tis true, we ought to have those Places in Reverence for the many learned Men they have sent us; but why must we go so far for Knowledge? why should a young Gentleman be sent raw from the Nursery to live on his own Hands, to be liable to a thousand Temptations, and run the Risque of being snapt up by sharping Jilts, with which both Universities abound, who make our Youth of Fortune their Prey, and have brought Misery into too many good Families? Not only the Hazard of their Healths from Debauches of both Kinds, but the waste of their precious Time renders the sending them so far off very hazardous. Why should such a Metropolis as *London* be without an University? Would it not save considerably the Expence we are at in sending our young Gentlemen so far from *London*? Would it not add to the Lustre of our State, and cultivate Politeness among us? What Benefits may we not in time expect from so glorious a Design? Will not *London* become the Scene of Science?[3] And what reason have we but to hope we may vye with any Neighbouring Nations? Not that I would have *Oxford* or *Cambridge* neglected, for the Good they have done: Besides, there are too many fine Endowments to be sunk, we may have Universities at those Places, and at *London* too, without Prejudice. Knowledge will never hurt us, and whoever lives to see an University here, will find it give quite another turn to the Genius and Spirit of our Youth in general.

How many Gentlemen pass their Lives in a shameful Indolence, who might employ themselves to the purpose, were such a Design set on foot? Learning would flourish, Art revive, and not only those who study'd would benefit by it; but the Blessing would be convey'd to others by Conversation.

And in order to this so laudable design, small Expence is required: The sole Charge being the hire of a convenient Hall or House, which if they please, they may call a College. But I see no necessity the Pupils have to lye or diet there; that may be done more reasonably and conveniently at home, under the Eye of their Friends: Their only necessary Business at College being to attend their Tutors at stated Hours, and (Bed and Board excepted) to conform themselves to College Laws, and perform the same Exercises as if they were actually at *Oxford* or *Cambridge*.

Let the best of Tutors be provided, and Professors in all Faculties encouraged, this will do a double good, not only to the Instructed, but to the Instructors. What a fine Provision may here be made for Numbers of ingenious Gentlemen, now unpreferr'd? And to what a heighth may even a small Beginning grow in time?

As *London* is so extensive, so its University may be compos'd of many Colleges, quarter'd at convenient Distances; for Example, one at *West-*

minster, one at St. *James's*, one near *Ormond Street*; (that part of the Town abounding in Gentry) one in the Centre of the Inns of Court; another near the *Royal-Exchange*; and more if Occasion and Encouragement permit.

The same Offices and Regulations may be constituted, Cooks, Butlers, Bed-makers, &c. excepted, as at other Universities. As for Endowment, there is no need, the whole may be done by Subscription; and that an easy one; considering nothing but Instructions are paid for.

In a Word, an Academical Education is so much wanted in *London*, that every Body of Ability and Figure, will readily come into it; and I dare engage the Place need but be chosen, and Tutors approved of, to compleat the Design at once.

It may be objected that there is a kind of University at *Gresham-College*,[4] where Professors in all Sciences are maintained and obliged to read Lectures every Day, or at least as often as demanded. The Design is most laudable, but it smells too much of the *Sine Cure*; they only read in Term-Time, and then their Lectures are so hurried over, the Audience is little the better. They cannot be turn'd out; 'tis a good Settlement for Life, and they are very easy in their Studies when once fix'd. Whereas were the Professorship during good Behaviour, there would be a Study to maintain their Posts, and their Pupils would reap the Benefit.

Upon second Thought, I think Colleges for University Education might be formed at *Westminster*, *Eaton*, the *Charter-House*, St. *Pauls*, *Merchant-Taylors*, and other Publick Schools, where Youth might begin and end their Studies; but this may be farther consider'd of.

I had almost forgot the most material Point, which is, that his Majesty's Sanction must first be obtain'd, and the University propos'd have Power to confer Degrees, &c. and other Academical Priviledges.

As I am quick to conceive, I am eager to have done, unwilling to over-work a Subject; I had rather leave part to the Conception of the Readers, than to tire them or my Self with protracting a Theme; as if like a Chancery Man,[5] or a Hackney Author, I wrote by the Sheet for hire: So let us have done with this Topick, and proceed to another; which is,

A Proposal to prevent Murder, Dishonour, and other Abuses, by erecting an Hospital for Foundlings.[6]

IT is needless to run into a Declamation on this Head, since not a Sessions passes, but we see one or more merciless Mothers try'd for the

Murder of their Bastard-Children; and to the Shame of good Government, generally escape the Vengeance due to shedders of Innocent Blood: For 'tis a common Practice now among them, to hire a set of Old-Beldams,[a] or pretended Midwives, who make it their Trade to bring them off for three or four Guineas, having got the ready rote of swearing the Child was not at its full Growth, for which they have a hidden Reserve, that is to say, the Child was not at Man's or Woman's Growth. Thus do these impious Wretches cheat the World, and damn their own Souls by a double Meaning, which too often imposes on a cautious, merciful and credulous Jury, and gives wicked Murderers means to escape and commit fresh Sins, to which their Acquitters no doubt are accessary.

I wonder so many Men of Sense, as have been on the Jury, have been so often impos'd upon by the stale pretence of a Scrap or two of Child-Bed Linnen being found in the Murderer's Box, *&c.* when alas! perhaps it was ne'er put there till after the Murder was committed; or if it was, but with a view of saving themselves by that devilish Precaution; for so many have been acquitted on that Pretence, that 'tis but too common a Thing to provide Child-Bed-Linnen before-hand for a poor Innocent Babe they are determin'd to murder.

But alas! What are the exploded Murders to those which escape the Eye of the Magistrate, and dye in Silence? Add to this procur'd Abortions, and other indirect means, which wicked Wretches make use of to screen themselves from the Censure of the World, which they dread more than the Displeasure of their Maker.

Those who cannot be so hard-hearted to murder their own Offspring themselves, take a slower, tho' as sure a way, and get it done by others, by dropping their Children, and leaving them to be starved by Parish-Nurses.[7]

Thus is God robb'd of a Creature, in whom he had breath'd the Breath of Life, and on whom he had stamp'd his Image; the World of an Inhabitant, who might have been of use; the King of a Subject; and future Generations of an Issue not to be accounted for, had this Infant lived to have been a Parent.

It is therefore the height of Charity and Humanity, to provide against this Barbarity, to prevent this crying Sin, and extract Good, even out of Evil, by saving these Innocent Babes from Slaughter, and bringing them up in the Nurture and Fear of the Lord;[8] to be of Benefit to themselves and Mankind in General.

And what nearer, what better way can we have, than to erect and endow a proper Hospital or House to receive them, where we may see them tenderly brought up, as so many living Monuments of our Charity; every one of them being a convincing Proof of a Christian saved, and a Murder prevented?

Nor will this be attended with so much Charge as is imagin'd, for we find in many Parishes, that Parents have re-demanded their Children, on encrease of Circumstances, and paid all Costs with a handsome Present in the Bargain; and many Times when a Clandestine Marriage is clear'd up, and openly avow'd, they would purchase the First-Fruits of their Loves at any Rate: Oftentimes a Couple may have no more Children, and an Infant thus sav'd, may arrive to inherit a good Estate, and become a Benefactor, where it was once an Object of Charity.

But let us suppose the worst, and imagine the Infant begot in Sin and without the Sanction of Wedlock; is it therefore to be murder'd, starv'd or neglected, because its Parents were wicked? hard Fate of innocent Children, to suffer for their Parents Faults! Where God has thought fit to give his Image and Life, there is Nourishment demanded; that calls aloud for our Christian and Human Assistance, and best shows our Nobleness of Soul, when we generously assist those who cannot help themselves.

If the Fault devolv'd on the Children, our Church would deny them Baptism, Burial, and other Christian Rites; but our Religion carries more Charity with it, they are not deny'd even to partake of our Blessed Sacraments, and are excluded no one Branch or Benefit accruing from Christianity; if so, how unjust are those who arraign 'em for their Parents Faults, and how barbarous are those Parents, who, tho' able, make no Provision for them, because they are not Legitimate: My Child is my Child, let it be begot in Sin or Wedlock, and all the Duties of a Parent are incumbent on me so long as it lives; if it survives me, I ought to make a Provision for it, according to my Ability; and tho' I do not set it on a Footing with my Legitimate Children, I ought in Conscience to provide against Want and Shame, or I am answerable for every Sin or Extravagance my Child is forc'd or led into, for want of my giving an Allowance to prevent it.

We have an Instance very fresh, in every ones Memory, of an ingenious, nay, a sober young Nobleman,[9] for such I must call him, whose either Father was a Peer, and his Mother a Peeress: This unhappy Gentleman toss'd from Father to Father, at last found none, and himself a Vagabond, forced to every Shift; he in a manner starved for many Years, yet was guilty of no capital Crime, till that unhappy Accident occur'd, which God has given him Grace, and Sense enough to repent: However, I cannot but think his hard-hearted Mother will bear her Portion of the Guilt, till wash'd away by a severe Repentance.

What a Figure might this Man have made in Life, had due Care been taken? If his Peerage had not been adjusted,[10] he might at least have been a fine Gentleman; nay probably, have fill'd some handsome Post in the Government with Applause, and call'd as much for Respect, as he does now for Pity.

Nor is this Gentleman the only Person begot, and neglected by Noble, or rather Ignoble Parents; we have but too many now living, who owe their Birth to the best of our Peerage, and yet know not where to eat. Hard Fate, when the Child would be glad of the Scraps, which the Servants throw away! but Heaven generally rewards them accordingly, for many Noble Families are become Extinct, and large Estates alienated into other Houses, while their own Issue want Bread.

And now, methinks, I hear some over-squeamish Ladies cry, *what would this Fellow be at? would not he set up a Nursery for Lewdness, and encourage Fornication? who would be afraid of sinning, if they can so easily get rid of their Bastards? we shall soon be over-run with* Foundlings *when there is such Encouragement given to* Whoredom: To which I answer, that I am as much against Bastards being begot as I am for their being murder'd; but when a Child is once begot, it cannot be unbegotten; and when once born it must be kept; the Fault, as I said before, is in the Parents, not the Child; and we ought to shew our Charity towards it as a Fellow-Creature and Christian, without any regard to its Legitimacy or otherwise.

The only way to put a stop to this growing Evil, would be to oblige all House-keepers, not to admit a Man and Woman as Lodgers, till they were certify'd of their being lawfully marry'd; for now-a-Days nothing is more common than for a Whore-monger and a Strumpet to pretend Marriage, till they have left a Child or two on the Parish, and then shift to another end of the Town.

If there were no Receivers there would be no Thieves: If there were no Bawdy-Houses there would be no Whores; and though Persons letting Lodgings be not actual Procurers, yet, if they connive at the Embraces of a Couple, whose Marriage is doubtful, they are no better than Bawds, and their Houses no more than Brothels.

Now should any Body ask, how shall this Hospital be Built? how endow'd? to which I answer, follow the Steps of the *Venetians*, the *Hamburgers*, and other foreign States,[11] &c. who have for Ages past prosecuted this glorious Design, and found their Account therein: As for building a House I am utterly against it, especially in the Infancy of the Affair: Let a Place convenient be hir'd: Why should such a considerable Sum be sunk in building as has in late publick Structures, which have swallow'd up part of the Profits and Dividend, if not the Capital, of unwary Stock-mongers?

To my great Joy I find my Project already anticipated,[12] and a noble Subscription carrying on for this purpose; to promote which, I exhort all Persons of Compassion and Generosity, and shall think my self happy, if what I have said on this Head, may any ways contribute to further the same.

Having said all I think material on this Subject, I beg pardon for leaving my Reader so abruptly, and crave Leave to proceed to another Article. *viz.*

A Proposal to prevent the expensive Importation of Foreign Musicians, &c. by forming an Academy of our own.

IT will no doubt be asked, what have I to do with Musick? to which I answer, I have been a Lover of the Science from my Infancy, and in my younger Days was accounted no despicable Performer on the Viol and Lute,[13] then much in Vogue. I esteem it the most innocent Amusement in Life; it gently relaxes, after too great a hurry of Spirits, and composes the Mind into a Sedateness, prone to every thing that's generous and good; and when the more necessary parts of Education are finish'd, 'tis a most genteel and commendable Accomplishment; it saves a great deal of Drinking and Debauchery in our Sex, and helps the Ladies off with many an idle Hour, which sometimes might probably be worse employ'd otherwise.

Our Quality, Gentry, and better sort of Traders must have Diversions; and if those that are commendable be denied, they will take to worse: Now what can be more commendable than Musick, one of the seven liberal Sciences,[14] and no mean Branch of the Mathematicks?

Were it for no other Reason I should esteem it, because it was the favourite Diversion of his late Majesty,[15] of glorious Memory; who was as wise a Prince as ever fill'd the *British* Throne. Nor is it less esteem'd by their present Majesties,[16] whose Souls are form'd for Harmony, and who have not disdain'd to make it a part in the Education of their sacred Race.

Our Nobility and Gentry have shown their Love to the Science, by supporting at such prodigious Expence, the *Italian Opera* improperly call'd an Academy;[17] but they have at the same time shown no small Partiality in discouraging any thing *English*, and over-loading the Town with such heaps of Foreign *Musicians*.[18]

An Academy, rightly understood, is a Place for the Propagation of Science, by training up Persons thereto from younger to riper Years, under the Instruction and Inspection of proper Artists: How then can the *Italian Opera* properly be call'd an Academy, when none are admitted but such as are, at least are thought, or ought to be adepts in Musick? If that be an Academy, so are the Theatres of *Drury-Lane*, and *Lincolns-Inn-Fields*:[19] Nay, *Punch's Opera* may pass for a lower kind of Academy. Would it not be a glorious thing to have an *Opera* of our own, in our own most noble Tongue, in which the Composer, Singers, and Orchestra, should be of our own Growth? Not that we ought to disclaim all Obligations to *Italy*, the Mother of Musick, the Nurse of *Corelli, Handel, Bononcini*, and *Geminiani*;[20] but then we ought not to be so stupidly partial, to imagine our Selves too Brutal a part of Mankind, to make any Progress in the Science: By the same reason that we love it, we may excel in it; Love begets Application, and Application Perfection. We have already had a *Purcel*, and no doubt, there are now many latent Genius's, who only want proper Instruction, Application, and ENCOURAGEMENT, to become great Ornaments of the Science, and make *England* emulate even *Rome* it self.

What a number of excellent Performers on all Instruments, have sprung up in *England* within these few Years? that this is owing to the *Opera*, I will not deny, and so far the *Opera* is an Academy, as it refines the Taste, and inspires Emulation.

But tho' we are happy in Instrumental Performers, we frequently send to *Italy* for Singers, and that at no small Expence: To remedy which, I humbly propose, that the Governours of *Christ's-Hospital*[21] will show their publick Spirit, by forming an Academy of Musick on their Foundation, after this or the like manner.

That out of their great number of Children, thirty Boys be selected, of good Ears and Propensity to Musick.

That these Boys be divided into three Classes, *viz.* Six for Wind-Instruments, such as the Hautboy,[22] Bassoon, and German-Flute.[23]

That sixteen others be selected for String-Instruments, or at least the most useful, *viz.* the Violin and Bass-Violin.[24]

That the remaining eight be particularly chosen for Voice, and Organ, or Harpsichord. That all in due time, be taught Composition. The Boys thus chosen, three Masters should be elected, each most excellent in his Way; that is to say, one for the Wind-Instrument, another for the String'd, and a third for the Voice and Organ, *&c.*

Handsome Salaries should be allowed these Masters, to engage their constant Attendance every Day, from eight till twelve in the Morning;

and I think a 100 *l. per Annum* for each, would be sufficient, which will be a Trifle to so wealthy a Body. The multiplicity of Holidays should be abridg'd, and only a few kept; there cannot be too few, considering what a hinderance they are to juvenile Studies. It is a vulgar Error that has too long prevail'd all over *England,* to the great Detriment of Learning, and many Boys have been made Blockheads, in Complaisance to Kings and Saints, dead for many Ages past.

The Morning employ'd in Musick, the Boys should go in the Afternoon, or so many Hours, to the Reading and Writing-School, and in the Evening should practice, at least two Hours before Bedtime, and two before the Master comes in the Morning. This Course held for seven or eight Years, will make them fine Proficients; but that they should not go too raw, or young, out of the Academy, 'tis proper, that at the stated Age of Apprenticeship, they be bound to the Hospital to engage their greater Application, and make them thorough Masters, before they launch out into the World; for one great hinderance to many Performers is, that they begin to teach too soon, and obstruct their Genius.

What will not such a Design produce in a few Years? will they not be able to perform a Consort, Choir, or Opera, or all three among themselves, and over-pay the Charge, as shall hereafter be specify'd?

For Example, we will suppose such a Design to be continued for ten Years, we shall find an Orchestre of forty Hands, and a Choir or Opera of twenty Voices, or admitting that of those twenty, only five prove Capital Singers, 'twill answer the Intent.

For the greater Variety they may, if they think fit, take in two or more of their Girls where they find a promising Genius, but this may be further consider'd of.

Now, when they are enabled to exhibit an Opera, Will they not gain considerably, when their Voices and Hands cost them only a College Subsistance? And 'tis but reasonable the Profits accruing from Operas, Consorts, or otherwise, should go to the *Hospital* to make good all former and future Expences, and enable them to extend the Design to a greater Length and Grandeur; so than instead of 1500 l. *per Ann.* the price of one *Italian* Singer, we shall for 300 l. once in ten Years, have sixty *English* Musicians regularly educated, and enabled to live by their Science.

There ought moreover to be annual Probations, and proper Prizes or Premiums allotted, to excite Emulation in the Youths, and give Life to their Studies.

They have already a Musick-School, as they call it, but the Allowance is too poor for this Design, and the Attendance too small; it must be every Day, or not at all.

This will be an Academy indeed, and in Process of Time, they will have even their Masters among themselves; and what is the Charge, compar'd with the profits or their Abilities?

One thing I had like to have forgot, which is, that with Permission of the Right Reverend the Lords Spiritual, some Performance in Musick, suitable to the Solemnity of the Day, be exhibited every Sunday after Divine Service: Sacred Poesy and Rhetorick, may be likewise introduc'd to make it an Entertainment suitable to a Christian and Polite Audience; and indeed, we seem to want some such commendable Employment for the better Sort: For we see the publick Walks and Taverns crowded, and rather than be idle, they will go to *Newport-Market*.[25]

That such an Entertainment would be much preferable to Drinking, Gaming, or profane Discourse, none can deny, and till it is proved to be prejudicial, I shall always imagine it necessary. The Hall at the *Hospital*, will contain few less than seven hundred People, conveniently seated, which at so small a Price as one Shilling *per* Head, will amount to 35 l. per Week; and if the Performance deserve it, as no doubt it will in time, they may make it half a Crown or more, which must considerably encrease the Income of the *Hospital*.

When they are able to make an Opera, the Profits will be yet more considerable, nor will they reap much less from what the Youths bring in during their Apprenticeship, when employ'd at Consorts, Theatres, or other publick Entertainments.

Having advanc'd what I think proper on this Head, or at least enough for a Hint, I proceed to offer,

That many Youths and Servants may be sav'd from Destruction, were the Streets clear'd of shameless and impudent Strumpets, Gaming-Tables totally suppress'd, and a stop put to Sabbath Debauches.

THE Corruption of our Children and Servants, is of Importance suffi-cient to require our utmost Precaution; and moreover, Women Servants (commonly call'd Maid-Servants) are such necessary Creatures, that it is by no means below us to make them beneficial rather than prejudicial to us.

I shall not run into a Description of their Abuses; we know enough of those already. Our Business now is to make them useful, First, by ascertaining[26] their Wages at a proper Standard.

Secondly, by obliging them to continue longer in Service, not to stroll about from Place to Place, and throw themselves on the Town on every Dislike.

Thirdly, To prevent their being harbour'd by wicked Persons, when out of Place; or living too long on their own Hands.

As for their Wages, they have topp'd upon us already, and doubled 'em in spight of our Teeth; but as they have had Wit enough to get 'em, so will they, I doubt not, have the same Sense to keep 'em: and much Good may it do those indolent over-secure Persons, who have given 'em this Advantage. However, if they are honest and diligent, I would have them encourag'd, and handsome Wages allow'd 'em; because, by this Means, we provide for the Children of the inferior Class of People, who otherwise could not maintain themselves; nay, sometimes Tradesmen, &c. reduced, are glad when their Children cease to hang upon them, by getting into Service, and by that Means, not only maintaining themselves, but being of Use in other Families. But then there ought to be some Medium, some Limitation to their Wages, or they may extort more than can well be afforded.

Nothing calls more for Redress than their quitting Service for every idle Disgust, leaving a Master or Mistress at a Nonplus; and all under Plea of a foolish old Custom, call'd Warning; no where practis'd but in *London*: For in other Places they are hir'd by the Year, or by the Statute, as they call it, which settles them in a Place, at least for some Time; whereas, when they are not limited, it encourages a roving Temper, and makes them never easy.

If you turn them away without Warning, they will make you pay a Month's Wages, be the Provocation or Offence never so great; but if they leave you, tho' never so abruptly, or unprovided, help yourselves how you can, there is no Redress: Tho' I think there ought, in all Conscience, to be as much Law for the Master as for the Servant.

No Servant should quit a Place, where they are well fed and paid, without assigning a good Reason before a Magistrate. On the other Hand, they should receive no Abuse which should not be redress'd: For we ought to treat 'em as Servants, not Slaves; and a Medium ought to be observ'd on both Sides. But if they are not restrain'd from quitting Service on every Vagary, they will throw themselves on the Town, and not only ruin themselves, but others: For Example, a Girl quits a Place, and turns

Whore; if there is not a Bastard to be murder'd, or left to the Parish, there is One or more unwary Youths drawn in to support her in Lewdness and Idleness; in order to which, they rob their Parents and Masters, nay, sometimes any Body else, to support their Strumpets; so that many Thieves owe their Ruin and shameful Deaths to Harlots. Not to mention the Communication of loathsome Distempers, and innumerable other Evils, to which they give Birth.

How many Youths, of all Ranks, are daily ruin'd? And how justly may be dreaded the Loss of as many more, if a speedy Stop be not put to this growing Evil? Generations to come will curse the Neglect of the present, and every Sin committed for the future may be pass'd to our Account, if we do not use our Endeavours to the contrary.

And unless we prevent our Maid-Servants from being harbour'd by wicked Persons when out of Place, or living too long on their own Hands, our Streets will swarm with impudent shameless Strumpets; the Good will be molested; those, prone to Evil, will be made yet more wicked, by having Temptations thrown in their Way: And to crown all, we shall have scarce a Servant left, but our Wives, *&c.* must do the Houshold-work themselves.

If this be not worthy the Consideration of a Legislature, I would fain know what is. Is it not Time to limit their Wages, when they are grown so wanton they know not what to ask? Is it not Time to fix 'em, when they stroll from Place to Place, and we are hardly sure of a Servant a Month together? Is it not Time to prevent the Encrease of Harlots, by making it penal for Servants to be harbour'd in Idleness, and tempted to Theft, Whoredom, Murder, *&c.* by living too long out of Place? And I am sure it is high Time to begin the Work, by clearing the publick Streets of Night-walkers, who are grown to such a Pitch of Impudence, that Peace and common Decency are manifestly broken in our publick Streets. I wonder this has so long escap'd the Eye of the Magistrate, especially when there are already in force Laws sufficient to restrain this Tide of Uncleanness, which will one Day overflow us.

The lewdest People upon Earth, ourselves excepted, are not guilty of such open Violations of the Laws of Decency. Go all the World over, and you'll see no such Impudence as in the Streets of *London*, which makes many Foreigners give our Women in general a bad Character, from the vile Specimens they meet with from one End of the Town to the other. Our Sessions-Papers[27] are full of the Trials of impudent Sluts, who first decoy Men, and then rob 'em: A Meanness the Courtesans of *Rome* and *Venice* abhor.

How many honest Women, those of the Inferior Sort especially, get loathsome Distempers from their Husband's Commerce with these Creatures, which Distempers are often entail'd on Posterity; nor have we an Hospital separated for that Purpose, which does not contain too many Instances of honest poor Wretches made miserable by Villains of Husbands.

And now I have mentioned the Villainy of some Husbands in the lower State of Life, give me leave to propose, or at least to wish, that they were restrained from abusing their Wives at that barbarous Rate, which is now practised by Butchers, Carmen, and such inferior Sort of Fellows, who are publick Nuisances to civil Neighbourhoods, and yet no Body cares to interpose, because the Riot is between a Man and his Wife.

I see no Reason why every profligate Fellow shall have the Liberty to disturb a whole Neighbourhood, and abuse a poor honest Creature at a most inhuman Rate, and is not to be call'd to Account because it is his Wife; this sort of Barbarity was never so notorious and so much encourag'd as at present, for every Vagabond thinks he may cripple his Wife at pleasure, and 'tis enough to pierce a Heart of Stone to see how barbarously some poor Creatures are beaten and abused by merciless Dogs of Husbands.

It gives an ill Example to the growing Generation, and this Evil will gain Ground on us if not prevented: It may be answer'd, the Law has already provided Redress, and a Woman abus'd may swear the Peace against her Husband, but what Woman cares to do that? It is revenging herself on herself, and not without considerable Charge and Trouble.

There ought to be a shorter way, and when a Man has beaten his Wife (which by the Bye is a most unmanly Action, and great Sign of Cowardice) it behoves every Neighbour who has the least humanity or Compassion, to complain to the next Justice of the Peace, who should be impowered to set him in the Stocks for the first Offence; to have him well scourg'd at the Whipping-Post for the second; and if he persisted in his barbarous Abuse of the holy Marriage State, to send him to the House of Correction 'till he should learn to use more Mercy to his Yoke-fellow.

How hard is it for a poor industrious Woman to be up early and late, to sit in a cold Shop, Stall, or Market, all Weathers, to carry heavy Loads from one End of the Town to the other, or to work from Morning till Night, and even then dread going Home for fear of being murder'd? Some may think this too low a Topic for me to expatiate upon, to which I answer, that it is a Charitable and a Christian one, and therefore not in the least beneath the Consideration of any Man who had a Woman for his Mother.

The Mention of this leads me to exclaim against the vile Practice now so much in vogue among the better Sort, as they are called, but the worst sort in fact, namely, the sending their Wives to Mad-Houses at every Whim or Dislike, that they may be more secure and undisturb'd in their Debaucheries: Which wicked Custom is got to such a Head, that the Number of private Mad-Houses in and about *London*, are considerably increased[28] within these few Years.

This is the heighth of Barbarity and Injustice in a Christian Country, it is a clandestine Inquisition, nay worse.

How many Ladies and Gentlewomen are hurried away to these Houses, which ought to be suppress'd, or at least subject to daily Examination, as hereafter shall be proposed?

How many, I say, of Beauty, Vertue, and Fortune, are suddenly torn from their dear innocent Babes, from the Arms of an unworthy Man, who they love (perhaps but too well) and who in Return for that Love, nay probably an ample Fortune, and a lovely Off-spring besides, grows weary of the pure Streams of chaste Love, and thirsting after the Puddles of lawless Lust, buries his vertuous Wife alive, that he may have the greater Freedom with his Mistresses?

If they are not mad when they go into these cursed Houses, they are soon made so by the barbarous Usage they there suffer, and any Woman of Spirit who has the least Love for her Husband, or Concern for her Family, cannot sit down tamely under a Confinement and Separation the most unaccountable and unreasonable.

Is it not enough to make any one mad to be suddenly clap'd up, stripp'd, whipp'd, ill fed, and worse us'd? To have no Reason assign'd for such Treatment, no Crime alledg'd, or Accusers to confront? And what is worse, no Soul to appeal to but merciless Creatures, who answer but in Laughter, Surliness, Contradiction, and too often Stripes?

All Conveniences for Writing are denied, no Messenger to be had to carry a Letter to any Relation or Friend; and if this tyrannical Inquisition, join'd with the reasonable Reflections a Woman of any common Understanding must necessarily make, be not sufficient to drive any Soul stark staring mad, though before they were never so much in their right Senses, I have no more to say.

When by this Means a wicked Husband has driven a poor Creature mad, and rob'd an injur'd Wife of her Reason, for 'tis much easier to create than to cure Madness, then has the Villain a handle for his

Roguery, then perhaps he will admit her distressed Relations to see her, when 'tis too late to cure the Madness he so artfully and barbarously has procured.

But this is not all, something more dismal Effects attend this Inquisition, for Death is but too often the Cure of their Madness and End of their Sorrows; some with ill Usage, some with Grief, and many with both are barbarously cut off in the Prime of their Years and Flower of their Health, who otherwise might have been Mothers of a numerous Issue, and surviv'd many Years. This is Murder in the deepest Sense, and much more cruel than Dagger or Poison, because more lingring; they die by Peace-meal, and in all the Agonies and Terrors of a distracted Mind.

Nay it is Murder upon Murder, for the Issue that might have been begot, is to be accounted for to God and the Publick. Now if this kind of Murder is conniv'd at, we shall no doubt have enough, nay too much of it; for if a Man is weary of his Wife, has spent her Fortune, and wants another, 'tis but sending her to a Mad-House and the Business is done at once.

How many have already been murdered after this manner is best known to just Heaven, and those unjust Husbands and their damn'd Accomplices, who, tho' now secure in their Guilt, will one Day find 'tis Murder of the blackest Dye; has the least claim for Mercy, and calls aloud for the severest Vengeance.

How many are yet to be sacrificed, unless a speedy Stop be put to this most accursed Practice I tremble to think; our Legislature cannot take this Cause too soon in hand: This surely cannot be below their Notice, and 'twill be an easy matter at once to suppress all these pretended Mad-Houses. Indulge, gentle Reader, for once the doting of an old Man, and give him leave to lay down his little System without arraigning him of Arrogance or Ambition to be a Law-giver. In my humble Opinion all private Mad-Houses should be suppress'd at once, and it should be no less than Felony to confine any Person under pretence of Madness without due Authority.

For the cure of those who are really Lunatick, licens'd Mad-Houses should be constituted in convenient Parts of the Town, which Houses should be subject to proper Visitation and Inspection, nor should any Person be sent to a Mad-House without due Reason, Inquiry and Authority.

It may be objected, by Persons determined to contradict every thing and approve nothing, that the Abuses complained of are not so numerous or heinous as I would insinuate: Why are not Facts advanced, they will be apt to[a] say, to give a Face of Truth to these Assertions? but I have two Reasons to the contrary; the first is, the more you convince them the more angry you make 'em, for they are never better pleased than when they have an Opportunity of finding Fault: Therefore to curry Favour with the Fault-finders, I have left 'em a loop Hole: the second and real is, because I don't care to bring an old House over my Head by mentioning particular Names of special Cases, thereby drawing my self into vexatious Prosecutions and Suits of Law, from litigious Wretches, who would be galled to find their Villainies made publick; and stick at no Expence or foul Play to revenge themselves. Not but I could bring many Instances, particularly of an unhappy Widow, put in by a Villain of a Husband, and now continued in for the sake of her Jointure by her unnatural Son, FAR from common Honesty or Humanity. Of another whose Husband keeps his Mistress in black Velvet, and is seen with her every Night at the Opera or Play, while his poor Wife, (by much the finer Woman) and of an Understanding far superior to her thick Skull'd Tyrant, is kept mean in Diet and Apparel, nay ill us'd into the Bargain; notwithstanding her Fortune supplies all the Villain's Extravagancies, and he has not a Shilling but what came from her: but a Beggar when once set on Horseback proves always the most unmerciful RIDER.

I cannot leave this Subject without inserting one particular Case.

A Lady of known Beauty, Vertue, and Fortune, nay more, of Wisdom, not flashy Wit, was, in the Prime of her Youth and Beauty, and when her Senses were perfectly sound, carried by her Husband in his Coach as to the Opera; but the Coachman had other Instructions, and drove directly to a Mad-House, where the poor innocent Lady was no sooner introduced, under pretence of calling by the way to see some Pictures he had a mind to buy, but the Key was turn'd upon her, and she left a Prisoner by her faithless Husband; who while his injur'd Wife was confined and us'd with the utmost Barbarity, He like a profligate Wretch ran through her Fortune with Strumpets, and then, basely, under Pretence of giving her Liberty, extorted her to make over her Jointure: which she had no sooner done but he laugh'd in her Face, and left her to be as ill us'd as ever. This he soon ran through, and (happily for the Lady) died by the Justice of Heaven in a Salivation[29] his Debauches had oblig'd him to undergo.

During her Confinement, the Villain of the Mad-House frequently attempted her Chastity; and the more she repuls'd him, the worse he treated her: till at last he drove her mad in good earnest. Her distressed

Brother, who is fond of her to the last Degree, now confines her in part of his own House, treating her with great Tenderness; but has the Mortification to be assured by the ablest Physicians, that his poor Sister is irrecoverably distracted.

Numberless are the Instances I could produce, but they would be accounted fictitious, because I don't name the particular Persons, for the Reasons before assigned; but the Sufferings of these poor Ladies are not fictitious, nor are the Villainy of these Mad-Houses, or the unnatural, though fashionable Barbarity of Husbands Chimira's, but too solid Grievances and manifest Violations of the Laws of God and Man.

Most Gracious and August Queen *Caroline*![30] Ornament of your Sex, and Pride of the *British* Nation! the best of Mothers, the best of Wives, the best of Women! Begin this Auspicious Reign with an Action worthy your illustrious Self, rescue your injur'd Sex from this Tyranny, nor let it be in the Power of every brutal Husband to Cage and confine his Wife at pleasure: A Practice scarce heard of 'till of late Years. Nip it in the Bud most gracious Queen, and draw on your self the Blessings of number-less of the fair Sex; now groaning under the severest and most unjust Bondage. Restore 'em to their Families, let 'em by your Means enjoy Light and Liberty: That while they fondly embrace, and with Tears of Joy weep over their dear Children, so long withheld from them, they may invoke accumulated Blessings from Heaven upon your Royal Head!

And you ye fair illustrious Circle! who adorn the *British* Court! and every Day surround our gracious Queen: Let generous Pity inspire your Souls, and move you to intercede with your noble Consorts for Redress in this injurious Affair. Who can deny when you become Suitors? and who knows but at your Request a Bill may be brought into the House to regulate these Abuses? The Cause is a Noble and a Common one, and ought to be espoused by every Lady who would claim the least Title to Vertue or Compassion. I am sure no honest Member in either honourable House will be against so reasonable a Bill; the Business is for some publick Spirited Patriot to break the Ice, by bringing it into the House, and I dare lay my Life it passes.

I must beg my Reader's Indulgence, being the most immethodical Writer imaginable; 'tis true, I lay down a Scheme, but Fancy is so fertile I often start fresh Hints, and cannot but pursue 'em; pardon therefore kind Reader my digressive way of Writing, and let the Subject, not the Stile or Method engage thy Attention.

Return we therefore to complain of destructive Gaming-Houses, the Bane of our Youth, and Ruin of our Children and Servants.

This is the most unprofitable Evil upon Earth, for it only tends to alienate the proper Current of Specie,[31] to maintain a pack of idle sharping Rascals, and beggar unwary Gentlemen and Traders.

I take the Itch of gaming to be the most pernicious of Vices, it is a kind of avaritious Madness; and if People have not Sense to command themselves by Reason, they ought to be restrained by Law: Nor suffered to ruin themselves and Families, to enrich a Crew of Sharpers.

There is no playing on the Square with these Villains; they are sure to cheat you, either by slight of Hand, Confederacy, or false Dice, *&c.* they have so much the Odds of their infatuated Bubbles, that they might safely play a Guinea to a Shilling, and yet be sure of winning. This is but genteel Pocket-picking, or Felony with another Name, and yet, so fond are we of it, that from the Foot-boy to the Lord, all must have a touch of gaming; and there are Sharpers of different Stations and Denominations, from *Southwark Fair* to the *Groom Porters*.[32] Shame, that Gentlemen should suffer every Scoundrel to mix with them for Gaming sake! And equal Shame, that honest laborious Tradesmen should be obstructed in crossing the publick Streets, by the gilt Chariots of Vagabond Gamesters; who now infest the Land, and brave even our Nobility and Gentry with their own Money!

But the most barbarous Part of this hellish Trade, is what they call setting of young Gentlemen, Apprentices, and others; this ought to be deem'd Felony, without Benefit of Clergy; for 'tis the worst of Thievery. Under Pretence of taking a Bottle, or spending an Evening gayly, they draw their Cull to the Tavern, where they sit not long before the Devil's Bones or Books are found accidentally on purpose, by the Help of which they strip my Gentleman in an Instant, and then generously lend him his own Money, to lose a fresh, and create a Debt, which is but too often more justly paid than those more justly due.

If we look into some late Bankrupcies, we shall find some noted Gamesters the principal Creditors; I think, in such Cases, 'twould be but Justice to make void the Gamester's Debt, and subject his Estate to make good the Deficiencies of the Bankrupt's Effects. If Traders have no more Wit, the Publick should have Pity on 'em; and make it as penal to lose as to win: And, in Truth, if Cards, Dice, *&c.* were totally suppress'd, Industry and Arts would encrease the more; Gaming may make a Man crafty, but not polite; one may understand Cards and Dice perfectly well, and be a Blockhead in every Thing else.

I am sorry to see it so prevalent in the City, among the trading Part of Mankind, who have introduc'd it into their Clubs, and Play so high of late, that many Bankrupts have been made by this pernicious Practice.

It is the Bane of all Conversation: And those who can't sit an Hour without Gaming, should never go into a Club to spoil Company. In a Word, 'tis mere Madness, and a most stupid Thing to hazard ones Fortune, and perplex ones Mind; nay, to sit up whole Nights, poring over Toys of pipt Ivory and painted Pasteboard,[33] making our selves worse than little Children, whose innocent Sports we so much ridicule.

To sum up all, I think 'twould be a noble Retribution, to subject Gamester's Estates to the Use and Support of the poor Widows and Orphans of their unfortunate Bubbles.

Sunday Debauches are Abuses that call loud for Amendment: 'Tis in this pernicious Soil the Seeds of Ruin are first sown. Instead of a Day of Rest, we make it a Day of Labour, by toiling in the Devil's Vineyard; and but too many surfeit themselves with the Fruits of Gluttony, Drunkenness, and Uncleanness.

Not that I am so superciliously strict, to have the Sabbath kept as rigidly here as in *Scotland*, but then there ought to be a Medium between the Severity of a Fast, and the Riot of *Saturnalia*. Instead of a decent and chearful Solemnity, our Taverns and Publick-Houses have more Business that Day than all the Week beside. Our Apprentices plume themselves; nay, some scruple not to put on their Swords and Tye Wigs, or Toupees;[34] and the loose End of the Town is their Rendezvous, *Sunday* being Market-Day all round the Hundreds of *Drury*.[35]

While we want Servants to do our Work, those Hundreds, as they call 'em, are crowded with Numbers of idle impudent Sluts, who love Sporting more than Spinning, and inveigle our Youth to their Ruin: Nay, many old Lechers (Beasts as they are) steal from their Families, and seek these Harlot's lurking Holes, to practice their unaccountable Schemes of new invented Lewdnesses: Some half hang themselves,[36] others are whipt, some lie under a Table and gnaw the Bones that are thrown 'em, while others stand slaving among a Parcel of Drabs at a Washing-Tub. Strange that the Inclination should not die with the Power, but that old Fools should make themselves the Prey and Ridicule of a Pack of Strumpets!

Some heedless Youths are wheedled into Marriage, which makes them and their unhappy Parents miserable all their Lives; others are drawn into Extravagancies, and but too often run into their Master's Cash, and for fear of a Discovery, make away with themselves; or at least run away and leave their distracted Parents in a Thousand Fears: Not to mention the Frustration of their Fortune, and the Miseries that attend a Vagabond Life. Thus honest Parents lose their Children, and Traders their

Apprentices, and all from a Liberty we have of late given our Youth of rambling Abroad on *Sundays*: For many, now-a-days, will lie out all Night, or stay out so late to give no small Disturbance in sober Families. It therefore behoves every Master of a Family to have his Servants under his Eye: And if the going to Church, Meeting, or whatever Place of Worship suited their Religion, were more enforc'd, it would be so much the better.

In short, the Luxury of the Age will be the Ruin of the Nation, if not prevented. We leave Trade to game in Stocks: We live above ourselves, and barter our Ready-money for Trifles; Tea and Wine are all we seem anxious for, and God has given the Blessings of Life to an ungrateful People, who despise their own Productions. Our very Plough-Fellows drink Wine now a-days: Our Farmers, Grasiers, and Butchers, are above Malt-Liquors; and the wholesome Breakfast of Water-gruel and Milk-pottage is chang'd for Coffee and Tea. This is the Reason Provisions and Corn, *&c.* are so dear; we all work for Vintners, and raise our Prices one upon another to such a Degree, 'twill be an Impossibility to live, and we shall, of Course, become our own Devourers.

We strain at a Gnat and swallow a Camel: And, in this Instance, the Publick Houses are kept open to furnish our Luxury, while we deny ourselves other Necessaries of Life, out of a Scruple of Conscience. For Example; in extreme hot Weather, when Meat will not keep from *Saturday* to *Sunday*, we throw, or cause to be thrown away, vast Quantities of tainted Meat, and have generally stinking Dinners, because the Butchers dare not sell a Joint of Meat on a *Sunday* Morning. Now, tho' I would not have the *Sabbath* so far violated as to have it Market-Day, yet rather than abuse God's Mercies by throwing away Creatures given for our Use, nay, for our own Healths and Cleanliness Sake, I would have the same Indulgence in extreme hot Weather, as there is for Milk and Mackrell; that is to say, that Meat might be kill'd in the cool of the Morning, *viz.* One or Two of the Clock, and sold 'till Nine, and no longer: Nor should villainous Informers have Power to molest them in this innocent and reasonable Amendment of a ridiculous vulgar Error.

I cannot forbear taking Notice of the extravagant use, or rather Abuse of that nauseous Liquor, call'd *GENEVA*,[37] among our lower sort. Those who deny, that an inferior Class of People are most necessary in a Body Politick, contradict Reason and Experience itself, since they are most useful when Industrious, and as pernicious when lazy. By their Industry our Manufactures, Trade, and Commerce are carried on: The Merchant in his Compting House, and the Captain in his Cabbin would find but little Employment were it not that many Hands carried on the different Branches of the Concern they superintended.

But now so far are our common People infatuated with *Geneva*, that Half the Work is not done now as formerly. It debilitates and enervates them, and they are not near so strong and healthy as formerly. This accursed Liquor is in itself so diuretick, it over-strains the Parts of Generation, and makes our common People incapable of getting such lusty Children as they us'd to do. Add to this, that the Women, by drinking it, spoil their Milk, and by giving it to young Children, as they foolishly do, spoil the Stomach, and hinder Digestion; so that in less than an Age, we may expect a fine Spindle-shank'd Generation.

There is not in Nature so unhealthy a Liquor as *Geneva*, especially as commonly sold: It curdles the Blood, it stupifies the Senses, it weakens the Nerves, it spoils the Eye-sight, and entirely ruins the Stomach; nay, some Stomachs have been render'd so cold by the Use of *Geneva*, that Lamp-Spirits have not been a Dram warm enough for 'em. Surely they will come to drink *Aqua-fortis*[38] at last!

On the contrary, our own Malt Liquors, especially common Draught Beer, is most wholesome and nourishing, and has brought up better Generations than the present: It is strengthening, cooling, and balsamick: It helps Digestion, and carries Nourishment with it. And, in spight of the Whims of some Physicians, is most pertinent to a humane, especially a good wholesome *English* Constitution. Nay, the honest Part of the Faculty deny not the Use of Small-Beer[39] well brew'd, even in Fevers. I my self have found great Benefit by it; and if it be good in its Kind 'tis the finest Julap[40] upon Earth.

If this Abuse of *Geneva* be not stopt, we may go whoop for[41] Husbandmen, Labourers, &c. Trade must consequently stand still, and the Credit of the Nation sink: Nor is the Abatement of the Excise, tho' very considerable, and most worthy Notice, any ways comparable to the Corruption of Manners, the Destruction of Health, and all the Train of Evils we are threaten'd with from pernicious *Geneva*.

An effectual Method to prevent Street-Robberies.

THE principal Encouragements, and Opportunity given to Street-Robbers is, that our Streets are so poorly watch'd; the Watchmen,[42] for the most Part, being decrepid, superannuated Wretches, with one Foot in the Grave, and the t'other ready to follow; so feeble, that a Puff of

Breath can blow 'em down: Poor crazy Mortals! Much fitter for an Alms-house than a Watch-house. A City watch'd and guarded by such Animals, is wretchedly watch'd indeed.

Nay, so little Terror do our Watchmen carry with them, that hardy Thieves make a mere Jest of 'em, and sometimes oblige even the very Watchmen, who should apprehend 'em, to light 'em in their Roguery: And what can a poor Creature do, in Terror of his Life, surrounded by a Pack of Ruffians, and no Assistance near.

Add to this, that our Rogues are grown more wicked than ever, and Vice in all Kinds is so much wink'd at, that Robbery is accounted a petty Crime. We take pains to puff 'em up in their Villainy, and Thieves are set out in so amiable a Light in the *Beggar's Opera*,[43] that it has taught them to value themselves on their Profession, rather than be asham'd of it.

There was some Cessation of Street-Robberies, from the Time of *Bunworth* and *Blewitt's* Execution,[44] 'till the Introduction of this pious Opera. Now we find the *Cartouchian* Villainies[45] revived, and *London*, that us'd to be the most safe and peaceful City in the Universe, is now a Scene of Rapine and Danger. If some of *Cartouch's* Gang be not come over to instruct our Thieves, and propagate their Schemes, we have, doubtless, a *Cartouch* of our own, and a Gang, which, if not suppress'd, may be full as pernicious as ever *Cartouch's* was, and *London* will be as dangerous as *Paris*, if due Care be not taken.

We ought to begin our Endeavours to suppress these Villainies; first by Heavenly, and then by Earthly Means.

By Heavenly Means, in enforcing and encouraging a Reformation of Manners, by suppressing of Vice and Immorality, and punishing Prophaneness and Licentiousness. Our Youth are corrupted by filthy, lewd Ballads, sung and sold publickly in our Streets: Nay, unlicens'd and unstamp'd, notwithstanding Acts of Parliament to the contrary.

Coachmen, Carmen, *&c.* are indulg'd in Swearing after the most blasphemous, shocking and unaccountable Rate that ever was known. New Oaths and Blasphemies are daily utter'd and invented, and rather than not exercise this hellish Tallent, they will vent their Curses on their very Horses; and, Oh stupid! Damn the Blood of a Post, rather than want something to curse.

Our common Women too have learn'd this Vice; and not only Strumpets, but labouring Women, who keep our Markets, and vend Things about Street, swear and curse at a most hideous Rate. Their Children learn it from the Parents, and those of the middle, or even the better Sort of People, if they pass through the Streets to School, or to play, catch the Infection, and carry home such Words as must consequently be very shocking to sober Parents.

Our Youth, in general, have too much Liberty; the Sabbath is not kept with due Solemnity; Masters and Mistresses of Families are too remiss in the Care of the Souls committed to their Charge. Family Prayer is neglected; and, to the Shame of Scoffers be it spoken, too much ridiculed. All Ages and Sexes, if in Health, should be obliged to attend publick Worship, according to their respective Opinions. Were it only to keep Youth out of Harm's Way, it would do well. But it is to be hoped, if their Parents, Masters, or Mistresses, should oblige their Attendance at publick Devotion, they would edify by what they should hear, and many wicked Acts would be stifled in their Infancy, and check'd even in the Intention, by good and useful Doctrine.

Our common People make it a Day of Debauch, and get so drunk on a Sunday, they cannot work for a Day or two following. Nay, since the Use of Geneva has become so common, many get so often drunk they cannot work at all, but run from one Irregularity to another, 'till at last they become arrant Rogues. And this is the Foundation of all our present Complaints.

We will suppose a Man able to maintain himself and Family by his Trade, and at the same Time to be a Geneva drinker: This Fellow first makes himself incapable of working, by being continually drunk; this runs him behind-hand, and he either pawns or neglects his Work, for which Reason no Body will employ him. At last, Fear of Arrests, his own Hunger, the Cries of his Family for Bread, his natural Desire to support an irregular Life, and a propense Hatred to Labour, turn but too many an honest Tradesman into an arrant desperate Rogue: And these are commonly the Means that furnish us with Thieves and Villains in general.

Thus is a Man, that might be useful in a Body politick, render'd obnoxious to the same: And if this Trade of Wickedness goes on, they will grow and encrease upon us, insomuch, that we shall not dare to stir out of our Habitations; nay, it will be well if they arrive not to the Impudence of plundering our Houses at Noon day.

Where is the Courage of the *English* Nation, that a Gentleman, with Six or Seven Servants, shall be robb'd by one single Highwayman? Yet we have lately had Instances of this; and for this we may thank our Effeminacy, our Toupee Wigs, and powder'd Pates, our Tea, and other scandalous Fopperies; and above all, the Disuse of noble and manly Sports, so necessary to a brave People, once in Vogue, but now totally lost among us.

Let not the Reader think I run from my Subject, if I search the Bottom of the Distemper before I propose a Cure, which having done, tho' indeed but slightly, for this is an Argument could be carried to a much greater Length, I proceed next to propose Earthly Means in the Manner following.

Let the Watch be composed of stout able bodied Men, and of those at least treble the Number now subsisting, that is to say, a Watchman to every Forty Houses, Twenty on one Side of the Way, and Twenty on the other; for it is observable, that a Man cannot well see distinctly beyond the Extent of Twenty Houses in a Row; if 'tis a single Row, and no opposite Houses, the Charge must be greater, and their Safety less. This Man should be elected, and paid by the Housekeepers themselves, to prevent Misapplication and Abuse, so much complain'd of, in the Distribution of Publick Money.

He should be allow'd 10 s. per *Annum*, by each Housekeeper, which at Forty Houses, as above specify'd, amounts to 20 l. per *Annum*, almost treble to what is at present allow'd; and yet most Housekeepers are charg'd at least 2 s. 6 d. a Quarter to the Watch, whose beat is, generally speaking, little less than the Compass of half a Mile.

This Salary is something of Encouragement, and a pretty Settlement to a poor Man, who, with Frugality, may live decently thereon, and, by due Rest, be enabled to give vigilant Attendance.

If a Housekeeper break, or a House is empty, the poor Watchman ought not to suffer, the Deficiency should be made up by the Housekeepers remaining.

Or, indeed, all Housekeepers might be excus'd, if a Tax of only 1 s. per *Annum* were levied on every Batchelor within the Bills of Mortality, and above the Age of One and Twenty, who is not a Housekeeper; for these young Sparks are a Kind of unprofitable Gentry to the State; they claim publick Safety and Advantages, and yet pay nothing to the Publick, nay indeed, they, in a Manner, live upon the Publick, for (on a *Sunday* especially) at least a Million of these Gentlemen quarter themselves upon the married Men, and rob many Families of part of a Week's Provision, more particularly when they play a good Knife and Fork, and are of the Family of the *Tuckers*.

I beg Pardon for this whimsical Proposal, which, ludicrous as it seems, has something in it; and may be improved. Return we, in the mean Time, to our Subject.

The Watch thus station'd, strengthen'd, and encourag'd, let every Watchman be arm'd with Fire-Arms and Sword; and let no Watchman stand above Twenty Doors distant from his Fellow.

Let each Watchman be provided with a Bugle-Horn, to sound on Alarm, or in Time of Danger; and let it be made penal, if not Felony, for any but a Watchman to sound a Horn in and about the City, from the Time of their going on, to that of their going off.

An Objection will be here made on Account of the Post-Boys, to obviate which, I had Thoughts of a Bell, but that would be too ponderous and troublesome for a Watchman to carry, besides his Arms and Lanthorn. As to a fix'd Bell, if the Watchman is at another Part of his Walk, how can he give Notice? Besides, Rogues may play Tricks with the Bell; whereas a Horn is portable, always ready, and most alarming.

Let the Post-Boys, therefore, use some other Signal, since this is most convenient to this more material Purpose. They may carry a Bell in a Holster, with Ease, and give Notice by that, as well as those who collect the Letters.

That the Watchmen may see from one End of their Walks to the other, let a convenient Number of Lamps be set up, and those not of the Convex Kind,[46] which blind the Eyes, and are of no manner of Use; they dazzle, but give no distinct Light: And farther, rather than prevent Robberies, Many, deceiv'd and blinded by these *Ignes fatui*,[47] have been run over by Coaches, Carts, &c. People stumble more upon one another, even under these very Lamps, than in the Dark. In short, they are most unprofitable Lights, and, in my Opinion, rather Abuses than Benefits.

Besides, I see no Reason why every Ten Housekeepers can't find a Lamp among themselves, and let their Watchman dress it, rather than fatten a crew of Directors: But we are so fond of Companies, 'tis a Wonder we have not our Shoes black'd by one, and a Set of Directors made rich at the Expence of our very Black-guards.[48] Convenient Turnpikes and Stoppages may be made to prevent Escapes, and it will be proper for a Watchman to be plac'd at one of these, fix'd at the End of a Lane, Court, Alley, or other Thoroughfare, which may happen in any Part of his Beat, and so as not to obstruct his View to both Ends thereof, or being able to give Notice, as aforesaid; for the Watch ought to be in View, as well as in the Hearing of each other, or they may be overpower'd, and much Danger may happen.

The Streets thus guarded and illuminated, what remains, but that the Money allotted by the Government be instantly paid on Conviction of every Offender; for Delays in this Case are of dangerous Consequence, and no Body will venture their Lives in Hopes of a Reward, if it be not duly and timely paid. If there is Reason of Complaint on this Head, it ought to be look'd into by those at the Helm; for nothing can be more vile than for Underlings to abuse the Benevolence of the Publick, or their Superiors, by sinking, abridging, or delaying publick or private Benefits. And it is by no Means below the Dignity, or Care, even of the greatest, to see the Disposal of their own Bounty and Charity, for it loses but too often by the Carriage: And where a Nobleman, or other generous Person, has order'd Five Guineas to be given, 'tis well if the proper Object has had even One.

Something allow'd by the Chamber of *London*,[49] to every Person apprehending a Robber, would have a good Effect, especially if it be not told over a Gridiron, but paid without Delay, or Abatement. And what if the fewer Custards are eat, so it augment the Publick Safety.

Some of our common Soldiery are (and I hope unjustly) suspected. This may be easily confuted, if strict Orders are enforc'd, that none but Commission, or Warrant Officers shall be out of their Quarters after Ten at Night. But if we consider, that neither *Blewit*, *Bunworth*, or their Gangs, were Soldiers, and that of those who have been executed for Ten Years past, not One in Ten were Soldiers, but, on the contrary, Seamen discharg'd, and thrown on the Publick, without present Subsistence, which made them desperate: But I hope the Act now depending[50] for the Encouragement of Seamen, *&c.* will sufficiently remove that Obstacle also. This, I hope, will stop the Mouths of censorious Persons, who unjustly arraign our Soldiery for the Vices of others: However, to make all easy, I believe the Generality of them will gladly submit to the Restraint propos'd, merely to show their Innocence.

Mean Time, would his most sacred Majesty let them partake of his Bounty, as the Officers, *&c.* have done, and raise their Pay, were it but One Penny *per Diem*, it would be a most Royal Bounty, would considerably contribute to their Support, and put them above any sordid Views: And there was never more Occasion than now, when Provisions of all Kinds are so excessive dear.

Having offer'd my little Mite to the Publick, I beg they will excuse the Deficiency of my Stile, and Multitude of my Errors, for my Intention's Sake. I write without prospect of Gain: If I am censured, 'tis what I can but expect; but if, among all my Schemes, One proves of Service, my Desires and Labours are amply answer'd.

Omissions.

IN my Scheme for an University in *London*, I proposed only a Hall or publick Room; on Recollection I find it should be a large House or Inn, in the Nature of a College, with store of convenient Rooms for Gentlemen, not only to study separately, but wherein to lodge their Books, for 'twould be most inconvenient to lug them backwards and forwards: They may indeed Breakfast, Sup, and Sleep at Home, but 'twill be highly necessary they should dine in Commons, or at least near the College; not that I would have Cooks, Butlers, Caterers, Manciples,[51] and the whole Train of College Cannibals retained; but for fear they should stay too long at Home, or be hindred from returning to Study in due time, some proper Place or Person might be pitch'd upon to keep an Ordinary[52] at a prefix'd Price and Hour, and for the Students only.

My Reasons are these:

First, A young Gentleman may live too far from College.

Second, The College Hours for Dinner, may not agree with those of the Family.

Third, Company may drop in and detain him.

These being, I think, the only material Objections could be offered, I hope I have amply provided against them, and rendered my Project more perfect and unexceptionable.

One Omission I made in the Discourse on Mad-Houses, *&c.* is, that Maiden Ladies as well as Widows and Wives, are liable to the Inquisition there complained of, and I am inform'd a good Estate is lately come to a worthless Family, by the Death, or rather Murder of an innocent young Creature, who being left very rich, chose to live with her Friends; but well had it been for her, had she taken up her Abode among Strangers, for they stav'd off all Proposals for Marriage a considerable time, and when at last they found the Lady would not be hindered from altering her Condition, she was hurried away to a Mad-House, where she miserably ended her Days, while they rioted in the Pillage of her Fortune. Thus neither Maid, Wife or Widdow, are safe, while these accursed Mad-Houses are suffered: Nay, I see no Reason, (if the Age improves in Wickedness, as in all Probability it may) but the Men, *per Contra*, may take their Turns. Younger Brothers, *&c.* may clap up their Elders and jump into their Estates, for there are no Questions ask'd at these Mad-Houses, but who is the Pay-master, and how much; give them but their Price, mad or not mad 'tis no matter whom they confine; so that if any Person lives longer than his

Relations think convenient, they know their Remedy, 'tis but sending them to a Mad-House and the Estate's their own.

Having answer'd all that I think liable to Objection, and recollected what I had omitted, I desire to stand or fall by the Judgment of the serious Part of Mankind; wherein they shall correct me I will kiss the Rod and suffer with patience; but if a pack of Hackney Scriblers shall attack me only by way of a get-Penny, I shall not be provoked to answer them be they never so scurrilous, lest I be accounted as one of them.

To Lieutenant-Colonel Samuel Robinson.[53]

SIR,

I Shall congratulate you on your Election into the Chamberlainship of the City of *London*, or otherwise, as you shall acquit your self in answering candidly and impartially to the following Queries.

I. Whether there is not Money sufficient in the Chamber of *London* to pay off the Orphan's Fund?[54] Or if not a sufficient Sum, What Sum it is, and what is the Deficiency? How long it has lain there, and what Interest has been made upon it?

II. If there are not considerable Arrears due from many Wards, and what those Arrears are?

III. Who are these poor Orphans we pay so much Money to? And whether they are not some of the richest Men in the City of *London*, who have got the Stock into their own Hands, and find it so snug a Fund, they do not care to get out of it?

IV. If it would not be much better to gather in the Arrears, join 'em to the Money in the Office, and collect the Overplus at once, rather than suffer the Tax to become eternal, and to pay so much Interest?

This is but a reasonable Request; and if Col. *Robinson* is the honest Gentleman Fame reports him to be, he will make no Scruple to give a ready Answer. And indeed it will be but a handsome Return made to his Fellow Citizens, for their Choice of him, to begin his Office with such an Act of Justice, Honesty, and publick Satisfaction. For many People don't know what is meant by the Orphan's Tax: They pay it with Remorse, and think themselves aggrieved. Even those who know the Reason of the Fund think it has been continued long enough, wish it were once paid off, suspect some Secret in the Affair, and give their Tongues the Liberty all Losers claim: *Our Fathers*, say they, *have eaten sour Grapes, and our Teeth are set on Edge, we are visited for their Transgressions, and may be to* the World's End, unless we find an honest Chamberlain who will unveil this cloudy Affair, and give us a Prospect of Relief.

Thus, Sir, it lies at your Door to gain the Applause of the whole City (a few Misers excepted) by a generous and Gentleman-like Discovery of this Affair. And you are thus publickly call'd upon, that your Discovery may be as publick and beneficial to all. If you comply, I shall think you an honest Man, above a Fellow-feeling, or being byass'd, and most worthy your Office: If not, give me Leave to think, the Citizens of *London* have made but an indifferent Choice. I am,

SIR,

Yours, as you prove yourself,

Sept. 23
1728

ANDREW MORETON.[a]

SOME

OBJECTIONS

Humbly offered to the

CONSIDERATION

OF THE

Hon. HOUSE of COMMONS,

Relating to the present intended

Relief of Prisoners.

LONDON:
Printed for R. WALKER, at the *White-Hart*, without
Temple-Bar, E. NUTT, at the *Royal-Exchange*, and sold by
the Booksellers of *London* and *Westminster*. 1729.
(*Price 6 d.*)

SOME OBJECTIONS, &c.

Part I.

Of the Fraud *made use of by* Insolvents *to bring themselves within the Reach of the Acts of* Parliament, *with some Limitations; humbly offered to be considered of, in order (not to prevent an Act of Favour to real* Insolvents, *but) to prevent the Abuse of it by improper Objects.*

IT is no wonder, if after so many Petitions from the several Prisons almost over the whole Kingdom, and such horrid *Cruelties* and Inhumanities, as appears to have been practised by some Jailors, especially by the *Warden of the Fleet*[1] and his *Agents*, upon several unfortunate Gentlemen who have fallen into their Hands; I say, 'tis no wonder if a Bill for Relief of Prisoners is become very popular.

By how much the ill Usage of the Prisoners, who are thus abused by the *Keepers of Prisons*, shocks the tender and charitable Part in every Man's Breast; by so much the Case of the *Prisoners*, even of those who have not been used ill, prevails upon the *Publick* in favour of the GRACE desir'd.

Nor shall one Word be said, or one Thought suggested, in this Tract in Prejudice of the *Charitable* Intention of the House, or any way to lessen the good and generous Disposition of any Person whatever, whether in the Legislature, or out of it, towards promoting so good a Work.

Far less shall I take one Step, or speak one Word, that so much as looks like a Plea for the *Cruelty* and Inhumanity of *Jaylors* and Prison-keepers; their Conduct in most, if not all the Jails in *England*, calls aloud for a like Inspection of Authority and for Justice upon the Persons, as well as a severe Censure of the Practices of the Delinquents, in order to have that rigid, tho' necessary Part of the Law, call'd *Imprisonment for Debt*, be executed with *Humanity* and with Equity, according to the natural Rights of the Unfortunate, as Men; and according to their *legal* Rights as *Englishmen*, which it is evident has not been observ'd hitherto.

And to conclude this Part; *least of all* shall I say one Word here in behalf of the Persons at this time detected openly in the *Cruelties*,

Inhumanities and Extortions, which they have practis'd upon the unhappy Gentlemen who have fallen into their Hands: I do not see they merit the least *Favour* from their Country; they have acted a *dreadful Part*, and they are in Hands, which I doubt not will have more *Mercy* than they have shewn to the Miserable, who have been under their Power; and tho' I shall not, on the other hand, prompt or push their *Misfortune*, yet this I may say without any Prejudice or Injury to them, that I hope they shall have such Justice, as will effectually disable them, and warn all others (of that *rough* Employment) from the *like* Practices.

Having laid down these *Postulata*, in order to prevent any prejudging my Design in this Work, or raising a *popular* Clamour, as if it was intended to lessen the intended *Grace* of the Government or Legislature, and to prevent the *Deliverance* of Prisoners; I shall with the more freedom lay down some Difficulties, which, as they occur to me on this Occasion, shall be worth the Consideration of the Legislature, not to lye as *Obstructions* in the way of the intended Bill, as a Reason *sine qua non*, but that the Parliament, taking them into their Hands, and *approving* or *disapproving* them, as they shall appear *important*, may find out such *proper Remedies* as to their great Wisdom shall seem meet.

Having thus, as I hope, remov'd the Prejudices which might lye against my present Design, I must also speak a Word or two, very briefly, to remove if possible a popular Objection (at least as it is used in the Mouths of some who are more particularly concern'd in that part) namely, that it is *unchristian* and inhuman, and inconsistent with a *generous* Nation abhorring Cruelty, as *England* professes to be, to confine poor miserable People in *Prison* for Debt, especially such as have nothing to pay.

As to the latter Part, *viz.* of *confining* People in Prison who have *nothing* to pay, I come readily into that part, and in doing so I confirm what I have said above, that I am not writing in order to intercept the intended *Grace* of the Parliament to the *Unfortunate*. The honest Debtor willing to pay, but *unable*; and willing to pay as far as he is *able*, and ready to give all reasonable Satisfaction, such as the Parliament may direct, that he is so unable, is certainly an *Object* recommending it self to the *Charity* and Compassion of the whole Nation; and whatever intervenes by the Fraud of others, these, and these only, are allow'd to be the Persons for whom the *Parliamentary Grace* which has been settled, and extended in so many Acts of Parliament already pass'd, has been *intended*.

That very great Numbers of *Fraudulent*, unqualify'd, wicked, and dishonest People have formerly receiv'd the Benefit of the like *Grace* by the Help of *false Oaths*, unjust Pretences, Connivance of Jailors, Bribery and Corruption of many kinds, has been loudly complain'd of, and I doubt is much easier to prove than to prevent; and not being willing, as I have said, to be any ways a Hindrance to the Relief of the *honest* and real Objects of *Grace*, who are indeed within the Intention of the Act, I cover all that Part with saying, Better *Ten* dishonest Debtors *escape*, than that *one* real Object of the intended *Good* should *perish*.

Yet I humbly propose it, as a Thing worthy the Consideration of the *British Parliament*, whether it is any Way probable, that there can be such a Number of miserable Insolvents in one Year, and that of but the *lowest* Class too; namely, not owing above 100 *l.* to any one Person, and all actually Prisoners, as have presented themselves yearly to the Magistrates, to be discharged by the *Grace* of Parliament, for these several Years past?

If it is true, as common *Fame* says it is, that notwithstanding there was an Act for Delivering such *Prisoners* but *two* Years past,[2] there are at this Time near ninety Thousand such *Insolvents*,[3] now on the Books of the several *Jails* in this Kingdom; I say, if this is *true*, is it rational to believe, that these are all really and fairly Prisoners, within the Intent and Meaning of the *intended Grace*.

It would be a noble Undertaking, and in my Opinion well worth the House of Commons, tho' it took up a good Part of a *Session*, to find out some effectual Means to *separate between the Sheep and the Goats*,[4] (speaking of that Allusion with due Regard) in this Case; and to discover, expose, and punish the *Frauds* which are put upon the NATION in this Affair.

It is true, the People are despicable; I mean, the *Guilty*; the Debts they lye for not large, at least not to particular Men, and some may suggest that it is not worth Notice; but I reply, the Number is great, surprizingly great, and the Injury to Trade is very *considerable*, nor is the Matter small among *Tradesmen*, tho' the Debts (as above) are not singly large. For as many of these *Insolvents* frequently fall within the Compass of one and the same Shopkeeper, it very often falls heavy; and as these *fraudulent* Debtors boldly run into Mens Books, with a Dependance upon such *Acts of Grace*, and with an evident Design to cheat and defraud their Creditors, and this *several* Times over, such People are, I think, very far from being Debtors who deserve Compassion, or within the Intent and Meaning of the *Parliamentary* Grace.

Likewise they are greatly injurious to Trade in general, as they *ruin innocent* Tradesmen by their Knavery; many Tradesmen having had thirty to fifty such Insolvents discharged by *one Act*, tho' they were never put in Prison, or so much as arrested at their Suit, or for any Part of their Debt.

The usual *Practice* of these People has been to run themselves into the *Tradesmens Books*, as it is called, in as many particular and different Places as possible; always taking Care that it be for small Sums, within the usual Restraint of the *Acts of Grace*; and then when the expected *Favour* is in Prospect, get themselves arrested, and put in Prison, or turn'd over by *Habeas Corpus*, so to be within the Reach of the Law, and then all the other *Creditors*, who have never offered them the *least* Violence, are paid with a SUMMONS.

Others by *Corruption* of Jailors, and by *Bribery*, have obtained those Jailors to own them as *Prisoners in Custody*, tho' not *really* so, for a certain antedated Time, so as to be brought within the Reach of the Act.

What *Perjury*, what *Forgery*, what foul Things are practised under this Head, deserves the Inspection of the like Authority as lately detected the *Frauds* of the *Fleet-prison*; a Committee, who are above the Reach of *Fraud* or *Corruption* themselves, and fully qualified to search those *Deeds of Darkness* to the Bottom; indeed it seems to be reserv'd to a House of Commons, and to them only.

It was the Saying of a known and judicious Writer, that no Man ought to complain in Print of any publick Grievance, unless at the same Time he proposed also the Remedies; I shall take the Hint, and offer something to the Purpose in this Case, that I may dismiss it as I go:

I. It would go a great Way towards preventing this Mischief, if it was provided in the *Act*, that no *Insolvent* should claim the Benefit *twice* over; it having been frequent to have them take *new Credit*, after their having been once *discharged*, seeking out new Places of Abode, and new Creditors, who, upon a Variety of Pretences, they insinuate themselves so far into, as to get Credit with them, their former Circumstances not being known.

II. That none should claim the Benefit of such an *Act*, who had *run* from their *Bail*, made *Escapes* from Officers or Prison-keepers upon their Parole, or that had committed any notorious *Fraud* punishable by Law, or that had obtained Credit upon Promise and express Conditions (before two or more Witnesses who shall attest the same) not to claim or take the Benefit of any such *Act of Grace*.

III. That none should claim such *Benefit* who shall conceal any of their Goods and Effects from their Creditors, notwithstanding their having made Affidavit as the Law directs, as in the Case of a Bankrupt.

These Proviso's, together with a *New Method* to be taken, to limit and restrain the *Prison-keepers*, to prevent their keeping Prisoners on their

Books after they have been *discharged, antedating* their Commitments, and giving *fraudulent* Certificates of their being *Prisoners*, when really they were not; I say these Methods, and such as these, under the farther Direction and Improvement of the Legislature, I perswade myself would go a great way to prevent the Abuse of *Parliamentary Grace*, and to make the future *Acts for Relief of Insolvents* effectually and truly, merciful and good, and the honest *poor* Prisoner, nobody repining at his Relief, would be deliver'd; the *knavish* designing Debtor remaining, *as he ought to do*, where the Law directs.

This leads me to enter a little into the Question so much insisted on by some, *viz.* that *no Man should be put in Prison for Debt*.

It is true, that this *Doctrine* has many Advocates, and some have pushed it so far, as to think the contrary Opinion *cruel* and unchristian; but I shall enquire more particularly into it in the next Part.

In the mean time, I take this Occasion to repeat again what I hinted at before, namely, that this is so far from *impeaching* the common Charity, and the Compassion of the *British* Nation to Prisoners, that it prompts and recommends it by the meer Nature of the Thing; for when I argue against the Knavery of the Debtor, in making himself a *voluntary* Prisoner, on purpose to defraud and delude his *Creditors*, it naturally follows that the Prisons should be purged from all such voluntary, fraudulent People, and those that remain would be the more real and unexceptionable Objects of the National *Grace*.

When the Prisoners were all really *Insolvent*, really miserable, and that without any room to charge either *them*, or the *Jailers* and *Keepers* with corrupt Practices, abusing the publick Mercy, and the like, the Parliament would always be the more ready to pass Acts for their Relief, as they should see Cause, so that this Proposal is evidently calculated to encourage and prompt the Mercy of the *Publick* to *Insolvents*, by removing all the just *Objections* which now lie in the way, and have so often obstructed it.

Part II.

Of the Necessity of Preserving to the Creditor the Right of arresting and imprisoning the Person of his Debtor; and how the Petty Credit given in all Retail Trade, and which is essential to the Support of our whole Commerce, depends upon it.

I Believe it will not be called *begging the Question* to lay it down as a *Foundation*, That as there is a greater Trade carried on in *England* than in any other Nation in *Europe*; so there is a larger Personal Credit given in Trade here than in any other Nation, not in *Europe* only, but in the whole World.

There are so many *Evidences* of the first, and so many Authors have written on that Subject, that I need only refer my Reader to them; and the last is evident to every MERCHANT now in Trade, who sees with the least Observation what Difference there is between the way of Trading here, and the like way of Trading in *Foreign* Countries, and between the Credit given in either.

Some would make it a Question, *tho' I think it is no Question*, whether the Greatness of our Trade is the Cause of giving this *large Credit*, or that the giving this large Credit is the Cause of the *Greatness of our Trade*.

I say there is no room to debate this Part; the latter is evident to Demonstration, namely, that the giving such large Credit is the true Spring of the Greatness of our Trade: This appears by comparing the Bulk of the Trade in this Kingdom with the Bulk of our *Current Stock* in Trade. If no *Credit* was given, the Trade could not go beyond the *Stock*; it is true, it might go beyond the Current Coin, because some Trade may be carry'd on by Barter, or exchanging one kind of Goods for another, without the Interposition of any *Medium* (which is Money). But no Trade can go beyond the *Stock* without *Credit*, because one Value must always be deliver'd for another, and they must be always equal too, otherwise the Exchange is not equal, nor the Payment compleat.

But in Credit the Case is quite different; for here the Seller delivers his Goods (which are a *real Value*) to the Buyer on his Note for Payment, or perhaps on his Verbal Promise, either of which, is an *imaginary Value* only; in a Word, the *Fame* or Reputation of a Buyer is put into the *Scale of Commerce* with the *real* Value and Substance of the Seller, and the one is deliver'd for the other: the Account in the Tradesman's Ledger stands as a Register of the Case; the Buyer stands Debtor on one side for the Value of the Goods sold and deliver'd to him against an open *Blank* on the contrary side, to be fill'd up to his *Creditor* when he pays the Money.

By this strange thing call'd *Credit*, all the mighty Wonders of an exalted Commerce are perform'd; a Tradesman beginning with a Thousand Pound Cash, and a good Character, shall store his Shop or Warehouse with 5000 *l.* in Goods, and may trade for 10,000, nay for 20,000 *l. per Annum*; and so long as he manages *prudently*, pays currently, and keeps up his Reputation, shall run almost what Length he pleases in his Trade, so much greater a Stroke in Trade does his *Character* furnish to him, than his *Cash*.

Upon the Foot of this very Article call'd *Credit*, as a private Man may trade for 10,000 *l. per Annum* with but 1000 *l.* Stock, so if the Stock of the whole Trade of *Great-Britain* be, as some insist, Ten Millions, the Trade may actually return a Hundred Millions of Pounds Sterling in a Year; an *immense* Sum, but not at all *improbable* to be true, and perhaps within Compass too.

But to bring it down to the Subject: Take the Credit given in smaller Articles; I mean, in *retailing* Goods to the *last* Consumer: This is what I call *petty Credit*, and is the particular thing which fills our Jails with *Insolvent* Prisoners. Even this *petty Credit* is, though small in the particular, immensely great in the general; and tho' it does not *encrease* the Stock of the Retailer, it certainly does *encrease* his Trade, and causes him to sell a great deal more Goods than otherwise he would find Customers for.

Thus the *Wholesale* Dealer trusts or gives Credit to the *Retailer*, and thereby encreases *his* Stock (for Credit in Trade is Stock in Trade) the *Retailer* gives Credit to the *Consumer*, and thereby increases *his* Sale.

Now upon what Foundation is all this Credit given? The *Retailer*, being a *Woollen-Draper*, trusts his Neighbour with a Suit of Clothes; how comes he to do it? perhaps the Man has no extraordinary Character; well but, says the *Retailer*, he is a Tradesman as well as I, and he must pay me, or he shall not be able to stand at his Shop Door, or sit behind his *Counter*, for I will *arrest* him and make him pay me; and upon this *Power* of *Arresting the Debtor*, and carrying him to *Prison*, or whether he is carry'd to *Prison* or no, the exposing him, disgracing him, and ruining his Credit; I say, upon this is founded the Freedom of the Tradesman to trust him.

If you destroy this Power of *Coercion*, you destroy the *Credit in Trade*; for if the Man cannot be *credited*, he cannot *buy*; and if the Tradesman cannot *arrest* him, he will not sell.

This particular Case merits to be *very well observ'd*; and there is more Weight in it than perhaps appears at first View.

1. I say if the Buyer cannot be trusted, he cannot buy, *that is to say*, he cannot buy at that time; he will make shift for a while, will wear his old Clothes longer, go without such or such *fine things* for himself, or Wife, or Children, and abate in his Expence, because he has not Money to buy, and the Shop-keeper will not trust him.

Even the *Drunkard* will abate his Liquor, if the *Alehouse* or *Tavern-keeper* will not admit him to score;[5] abundance of *Luxury* and *Gaiety*, as well in *Food as fine things*, must abate for want of ready Money; whereas Men will venture to buy if they have Credit with the Tradesman.

To say, let Luxury and Extravagance *abate*, it will perhaps reform the Town, is to say nothing; for the *Question* does not lye that way: It is not whether the Luxury will abate, but will our *Trade* abate or not; if the *Trade abates*, as it certainly will, my Argument is good.

2. On the other hand, if the *Buyer* cannot *buy*, the *Seller* cannot *sell*; then his Stock lyes dead on his Hands, the Money for it, and for which perhaps he has been trusted himself, grows due, and he cannot pay; he had better sell, and give some *Credit*; but he is afraid to do that, because if his Debtor refuses to pay, he cannot force him to it. In short, he must *trust*, or *shut* up Shop, and *break*; and thus if a LAW should be made to prevent *arresting* the *Person* of the *Debtor*, you at once destroy *Personal Credit* and *ruin* the Tradesmen.

I remember an Attempt ignorantly made, (as it appear'd afterwards) even by the *Tradesmen* themselves, to destroy this *Petty Credit*: The Shop-keepers mightily affected to write over their Shop-Doors, NO TRUST BY RETAIL. But the Consequence soon appear'd, to the opening their Understandings; for *Thousands* of Buyers, who laid out their Money freely, and who, tho' they might not always pay down upon the *Spot*, yet paid tolerably well, went from their Shops, and bought where they knew they could be *trusted*.

In a Word, any LAW which abates *Petty Credit*, or Trust by Retail, will be fatal to TRADE, and would give such a *Blow* to our Commerce in general, as it would be impossible for all our Heads put together to retrieve.

Therefore if we will support *Trade*, we must encourage *Petty Credit*: and if you will support *Petty Credit*, you must not take away the *Security* to the *Creditor*; the Security of the Tradesman's trusting his Neighbour is the Power he has by Law to *enforce* his Payment, and of arresting and imprisoning the Debtor if he fails or refuses: The Law is the Tradesman's *Security*, and if you take away the *Law*, which is his *Security*, you take away his Trade.

What is the Reason why in *Scotland*,[6] and in other Countries, they have so *little* Trade? 'tis because you cannot *enforce* your Demand of Debt, you can't send the Debtor to Prison; and therefore no Man *buys* till he has *Money* to pay; if you will imprison the Debtor, you must allow him a Maintenance, or he will come out before your Face.

It may be true, that there is some *Humanity* in such a Law, but I cannot say there is any *Policy* in it; for it overthrows *personal* Credit, and that in effect sinks Trade, lessens the *Consumption* of Goods, and *ruins* the Tradesmen themselves: I cannot but think it were much better to have an *Act of Mercy* every Year, to release poor Insolvents upon reasonable Conditions, than not have it in the Tradesman's Power to *imprison* them when they do not pay; for this *Mercy* will not be so prejudicial to the *particular* Creditors, as the other would be to the *general* Credit.

It is our Business to *increase* our Trade to the utmost by all lawful Methods; nay, wise Men in Commerce tell us, some Errors, even in Morality, had better be wink'd at, than the Trade be ruin'd, or than any *general* Head of Trade be impair'd; the Meaning is, that, in some Cases, even our Luxury or High-living, *I do not mean our Drunkenness and Vice,* is so essential to our Trade, that it were better *continued,* than be entirely *supressed,* the Trade would suffer so much.

It must be confess'd, a Set of *Sumptuary* Laws,[7] as they are called, to reform our Extravagancies in Equipages and Dress, House-Furniture and Diet, would effectually *ruin* our Commerce, starve and leave unemploy'd our *Poor,* and reduce the whole Nation to a most deplorable Condition of Misery and Distress.

It would be the like, in Case of a Stop to *Credit,* for it would be an Abatement of the Consumption in all Sorts of Goods, as well our Manufactures and Home Product, as our importation from abroad; for as the last Consumer is the Life of all, if Credit abates, he abates his Expence, and buys less; consequently Trade declines, and less is consumed. By Credit here, *that I may explain Things as I go,* I must be understood to mean not *publick* Credit, I have nothing to do with that Part here; but *personal* Credit, the *ordinary* Credit given by one Tradesman to another, as well in *wholesale* Dealing and Merchandizing, as in Retailing from the Shopkeeper to his Neighbours and Customers, and indeed chiefly the *last*; for on that does the Wholesale Part depend.

Upon this Foundation I build the Consequences which I insist upon, as above; this *Trust by Retail,* this *petty* Credit entirely depends upon the Right which every Citizen thus selling his Goods to his Neighbour *upon his Word,* that is, upon his *personal* Credit, has by *Law to sue, arrest, imprison,* and *keep in Prison his Debtor,* if he delays or refuses to pay the Money when it is due.

If you take away this *Right,* you take away the *Credit*; for no Man will sell his Goods upon a *Faith* which the Debtor is not obliged to *keep.*

It is a great Mistake to say, *personal* Credit is given upon the *Honour* and *Faith* of the Debtor; the case is quite otherwise, the *Credit* is given to the *Law*; 'tis my being able to prosecute the Debtor in a Course of Law, and (*as we call it*) make him pay me, that encourages me to trust him; and therefore 'tis the ordinary Enquiry of a Tradesman, when he would *inform* himself about a Man he deals with, not whether he be *honest*, but whether he is *able*; if you tell him he is a *Knave*, and won't pay any body if he can help it, *O*, says the *Tradesman, I don't value that; I am willing to get off the Goods, and if he is* able, *I'll venture; for I know how to make him willing.*

Nor does any Part of this Discourse, to repeat it again, tend in the least to prevent our *Tenderness* to any of these *Debtors* who are thus *impris-on'd*, if by Disasters, Losses, Misfortunes, or any visible Accident they are render'd really poor and unable, but that such should always be reliev'd; and if the Creditor be *cruel* and inexorable, as some perhaps will always be, the Parliament will, on all just Occasions, *of which also they are the proper Judges*, deliver such Insolvents by *Acts of Clemency and Grace*, as they do *now*, and no Christian Tradesman can, I think, repine at their commiserating and relieving *unfortunate*, tho' otherwise *honest Insolvents*.

EXPLANATORY NOTES

An Essay upon Projects (1697)

Advertised as published 'this day' in the *Flying-Post*, 19–21 January 1697.

page

29 1 *Dalby Thomas*: For Defoe's involvement with Dalby (later Sir Dalby) Thomas, see Introduction, p. 4. A well-connected and wealthy merchant, Thomas had extensive business interests in the West Indies, and later, in 1703, was appointed Agent-General of the Royal African Company's settlement at Cape Coast, on the Gold Coast, where he died in 1711.

  2 *Projector*: At the time Defoe was writing, the word projector could have strongly pejorative overtones, implying one who cheats, or speculates, or schemes. See Introduction, p. 4–6.

  3 *present War with France ... Sufferers*: England had joined the War of the League of Augsburg against France in 1689. A feature of the war was the campaign waged by both sides on merchant shipping. Something like 4000 English merchant vessels were lost, many more than were lost by France, and in one twelve-month period alone, between September 1694 and September 1695, English shipping losses amounted to over £2,000,000 in value. In the *Review*, 9 January 1705, Defoe claimed that he himself had lost the first ship to be taken by the French. See further note 20 below.

  4 *Act for Registring Seamen*: The Act for the Increase and Encouragement of Seamen (7 & 8 William III, c. 21) set up a system of registering seamen aged above eighteen and under fifty, who would receive forty shillings a year, and could be called up for service in the Royal Navy.

  5 *Advice to the Ladies*: Mary Astell's *A Serious Proposal to the Ladies, for the Advancement of their True and Greatest Interest* (1694) had argued in favour of education for women, and proposed the establishment of a college for females, a 'Protestant nunnery'.

  6 *Notions about County Banks*: Defoe is probably referring here to Dalby Thomas's *Propositions for General Land-Banks* [London, 1695].

30 7 *Friendly Society for Widows*: A Friendly Society for Widows had been established in November 1696 and over the next few years several others were formed on a joint-stock basis. See W. R. Scott, *The*

Constitution and Finance of English, Scottish and Irish Joint-Stock
Companies to 1720, 3 vols (Cambridge, 1910–12), Vol. III, p. 389.

30   8   *the Coin . . . great Heads*: In the early 1690s there had been an enormous
debate over the state of the coinage, and a Recoinage Act, by which bad
and clipped money was to be exchanged, had been passed in 1696.

9   *Ways and Means*: a Parliamentary phrase referring to methods of raising
public funds.

10   *by Composition*: by agreement.

31   11   *the Land-Tax*: This was a yearly tax, based originally on assessments
of personal wealth as well as the value of land, but which came to fall
entirely upon land. It was introduced in 1692 (3 William and Mary,
c. 5) as a way of helping to finance the war with France. As Defoe
argues here, there were great inequities throughout the country in the
way the Land Tax was administered.

12   *Constantinople*: cf. Richard Knolles, *The Turkish History*, with a contin-
uation by Sir Paul Rycaut, 2 vols (sixth edn, 1687), Vol. I, p. 235:
'such was the disloyalty of the Citizens . . . that many times they could
hardly be drawn from their private Trades and Occupations, unto the
Walls to withstand the Enemy . . . [T]he poor Emperor . . . had many
times before with tears, in vain requested to have borrowed money
of his covetous Subjects, to have been employed in the defence of the
City; but they would still swear, that they had it not, as men grown
poor for want of Trade; which in few days after, their Enemies found
in such abundance, that they wondered at their Wealth, and derided
their folly, that possessing so much, they would bestow so little in
defence of themselves and their Country'.

32   13   *War*: King William had joined the War of the League of Augsburg
in May 1689. The war ended in September 1697 with the signing of
the Treaty of Ryswick.

14   *Sir J— C—*: Sir Josiah Child (*c.* 1630–99), Member of Parliament, a
director and afterwards chairman of the East India Company, was one
of the richest men in England.

15   *procure a Farm*: Defoe seems to mean that he could envisage the collection of taxes from merchants, for the purposes of his scheme, being
very successfully farmed out.

34   16   *Negoce*: mercantile trade.

17   *this Long . . . War*: see notes 3 and 13 above.

18   *Fougades*: small underground explosives.

19   *Lodgments*: temporary defensive works made on a captured portion of
an enemy's fortifications.

35   20   *Bill . . . for the Relief of Merchant-Insurers*: On 13 December 1693 a
Bill was presented to the Commons to give 'Merchants Insurers', i.e.
merchants ruined by insuring vessels during the present war, relief
against their creditors by making any composition accepted by two-
thirds of the creditors binding upon all of them. In February 1694,
while the Bill was being considered by a select committee, Defoe, who
had recently been bankrupted, petitioned to have his name included
in the list of petitioners, on the grounds that he had 'sustained divers

losses by insurance since the war with France'. His petition was accepted, but the Bill was rejected in the Lords.

36   21   *I'le*: variant spelling of 'I'll'.

37   22   *Linnen-Manufactures . . . Dipping*: Details of the financial problems of the companies listed by Defoe may be found in Scott, *The Constitution and Finance of . . . Joint-Stock Companies*. For linen manufacturing in the 1690s, see Vol. III, pp. 90-7; for various saltpetre companies, see Vol. II, pp. 471-4; for the Company of the Copper Miners in England, see Vol. II, pp. 430-3; for numerous diving machine companies formed in the wake of Sir William Phipps's success, see Vol. II. pp. 486-9; for a metal dipping company formed in 1694, see Vol. III, p. 108.

23   *History of a Patent-Monger*: In October 1691 a Cornishman named Joseph Williams patented a diving-bell and Defoe invested £200 in the company formed to promote it, also being appointed secretary-treasurer. The venture failed, and Defoe lost not only his £200 but some further money he had advanced on Williams's behalf, Williams having repaid it in worthless notes.

24   *Cully*: dupe.

38   25   *Patents*: A statute of the reign of James I (21 James I, c. 3) provided that the Crown might grant letters patent for fourteen years or under reserving 'the sole working or making of any manner of new manufactures within this realm to the true and first inventor'.

26   *Mysteries*: crafts.

27   *Deceptio Visus*: optical illusion.

28   *Sir William Phips's Voyage*: In 1686-7 William Phipps (1651-95), the first royal governor of Massachusetts, set up a small company to search for a Spanish plate ship wrecked off the Bahamas. The expedition was eventually successful in salvaging treasure worth nearly £300,000. Over £20,000 was paid to the Crown, Phipps himself received £16,000, and shareholders in the company received dividends of about 10,000 per cent. Phipps was knighted by James II.

29   *Endeavour . . . Wise*: Defoe included these lines in *More Reformation: A Satyr upon Himself* (1703), p. 39.

40   30   *Babel*: see Genesis 11:1–9.

41   31   *Thus when . . . Know*: A version of these lines formed part of an ode by Defoe first published in 1692, prefixed to Charles Gildon's *History of the Athenian Society*.

32   *Solomon*: see Ecclesiasties 1:9–10.

33   *Tubal Cain*: son of Lamech (see Genesis 4:22). He was regarded as the legendary founder of metalworking.

34   *Jubal his Brother*: see Genesis 4:21.

35   *Knitting Frame*: The iron knitting-machine, or 'stocking-frame' as it was called, was a remarkable piece of pre-industrial revolution technology, invented in 1589 by William Lee.

36   *Water-houses*: Presumably Defoe means the water-mills, used to raise water, which had been set up under two of the arches of London Bridge. The works were destroyed in the Great Fire of London in 1666, but quickly rebuilt.

41   37   *New-River*: The New River, a canal beginning at Ware, was constructed in 1609-13 to supply the City with water. An account of the New River Company may be found in Scott, *The Constitution and Finance of . . . Joint-Stock Companies*, Vol. III, pp. 18–26.

42   38   *Engine to Quench Fires*: Following the Great Fire in 1666 efforts were made to improve fire engines. In 1688 several Dutch engines were imported, and by the end of the seventeenth century there were several competing manufacturers of fire engines in London. For details, see Scott, *The Constitution and Finance of . . . Joint-Stock Companies*, Vol. II, pp. 479–83.

39   *Prince Rupert*: Prince Rupert of Bavaria (1619–82), third son of Frederick V, Elector Palatine, by Elizabeth, daughter of James I. Among other scientific achievements he invented a compound of copper and zinc known as 'Prince's metal'.

40   *Bishop Wilkins*: John Wilkins (1614–72), bishop of Chester and one of the founders of the Royal Society. His works include *Mathematical Magick* (1648) and *An Essay towards a Real Character and a Philosophical Language* (1668).

41   *Captain Phips*: see note 28 above.

42   *Lord Mordant*: Charles Mordaunt (1658–1735), third Earl of Peterborough, famous for his role in the War of the Spanish Succession. In 1687 he commanded a small Dutch squadron in the West Indies and joined Sir John Narbrough in the attempt to rescue treasure from a wrecked ship off St Domingo.

43   *Sir John Narborough*: Sir John Narbrough (1640–88), admiral. He conducted an expedition through the Straits of Magellan and died shortly after recovering treasure from a Spanish wreck off St Domingo.

44   *Penny-Post . . . Mr. Dockwra*: William Dockwra (*d.* 1716), a London merchant, set up a penny post system in the City in 1680. He was opposed by London porters and others, and suits were brought against him by the Duke of York, who received revenue from the General Post Office. In 1682 the Post Office stopped his operations and took over his system themselves. Dockwra was granted an annual pension of £500 in compensation.

43   45   *William Pen*: William Penn (1644–1718), a Quaker, founded the colony of Pennsylvania in 1681 for his persecuted co-religionists.

46   *Lord Shaftsbury*: Anthony Ashley Cooper (1621–83), first Earl of Shaftesbury, famous Whig statesman. He was one of eight to whom Charles II made a grant of Carolina in 1663 and was active in managing the colony; he also was one of five granted the Bahamas in 1670.

47   *Dr. Cox*: Dr Daniel Coxe (1640–1730), physician and colonial adventurer. In the 1680s he acquired extensive interests in West New Jersey, and in the 1690s he acquired the title to the province of Carolana – present-day North and South Carolina, Georgia, Florida and Louisiana – and attempted to organise settlements there.

44   48   *Mint*: A mint established about 1543 by Henry VIII at Suffolk Place in Southwark, near the King's Bench Prison, had been demolished in 1557, but the area around it was a recognised sanctuary for debtors and thieves, who sheltered there from justice on the pretext that it

was an ancient royal palace. The privilege of sanctuary was removed from the Mint in 1723.

44   49   *Friars*: A Carmelite monastery founded on the south side of Fleet Street gave its name to a district known as Whitefriars or Alsatia, for long a sanctuary for criminals and debtors. It was abolished by Act of Parliament in April 1697.

45   50   *Nascitur ridiculus mus*: a ridiculous little mouse is born. (Horace, *Ars Poetica*, l. 139.)

51   *the Saltpeter-Maker ... Tom T—ds Pond*: Saltpetre companies which claimed to have developed methods of obtaining saltpetre from manure and earth had proliferated in the 1690s. 'Tom Turdman' was the name given to a night-soil collector.

52   *Premio's*: bonuses, or rewards.

53   *Royal Bank Establish'd*: The Act establishing the Bank of England was passed in 1694 (5 & 6 William and Mary, c. 20).

54   *Fund upon the Orphans Stock*: In 1695 William Paterson and others established an Orphan's Fund Bank, but it was not a success. See J. Keith Horsefield, *British Monetary Experiments 1650–1710* (London, 1960).

46   55   *Four or Five Banks*: Various banks had been founded in the 1690s, including several Land Banks, the Orphans' Bank, and the Million Bank. See Scott, *The Constitution and Finance of ... Joint-Stock Companies*, Vol. III, pp. 246–52, 275–87; Horsefield, *British Monetary Experiments*, pp. 150–217.

47   56   *Lotteries*: Many lotteries had sprung up in the 1690s offering those who purchased tickets the chance of a massive win, or payment of annuities over a longer time-scale. One of the leading private lottery sponsors was Thomas Neale, groom-porter at the palace, who was appointed as manager of the state-sponsored Million Lottery, established by Act of Parliament in 1694. Defoe was among the trustees of another lottery organised by Neale in 1695.

57   *less than* [blank]: Subscriptions amounting to £1,200,000 had been received by 2 July, only ten days after the subscription opened.

51   58   *Tallies*: Tallies were the notched pieces of wood used by the Exchequer for accounting.

52   59   *some Gentlemen who have had thoughts of the same*: Various schemes for banks were put forward in the late seventeenth century. See Horsefield, *British Monetary Experiments*, pp. 144–50.

53   60   *Rents of the Town-House in France*: i.e. the public loans administered on behalf of the French Crown by the Hotel de Ville in Paris. (The first of these was floated during the reign of Francois I.) The word 'rents' ('rentes') refers to the annual interest-payment to investors.

55   61   *John Asgill of Lincolns-Inn*: John Asgill (1659–1738,), who was called to the Bar in 1692, founded a Land Bank in 1695 along with Nicholas Barbon. He published *Several Assertions Proved, in Order to Create Another Species of Money than Gold and Silver* in 1696, arguing that another species of money was needed, and that land securities could be more useful and valuable for this purpose than gold and silver.

56   62   *Watling-Street ... London-Stone*: Defoe is referring here to the famous Roman Watling Street which ran from Dover to St Albans, and also

page

to the Watling Street in the City, which ran parallel to Cannon Street. The 'London Stone' was a round-topped stone, probably of Roman origin, which had been in place since early medieval times, and was set into the wall of St Swithin's Church, Cannon Street. It was believed that all measurements in the Roman province of Britannia were taken from this stone.

56 63 *Mr Cambden*: William Camden (1551–1623), antiquary and historian, whose great work *Britannia*, a county-by-county archaeological, physical and historical guide to the British Isles, was first published in Latin in 1586. The first translation appeared in 1610, and a handsome new edition, translated and augmented by Edmund Gibson, was published in 1695.

64 *The Fosse*: Fosseway, so called from the foss (from Latin *fossa*, ditch) on either side, was one of the most important military roads constructed by the Romans. It ran from Lincoln to Exeter, via Leicester and Bath.

65 *King's new Road through Hide-Park*: i.e. Rotten Row, sometimes described as the *Route du Roi*, a road to William III's new palace at Kensington.

57 66 *Cart-routs*: 'routs' was a variant spelling of 'ruts'.

59 67 *Houses of Correction*: An Act of 1607 had required Houses of Correction to be provided in every county. They were used partly as prisons for beggars and vagrants, and partly as workhouses for the unemployed.

62 68 *Rod*: a measure of length, equal to five and a half yards, also called a perch or a pole.

64 69 *Drift-ways*: roads along which animals are driven.

67 70 *the Guinea-Company*: another name for the Royal African Company, which held the monopoly on the Guinea Coast slave trade.

69 71 *Stone-street*: The Roman road of this name ran in fact from Dorking to Chichester, but a branch went down to Arundel.

70 72 *Prescription*: traditional custom.

71 73 *Dr. Barebone*: Nicholas Barbon (d. 1698), a physician by training, had become one of the largest house builders in London after the Great Fire of 1666. He was the originator of fire insurance, setting up an Insurance Office for Houses, based on a large fund, in 1681.

74 *Friendly Society*: A Friendly Society for Securing Houses from any Considerable Loss by Fire was founded by William Hale and Henry Spelman in 1683. As 'undertakers', they received 1s. 4d. per annum on each £100 insured. See Scott, *The Constitution and Finance of . . . Joint-Stock Companies*, Vol. III, pp. 378-99.

75 *a Design in hand*: In 1696 John Asgill, Nicholas Barbon and John Briscoe had published *A Scheme for a National Land-Bank*. See Horsefield, *British Monetary Experiments*, pp. 202–5.

73 76 *Chest at Chatham*: A fund including monthly contributions from sailors, and known as the Chatham Chest, was set up by Sir John Hawkins and Sir Francis Drake in 1590. The proceeds were used to build a hospital for ex-seamen and ex-shipwrights of the Chatham and Sheerness dockyards.

77 *Les Enfans Perdue*: (properly *perdus*), literally, 'the lost children'.

78 *the Forlorn hope*: in military use, the vanguard, or group of soldiers sent first into battle.

78 79 *Volenti . . . injuria*: 'One who is willing cannot be injured'.

80 *Sir William Petty*: Sir William Petty (1623–87) was a noted statistician and political scientist, and one of the founders of the Royal Society. In *Another Essay in Political Arithmetic, Concerning the Growth of the City of London* (London, 1683) he calculated the rate of deaths at one in thirty for London, one in fifty for the rest of the country, and therefore one in forty over the nation as a whole. See *The Economic Writings of Sir William Petty*, ed. Charles Henry Hull, 2 vols (Cambridge, 1899), vol. II, pp. 459–63. In *A Plan of the English Commerce* (1728), Defoe expressed scepticism about Petty's methods and figures (pp. 171–2).

79 81 *a Million of People*: In fact Petty estimated the population of London as being about 670,000 in 1682.

83 82 *Thus Calculated*: Defoe's arithmetic here, and over the next few pages, is not always easy to follow, and is in some places inaccurate. For a thorough discussion of the problems, to which it seems unnecessary to add anything here, see *An Essay upon Projects*, ed. Joyce D. Kennedy et al, in The Stoke Newington Daniel Defoe Edition (New York, 1999), pp. 180–4.

85 83 *Sir William Petty*: see note 80 above.

88 84 *Two*: In fact Defoe goes on to list three points.

89 85 *Million Lottery Tickets*: In 1694 the Chancellor of the Exchequer, Charles Montagu, set up a lottery designed to raise £1,000,000. Tickets cost £10 each, and holders were to receive interest at varying rates for sixteen years. The scheme proved immensely popular, and 'shares' in tickets were sold for as little as a few shillings each.

90 86 *Gaged*: staked, wagered.

87 *second Siege of Limerick*: Limerick was besieged unsuccessfully by William III during his Irish campaign in 1690, but was taken the following year after a second siege by General Ginkel.

88 *Return . . . deserv'd*: In 1696 there had been a conspiracy to assassinate King William, but it was frustrated and most of the conspirators were arrested.

89 *Groom-Porter's*: A groom-porter was a court official who oversaw gaming within the precincts of the court. Thomas Neale held this post under William III (see Introduction, p. 4).

90 *Gaming-Ordinary*: gambling establishment.

91 *Polities*: or policies, conditional promissory notes, depending on the outcome of a wager.

92 *he is your Humble Servant*: i.e. with a mocking bow he removes himself from this City scene.

91 93 *in such a Knot*: i.e. the thing is so well tied up.

92 94 *Bedlam*: properly Bethlehem Royal Hospital, a lunatic asylum from about the end of the fourteenth century. In 1675–6 it was moved to a splendid new building in Moorfields designed by Robert Hooke.

95 *no Brute . . . a Man*: Defoe is alluding to Boileau's 'Satire VIII', line four of which runs 'Le Plus sot animal, à mon avis, c'est l'homme'. Defoe knew Boileau's work well, for he devoted a whole number of the *Review* (6 December 1711) to a parody of Boileau's 'Satire IX' as applied to himself.

page
93   96   *Chamber of London*: an apartment in Guildhall where City money was kept.

        97   *mean*: modest.

94   98   *the Million-Lottery*: see notes 42 and 85 above.

95   99   *Tallies*: see note 58 above.

       100   *shamefully allow'd in Bedlam*: Bedlam (Bethlehem Hospital, see note 94 above) was one of the sights of London in the seventeenth century. Visitors paid fees to see the inmates, who were chained in cells in galleries. In 1770 admission was restricted to ticket-holders.

96   101   *be in Commission of the Peace*: i.e. have the powers of a magistrate.

       102   *This Chapter*: Defoe quoted long extracts from this chapter in the *Review* for 12, 14 and 16 February 1706, when a Bill for Preventing Frauds Frequently Committed by Bankrupts was going through Parliament.

97   103   *a Statute*: a legal instrument by which a person might be declared a bankrupt.

98   104   *the Friars*: see note 49 above.

       105   *the Mint*: see note 33 above.

100   106   *sui juris*: legally his own master.

102   107   *de Die in Diem*: from day to day.

103   108   *fieri facias*: a writ of execution to a sheriff to levy a sum from a debtor by seizure of his goods.

104   109   *Parcels*: lots.

106   110   *Savoy*: Originally a palace built by the Count of Savoy in 1246, then rebuilt as a royal hospital, it had by Defoe's time become a warren of lodgings with right of sanctuary for debtors. The right of sanctuary was abolished in 1697.

       111   *Rules*: areas surrounding the King's Bench Prison in Southwark and the Fleet Prison in the City of London where wealthy debtors could pay to live unguarded and unsupervised in a house or apartment.

       112   *Train'd-Bands*: 'Trained bands' (or 'train bands') was from the sixteenth century the name given to the militia. By an Act of 1662 the system was discontinued in the shires, but the London Trained Bands survived until 1794, when they were reorganised as the City of London Militia.

108   113   *two great Seminaries*: i.e. the universities of Oxford and Cambridge.

       114   *the Academy of Paris*: the Académie française was founded in 1634 on the initiative of Cardinal Richelieu. From 1676, under Louis XIV, the French king was 'protector' of the Académie. Its principal concern was to be the French language, and the first edition of the *Dictionnaire de l'Académie Française* finally appeared in two volumes in 1694.

       115   *Richlieu*: Armand du Plessis (1585–1642), cardinal de Richelieu, first minister of Louis XIII from 1628 to 1642. A notable patron of science and the arts, he rebuilt and endowed the Sorbonne, founded the royal printing press at Paris, and was chiefly responsible for the establishment of the Académie française.

       116   *Rapin*: René Rapin (1621–87), poet and critic.

       117   *St. Evremont*: Charles de Marquetel de Saint-Denis (1613–1703), sieur de Saint-Évremond, poet, essayist and playwright. He spent the later part of his life in England, and praised the English theatre at the expense of the French.

page

108 118 *Lord Roscommon*: Wentworth Dillon (*c.* 1633–85), fourth Earl of Roscommon, author of a blank verse translation of Horace's *Ars Poetica* (1680). The often-quoted lines repeated here by Defoe come from *An Essay on Translated Verse* (1684).

109 119 *present King of England*: William III, who had won a great victory at Namur in 1695.

114 120 *Acts of Parliaments*: An Act for the more Effectual Suppressing Prophane Cursing and Swearing was passed in 1695 (6 & 7 William and Mary, c. 11). It imposed fines for bad language.

115 121 *The Two Theatres*: In 1660 Charles II had granted patents to two theatrical companies, the King's Men and the Duke's Men, playing at Drury Lane and Lincoln's Inn Fields. The two companies combined in 1682 and made Drury Lane their headquarters. In 1695, however, the leader of the United Company, Thomas Betterton, quarrelled with the manager of Drury Lane and broke away to return with most of the veteran actors to Lincoln's Inn Fields.

116 122 *Schomberg, Ginkel, Solms, Ruvigny*: Friedrich Herman von Schonberg (1615–90), Earl of Brentford and Duke of Schomberg, one of the greatest military commanders of his day, volunteered his services to William in 1668. He commanded William's armies in Ireland, and died at the Battle of the Boyne. Godart van Ginkell (1630–1703), first Earl of Athlone, was a Dutch general who fought under William in Ireland, and was appointed general-in-chief after the death of Schomberg. Heinrich Maastricht (1636–93), Count of Solms–Braunfils, was a relation of William III who accompanied him to England and fought with him in Ireland. Henri de Massue (1648–1720), second marquis de Ruvigny, first Earl of Galway, was a Huguenot émigré who fought with William in Ireland and was appointed Lord Justice of Ireland in 1697.

123 *Dunbar Fight*: Cromwell's victory over the Scots at Dunbar, on 3 September 1650.

117 124 *Long Perukes . . . Piqued Beards*: Pointed ('piqued') beards were fashionable in the earlier seventeenth century. Under Charles II full wigs came into fashion.

118 125 *Artists*: technicians.

126 *Chelsea-College*: i.e. Chelsea Hospital, built by Sir Christopher Wren as a hospital for veteran soldiers on the site of an unsuccessful college of theology, founded in 1618. Charles II laid the foundation stone in 1681, and the building was finished in 1692.

119 127 *Exempts*: It is not clear what Defoe means by this term, but it may be relevant that in military usage, an exempt was a sub-officer of cavalry. In French the word is used for an adjutant or policeman.

121 128 *pump'd*: i.e. put forcibly under the pump.

123 129 *Dialing*: surveying with the aid of a miner's compass (or 'dial').

130 *the Siege of Limerick*: see note 87 above.

124 131 *Buts*: Butts were the erections or mounds against which targets were placed, and thus by extension the place where practice-shooting took place.

132 *Cocking*: cock-fighting.

page
124   133   *Firelock*: a musket with a lock in which sparks were produced to ignite the priming.

125   134   *Battel of Agrim*: In July 1691 at the Battle of Aughrim the forces of King William won a decisive victory over an Irish army supporting King James.

126   135   *Advice to the Ladies*: Mary Astell's *A Serious Proposal to the Ladies, for the Advancement of their True and Greatest Interest* (1694). See note 5 above.

127   136   *Jettings*: projections, juttings.

       137   *Bearing-Work*: corbels or buttresses.

       138   *Coin*: corner-stone (now usually quoin).

128   139   *Felony without Clergy*: persumably short for 'felony without benefit of clergy'. Benefit of clergy was a privilege enjoyed by the clergy and the literate generally not to be tried for certain offences by a regular court; but here no more is meant than 'a heinous offence'.

131   140   *Souls equally capable ... Education*: Defoe makes the same point in *Mere Nature Delineated* (1726), p. 18: 'this Soul is ... at Liberty to act, and not interrupted by the Defects of Nature, only wanting Culture, and Improvements'.

132   141   *Court-merchant*: i.e. a court for settling disputes between merchants.

133   142   *Factorage-Account*: a set of accounts between a merchant and his factor.

134   143   *Demoreage*: an obsolete form of demurrage, which in commerce referred to the detention of a ship by the freighter longer than had been agreed.

137   144   *Avarages*: i.e. averages, losses arising from damage at sea to a ship or cargo.

138   145   *Ports*: carriage charges; or perhaps simply 'things carried'.

       146   *Tonnage*: or tunnage.

139   147   *Tinmouth-Bar to the River*: i.e. from Tynemouth to the River Thames.

       148   *Chaldron*: a dry measure, of thirty-six bushels, used only for coals.

       149   *the Pool*: i.e. the reach of the Thames known as the Pool of London, where ships would unload their cargoes.

       150   *late methods of ... registring Seamen*: see note 4 above.

An Essay on the Regulation of the Press (1704)

Advertised as published 'tomorrow' in the *Daily Courant*, 6 January 1704. For the circumstances, see Introduction, pp. 9–10.

page
145   1   *Asgill ... B—t's Theory*: John Asgill (1659–1738) published *An Argument Proving, that According to the Covenant of Eternal Life, Revealed in the Scriptures, Man may be Translated from Hence into that Eternal Life without Passing through Death* (1700). The book was regarded by many as blasphemous. Defoe wrote *A Enquiry into the Case of Mr Asgil's General Translation* attacking Asgill's theories, but laid it aside and only published it in 1703, following Asgill's expulsion from the Irish House of Commons. William Coward (*c.* 1657–1725), a physician, was best known as the author of a pamphlet entitled *Second Thoughts Concerning*

Human Soul (1702), in which he argued that there was no such thing as a separate soul. In 1704 the House of Commons ordered it to be publicly burnt as containing offensive doctrines. It is not clear whose book on polygamy Defoe may have had in mind. He frequently accused the deist John Toland (1670–1722) of being against the Trinity; see, for example, *To the Honourable the C—s of England*, above, p. 166. Thomas Burnet (*c.* 1635–1715) published in Latin in 1681 the first part of his celebrated *Telluris Theoria Sacra*, in which he offered a novel explanation of the Genesis Flood. A somewhat modified English version was published as *The Theory of the Earth* (1684, 1689).

145   2   *Messenger of the Press*: an official employee of the Secretary of State with authority to search for and seize unlicensed publications and to make consequent arrests. The most notorious of the Messengers of the Press was Robert Stephens (*c.* 1643–97), formerly a printer and member of the Stationers Company, known to his enemies as 'Robin Hog'.

146   3   *Under-spur-leathers*: menials, subordinates.

150   4   *the King of France*: One of the main projects of the Académie française (see note 114 on *An Essay upon Projects*, above p. 308) was to promote translation. With the encouragement of Valentin Conrart, the first 'Perpetual Secretary', translators such as Perrot d'Ablancourt produced French versions of Cicero, Tacitus, Zenophon, Caesar, Lucian, Thucydides and others.

151   5   *Anglicè*: in plain English.

153   6   *Mr. Delaun*: Thomas Delaune (d. 1685) was a Dissenting schoolteacher and translator, who published *A Plea for the Nonconformists* in 1683 as a response to Benjamin Calamy's *A Discourse about a Scrupulous Conscience* (1683) which claimed that Dissenters could give no good reasons for their nonconformity. Delaune was convicted in 1684 of publishing a seditious libel, and, unable to pay his fine, he died in Newgate together with his wife and children. In 1706 Defoe wrote a Preface to a new edition of the *Plea*, in which he described it as the best statement of the Dissenters' case ever written. See *Political and Economic Writings*, volume 3.

154   7   *Baxter's Comment ... Anderton's two Books*: Richard Baxter (1615–91), one of the most eminent Puritan divines, was imprisoned in 1685 after being found guilty by Jeffreys of libel in his *Paraphrase on the New Testament, with Notes* (1685). Algernon Sidney (1622–83), the Whig leader, was executed for his part in the Rye-House Plot to murder Charles II. Among the evidence used to convict him was that he had written a treasonable libel, under the pretence of answering Filmer's *Patriarcha*. On Delaune, see note above. William Anderton (*c.* 1663–93), a Jacobite printer, was executed in 1693 for printing two pamphlets, *Remarks upon the Present Confederacy, and Late Revolution in England* (1693) and *A French Conquest Neither Desirable nor Practicable* (1693).

       8   *post Factum's*: retrospective incrimination or revisions of verdicts.

156   9   *trapann'd*: trapped.

   10   *Marks*: A mark in England was not an actual coin, but money of account representing 13*s.* 4*d.*

page
157   11   *to instance in*: to give examples of.

       12   *Abridgments of . . . Life*: An abridged edition of Richard Knolles's *The Generall Historie of the Turkes*, first published in 1603, was published in two volumes in 1701; an edition of *The Wars of the Jews*, 'Epitomiz'd from the Works of Flavius Josephus, Translated into English by Sir Roger L'Estrange', was published in 1703; Edmund Calamy published *An Abridgment of Mr Baxter's History of his Life and Times* in 1702.

158   13   *Pasquinadoes*: A pasquinade was a squib, or a libel. (Defoe gives an account of the origin of the term from the custom of posting satirical verses on the statue of Pasquin in Rome, in the *Review* for 13 May 1712.)

To the Honourable the C—s of England Assembled in P—t [1704]

Probably published in late March 1704. See Introduction, p. 10.

page
164   1   *Ultra Tenementum*: beyond (i.e. out of proportion to) one's estate. Defoe frequently used the phrase about the fine imposed on him for *The Shortest Way with the Dissenters*.

       2   *Shortest Ways*: A reference, the first of several, to Defoe's famous tract, *The Shortest Way with the Dissenters* (1702). See *Political and Economic Writings*, Volume 3.

       3   *Golden Ages*: Probably a reference to William Walsh's poem *The Golden Age Restor'd*, published in January 1703 as a Whig answer to the earlier High Tory poem, *The Golden Age* (1702).

       4   *Auctions of Books*: unidentified.

       5   *New Associations*: In 1702 the High-Church polemicist Charles Leslie published a pamphlet entitled *The New Association* in which he argued that Dissenters should be excluded from any part in government, and even from voting for Members of Parliament. By 'New Association' he meant the combination of Low-Churchmen and Dissenters.

       6   *Occasional Bills*: In November 1702 and again in November 1703, High-flying Tories introduced bills to outlaw the practice of Occasional Conformity, as they would again in November 1704. The device of occasionally taking communion in the Anglican church was used by some Dissenters as a way of getting round the provisions of the Test Act, which required that anyone appointed to a public office take the sacrament according to the rites of the Church of England. All three Occasional Conformity bills were rejected in the Lords.

165   7   *B—s*: bishops.

       8   *private-Academys*: High-Churchmen often called for Dissenting Academies, which were not covered by the Toleration Act, to be suppressed.

       9   *Westly*: Samuel Wesley (1662–1735) had been brought up as a Dissenter, and was educated with Defoe at Charles Morton's Academy at Newington Green. He subsequently conformed, and became Rector of Epsworth in Lincolnshire. Two pamphlets by Wesley attacking Dissenting academies were answered by Defoe in *More Short-Ways with the Dissenters* (1704).

166 10 *Convocation*: Convocation is the name given to an assembly of clergy in the Church of England called together to discuss ecclesiastical matters. Strictly speaking there was a Convocation of York as well as a Convocation of Canterbury, but the latter was much more important and was simply referred to as 'Convocation'. There were two Houses, the Upper House of bishops, and the Lower House of parish clergy. The Lower House was dominated by High-flyers.

11 *Lesly, alias White*: Charles Leslie (1650–1722), the nonjuror, was a leading High-Church controversialist with whom Defoe frequently clashed. He had Jacobite affiliations, and sometimes used the alias of 'Mr White'. In *Royal Religion* (1704), p. 19, Defoe also referred to 'Mr. *L. alias W.*'

12 *Toland*: John Toland (1670–1722), the notorious deist. Parliament ordered his most famous book *Christianity Not Mysterious* (1696) to be burnt by the common hangman.

13 *Dr. B—*: Joseph Browne, who was born about 1673, styled himself 'Dr' and practised medicine in London. A violently Tory polemicist, he became one of Defoe's most persistent and virulent critics, in works like *The Moon-Calf* (1705), and *A Dialogue between Church and No-Church* (1706), a short-lived periodical whose sole purpose was to attack the *Review*.

14 *Sachaverel ... Bloody Flag*: Henry Sacheverell (1674–1724) was perhaps the most notorious High-Churchman of the early eighteenth century. In May 1702 he preached a fiery sermon at Oxford, calling on all true sons of the Church of England to 'Hang out the *Bloody Flag* ... of Defiance' against the Dissenters and their Low-Church sympathisers. The sermon was published the following month as *The Political Union* (1702).

15 *Legion Papers*: In 1701 Defoe published a tract known as *Legion's Memorial*, and another entitled *Legion's New Paper*. See *Political and Economic Writings*, Volume 2.

16 *Kentish Petitions*: In 1701 a petition was delivered to the House of Commons by five Kentish gentlemen. They were immediately thrown into prison. Defoe published *The History of the Kentish Petition* (1701), vigorously defending them. See *Political and Economic Writings*, volume 2.

17 *Observators*: The *Observator* was a twice-weekly Whiggish journal conducted from April 1702 by John Tutchin.

18 *Shortest Ways*: see note 2 above.

19 *Challenges to Peace*: In November 1703 Defoe published a pamphlet entitled *A Challenge of Peace, Address'd to the Whole Nation*.

20 *Hymns*: probably a reference to Defoe's *Hymn to the Pillory* (1703).

21 *Ballads*: perhaps a reference to Defoe's satirical ballad *The Address*, which was published in March or early April 1704. See *Political and Economic Writings*, volume 2.

22 *Packingtonian*: Sir John Packington (1671–1727), MP for Worcestershire, was a leading High-Church Tory.

23 *Stubbs*: Philip Stubbs (1665–1738) was Rector of St Alphage, London Wall, and later Archdeacon of St Alban's. He preached a famous sermon against Occasional Conformity, published as *For God or for Baal: or, No Neutrality in Religion* (1702).

page
166   24   *Sir H. M.*: Sir Humphry Mackworth (1657–1727), High Tory MP for Cardiganshire in Wales. Defoe attacked him several times in pamphlets and in the *Review*.

25   *Mr. D.*: probably a reference to James Drake (1667–1707), physician and leading Tory propagandist, who was several times arrested and tried for seditious libel. In 1705 he was suspected of authorship of the notorious *Memorial of the Church of England*.

26   *Mr. S.*: probably Henry Sacheverell; see note 14 above.

Giving Alms no Charity (1704)

Advertised in the *Review*, 18 November 1704. See Introduction, pp. 12–14.

page
167   1   *Corporations*: The setting up of a Corporation of the Poor in Bristol in 1696 was quickly imitated in a number of other towns. It essentially was a method of transferring responsibility for poor-relief from the parish to the city as a whole, under the surveillance of a body of 'Guardians of the Poor', and was the origin of the eighteenth-century workhouse system.

2   *Parish-Stocks*: Sidney and Beatrice Webb, in their *English Local Government*, Vol. 7: *English Poor Law History, Part I. The Old Poor Law* (London, 1927), p. 9, mention entries in parish records concerning the 'Church Stock' or 'Parish Stock' – in some cases a flock of sheep, in others a herd of cattle, maintained to yield an annual revenue for the common purposes of the parish.

3   *a late Pamphlet*: *A Bill for the Better Relief, Imployment, and Settlement of the Poor, as the Same was Reported from the Committee to the Honourable House of Commons; in order that (by Reason of the Great Importance and Universal Concerns of the said Bill) the Same be Farther Consider'd against the next Session of Parliament* (London, 1704). According to the imprint this was 'Printed by the Directions of Sir Humphry Mackworth'. The bill was introduced in the Commons in 2 November 1704 and was passed there, but was thrown out by the Lords.

170   4   *Pauper Ubique jacet*: paupers are to be found everywhere.

5   *the Dutch being not yet Revolted*: The Netherlands declared their freedom from Spanish rule in 1581.

171   6   *Staple*: principal centre from which a commodity is distributed.

7   *Stuffs*: woollen fabric.

8   *Bays*: i.e. baize.

9   *Says*: a distinct two-and-two twill with a single weft.

10   *Serges*: a very durable twilled cloth of worsted.

11   *Duke D'Alva*: Fernando (1507–82), Duke of Alva (or Alba), Spanish soldier and statesman, was appointed Governor-General of the Netherlands by Philip II in 1567. He ruled with great savagery, condemning thousands for rebellion, and his name became a byword for cruelty and tyranny.

172   12   *10th. Penny*: The Duke of Alva attempted to impose a ten per cent sales tax (known as the 'tenth penny') on the Netherlanders, but without success.

page

173   13   *True born English Families*: cf. *The True-Born Englishman*, ll. 412–14.

       14   *late Persecution*: There was a flood of French Protestant refugees to England at the time of the revocation of the Edict of Nantes in October 1685.

       15   *Perpets*: i.e. perpetuanas, a light, smooth, inexpensive fabric.

174   16   *Corporations*: see note 1 above.

175   17   *Parish Charges, Assessments*: Assessments for the poor-rate were a constant source of local controversy. Defoe discusses the matter in his 'Andrew Moreton' pamphlet *Parochial Tyranny* (1727).

178   18   *Laws against sturdy Beggars*: The laws against vagabonds and 'sturdy beggars' were made harsher under Queen Elizabeth, though the same period saw the setting up of a system of poor-relief, based on a parish rate.

179   19   *the Learned Gentleman . . . been Printed*: see note 3 above.

       20   *Overseers*: officers appointed annually to oversee poor relief.

       21   *raise Stocks*: see note 2 above.

181   22   *on the Tenters*: on the stretch (a tenter was a wooden framework on which cloth was stretched to dry).

182   23   *Arcanas*: (trade) secrets.

       24   *Shaloons*: says woven from line yarns, often glazed.

       25   *Druggets*: a loosely woven plain cloth.

183   26   *the Frame*: see note 35 on *An Essay upon Projects*, above, p. 303.

184   27   *Voiture*: carriage.

       28   *Corporations*: trade guilds.

       29   *present Trade to Muscovy*: Defoe makes the same criticism of the trade with Russia in the *Review* for 25 March 1707.

187   30   *Silk Throwsters*: operatives who twisted silk fibres into raw silk or raw silk into thread.

       31   *Cur Moriatur Homo*: why does a man languish and die?

       32   *Tile making*: Defoe in 1694 set up what was for several years a prosperous business in brick-and-tile-making on the Thameside near Tilbury.

188   33   *List*: enlist.

Remarks on the Bill To Prevent Frauds Committed by Bankrupts (1706)

Advertised as 'just published' in the *Review*, 18 April 1706. See Introduction, pp. 16–18.

page

195   1   *a long War*: i.e. the War of the Spanish Succession, which had begun in 1702.

       2   *the Great Storm*: Defoe's account of this, *The Storm*, was published in 1703.

196   3   *Rules*: see note 111 on *An Essay upon Projects*, above, p. 308.

       4   *Escape Act*: Defoe seems to be referring here to an Act of 1702, For the Better Preventing Escapes out of the Queen's Bench and Fleet Prisons (1 Anne, sess. 2, c. 6). See Introduction, p. 16.

       5   *Pitkin*: for the case of Thomas Pitkin, see Introduction, p. 16.

page
199   6   *the Mint or Rules*: see notes 48 and 111 to *An Essay upon Projects*, above, pp. 304, 308.
200   7   *19th of March, 1705*: i.e. 1706, new style.
      8   *discover*: divulge, reveal.
204   9   *swear as thro' a 10 Inch Plank*: swear with enormous force.
206   10   *even from the Horns of the Altar*: an allusion to 1 Kings 2:28–9.
207   11   *Lord Keeper*: William Cowper (*c.* 1664–1723), first Earl Cowper, became Lord Keeper in October 1705.
214   12   *Setters*: informers, spies.
      13   *Appraisers*: licensed valuers.
      14   *Spunging Houses*: privately-run secure houses in which debtors were held pending trial.
      15   *White-Fryers*: see note 49 to *An Essay upon Projects*, above, p. 304.
      16   *Hackney-Bails*: men who made a living by fraudently pretending to stand bail.
      17   *Catchpoles*: sheriff's officers, especially bum-bailiffs.

Every-Body's Business is No-Body's Business (1725)

Advertised as published 'this day' in the *Post Boy*, 1–3 June 1725. See Introduction, pp. 20–2.

page
219   1   *three Answers*: for details, see Introduction, p. 22.
      2   *The Good . . . Laws*: source unidentified.
220   3   *their Wages*: see Introduction, p. 21.
221   4   *Herb-Woman or Chandler-Woman*: woman who sells herbs, or groceries.
      5   *Vails*: tips or gratuities given to servants.
      6   *Neat's Leathern*: leather made from the hides of meat cattle, i.e. bullocks, cows or heifers.
      7   *Clocks*: bold ornamental patterns on the sides of stockings.
      8   *Wooden Pattens*: overshoes worn to raise ordinary shoes an inch or two above the mud.
      9   *Leathern Clogs*: shoes with wooden soles.
      10   *Hoop*: a circle made of whalebone or some such material, designed to push out the skirt of a woman's dress.
      11   *Linsey-Woolsey*: a coarse textile material of mixed wool and flax or cotton.
222   12   *whip*: in a trice, forthwith.
      13   *Inch-meal*: little by little, by inches.
      14   *cribbing*: pilfering.
      15   *Factors*: a factor is one who buys or sells for another on commission.
      16   *Brokeridge*: commission.
223   17   *Jonathan Wild*: Jonathan Wild (1683–1725), the most notorious criminal of his time, recruited and directed the activities of a vast network of gangs of thieves. He was hanged at Tyburn on 24 May 1725.
224   18   *enhauncing*: increasing.
      19   *Dabs*: dirty clothes.

page

224 20 *Custom of Warning*: i.e. giving notice of a decision to leave employment.

226 21 *Jus Trium Liberorum*: i.e. 'the law of three children'. Suzanne Dixon, in *The Roman Family* (Baltimore and London, 1992), p. 120, writes: 'The full privileges of the *ius liberorum* ... were secured by producing three, four, or five children, depending on the status of the parent. The privileges included earlier candidacy for political office for men and freedom from *tutela* (quasi-guardianship) and the restrictions of the testamentary *Lex Voconia* for women'.

22 *Yard-wide Stuff*: woollen fabric.

23 *Callimanco*: i.e. calamanco, 'a glossy woollen stuff of Flanders, twilled and chequered in the warp, so that the checks are seen on one side only' (*OED*).

228 24 *slop*: slobber over.

25 *Cullies*: see note 24 to *An Essay upon Projects*, above, p. 303.

230 26 *amerc'd*: fined.

27 *Never a Barrel the Better Herring*: i.e. there is nothing to choose between them; proverbial.

28 *Trulls*: prostitutes, mistresses.

231 29 *Societies for Reformation*: The first 'societies' for reformation of manners appeared in London in the early 1690s. Their initial aim was to bring prosecutions against the owners and frequenters of bawdy-houses, though they soon widened their scope. Their use of informers made them unpopular.

232 30 *Task-Masters*: overseers.

31 *docible*: teachable, tractable.

32 *Stannaries*: tin mines in Cornwall and Devon.

33 *Ballast-Men*: men who supply the heavy sand and gravel used for ballast in ships.

34 *Watermen*: boatmen who plied for hire on the Thames.

233 35 *Dagenham-Breach*: The Thames burst its banks at Dagenham and Havering in 1707, and was not finally dammed until 1720.

36 *Pepper-Alley-Stairs*: These were beside Southwark Cathedral, on the south bank of the Thames.

37 *the Hall*: Watermen's Hall, the hall of the Watermen's Company, which in the seventeenth century was in Upper Thames Street. Burnt down in the Great Fire of 1666, it was rebuilt on the same site in 1670, and again in 1720.

234 38 *House of Correction*: see note 67 to *An Essay upon Projects*, above, p. 306.

39 *Link-Boys*: boys employed to carry links, torches made of tow and pitch, to light people along the streets.

40 *Thimbles and Balls*: a reference to thimbling, a swindling game in which a pea is ostensibly placed under one of three thimbles, which are then moved around, and bystanders are challenged to lay bets on which thimble the pea is under.

41 *Bills of Mortality*: From the sixteenth century onwards, weekly returns of deaths, known as Bills of Mortality, were compiled by the Company of Parish Clerks, representing 109 parishes in and near London.

42 *Knot*: A porter's knot was a double shoulder-pad used by market porters for carrying burdens.

The Protestant Monastery (1727)

Advertised as published 'this day' in the *Post Boy*, 19–22 November 1726.

page
239 1 *subject to the Higher Powers*: see Romans 13: 1.

2 *Projector*: see note 2 on *An Essay upon Projects*, above, p. 301.

3 *Non nobis nati sumus*: 'We are not born just for ourselves'.

240 4 *my 67th Year*: Defoe himself would have been about 66 in 1726.

241 5 *Honour ... Saviour*: see Exodus 20: 12; Matthew 15: 4–6.

242 6 *Quo ... diu*: 'Once an impression has been made, it will retain its odour as evidence for a long time'.

7 *an Old Woman*: Defoe himself frequently makes play with this phrase. See, for example, the *Director* for 18 and 21 November and 2 December 1720, in *Political and Economic Writings*, Volume 6.

8 *Jane Wenman*: Jane Wenham was charged with witchcraft at Hertford in 1712. Although condemned, she was subsequently reprieved. She was the last person to be convicted of witchcraft in England.

244 9 *Chariot*: a light four-wheeled carriage with only back seats.

10 *Whet*: a small draught of liquor as an appetiser.

11 *Fritters*: portions of fried batter, sometimes containing meat or apple.

245 12 *spawling*: spitting copiously or coarsely.

246 13 *Charter-House*: a former Carthusian priory, which in the seventeenth century had become a generously endowed hospital for well-born male pensioners and a school.

14 *the Penny-Post*: a private post service set up in 1680 by William Dockwra to serve the Cities of London and Westminster and the Borough of Southwark. It was so successful that in 1682 it was taken over by the Post Office, who regarded it as an infringement of their monopoly.

247 15 *riv'd*: broken or burst with sorrow.

16 *prevented by a Ticket ... Pall*: forestalled by a printed invitation to serve as a pall-bearer at his funeral.

17 *Quis ... Lachrymis?*: 'Who relating such things could refrain from tears?' (Virgil, *Aeneid*, book II, ll. 6–8).

248 18 *a Man of Clouts*: The phrase 'a king (or lord, master) of clouts' was proverbial.

19 *Hobbydehoy's*: clumsy, awkward youths.

20 *Tye-Wig*: a wig with the hair gathered behind and tied with a ribbon.

21 *Now little Miss ... Year*: The lines are from Henry Carey, 'Epilogue to *The Puritan, or, Widow of Watling Street*', in his *Poems on Several Occasions* (London, 1720), p. 71; slightly misquoted ('bare fifteen').

249 22 *Top-Knots*: A topknot was a bow of ribbons worn by women on top of the head.

23 *a foul Bird ... Nest*: proverbial.

250 24 *Spare ... Child*: proverbial, based on Proverbs 13: 24.

251 25 *Nurture ... Lord*: see Ephesians 6: 4.

254 26 *Tillotson ... Scot ... South*: John Tillotson (1630-94), Archbishop of Canterbury, was one of the most famous preachers of his day, and numerous editions of his sermons were published. Dr John Scott (1639–95), Rector of St Giles-in-the-Fields, was the author of volumes of sermons and devotional works. Dr Robert South (1634–1716) was

celebrated for his humorous style in the pulpit; many of his sermons were published separately and in collected editions.

Augusta Triumphans (1728)

Advertised in *Mist's Journal,* 16 March 1728.

page
259 1 *Augusta Triumphans*: (literally, 'the female sovereign triumphing'), a reference to Queen Caroline, consort of George II who succeeded to the throne in 1727 (see note 30 below).

      2 *Schemists*: projectors.

260 3 *Science*: learning, knowledge.

261 4 *Gresham-College*: In his will, Sir Thomas Gresham (1519–79) made provision for founding Gresham College, where public lectures on divinity, music, astronomy, geometry, physics, law and rhetoric were delivered by resident professors. The weekly meetings of the seven professors led to the development of the Royal Society, which was formally instituted in 1662, and met at the College until 1710.

      5 *Chancery Man*: legal copyist.

      6 *Hospital for Foundlings*: Since the early 1720s, Thomas Coram (*c.* 1668–1751) had been campaigning for the establishment of a hospital for London's foundlings, against criticism that caring for illegitimate children would encourage vice. In 1737 George II, moved by a petition from Coram, gave his approval to the plan. Funds were raised by a committee of Governors, among them William Hogarth, and eventually, in 1741, the hospital was opened and the first babies admitted.

262 7 *Parish-Nurses*: These were nurses hired by parishes to take care of foundlings, but who often simply allowed them to die. In 1715 it was reported by a Parliamentary committee that three-quarters of the foundlings in the parish of Martin-in-the-Fields died while in the care of parish nurses.

      8 *Nurture . . . Lord*: see note 25 on *The Protestant Monastery*, above, p. 318.

263 9 *young Nobleman*: Defoe is referring here to the case of Richard Savage (*c.* 1697–1743), the poet who claimed to be the illegitimate son of Richard Savage, fourth Earl Rivers, and Lady Macclesfield. In 1727 he had killed a man in a tavern brawl, but, although convicted of murder, had been granted a royal pardon on 6 January 1728. The case attracted enormous public attention, and a confessional poem, *The Bastard*, published by Savage in April 1728, ran to five editions.

264 10 *If his Peerage had not been adjusted*: even if he had not been allowed to succeed to the Peerage.

      11 *Venetians . . . other foreign States*: Foundling hospitals, supported by Church and State, had been established in many European cities, including Paris, Rome, Lisbon and Amsterdam. The earliest seems to have been the Spedale degli Innocenti, opened in Florence in 1445.

265 12 *my Project already anticipated*: see note 6 above, and Introduction, p. 24.

      13 *Viol and Lute*: The viol was one of the most popular Renaissance and Baroque instruments, but although it survived into the middle of the eighteenth century, little new music for solo viol was written after the

page

1680s. The lute also declined in popularity during the seventeenth century, with almost the last English lute music being published in 1674.

265　14　*seven liberal Sciences*: In the middle ages the quadrivium (arithmetic, music, geography and astronomy) and the trivium (grammar, rhetoric and logic) formed what was known as the 'seven liberal arts'.

　　15　*his late Majesty*: King William III.

　　16　*their present Majesties*: King George II and Queen Caroline.

　　17　*Italian Opera ... Academy*: In 1719 a Royal Academy of Music was established in London by a group of noblemen led by the Earl of Burlington. Its purpose was to promote Italian opera, and especially the operas of Handel.

　　18　*Foreign Musicians*: Italian opera was all the rage in the early eighteenth century, and the King's Theatre, opened in 1705, was almost entirely given over to performances by Italian singers, particularly castratos.

266　19　*Drury-Lane, and Lincolns-Inn-Fields*: Drury Lane (or, properly, The Theatre Royal, Drury Lane) was opened in 1663 but burnt down in 1672. A second theatre, designed by Wren, was opened in 1674. Lincoln's Inn Fields Theatre in Portugal Street, off Kingsway, was opened in 1661. In 1695 a new theatre was built on the same site, followed by a third in 1714. It was the home of the Opera of the Nobility, under the patronage of the Prince of Wales.

　　20　*Corelli ... Geminiani*: Arcangelo Corelli (1653–1713), Italian violinist and composer, best known for his chamber music. George Frideric Handel (1685–1759) arrived in London in 1710 and became the musical director of the newly-founded Royal Academy of Music in 1718. Giovanni Bononcini (1670–1747), composer and cellist, was famous throughout Europe for his operas and cantatas. In 1719 the Earl of Burlington persuaded him to come to London as a composer for the Royal Academy of Music. At first extraordinarily successful, his reputation later suffered through his acquaintance with notorious Jacobites. Francesco Geminiani (1687–1762), Italian violinist and composer, and follower of Corelli. He came to England in 1714 and later settled in Dublin.

　　21　*Christ's Hospital*: Christ's Hospital in Newgate Street was founded in 1553 by Edward VI as a refuge for orphans. It became known as the Blue Coat School from the uniform worn by the boys. Many of the buildings were destroyed in the Great Fire of 1666, but were rebuilt under the superintendance of Sir Christopher Wren.

　　22　*Hautboy*: oboe (French, hautbois).

　　23　*German-Flute*: In the early eighteenth century the flute was often specified in English music as 'German flute' (from the French 'flute d'Allemagne') to distinguish it from the recorder, which was also called 'flute' in this period.

　　24　*Bass-Violin*: double bass.

268　25　*Newport-Market*: Newport Market was a meat market and shopping area which had been developed in the 1690s, when the estate of Mountjoy Blount, Earl of Newport, was sold to the builder Nicholas Barbon.

269　26　*ascertaining*: fixing.

page

270   27   *Sessions-Papers*: These were the printed reports of court proceedings at Quarter-Sessions and the like.

272   28   *private Mad-Houses . . . increased*: In the early years of the eighteenth century there was a marked increase in the numbers of institutions for the confinement of lunatics privately run for profit. Partly because of the profit motive (it was in the interest of the proprietors to retain patients), these private madhouses attracted much criticism. See William Parry-Jones, *The Trade in Lunacy: A Study of Private Madhouses in England in the Eighteenth and Nineteenth Centuries* (London and Toronto, 1972).

274   29   *Salivation*: Mercury, often prescribed for venereal disease, could cause the production of an excessive flow of saliva.

275   30   *Queen Caroline*: Caroline Wilhelmina of Anspach (1683–1737), wife of George II, who succeeded to the throne in 1727. She was a highly educated woman, with wide intellectual interests, who exercised considerable political power.

276   31   *alienate the proper Current of Specie*: misapply the nation's currency.

      32   *from Southwark Fair to the Groom Porters*: Southwark Fair, the subject of the great picture by Hogarth in 1733, was a popular jamboree, held each September, and with entertainments of all kinds. The Groom Porters looked after gaming on royal premises, and hence were socially exclusive.

277   33   *pipt Ivory and painted Pasteboard*: i.e. dice and playing cards.

      34   *Tye Wigs, or Toupees*: A tie-wig was one where the hair was gathered behind and tied with a knot of ribbon. A toupee was a periwig with a high curl of hair tied with a bow on top of the head.

      35   *round the Hundreds of Drury*: in the vicinity of Drury Lane. A 'hundred' is a territorial division, the word being used loosely here.

      36   *half hang themselves*: A form of masochism called hypoxyphilia involves sexual arousal by oxygen deprivation by means such as a noose.

278   37   *GENEVA*: i.e. gin, the spirit flavoured with juniper berries. It was drunk in vast quantities at this time in England.

279   38   *Aqua-fortis*: nitric acid.

      39   *Small-Beer*: weak beer.

      40   *Julap*: (more usually, julep), a sweet drink.

      41   *go whoop for*: search in vain for.

      42   *Watchmen*: Before Peel's Police Act of 1829, law and order in London were upheld by constables of the watch, who patrolled the streets at night. By law, all freemen had to serve a turn in this unpaid post, though they could evade this by paying for a substitute. The system was widely recognised to be ineffective.

280   43   *Beggar's Opera*: John Gay's *The Beggar's Opera* (1728) was an immensely successful musical drama set in the underworld of London's criminals.

      44   *Bunworth and Blewitt's Execution*: Edward Burnworth and William Blewit were members of a daring gang of pickpockets and housebreakers. They and their associates were eventually hanged at Kingston on 12 April 1726.

      45   *Cartouchian Villainies*: Louis-Dominique Cartouche (1693–1721) was the leader of a band of robbers in France. He was eventually caught and broken on the wheel.

page
283 46 *the Convex Kind*: In 1684 one Edward Wyndus patented a new kind of street-light which used a convex (bull's eye) lens to throw out long rays of light. These 'New Lights', or 'Convex Lights', as they were called, were widely regarded as the best so far invented, and in 1694 the Convex Lights Company's monopoly for the City and Liberties was established by Act of Parliament, and renewed again in 1716.

  47 *Ignes fatui*: will-o'-the-wisps.

  48 *Black-guards*: street shoe-blacks.

284 49 *Chamber of London*: see note 96 to *An Essay upon Projects*, above, p. 307.

  50 *Act now depending*: On 17 May 1728 the House of Commons debated a bill granting the King £500,000 for the better payment of seamen's wages. George II, in his first speech from the throne in January 1728, had said that he was anxious for seamen to be encouraged, rather than press-ganged.

285 51 *Manciples*: officers responsible for buying provisions for an institution such as a college or monastery.

  52 *Ordinary*: dining room.

286 53 *Samuel Robinson*: Samuel Robinson, clerk and later master of the Joiners Company, was elected to the office of Chamberlain of the City of London on 13 February 1728. Elections to this prestigious office were keenly contested, though not always strictly along Whig and Tory lines. On his election, Robinson became treasurer of the Orphans' Fund (see note below). He died in office on 13 March 1734.

  54 *Orphan's Fund*: The Orphans' Act of 1694 (5 & 6 William and Mary, c. 10) set up a 'perpetual fund' of £400,000 a year, charged upon certain City of London revenues. See Horsefield, *British Monetary Experiments*, pp. 150-1.

Some Objections ... to the Present Intended Relief of Prisoners (1729)

Advertised as published 'this day' in the *Daily Post Boy*, 7 May 1729.

page
291 1 *Warden of the Fleet*: In August 1728 Thomas Bambridge, an attorney, purchased the Wardenship of the Fleet prison for £5000. He rapidly became notorious for the atrocious cruelties he inflicted on prisoners, and in February 1729, following the highly critical report of a committee of the House of Commons looking into the state of prisons, he was removed from office and taken into custody. He was subsequently tried (twice) for the murder of a prisoner, but was acquitted. The report of the Committee, which was chaired by James Oglethorpe, was published on 14 May 1729. See Introduction, p. 19.

293 2 *an Act ... but two Years past*: Defoe is referring in fact to an Act of Grace which was passed in 1724, permitting the release of prisoners for debt who owed less than a certain sum and had been imprisoned for more than a certain length of time.

  3 *near ninety Thousand such Insolvents*: According to Paul H. Haagen, 'Eighteenth-Century English Society and the Debt Law', in *Social*

Control and the State, eds Stanley Cohen and Andrew Scull (Oxford, 1983), p. 228, most contemporary estimates put the figure at between 20,000 and 60,000 but with some insisting that it was closer to 100,000.

293   4   *separate between the Sheep and the Goats*: see Matthew 25: 32-3.

297   5   *admit him to score*: give him credit.

298   6   *in Scotland*: The law concerning imprisonment for debt was quite different in Scotland. As Defoe says, a creditor in Scotland could not have the body or goods of a debtor seized before he was aware that action was being taken against him (what in England was known as the 'mesne process'), and also, by an Act of Grace passed by the Scottish Parliament in 1696, the creditor was made responsible for paying for the upkeep of a debtor while in prison. For a detailed description of the Scottish system, see William Chambers, *The Book of Scotland* (Edinburgh, 1830), pp. 150–73. Chambers makes the point that an effect of the law in Scotland was to reduce the giving of credit (p. 163).

299   7   *Sumptuary Laws*: laws regulating expenditure on food, clothing and luxury goods. Those of England were repealed in the early seventeenth century (1 James I, c. 25).

TEXTUAL NOTES

The textual policy for *Political and Economic Writings of Daniel Defoe* is described in the General Editors' Preface printed in Volume 1, pp. 3–4. Bibliographical details of each work will be found in P. N. Furbank and W. R. Owens, *A Critical Bibliography of Daniel Defoe* (London: Pickering & Chatto, 1998), referred to as 'F&O' in the notes that follow. The numbers in the left-hand column refer to the Pickering & Chatto page numbers.

An Essay upon Projects

The copy-text is the first edition of 1697 (F&O 5). Corrections listed in an Errata on p. 336 have been carried out.

139a at a] a

An Essay on the Regulation of the Press

The copy-text is the first edition of 1704 (F&O 51(P)), the only one published.

153a or] of

To the Honourable the C—s of England Assembled in P—t

The copy-text is the first edition of 1704 (F&O 55), the only one published.

165a pleased not] pleased

Giving Alms no Charity

The copy-text is the first edition of 1704 (F&O 62). This has been collated with the text included in *A Second Volume of the Writings of the Author of the True-Born Englishman* (1705). When a passage from p. 17 of the first edition was reprinted in the *Review* for 22 March 1707, the word 'buy' was changed to 'have', and this reading has been adopted here.

181a have] *Review*; buy 1704, 1705

Remarks on the Bill to Prevent Frauds Committed by Bankrupts

The copy-text is the first edition of 1706 (F&O 77), the only one published.

206a 3] 4
207a if he] he
208a Commissioners] Commissions
213a Commissions] Commissioners

Every-Body's Business is No-Body's Business

The copy-text is the first edition of 1725 (F&O 222), referred to as 1725a in the list below. This has been collated with the second, third, fourth, and fifth editions, all of 1725, and referred to below as 1725b, 1725c, 1725d, and 1725e respectively. A 'Preface' which appeared for the first time in the fifth edition (published on 22 July 1725) is included here.

220a thirty and forty] 1725b–e; 30 and 40 1725a
220b six . . . eight] 1725b–e; 6, 7, and 8 1725a
220c Matter now] 1725b–e; Matter 1725a
220d for nothing] 1725b–e; for now nothing 1725a
220e Wenches . . . they] 1725b–e; Wenches, and it is to support this intoller-
        able Pride, that they 1725a
221a fifty] 1725b–e; 50 1725a
221b three] 1725b–e; 3 1725a
221c four or five] 1725b–e; 4 or 5 1725a
221d four or five] 1725b–e; 4 or 5 1725a
221e young prinkt] 1725b–e; young wanton prinkt 1725a
222a these] 1725b–e; your 1725a
222b mighty] 1725b–e; very 1725a
222c three . . . pence] 1725b–e; 3 *d.* or 4 *d.* 1725a
223a punish'd . . . *Wild.*] 1725b–e; punish'd. 1725a
223b Folk . . . Shoe-cleaners] 1725b–e; Folk, or Servants out of Place, or whether
        they are Shoe-cleaners 1725a
223c their] 1725b–e; her 1725a
223d eight] 1725b–e; 8 1725a
224a Comer] 1725b–e; Servant 1725a
224b Ease; which] 1725b–e; Ease, yet 1725a

224c 20 *l.*] 1725b–e; twenty Pounds 1725a
225a and make] 1725b–e; and so make 1725a
225b But] 1725b–e; And 1725a
225c and therefore] 1725b–e; so 1725a
225d What] 1725b–e; Therefore, what 1725a
225e Forty Shillings] 1725b–e; 40 *s.* 1725a
225f No-body's … I] 1725b–e; No-body's, for I have not 1725a
226a Years. A] 1725b–e; Years, a 1725a
226b which] 1725b–e; that 1725a
226c be … obliged] 1725b–e; be avoided, if our Servant-Maids were to wear
       Liveries, as our Footmen do; or if they were oblig'd 1725a
226d not suffer'd to] 1725b–e; not 1725a
226e but oblig'd to] 1725b–e; but 1725a
226f the last] 1725b–e; a Servant 1725a
226g self. The] 1725b–e; self as a Servant; the 1725a
227a more] 1725b–e; and more 1725a
227b she] 1725b–e; and she 1725a
227c ran] 1725b–e; runs 1725a
227d Affairs; mean] 1725b–e; Affairs with Madam; mean 1725a
227e any Work] 1725b–e; any 1725a
228a dismiss'd] 1725b–e; so dismiss'd 1725a
228b Devil. It] 1725b–e; Devil; and it 1725a
228c Creature] 1725b–e; Servant-Maid 1725a
229a This] 1725b–e; But this 1725a
229b Being] 1725b–e; I was 1725a
229c I] 1725b–e; and 1725a
230a And] 1725b–e; For you 1725a
230b it] 1725b–e; your Table 1725a
231a those Servants who] 1725b–e; such Servants as 1725a
233a *April*-Day] 1725b–e; *May*-Day 1725a
233b but … attend] 1725b–e; and was gone, so they appointed 1725a
233c again and again] 1725b–e; again 1725a
233d deter] 1725b–e; defer 1725a
234a would] 1725b–e; might 1725a
234b may] 1725b–e; will 1725a
234c knock] 1725b–e; so knock 1725a
234d or] 1725b–e; and 1725a
234e others … I] 1725b–e; others, or perform any other Part of the thieving
       Function, I 1725a
234f even such] 1725b–e; these 1725a

The Protestant Monastery

The copy-text is the first edition, dated 1727 on the title page (F&O 232).

246a for] in

Augusta Triumphans

The copy-text is the first edition of 1728 (F&O 243). This has been collated with the 'second edition' of 1729.

262a Old-Beldams] *ed.*; Old-Bedlams 1728, 1729
274a apt to] *ed.*; apt 1728, 1729
287a *yourself,* / *Sept.* 23 / 1728 / ANDREW MORETON.] 1729; *yourself.* /
        February 28, / 1727–8. 1728

Some Objections Humbly Offered . . . Relating to the Present Intended Relief of Prisoners

The copy-text is the first edition of 1729 (F&O 248(P)), the only one published. No substantive emendations have been made to the text.

CUMULATIVE INDEX

Writings by Defoe appear directly under title; works by others appear under author's name, where known. 'DD' indicates Defoe. Index prepared by Douglas Matthews.

Louis XIV promotes, **5**.279–80
and membership of Parliament,
  2.50
parliamentary strength, **2**.363
and potential English war with
  Dutch, **5**.260, 265
proposed rising in Scotland (1703),
  3.370n39
Protestant supporters, **2**.33
rebellion (1715), **2**.21, 361, 365–6,
  405, **6**.302nn21, 5, 304n18
and religion, **1**.218–19
and Roman Catholicism, **1**.178
and Scottish Squadroni, **2**.151
and Scottish union with England,
  4.202
as threat in event of abolition of
  standing army, **1**.40, 46, 56–7
threat of revolution over South Sea
  Bubble, **6**.287–8, 290
and Triennial Act, **2**.369
under Queen Anne, **1**.212
Jamaica
  storms, **8**.196
  trade, **7**.76, 268, 287, 296, 301–2,
    312, 314
James I, King
  accession to English Crown,
    4.41
  brings Scots to English court,
    4.42
  dissolves Parliament (1621),
    5.319n49
  and divine right, **1**.23
  fails to support Bohemian
    Protestants, **5**.6
  and failure of 1604 union
    commission, **4**.363n8
  and historical liberties, **1**.35
  Locke cites, **1**.33n
  peace policy, **1**.68, 95
  persecutes Dissenters, **3**.63,
    99–100
  and public finances, **6**.5
  requests Bishop Overall draw up
    canons on civil government,
    3.359n22
  Scots benediction on, **3**.147
  in standing army controversy, **1**.87

and struggle of Frederick, Count
  Palatine, against Spain **5**.79
James I, King of Scotland, **4**.361n2
James II, King
  abdication question, **2**.387n1
  accession, **2**.30
  Anglican clergy's allegiance to,
    3.7
  Catholic innovations, **1**.25
  challenge to Church of England,
    3.196
  Charles Leslie supports, **1**.25
  Church opposition to, **1**.26, **3**.75,
    212
  DD opposes, **2**.22
  death, **1**.12, **5**.14, 170
  Declaration of Indulgence (1687),
    3.3–5, 30–1, 362n8, 375nn18,
    19
  deposed and exiled, **1**.58, 89, 104,
    113, 124, 142–3, 183–5, 224, **2**.5,
    100, **3**.6–7, 14, 100, 205, 251,
    5.159
  Dissenters under, **3**.21, 100, 196–8,
    221, 272, 286–8, 343
  'dry martyrdom', **1**.27
  Episcopalians' loyalty to, **4**.30
  escapes execution, **3**.65
  establishes Commission for
    Ecclesiastical Causes, **2**.374n9
  exclusion bills against succession,
    2.5, 373n7, **3**.372n26, **6**.312n58
  favours Royal African Company,
    7.343n1
  High Church addresses to, **6**.102
  introduces religious toleration,
    3.1–6, 26, 249, 288
  invades Ireland, **1**.52
  and legitimacy of son James,
    1.182–3, 185–6, 190, 231,
    4.392n21
  Louis XIV supports, **5**.45
  and Occasional Conformity, **3**.91
  and passive obedience, **3**.251
  potential return from exile, **1**.53,
    58
  proposes repeal of Test Act, **3**.343
  religious aims, **1**.43, 179, **3**.274,
    5.66

For Product Safety Concerns and Information please contact our EU
representative GPSR@taylorandfrancis.com Taylor & Francis Verlag GmbH,
Kaufingerstraße 24, 80331 München, Germany

Printed and bound by CPI Group (UK) Ltd, Croydon, CR0 4YY
08/05/2025
01864496-0001